EMPIRE OF VINES

NATURE AND CULTURE IN AMERICA

Marguerite S. Shaffer, Series Editor

Volumes in the series explore the intersections
between the construction of cultural meaning and
perception and the history of human interaction
with the natural world. The series is meant to
highlight the complex relationship between nature
and culture and provide a distinct position for
interdisciplinary scholarship that brings together
environmental and cultural history.

EMPIRE OF VINES

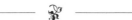

WINE CULTURE IN AMERICA

ERICA HANNICKEL

PENN

UNIVERSITY OF PENNSYLVANIA PRESS

PHILADELPHIA

Published by
University of Pennsylvania Press
Philadelphia, Pennsylvania 19104-4112
www.upenn.edu/pennpress

Printed in the United States of America on acid-free paper
10 9 8 7 6 5 4 3 2 1

Library of Congress Cataloging-in-Publication Data
Hannickel, Erica.
Empire of vines : wine culture in America / Erica Hannickel.
— 1st ed.
p. cm. — (Nature and culture in America)
Includes bibliographical references and index.
ISBN 978-0-8122-4559-2 (hardcover : alk. paper)
1. Viticulture—United States—History—19th century.
2. Wine and wine making—United States—History—19th
century. 3. Grapes—United States—History—19th century. I.
Title. II. Series: Nature and culture in America.
TP557.H358 2013
663'.20973—dc23   2013015746

For my grandmothers

The first record of America is also a record of its grapes.

> Liberty Hyde Bailey
> *Sketch of the Evolution of Our Native Fruits*, 1898

How beautifully prophetic is the emblematic vine of the destiny of man.

> Jno. S. Reid
> *The Horticulturist*, 1862

The vine and the American people are not unlike [one another]. They require room to spread themselves, and do not thrive under restraint.

> G. W. Campbell
> *The Horticulturist*, 1874

The gold of the Sierra did not build cities as surely as will the vines of its foothills.

> Charles A. Wetmore
> *Californian*, 1880

CONTENTS

Grape Culture, National Culture

C ARRYING WITH IT a picture of rustic elegance, sun-drenched hillsides, and verdant grapevines running parallel in organized prospect, wine growing easily outpaces romanticized images of other agricultural goods. To many Americans, vineyard scenes represent the trappings of a noble society. A 2005 PBS documentary, *The Cultivated Life: Thomas Jefferson and Wine*, argues as much. The narrator, over images of vines heavy with luscious grapes, explains that "Jefferson's vision for the quality of American wine has been realized, but his dream of a genteel agrarian society has largely been relegated to the pages of history books. Except in one instance—the American vineyard." Jefferson's ideal "agrarian society" was one populated by independent farmers, men removed from the cash economy who owned their own land, performed their own labor, and were stalwart in the face of economic change and political tomfoolery. Although it has been two centuries since Jefferson planted his own (largely failed) vineyards at Monticello, several contemporary winemakers interviewed in the documentary agree that Jefferson's ideals are embodied today in American vineyards.[1]

The suggestion that wine growing is still a yeoman enterprise is, to put it plainly, wildly inaccurate. Against PBS's minikin scene, wine is actually a $122 billion-dollar industry in America, and the United States is currently the world's fourth-leading wine producer, behind France, Italy, and Spain. As of 2010, California made 90 percent of all American wine, and 21 million tourists visit the state's 535,000 acres of vineyards annually. (The next largest wine-producing states are Washington, Oregon, and New York.) Although many growers might be loath to admit it, the contemporary U.S. wine industry reflects global industrial agribusiness at its most successful. Large wine producers are deeply dependent on national and international markets, and advanced technology is used throughout the many stages of production. One of the most distinctive features of industrial agriculture—monocropping, growing only one type of plant across a wide area—is ubiquitous in grape production, and its benefits and risks are no different than for any other crop. As with all monocrops, a variety of pests and diseases plague contemporary vineyards, and most growers still find chemical pesticides the easiest and most effective method of pest control. Methyl bromide, a highly toxic, ozone-depleting pesticide, is used regularly as a fumigant to sterilize soils prior to planting wine grapes. Its use in California was at a record high in 1992, with over 18 million pounds administered, and though its application has been on the decline since then, in 2009 over 5.4 million pounds were still spread annually.[2] One especially egregious example of the suspected overuse of the pesticide includes Francis Ford Coppola's 115-acre vineyard in California wine country, where in 2009 over 42,000 pounds of methyl bromide was administered. Sulfur is another major vineyard additive, used since the nineteenth century to prevent grape mildew and rot. The Pesticide Action Network of North America reports that over 60 million pounds of fumigants and pesticides a year are used by California farmers, 6–10 million being sulfur. According to the network, "Agricultural workers face greater risks of suffering from pesticide-related illnesses—including acute poisonings and long-term effects such as cancer and birth defects—than any other sector of society. . . . Grapes continue to rank first in reported illnesses, attributed in part to frequent high level applications of sulfur." The ill effects of sulfur are not believed at this time to be life threatening; the ill effects of methyl bromide, however, are. Californians for Alternatives to Toxics has characterized the wine business as "a lucrative industry heavily reliant on industrial poisons."[3]

This less-than-flattering industry overview comes on the heels of decades of high-profile vineyard labor activism in California, headed by Cesar Chavez from 1965 to 1993. Immigrant bracero programs, in effect throughout the postwar Southwest, had brought hundreds of thousands of Mexican laborers into the United States. Suffering poor pay, harassment, and often dangerous working conditions, by the 1960s, Chavez and the United Farm Workers drew inspiration from the civil rights movement, and mounted a successful table grape boycott in 1970. It resulted in 150 contracts with growers who at the time produced 85 percent of California's table grapes. The contracts covered 20,000 farmworker jobs. Provisions included union worker security, grievance procedures, and health plans; an improved work environment, including rest breaks, field toilets, and drinking water; and finally, strictly enforced pesticide use, including banning DDT. These contracts, however, have been under assault by conservative lawmakers from their beginning, and although the UFW mounted other successful lettuce and grape boycotts (including one against Gallo brand wines) over the decades, its organizing power has been in steady decline since 1973.[4] From health, safety, and environmental standpoints, many would agree that industrial vineyard labor conditions today, just as temporary labor conditions for any other industrial monocrop, leave much to be desired.

In the midst of these industry realities, the Wine Institute, the major advocacy group for more than a thousand wineries and affiliated businesses in California, is keen to capitalize on wine's continuing, if inaccurate, yeoman pastoral image. Wine's sylvan narrative has been perpetuated internationally for centuries, and is the basis for what journalist Mike Weiss has called "the Story" of contemporary wine growing.[5] This vision of wine production, in which nothing is corporate and everything is personal, local, and hand-crafted, is bolstered by winegrowers and the wine industry. For example, in "California Wine Profile 2010," the key wine industry flyer, the institute lists what it purports are the most important details of the contemporary wine economy. The flyer states that vineyards "preserve open space and wildlife habitats," and are "predominantly family-owned, multi-generational businesses." It attests that local winegrowers are "committed to California with deep roots in the soil and communities." Above all, California wine "creates scenic, pastoral landscapes. . . . California wineries are good neighbors."[6] In the Wine Institute's vision of wine growing, there is continuous cultivation of natural abundance, Old World refinement reinvigorated in the New World, and local craft rooted in the land. Supposedly, repeating yeoman lore of old, American viticulture comes from, and helps build, healthy natural spaces and communities. The Wine Institute is of course a booster organization for the industry, and this flyer reflects its central sales pitch. Yet it would be hard to underestimate the power of the story they sell.

It is not my intent in this book to take the contemporary wine industry to task for publicizing and profiting from what amounts to an egregious mischaracterization of how wine is actually made. Many other industries profit from similar stories. Rather, I hope to illuminate how the American grape's mythology came to be, and how, in reality, it has been inextricably linked with continental expansion and economic and environmental exploitation. The American winemaking myth extends well beyond contemporary industry advertisement and deep into the nation's past. Here we find the roots of this still-prolific vineyard mythos in nineteenth-century America, roots deeply tangled with the ideology of national expansion and its ideological foundation in manifest destiny.

Three elaborate and seemingly timeless cultural myths coalesce around American grape cultivation: the seductive image of Bacchanalian revelry associated with wine since antiquity, the persistence of the cult of *terroir* within winemaking, and an imagined culture of refined empire surrounding grape cultivation. These three myths informed the American public's understanding of vineyards in the nineteenth century, and imbued grape cultivation with larger aspirations of continental expansion and international prestige. They also worked together to cast American expansion as a process that was enacted at the creative selvage between nature and culture. Cultivating grapes ultimately assured the transformation of wild nature into sophisticated social refinements, while simultaneously pledging to unsettle a staid culture of gentility. Old World and New World methods combined to prove that America had gracefully fulfilled the seemingly paradoxical dream of a "republican empire." Grape growers promised a uniting of opposites: to craft the nation and its landscape as simultaneously lush and controlled, at once subtle and powerful, both wild and descendent of the best stock—much like they had crafted their wine.

Ambitious winegrowers of the 1850s would be very pleased with the U.S. wine industry today. In 1858, Marshall P. Wilder, president of the American Pomological Society (APS), delivered a rousing speech on the significance of his field at the society's national meeting in New York. He argued that fruit growers had a "divine charter," as Adam and Eve once had, "to dress and keep the garden." The biblical couple's first "primitive food" was fruit: "*all* its trees save one." The Creator in this way, he explained, intended for the growth of the horticultural arts through the ages. Wilder, calling horticulture one of the "most refined and honorable of human pursuits," further argued that the great gift of cultivating fruit had been "reserved for the present century, for our own time and country." He reasoned:

> Our country, vast in extent, containing every variety of soil and climate, fast filling up with an intelligent and enterprising population, is already a pioneer in other useful arts, and is doubtless destined to sustain a corresponding superiority in the cultivation of fruit. The cause we seek to advance will, ere long, adorn her hills and vales with the choicest fruits of the earth, and tune to grateful lays the voices of happy millions who shall succeed us. . . . It is, therefore, our duty, as

benefactors of our race, to develop these wonderful resources of our land, and to increase them to their utmost extent.[7]

Grape growing thus carried layered meanings and directives: of middle-class refinement, of honor and prestige, but perhaps most of all, of power to cultivate the continent. As "benefactors of [their] race" of fruit growers, and more largely, the white race that was multiplying across the continent, viticulturists imagined themselves the vanguard of "happy millions" to follow. Wilder was far from alone in using the language of expansion when discussing grapes.

APS records and hundreds of other published writings in the nineteenth century discussed grape growing as the premier practice for the fruition of an American culture of empire. When horticulturists and *vignerons* discussed "vine culture," or the "culture of the grape," they referred to the technical aspects of how best to tend grapevines at various life-cycle stages. Yet growers' technical language often wandered into more flowery rhetoric. Beyond giving advice on planting, trimming, trellising, harvesting, and propagating vines, viticulturists' practices and publications also went so far as to construct a larger "wine culture," a community of taste that was an essential and active part of an imperial horticultural imagination in nineteenth-century America.

While a few historians and several vinophiles have written devotedly and zestfully about wine, this is an attempt at a critical treatment of wine—especially in its connections to national expansion and cultural empire. In the past, grape and wine history has been told in vinophilic and boosterish narratives, as a subtopic within religious history, or within histories of prohibition politics.[8] Here I move away from those frames to situate U.S. horticulture and viticulture in the history of U.S. geographic and capitalist expansion. In the United States by the mid-nineteenth century, a potent wine culture acted as both a civilizing practice and one that strengthened Americans' grip on the continent. Mid-century grape guides had an uncanny way of evoking both the deeper mythology of grapes and the more grounded socioeconomic place-making that made viticulture so powerful—a combination that has been at the center of grape writing for generations. In turn, the narrative and visual trope of the grapevine offered the nation a powerful way to see and understand the world—and Americans' place in it—through a refined and seemingly timeless, civilized, horticultural lens. Indeed, as the APS's Wilder explained, vinegrowers' "divine charter" demanded it.

A word on terminology. While *agriculture* is a catchall term for the science or practice of farming of fibers and foodstuffs, *horticulture* is, more specifically, the science or practice of *gardening* and includes specialty crops like fruits and flowers, as well as landscaping plants. (As will be detailed, horticulture in the nineteenth century took on a specific class valence: claiming to be a horticulturist was different and more refined than being a farmer or agriculturist.)[9] *Pomology* is the science of growing fruit; *pomologists* are professionals in the fruit-growing industry. *Viticulture* is the art of growing grapes for fruit or drink, while a person who tends grapevines is a *vineyardist, viticulturist,* or *vigneron. Viniculture* or *vinoculture* is the art of growing grapes specifically for wine. *Vinifera* is the grape species that originated in Europe and whose varieties are used expressly for making wine.[10] I focus here on viticulture—the activities of nineteenth-century grape growers in general—most often, but not always, growing for wine. Grape enthusiasts across the period used the term "viticulture" over other terms because it best incorporated all activities of the vineyard: site selection and soil dressing, as well as trellising, propagation, cultivation, harvest, and grape processing. Each of these activities was also woven into several forms of literary and visual culture across the nineteenth century.

These terms and the differences between them were well known by growers and the lay public. Liberty Hyde Bailey, one of the most famous late nineteenth- and early twentieth-century professional gardeners, further defined horticulture as a high art in his *Cyclopedia of American Horticulture* (1900): "Horticulture is a composite of botanical and agricultural subjects. But Horticulture is more than all this. It is a means of expressing the art-sense. Plant-forms and plant-colors are as expressive as the canvas work of the painter. In some respects they are more expressive, since they are things themselves, with individuality and life, not the suggestions of things. Landscape making is fundamentally a fine art."[11] As an artistic medium, then, as well as one that put food on the table and had countless other uses, horticulture—and its star, viticulture—were full-fledged subcultures connecting nature and culture in the nineteenth century. Here, horticulture was a specific and shared way to define oneself, one's livelihood, and one's interests as a consumer.[12] Viticulture, as a primary subcategory within horticulture and with an active mythos and markets all its own, also became a subculture in its own right. Although diffuse, viticultural society shared overlapping worldviews and included communities of vine hybridizers, growers and nurserymen, vineyardists, vineyard tourists, avid wine drinkers, and literary vineyard romance readers. Indeed, these practices continue today in bridging the "natural environment and cultural tradition."[13] Then, as now, these groups employed a cadre of elite tastemakers, growers, and distributors who produced and supported a prolific horticultural industry and press.

It is my contention that grape culture was more explicitly expansionist than other agricultural products and practices of the nineteenth century. This was partly due to its central place in Western culture since the ancient Greeks and Romans, and its reemergence in the seventeenth and eighteenth centuries through a growing American interest in neoclassical design and culture. James Fenimore Cooper's *The Headsman or, the Abbaye des Vignerons* (1833), among other writings, helped establish a literary canon for viticulture, claiming ancient European roots for the nineteenth-century American wine grape movement. Grapes' importance in a new and growing nation was also made explicit in the most important landscape gardening journal of the day, Andrew Jackson Downing's *The Horticulturist* (1846–1875). The journal's focus on grapes came to its peak in "Grape Cuttings from History," a monthly column in 1865 and 1866 devoted to the history of vinoculture in sacred texts and ancient empires. The Bible's references to viticulture were the topic of the first column, with discussions on Greece, Rome, Persia, western Europe, and many Asiatic state histories following in subsequent columns. Each column details that all of the most powerful nations in world history had booming wine industries, and intimates that the United States should work to follow suit. The author, John Reid, writes that Greece, "in the days of its early nationality . . . was the LIGHT of the world . . . [they perfected] the 'nectar of the gods.'"[14] In context, the idea that the United States could imitate Greece's cultural prestige seems a bit forced—of course, by 1865 the United States had ripped apart at the seams. *The Horticulturist* had previously made a concerted effort to stay out of matters of war: there are only brief references to battles in readers' letters throughout the Civil War period, and there are no significant statements concerning slavery. Although the journal does not make specific reference to the war, "Grape Cuttings from History," with its focus on great nations and their genteel wine industries, reads as an ameliorator, an attempt to bring the nation metaphorically back to its senses, stitching it back together with grapevines. "Grape Cuttings" was one of many direct attempts of horticulturists to associate U.S. viticulture with the promise of an American empire on par with ancient Greece, just one example of how in nineteenth-century America grape cultivation and a sense of cultural nationalism rose in tandem. Time and again, growers argued that establishing a powerful wine industry was of utmost importance for the construction of an elite, imperial nation and American identity. The deep history and cultural cachet of wine had a large part in this, but here I find the literary heritage, the artistic trope of the grapevine, and the physical space of the vineyard were also key in articulating Americans' evolving cultural imperialism.

Grape Biology, Climate, and Industry Growth

The distinctiveness of American grapes by contrast with international grapes helped energize and delineate a national vine culture. In *The Fruits and Fruit Trees of America* (1845), Andrew Jackson Downing described the state of American grapes: "The wild grapes of our own country are quite distinct species from the wine grapes of Europe—[they] are usually stronger in their growth, with larger and more entire foilage, and in their native state, with a peculiar foxy odour or flavour, and more or less hardness of pulp. These traits, however, disappear in the process of cultivation, and we have reason to hope that we shall soon obtain, from the wild type, new varieties of high quality, and of superior hardiness and productiveness in this climate."[15] Downing was stating a truth: American grapes (*Vitis labrusca, aestivalis, girandia, rotundifolia*, and others) were different from traditional European wine grapes (*Vitis vinifera*). New World grapes differed from Old World grapes in significant ways, especially for winemakers concerned with their base ingredient's sugars, flavors, and yield. Relative to other species, *V. vinifera* generally produced larger berries and sweeter fruit, benefiting from thousands of years of human selection and cultivation. When compared with popular European wine grapes, most grapes found in the United States had smaller berries (and therefore reduced yield), lower sugar and higher acid levels, as well as different chemical compounds. American winegrowers were intent on developing American grapes that could stand up to *vinifera*'s prestige. (And in some respects grape breeding was out of their control: once *vinifera* was brought to the United States, its pollen began mixing with American species, and soon created the Isabella, Norton, and Concord, popular nineteenth-century American natural hybrids.)[16] Downing was also stating a falsehood: American grapes' unfavorable traits would not disappear as quickly as promised. Yet Downing's focus on the "process of cultivation" in an effort to make "superior" American grapes had many cultural effects. Prized new technologies in vine care spearheaded this process, and their trials and results were constantly reported to the grape-growing public through an expanding print industry.

Viticulturists also quickly found that due to climate and topography, growing grapes in America rather than Europe would require adjustments. Although many past and current scientists purport that the European *V. vinifera* is adaptable to a fairly wide range of environments, most also agree that it "reaches perfection" within a much narrower range of physical conditions. New York, for instance, like most of the East Coast, has ample rainfall and acceptable soils, so vineyards there did not need irrigation. But too much rainfall at the wrong time (especially during flowering and just before harvest) meant disaster for some grape crops. Many early eastern vineyard sites were also quite humid, a detriment to most vines because humidity encourages harmful fungi. Prior to the 1860s, trellising was not widely practiced, and unsupported vines that sprawled on the ground often did not receive sufficient air flow to combat fungal disease. Also, the eastern United States' seasonal variations were far more drastic than in most of the winemaking countries in Europe. Most popular wine grapes ripen best in moderate daytime and nighttime temperatures, so extremes in temperature were a problem for growers on most of the East Coast. For example, temperatures in New York soared regularly in July and August, but then dropped much more quickly in the following months than in popular European wine-growing regions.[17] Growers also found that vineyards did best when planted on hillsides overlooking lakes or rivers. These spaces granted the drainage grapevine roots preferred, and the bodies of water below often mitigated hot summers and cold winters. Because large bodies of water hold their mean temperatures longer than their surrounding landscapes, lake- and riverside growing areas stayed cooler longer in the spring and warmer longer in the fall. This was advantageous for grape culture because the moderation in temperatures often delayed grapevine bud break to a point past dangerous last frosts in spring, and extended fall seasons for maximum ripening.[18] Also, while seriously overstressed vines suffered and eventually died, winemakers believed that some amount of stress aided in wine production, adding "character" to the beverage by limiting the crop and enhancing the taste of premium grapes. Popular wisdom attributed various stressors to different regions: in Europe, poor soil had long been the beneficial stressor; in New York, it was cold temperatures; and in California, it would be lack of water.[19] While the eastern United States had many natural advantages for growing grapes, its disadvantages prompted winegrowers to engineer and experiment for better yields and higher-quality fruit.

Within this variety of experience, precisely quantifying vine culture throughout the century proves somewhat difficult. A look at vineyard acreage and publication numbers at various moments throughout the century relays partial evidence to the size and growth of interest in viticulture in the United States. In 1830, there were at least 5,000 acres of vineyards operating in the United States; in that decade, the aggregate agricultural press, containing separate and special sections on viticulture, had an estimated 100,000 subscribers. In 1858, the annual Patent Office *Report* included several chapters of information on viticulture, and 210,000 *extra* copies were printed, in light of public demand (the original number of printed copies is unknown). By the early 1860s, sixty journals covered horticultural interests, with an estimated circulation of 250,000. At this time, there were also more than forty books in publication dedicated solely to U.S. viticulture. The interest in viticulture was so great that by 1890 there were more than 400,000 acres of grapes in the United States, a hundred-fold expansion in just sixty years. International expositions were a primary space for experiencing new agricultural products in the nineteenth and early twentieth centuries, and winemakers constructed ever-more lavish displays at successive world's fairs. Their advertisements and models were most luxurious at the 1915 Panama-Pacific International Exposition in San Francisco, where more than 100,000 people experienced the wine exhibit. In our own time, the wine-soaked romantic comedy *Sideways* (2004) grossed $110 million in domestic and international box offices, and today national wine tourism, already a $100 billion-dollar industry, continues to grow.[20] These statistics and others in later chapters should give the reader some clues to the size and importance of viticulture over the past two centuries. Although wine is not nearly as popular as beer or spirits, U.S. wine consumption nearly doubled (from 1.2 to 2.2 liters per capita annually) in the half-century prior to World War I.[21] And beyond quantifiable numbers, the centuries-old legends about grapes and wine continued their popular circulation to untold numbers of American readers. The grape as symbol in nineteenth-century America gained a cultural significance far exceeding its economic significance at the time.

Dionysus, Terroir, and Empire

The foundational literary heritage concerning grapes and wine for a nineteenth-century audience was the Greco-Roman myth of Dionysus and stories of debauched and dipsomaniacal celebrations held in his honor. Since late Greek times, Dionysus, a lesser god in the house of Cadmus, has been affiliated with vegetative growth, fruits, and the vine. As a deity of autumnal fertility associated with masculine and feminine genders, Dionysus also symbolized the parallel powers of human reproduction—at once the creative and destructive forces that bring new life. Ancient Bacchanalian worship centered on the mystic ecstasy that imbued the "sap of life" into plants, animals, and humans: celebrations that very often and very easily vacillated from the gloriously elysian to the hellishly grotesque. In Dionysian tales, society's delicate veneers shatter. As one classical mythologist writes, the "basic impulses toward the bestial and the sublime are terrifyingly and wondrously interrelated" in classic works like Euripides' *Bacchae*.[22] The plots of most Dionysian tragedies center on the thin line between worship and madness: the spectacle and horrifying threat of men, and especially women (Bacchus's maenads or votaries) who became "unyoked" from civilization.[23] For many nineteenth-century readers, homage to Dionysus was befuddling. It was, on the one hand, understood through the ages as a legitimate cry for an individual's release from the bounds of society—a return to the freedom and purity found in mystic nature. On the other hand, most celebrations ended as berserk and bestial orgies of self-indulgence, reminders of the importance of self-control.

Among the many ways in which the stunningly symbolic myth of Bacchus may be analyzed, it is this last idea, the dissolution of social order and boundaries, that seems most prevalent in nineteenth-century Americans' fascination with the tale. Andrew Lang's *Custom and Myth* (1885) explains that the "Great Dionysiak Myth" turns on "the ripening power of the harvest" under a "wily and savage god." Lang writes for a U.S. audience perturbed by the idea that this "savage nature-myth" not only crossed the boundaries of accepted social order but also pointedly attacked those customs—and that bloody ruination was the story's inevitable end.[24] The myth, and especially Euripides' *Bacchae*, was understood as a narrative intent on ripping asunder accepted lines between divinity and bestiality, reason and madness, self and other. U.S. popular literature in the nineteenth and twentieth centuries contained dozens of similar vineyard romances, most of them plotted in reference to the basic themes in the myth of Bacchus. Works in the U.S. vineyard romance subgenre also contain significant and similar themes of boundary crossing. But in the American context, these more timeless boundaries were refashioned to focus on contemporary social and sexual boundaries, as well as meditations on the often-distressing geographic boundaries of the growing nation. The Bacchanalian myth that framed vineyard romances highlighted the vagaries of Americans' efforts to be "nature's nation": the landscape and its timeless protean deity led them through abundant cornucopias as well as devastating wilderness.

As such, in attempting to transcend the division of the bestial and the civilized, the Dionysiac myth is situated at the crux of nineteenth-century America's most fecund and haunted ideas of the interplay of nature and culture. Belgian literary historian Marcel Detienne has argued that the figure of Dionysus "oscillates between beast, plant, and human appearance, [and] straightaway found himself at the center of the problems of partition between man and the animal or vegetal world."[25] In the U.S. context, Dionysus's liminal identity has been culturally generative. Nineteenth-century Americans, if regularly concerned with understanding and apprehending nature under a nationalist banner, found a teeming and useful, if also beguiling and bewildering, story about the promise, pleasures, and threat of American wine growing within the myth of Bacchus.

Terroir was a second myth that drove Americans' imaginative understanding of vine cultivation. As they had learned from the Greeks and many other later European wine cultures, Americans knew that varying landscapes and soil types produced differences in their wines. For centuries, international winemakers from different agricultural regions developed their own styles and tastes, and over time the quality and uniqueness of particular wines gained social cachet. Grape culture continued over the centuries to offer various nations' viticulturists an attachment to the land, and a deeper sense of cultural permanence. The best description of this is the French term *terroir*, in use since the thirteenth century, denoting a kind of totalizing ecology of the vineyard. Within the cult of terroir, every aspect in the vineyard was believed to be important to the life of the vine. Soil, weather, the location in which grapes are grown, the methods by which they were tended, and indeed even the soul of the vigneron are all crucial aspects of the grape's transformation into wine.[26] The image of the landed yeoman farmer that accompanied viticulture was thereby in part a societal construction, but it also seemed to be a natural by-product of the necessities of the crop. American vignerons had participated in an international cult of terroir (though they did not use the specific word) since the trade in Madeira and other wines in the seventeenth and eighteenth centuries.[27] Americans believed if they could make good wine, everything else in terroir's web would be legitimated for their new country—including its land, methods, farmers, and claim to international prestige. Grapes and the myth of terroir rooted the nation's imperial sense of itself. But, as we will see, far beyond location and a nation's "inherent" terroir, national interest and historical circumstances made "good" wine happen in the nineteenth century.

The third formative myth of grape cultivation is that of grape growing as an essential part of U.S. empire. It begins with Thomas Jefferson's conception of America as a republican empire, an "empire for liberty." For Jefferson and his cohort, "empire" did not so clearly suggest, as it does today, attempts at world domination. Instead, it meant the opposite of European monarchy. A democratic empire was an "expanding union of republics held together by ties of interest and affection," an expansive, dynamic "union of free peoples." For many, "empire" in these early days of the republic evoked an idealized history, and an inclusive—but expansive—democratic civilization on par with dreams of nonesuch Rome.[28]

But other leaders at and since the nation's founding were vexed by the idea of an imperial America, for evolving definitions of empire didn't sit easily with basic theories of republican government. For one, Native Americans did not disappear from the continent as the Founders surmised, nor as Jefferson's ideal empire required. Instead, many leaders soon found that "empires traditionally entailed militarism, colonialism, and exploitation—practices that were anathema to self-determination and self-government." By the Jacksonian period, expansionist presidents and their cabinets had developed an aggressive and "elaborate ideology of republican empire."[29] They believed democracy would surely only strengthen as the nation's borders grew, and that America was an exceptionally blessed nation, with astoundingly fertile soils and facile people. Jacksonians clung to the idea that the United States could be an empire without parallel, without precedent—one that would not lose its power, like earlier empires' cycles of rise and fall. Viticulture here offered an active and graceful way to navigate America's core problems: enswathed in vineyards, the United States could continue to grow, yet in a cultivated manner. As long as its independent farmer mythos held strong, "republican empire" would not be an oxymoron. Nineteenth-century viticulturists attempted to model a type of benevolent empire, and actively hewed a path through the moral vagaries of nation building. Viticulture was thus part of the elaborate, ever-evolving ideology that sanctioned imperial growth in the nineteenth and twentieth centuries.

In the grape culture context, I have used the terms *imperial* and *empire* while describing a sense of the prevailing cultural mindset of American viticulturists, including a basic will to power over markets, international social standing, and national expansion. While the issues here are more indicative of detailing a growing domestic "culture of imperialism," I ask that readers not forget the growing U.S. territorial domination and the pervasive "empire over nature" that was also basic to nineteenth-century agricultural and political thinking.[30] This more malleable application of empire, as variously meaning formal international imperial holdings, true colonization, control of nature, and/or a more culturally encompassing "spirit of empire," has been in flux in American dictionaries since the 1820s. As art historian Angela Miller has written, sometime between 1860 and 1870 (also a crucial period for U.S. grape culture), the definition of *empire* in *Webster's* began to include "the spirit of empire." Americans believed they had "transformed empire building from an arrogant autocratic policy into a benign democratic program."[31]

The worlds of professional horticulture and private gardening often served as sites of everyday empire building. For the thousands of people concerned with growing grapes and making wine, and for the people represented by a growing market interest in wine throughout the nineteenth century, the idea of empire through viticulture was transmitted in several arenas. It took shape within the pages of horticultural journals as well as other popular media, such as the visual arts and the era's literary expressions. Through these, grape growing had a powerful ideological place in the emerging panoply of nineteenth-century U.S. agricultural endeavors and products.

Agriculture at large has been a perennial form of geographic expansion in America. Farming and horticulture deserve cultural historians' close attention because of their ability, in diverse forms and locations, to precede and perpetuate U.S. imperialism. I and many others have found academic inspiration in Frieda Knobloch's statement that "colonization is an agricultural act; it is also an agricultural idea."[32] Growing grapes was not just a material practice, it was a powerful ideology, set of aesthetics, and ubiquitous discourse of national power. Historians have long since taken it for granted that the United States was an imperial power well before its self-described imperialism of the 1890s in Central America, the Caribbean, and the Pacific—Indian removal and Mexican cession from the 1830s through the 1870s being the most significant examples. A parallel project for cultural historians, then, has been seeking out the various ways in which the American public was complicit with, and sometimes drove, this imperial expansion in their everyday lives.

Developing a productive, beautiful sense of place has always been central to the practice of growing grapes. Part of a nineteenth-century culture of the grape, as well as the centuries-old mystique of the vineyard, was also a specific understanding about, and interaction with, the land. The largely middle-class public contributing to this ethic of cultivation believed that attractive plants and landscapes, as well as learned fruit culture, were key characteristics comprising American gentility and their sense of landed power.[33] Taken together, in the same way that travel writing was a key ideological apparatus of empire, antebellum vineyard construction, grape cultivation, and horticultural publications provide for another such apparatus. For centuries, colonial powers have used grapes and wine to legitimate their empires. When the British colonized Australia and the French colonized Algeria in the nineteenth century, for example, both colonizers immediately established wine industries, and often marketed their wines internationally. By virtue of being graced with grapevines and a particular vision of labor, U.S., Australian, and Algerian landscapes could be solidly located within the accepted Western narrative of world history that claimed all powerful nations, since antiquity, had transcendent grape cultures. In this way, viticulture was an international set of colonial tactics for transforming landscapes and for propagating a particular worldview of cultivation and control.[34]

Not coincidentally, the middle decades of nineteenth-century wine production reveal a deep-seated fear that America would never approach the culture, refinement, or power of Europe. Grape growers developed a language of viticultural nationalism in part to combat the dominance of European wine and the continent's age-old colonial and cultural prestige. The centers of the U.S. grape industry (New York, the Ohio Valley, and California), far from predestined or natural, helped spearhead manifest destiny's ideological push, and were established precisely at sites that needed to provide "proof" of the success of America's evolving and expanding agricultural empire. Viticulture was only made possible, however, through constant agricultural and technological adaptations to new environments and labor conditions. This required dedicated federal and state spending, as well as public interest and consent. Although this book examines major U.S. grape-growing regions roughly from east to west, it ultimately problematizes the history of frontierism and the sequential westward movement of the "frontier line" that the ideal picture of manifest destiny represented. Instead, grape culture flourished in several locations at once across several decades. Grape culture was disseminated through rootstocks, vineyard tourism, the growing availability of grape products, and print and visual materials; it ultimately provided a grounded practice and new ways of seeing that were easily conveyed to middle-class audiences.

It should be clear, then, that this project is more concerned with grapes, the grape industry, and the establishment of vineyards within the context of national expansion, broadly construed, than a focused study on the cultural cachet of wine. Many other excellent books have addressed wine drinking in the United States.[35] I am more concerned with who grew the grapes and where, as well as the stories Americans told themselves about their vineyards. Wherever middle-class Americans wanted to prove a new legitimate hold on land, markets, or taste, they turned to horticulture—and more pointedly, grape growing—no matter the odds. I illuminate elements of grape culture that were performed for a larger market industry, which increasingly also became schemas for surplus capital investment. Said another way, I have chosen particular moments, personalities, and texts because they best situate grape culture as a means by which the country's cultural imperialism could be constructed and performed, and further, a way to mystify the means by which capital from other sources was accumulated. Given this focus, I do not explore all regions or personalities, nor the winemaking endeavors of various ethnic subcultures in America throughout the century. Although ethnic growers themselves do not often appear here, issues of the social construction of race and racism compose major sections of many chapters, as they are central to the American grape myth. Thus, one of the book's central concerns is indeed race in the American vineyard—but race as perceived from primarily the white perspective.

Ultimately, this book finds that the history and logic of nineteenth-century grape culture is located somewhere between the early ideology of manifest destiny and larger, final imperial control of lands and trade—a crucial middle step between the dream of laying claim to the continent and actually controlling national and international agricultural markets. The centers of wine production in the United States moved through three major regions, each of which was serially imagined at the heart of America's agricultural Eden. The history of grape culture, which was neither at the bloody edge of empire, nor the final symbol of U.S. agricultural dominance, reveals unexplored ideologies and practices at work through the long nineteenth century, the gestation period of American imperialism. The grape's roots and trunk, providing evidence of the age, stability, and strength of its vines, along with the grape's looping, sweet, cursive tendrils and fruits, are perfect symbols for the nation's historical, literary, and artistic attempts in cultivating a "natural" empire of bourgeois taste. That fine wine sometimes takes decades to ripen is perhaps an apt metaphor for this larger historical narrative of power and refinement.

1

Tributaries of the Grape

NEW YORK STATE was the center of the mid-nineteenth-century U.S. plant empire. As the nation's primary hub of print culture production and distribution, as well as the terminus of the Erie Canal, the region was home to thousands of investors, plantsmen, and horticultural writers.[1] Although Boston and Philadelphia had led the nation's botanical efforts in previous decades (with the Peales and Bartrams and others in operation, as well as horticultural societies, exhibitions, and libraries functioning in those cities), by the 1840s, the locus and drive of national horticultural pursuits had recentered in New York City. Indeed, by 1860 the city controlled one-third of the national periodical circulation, which was two times that of second-place Philadelphia. In this regard, New York publishers and nurserymen delivered plants and reading materials to the rest of the nation. Coupled with its agricultural publishing monopoly, New York was the nation's horticultural epicenter between 1835 and 1865.[2]

Within this sphere, an alliance of country gentlemen, urban nurserymen, and horticultural writers throughout the state pioneered a nationalist grape culture. Antebellum nurserymen such as the William Prince family and Andrew Jackson Downing were central to the New York network of plant distribution, vine grafting, and the publication of new grape information that extended into "far western" locations like Ohio and California. In addition, James Fenimore Cooper, a devoted gardener, lover of landscape architecture, and one of the most widely read American fiction and travel writers of the nineteenth century, popularized an Old World mythos about vineyards and wine. Through their plants and writings, the Princes, Cooper, and Downing propagated a worldview that was generative of nineteenth-century American national identity and ideal visions of urban and rural life.

The antebellum obsession with creating good U.S. wine was part and par-
cel of other classical impulses at the time. Americans reconceived architecture, dress, leisure reading material, and other cultural forms at mid-century
in an attempt to revive and adapt ancient Greek and Roman lifeways. Farming was understood as a continuous font of classical republican virtue. The
U.S. public lauded ancient civilizations because they were seen as incorrupt-
ible, and Americans yearned to live with the vitality, simplicity, and wonder they believed their bygone forbears had. Several leaders argued that the
United States was an heir to the ancients, both for good and for bad. President
Andrew Jackson, for example, was negatively compared to Julius Caesar, as
both men were generals who were popular with the masses and often accused
of imperial overreach. Jackson was also thought to be neoclassically inclined
in that he kept a large wine cellar at his Hermitage home in Tennessee.[3] Vine
culture, then, seemed to deliberately and materially link its practitioners to
matters of history and imperial legacy. Grape growing and wine making became a major part of America's classical revival.

Princely Nurseries and Their Businessmen-Botanists

William Robert Prince, of Flushing, New York, is one of the best representatives of the neoclassical grape movement. In 1830 and 1831, Prince published
a series of articles titled "The Vine" in the short-lived journal *The Naturalist*.
For thirty pages, Prince mapped grape history around the world as one long
tale of empire. Beginning with the Bible, Greek mythology, and Roman rule,
"the vine" became "an emblem representing the riches of a country, or the
flourishing condition of a nation, tribe or family." Kings and conquerors of
upper Asia and all of Europe each had their days in the sun with grapes and
wine, the vines "trained upon trees . . . so as to display all their luxuriance," as
well as strewn about their tables for feasting, and wreathed upon their heads
in victory. In his own time, Prince complained that "the French boast that
their country possesses greater advantages than any other for the culture of
the vine, and that for centuries her vineyards have been regarded as one of the
principal sources of her territorial riches." He continues, "but when we recur
to our own happy country, combining every variety of clime and soil, with
the conscious knowledge that she is yet but in her infancy, and look forward
with the gaze of anxious hope to her high destiny, can we as Americans fail to
reply to that nation in her own language, '*Voila l'Amerique la rival!*' ('Behold,

America thy rival!')." This long, valiant grape history and its "anxious" American future was capped with reference to Prince's own efforts in vine culture at his "Linnaean Botanic Garden, New York, contain[ing] 513 varieties, 87 of which are natives of America."[4] In later pages, he describes grape projects in the "vicinity of New York," where grapes "succeed perfectly," cultivated on new trellises and in graperies of all sizes. Prince narrates grape history as an extended story of empire, finally imagining U.S. grape culture in its lineage, himself at the helm.

Prince was the most successful in a family line of New York nurserymen. As the fourth proprietor of Prince Nursery, in operation since the Revolutionary War, he continued from the 1820s to the 1860s to build the nursery's reputation as the largest and most important in the antebellum United States. Yet he did not operate in a vacuum: plantsmen William Reynolds and Michael Bateham began a nursery in Rochester in 1834, which was sold to George Ellwanger and Patrick Barry in 1840, who, by the mid-1850s, had over one million grapevines on six acres in Mount Hope, New York.[5] Between the 1840s and 1850s, a network of nurseries bloomed in western New York, including Asa Rowe Nurseries, W. & T. Smith Company, and T. C. Maxwell & Brothers. The Princes, leading the pack as some of the nation's earliest grape hybridizers, were constantly creating and selling new types of grapes. William Prince (1725-1802), William Prince Jr. (1766-1842), and William Robert Prince (1795-1869) were crucial to the success of grapes and horticulture in the United States, as well as the period's broader grape culture.[6] Their nurseries remained America's foremost for a century. This family of nurserymen was exemplary not only for its social position, but for its stance on the potential power of viticulture. Beyond supplying viticulturists with hundreds of thousands of grapevines to cultivate in all national regions and upon all types of land, the Prince family was important—through a matrix of horticultural journals and books, agricultural societies, landscape designers, and the national government—in making grape culture a national concern for the United States, and indeed, they argued, any developing nation. The Prince family propagated and sold grapes as a tool for rooting and expanding national identity.

William Prince Jr.'s *A Short Treatise on Horticulture* (1828) devotes thirty pages to the "varieties and culture of grapes," while most other fruits get two to three pages of description. For no other fruit but the grape does he offer "Concluding Remarks," comparing U.S. ventures in grapes with German, Russian, and Swiss vineyard and wine production. His writing amounts to a national call for action:

Shall, then, America alone be debarred from this, one of the bounti-
ful gifts of nature? . . . Shall it be said that a plant, which culture has
accommodated to almost every other clime to which it has been induced, can find no spot whereon to flourish, in a country extending
from the 25th to the 47th degree of latitude, and that we can boast no
such congenial soil in an empire, whose bounds are the St. Lawrence
and the Gulf of Mexico, and whose settlements already extend from
the shores of the Atlantic to the sources of the Missouri? It is high
time such delusions of blinded theorists should give way to the lights
of reason and of judgment, and that the culture of the vine, to *every
variety of which* we have a soil and climate suitable to offer, should
assume that importance to which it has already attained in countries
possessing comparatively few advantages. Let, then, the beams of in-
telligence, which are imparting so much benefit to mankind by their
wide diffusion, disperse these clouds of ignorance and error from the
enlightened horticulturists of the American republic![7]

In the *Treatise*, America at large will flourish through its natural productions.
In this way, Prince pointedly disproves the French Enlightenment philoso-
pher Comte de Buffon's stinging claims from decades earlier that the American environment was inherently degenerate; for Prince, the sweeping country
had many "advantages" for the vine. Yet, Prince also turns an ideological cor-
ner in this piece: he describes the panorama of latitudinal and longitudinal
coordinates to evoke the grand sweep of the continent and to claim it all as
land on which grapes could be grown. Writing in 1828, when the national
borders of the United States did not yet include the Southwest or the West
Coast, he posits that the U.S. empire's "bounds" were the St. Lawrence River
and the Gulf of Mexico, the Atlantic to the "sources of the Missouri." Reason
and judgment, he argues, would prove to unnamed naysayers that grapes of
all kinds from all nations could somewhere take root in America's diverse
expanse of "congenial soil." Prince believed it a problem that the United States
had not yet fully secured these boundaries. Indeed, the final inclusion of all
lands north to south, east to west, in one great American empire would be
the only guarantee that an immense variety of the best-quality grapes would
flourish here, as they did in an ever-idealized Europe. To Prince, the evidence
of grapes in the United States was more than fodder for Enlightenment theorists' debates over New World biology and geography; it was simple, intrac-
table evidence of a growing empire.

Horticulturists like the Princes relied on a geographical vision of the "high destiny" of American power, a "destiny" that prefigured manifest destiny, a term not coined until the 1840s. One of the tenets of this ideology was the theory of the "isothermal zodiac," a finite latitudinal band about thirty-five degrees in width, stretching across the fortieth degree of latitude around the world, where every great empire throughout time (including China, India, Persia, Greece, Rome, Spain, and Britain) had flourished. Here, as in other grape writing of the period, reliance on numerical continental geography legitimated American claims to the continent through horticultural expansion. The logic behind the isothermal zodiac was at once world-totalizing and microscopic in its deployment—and it was not new. Arguments concerning America's exceptional physical geography had been utilized by William Gilpin and other major eighteenth- and nineteenth-century explorers. In this line of thinking, American claims to a perfect range of geographic latitudes were essential to viticulturists' discussions of "divine providence" and "cosmic burden" in fulfilling a national project of empire.[8] Other grape writers as far back as 1819 never failed to open their works with similar rhetorical flourishes detailing the sweep of the continent before reporting on updates in viticultural matters. For example, in a piece published in the *National Intelligencer,* later reprinted in the compendium *American Farmer,* the author exhorts:

> The vine country of the United States . . . is much larger than that of France, the most extensive and valuable vine country owned by any one people of the world... from 26 degrees north latitude, to 38 degrees 40 minutes in North America, prove the natural and present capacity of all that region, of nearly nine hundred common miles from south to north, for the production of the grape, as a crop; and as our country shall be cleared of its woods and forests, and drained in its great and small swamps, marshes, and alluvial grounds, the sphere of the vine will be improved and extended one thousand miles.[9]

The "sphere of the vine" was at once large, and growing, and yet it would spread itself over the land astonishingly fast and in highly localized forms. Dozens of publications included references to this continental sweep.

The Princes chided readers for not believing in the grape's power to transform the nation, and in doing so, implied that such readers were not following the Enlightenment's key principles. This was an especially weighty allegation coming from the Princes, proprietors of the New York "Linnaean Botanic

Garden and Nurseries." Its namesake, Carl Linnaeus (1707–1778), a Swedish botanist and minister, continued his significance in the nineteenth century as one of the key figures of the Enlightenment and botany. Born Carl Linné, he changed his name to Linnaeus to mimic his scientific naming model and to make it sound Latin, and therefore classical and international.[10] Linnaeus's claim to world fame, his *Systema Naturae* (1735), was a plant-naming schema that offered instant recognition and hierarchy of plant species to anyone operating in the international plant trade. With the *Systema Naturae* in hand, botanists acted as agents of colonization, linking far-flung locales with metropolitan centers, delivering marked and hierarchized plant materials to western European and U.S. botanical gardens. When utilized by eighteenth- and nineteenth-century botanists and gardeners, the Linnaean classification system for known and unknown plant life helped reify what has been called a burgeoning international "hegemonic reflex" of Europe over its colonial interests. In this way, Linnaeus was a key "ambassador of empire," offering European plant explorers a "planetary consciousness" for comprehending— and apprehending—continental interiors around the globe. The scientific systematization of nature was an integral component of the period's imperial conquests at the "height of the slave trade, the plantation system, [and] colonial genocide in North America and South Africa."[11]

Enlightenment techniques of naming and mapping deftly subsumed native cultures and history into nature, establishing a place for literally everything in a "universal" classification scheme. Ultimately eliminating (or at the very least, rewriting) the cultural and historical context the specimens were extracted from, both history and biology were viewed through one world-totalizing and hierarchized system. Much like the Princes, Linnaeus believed collecting the globe's various biota was crucial to any nation's self-sufficiency. As such, he sought to build a transoceanic natural empire within Sweden's limited national borders. As he wrote in 1746, "Nature has arranged itself in such a way that each country produces something especially useful; [our task] is to collect from other places and cultivate at home such things that don't want to grow but can grow [here]." Linnaeus organized nature to service his contemporary international political culture: that which was exotic and natural could be groomed to produce wealth and prestige at home.[12]

In New York, the Princes and their fellow "enlightened horticulturists" marked their own claims to international power through the figure of Linnaeus. The family's botanical garden, much like larger versions in France, Sweden, and England, was a carefully ordered, large-scale public spectacle for showing and selling national grapevines and plantstuffs. Scientific naming meant the constant elevation of one's national plant species, and presenting those plants on an international stage. The distribution of plants to large botanical gardens and collectors, and ultimately to farmers and landscape designers on several continents, was key to manifesting this power. The Princes were instrumental propagators of the colonizing Linnaean system and distributed it to anxious American consumers.

Varietally, however, William Robert Prince always advocated that native grapes be given American names and not carry any taint of European reference. Linnaean Latin was an international (albeit Eurocentric) language used to delineate grape species (for example, *Vitis vinifera* or *Vitis labrusca*). But for the variety, Prince demanded in his *Treatise on the Vine* "that the foreign titles [of grapevines] be dropped in every case and appropriate ones substituted." Although he was launching an effort to hybridize native and European grapes, he was well aware that vines signified Old World culture and control in the New World.[13] Linnaean methods of collecting, nationalist advertising, and local and domestic techniques of enhancing investments in landed capital were intertwined practices for the Princes and other nurserymen. In their catalogues and publications, the Princes offered Linnaean science's "correct" hierarchical organization of plants, as well as information and tools for grape cultivation. They also included tips on the best methods of plant deployment in the landscape and helped determine what people grew, where and how they grew it, and how they understood and evaluated their surroundings. The Princes sold seeds, plants, and vines in every town in the Hudson River Valley, and "almost to every farmer," for one hundred years.[14] Their mail-order business and publishing ventures further extended this reach. As an ornamental and useful landscape of power, the vineyard could be bought and reproduced in physical form only under the aegis of nurserymen—the businessman-botanist was the necessary funnel through which several streams of rhetorical and material power flowed to the American public.

Continuing the grape's imperial destiny in the United States was crucial to the Prince family, and that meant wresting that destiny from Europe. This central project was most fully articulated in the second installment of William R. Prince's series in *The Naturalist*, where he again makes the case for expanding U.S. viticulture.

Too long indeed have Americans listened to the counsel of strangers to their country and its interests, rather than seek for facts in the

bosom of her grateful soil, thereby allowing their own reason and in-
telligence to be the dupe of foreign ignorance, envy and rivalry. . . .
And what country ever presented a more eligible theatre for agricultural pursuits than the United States? . . . The land is both fertile and
cheap, and the great diversity of soil and climate seem to invite the
introduction of the varied products of other climes. The country penetrated in every direction, even to its remotest bounds, by navigable
rivers, and intersected by canals and artificial roads, offers every advantage for the speedy transmission of its productions.

The "strangers" to whom Prince alludes are the French, long recognized the
world over for wine production. In Prince's view, the grapevine and its culture
are tropes for the nation: the United States would spread like vines colonizing a hillside. The land is "penetrated" by transportation routes, just as vine
culture digs its roots in the soil. The "theatre" and its "productions" (that is,
the national landscape and its grapes) have every "advantage" for continued
growth. Rivers and canals symbolize the flow of goods and power and enable
the grapevines to spread "luxuriantly," while offering access to markets on
a world stage. Prince's key point remains that the United States alone could
sustain all the best grape varieties of the world, since such climate and soil
variation was present in North America. Prince ends the section with a gloss
on these central issues: "We may hope that the day is not far distant, when
America will fully establish and claim a rivalry with the most favored lands
of the vine . . . and proudly disclaim being tributary to any foreign clime."[15]
Although he imported various vines for experimentation for years, Prince
wanted to dislodge the United States from continuing as a "tributary" to
foreign countries—he specifically wanted to break other nations' grasps on
American pocketbooks for agricultural goods. In using the term "tributary,"
he returns to canal and fluvial transportation references, terms especially potent in the aftermath of America's early nineteenth-century transportation
revolution. Through these metaphors of national expansion, Prince developed his central theme that power and empire are accessed and developed
only through agricultural development. Waterways and transportation are
presented as mechanisms for the flow of "productions"—goods, people, and
monetary interests—all of which tied the nation together. The "flow" of goods
down waterways is also reminiscent of "luxuriantly" spreading grapevines:
the vines themselves naturally ripple into market profit.[16] Presented in this
way, grapevines were an essential part of the stream of national power, both

pathway and product, mapping and legitimating America's stake in the history of empire.

William R. Prince continues the imperial trope in his 350-page *Treatise on the Vine*. For him, grape culture was to be "calculated to develop our internal riches, by bringing into useful action those vast domestic resources which have too long lain dormant in the bosom of our soil; a proper attention to which would place us in an attitude of independence of foreign supply."[17] In *Vitis labrusca, Isabella* (Fig. 1), drawn by William Prince as the frontispiece to William Robert's *Treatise*, the artistry is basic, but the visual effect extends his written argument.[18] The grapes are shiny and distinct; each grape makes its own claim to space and light. Stems, each grape's tributary from the larger vine, are also fully visible, an unusual addition when compared with other pictures of grapes at the time, which show grapes crowded together, no stems visible. In rhetoric and art, Prince argues that accessing and exploiting America's own natural "tributaries," by investment in and construction of transportation and agricultural goods, was the answer to American ambitions. That these items had a natural, flowing, connective quality signaled that all actions toward their enhancement would be justified.

Although they loved mounting the family soapbox to decry Americans' lack of grape interest, the Princes must have known through their own nursery sales that grape growing in the United States was expanding briskly in the 1830s. Another writer on American grapevines and wine, C. S. Rafinesque, quantified this surge in vineyard establishment. In 1825, he found small vineyards operating in Georgetown in Washington, D.C.; Vevay, Indiana; Pendleton, South Carolina; and York, Pennsylvania. Rafinesque estimated that there were sixty vineyards of "1 to 20 acres each, altogether 600 acres" across the states. By 1830, these acreages had grown to "200 of 3 to 40 acres, or nearly 5,000 acres of vineyards." He found that vineyards of good size had been established in New York, Delaware, Maryland, Virginia, Georgia, New Jersey, Ohio, and Alabama, and more in Indiana, Pennsylvania, and the Carolinas. According to Rafinesque's estimates, vineyard grounds had increased tenfold in the space of five years, and would only hasten on that trajectory in later decades.[19] In addition to this growth was burgeoning grape experimentation in cities. Small indoor and outdoor vineyards were established up and down the eastern seaboard, and they stretched out into new western states.

By 1844, Prince Nursery sold 420 varieties of native and foreign grapes. The sheer number of varieties was fodder for international bragging rights. Likewise, the length and strength of certain grapevines (attested to in detailed

Figure 1. "*Vitis labrusca*, Isabella. Drawn by W. Prince," frontispiece to *Treatise on the Vine* (1830). Courtesy of Special Collections, University of California Library, Davis.

monthly journal columns) enhanced the extent to which grape advocates believed themselves and their grapes to be truly cultured and cultivated. In 1847, William R. Prince was still entreating Americans to take up grape growing:

> It seems a matter of amazement that so much apathy should exist in regard to Vine culture . . . when we have thousands of acres of idle lands that might be most lucratively devoted to the production of an article for which we are paying an annual tribute of millions to foreign nations less favorably situated than ourselves . . . here, partaking, as it were, of the general character of our country, the Vine extends its tendrils far and wide, impatient of restraint; whilst nurtured and warmed by the richness of our soil . . . it presents to the mind in its wide expansion and ample development, another emblem of the genius of our country.[20]

Again, Prince overstates the case. By the time he wrote this article for *The Horticulturist*, his own nursery's catalog contained more than five hundred varieties of grapes, each promising a different bouquet when made into wine—and conspicuous elegance when growing in an antebellum garden. Certainly not suffering from "so much apathy," American viticulture had expanded rapidly throughout the early manifest destiny period. Yet Prince's tract reveals much more than the state of grape growing in the United States. It also highlights his investment in producing American wine so that foreign nations (such as France, Italy, and Germany) would receive no more "tribute"—in the form of money or respect. American vinoculture, for Prince and his contemporaries in the horticultural trade of New York, was bathed in the residue of Jeffersonian agrarian nationalism. Yet this nationalist call to deny other nations "tribute" for grapes and wine was groundwork for national expansion as well. In his description of the vine "extending its tendrils far and wide," Prince distills the discourse of agricultural production into one about the furtherance of American empire. The "genius of the country," although found specifically in the "richness of the soil," was really the "genius" of a national and continental paradise. Prince's call for vine "cultivation" in this way held second and third meanings: by cultivating grapes, Americans were also cultivating a distinctive (bourgeois, republican) character and, more importantly, national power. By the 1840s, Prince's rhetoric and desires for the country were in lockstep with prominent national Democratic expansionists. Like them, he had reservations about rapid modernization, and to that end idealized a pastoral Jeffersonian past. Expansionists throughout the decade argued for the acquisition of new lands to encourage all types of agriculture and to promote foreign markets for U.S. goods.[21]

As seen here, American nineteenth-century botanical exploration and experimentation was a political project as well as an art and a science. As such, the development of a powerful agricultural program was vital not only to the national economy, but to the United States' perceived cultural standing among elder European nations. Like many other prominent examples of Americans' developing cultural nationalism—as found in literature, landscape painting, technological advancement, and newly advertised natural wonders—U.S. horticultural development carried within it a programmatic nationalism, one that assured Americans that their country and its natural accoutrements would soon best their venerated rivals' botanical wardrobes. Much like landscape painting specifically, the horticultural arts' central concerns paralleled nation-building itself, creating a nationalism that was intensely conscious (and apprehensive) of continued European authority. As we will see, horticulture and nation-building's overlapping programs included the development of a biological national character and institutions "naturally" suited to it, the cultivation of ever more beautiful and profitable landscapes, the removal of "native" and/or otherwise "foreign" bodies, and a vision of nature writ large as a civic and moral primer. Horticulture's effects were thus more than simply aesthetic—as a cultivated component of "nature's nation," learned gardening's cultural work was similar to other arts that also promised to be forward-looking economic programs.[22] American civilization could be judged through grape growing; the nation's aesthetic and botanical adroitness would propel her to new heights. With the Prince family at the helm, horticulturists proved excellent translators and cheerleaders of national expansion.

Gentlemen, Journals, and a Powerful Taste for Grapes

Antebellum Americans had growing access to grape information. As viticulture expanded, so did the print industry in agricultural and horticultural information. Historian Hamilton Traub explains that viticultural writing was a "vigorous pomological branch of horticultural literature [in the United States] . . . [and] differentiated from the main trunk in 1817."[23] Print culture's explosion in the market revolution of the 1820s and 1830s laid the groundwork for what scholars have called the era of the "industrial book." It also enabled New York horticulturists to reach a national and international audience. From 1850 to 1880, book manufacturing establishments rose in number by 66 percent, and a coordinated national book trade system emerged. Increasingly, authors and artists were connected to publishers, who were connected to dealer/jobbers, who were connected to booksellers, who were connected to advertisers, who were connected to readers, all of which in turn developed into a great web of the book and journal trade.[24] The U.S. agricultural press began as the publishing arm of agricultural societies that were well established by the 1840s. The *New England Farmer, Plough Boy, American Agriculturist,* and *American Farmer,* published in Boston, Albany (New York), New York City, and Baltimore, respectively, were among the most popular. In 1834, there were fifteen agricultural journals in the country, but most were short lived. By the end of the 1830s, the weekly and monthly journals numbered more than thirty, with an estimated 100,000 subscribers in 1839.[25] By the 1850s, many journals were popular enough to stand alone, without the help of state agricultural societies. The *Genesee Farmer* and *Southern Planter* each had about three thousand weekly subscribers, while the monthly *American Agriculturist* sold up to 80,000 copies per issue. By 1852, there were forty-three U.S. agricultural journals, for general farmers and anyone reading for "rural interest," in northern and southern seaboard states, as well as the "western" states, especially Ohio.

Early in the century, journal content was typified by the sharing of "useful" information through largely amateur sources. The role of professional scientists became significant in the 1830s with the rise of agricultural chemistry and geology. Increasingly after the Civil War, journals claimed to convey the knowledge of experts.[26] At that point, agricultural writing professionalized, allowing the most respected journals to claim expertise in questions about farming techniques. Both practical and aesthetic aspects of rural and farm life were central to this genre of journal writing until late in the century. By the early 1860s, the national agricultural press had expanded to nearly sixty journals, with circulation numbers of more than 250,000. But the reading public at large, not just horticultural magazine subscribers, were getting good doses of agricultural writing, too.

Grapevines had a presence in many general magazines, as the topic claimed significant layout space in *The National Recorder* and *Harper's Weekly,* as well as others.[27] One example is Mrs. H. H. Dodge's "The Cottage of the Vine," written for the *Saturday Evening Post* in 1830. She describes the setting of her brief romantic tale: "In Italy, glowing Italy . . . perhaps there never was a more lovely scene . . . the grape vines clustered thickly over its thatched roof, all interwoven with bunches of their delicious fruit." Along with James Fenimore Cooper and dozens of other American authors of the nineteenth and twentieth centuries, Dodge exemplified the romance, charm, intrigue, and gentility found in vineyard prose and travel narratives. She continues, "Here were neatness and order in their perfection—and here were piety, harmony and love. . . . [The vines] yielded a superabundance of the richest fruits of the country, and extended to the banks of a clear and gentle river, which seemed more like the fabled streams of the ancients than a beautiful modern reality."[28] Dodge's vineyard cottage holds natural abundance and, although reminiscent of ancient spaces and cultural rituals, prompts a present-day piety and love for its "chaste" Euro-American occupants. Although presented in the language of a virtuous middle-class woman of the early nineteenth century, Dodge's piece of vineyard fiction is not unlike what was to follow it. As we will see, James Fenimore Cooper was a cheerleader for U.S. viticulture through his fiction and travelogues, the progenitor of the novel-length vineyard romance for an American audience. These and other vineyard voices constitute an American literary subgenre that has remained an active part of the American imagination about grape and wine culture since the 1830s.

With the popularity of journals for horticultural enthusiasts and general readers came a wave of viticultural manuals. Up to 1840, only three books had been published in the United States on the art of grape growing. Through the 1850s and 1860s, thirty-seven more books were added to the shelves.[29] This number does not include the dozens of works imported from other countries in wide circulation, nor works translated and published by American printers. By 1900, Liberty Hyde Bailey, in his behemoth *Cyclopedia of American Horticulture*, claimed that "the American book literature of the Grape is nearly as large as that of all the tree fruits combined." Bailey believed the grape was important to U.S. society because it was civilization's "oldest of domesticated fruits."[30] Its presence on the page included straightforward methods of propagation as well as, per usual, much more historical and ideological detail than other fruits detailing *why* Americans must practice grape culture in the first place: viticulture alone would place the nation in the long, distinguished line of empires adorned with grapes and power.

American agricultural journalism began in New York with the publishing of *The Plough Boy* in 1819. With New York being the nursery center as well as the publishing capital of the continent, these practices merged in the nineteenth century to create a robust market for agricultural and horticultural journals. A brief list of periodicals published in New York devoted to agriculture through 1870 (with varying success) includes *The Country Gentleman, The New York Farmer and Horticultural Repository, Genesee Farmer, New Genesee Farmer and Gardeners' Journal, Dairyman's Record, The Cultivator,*

American Agriculturist, The Farmer and Mechanic, The Plow, American Fruit Culturist, Central New York Farmer, Working Farmer, American Farmers' Magazine, Rural New Yorker, and *The Farm and Garden.* The *American Agriculturist* had offices in downtown New York City, situated just below the offices of the *New York Times.* The journal boasted its prime location through an image run in 1860 (Fig. 2).[31] New York's urban landscape, print technologies,

Figure 2. "Office of the *American Agriculturist*, No. 41 Park Row, New York City," *American Agriculturist* 19 (October 1860), 304. Courtesy of Steenbock Memorial Library, University of Wisconsin–Madison.

and publishing influence were central to agricultural experimentation and expansion.

Journals and presses were very competitive, critiquing one another's work and buying each other out at the first sign of failure. Periods of quick consolidation and even faster expansion marked the agricultural press industry at the middle of the century.[32] Magazine content is generally revealed by each publication's title, but consistent attention to grapes was present in nearly all agricultural journals. Grapes were a central item of concern for the *New-York Farmer* from its inception in 1828. The journal's first article in Volume 1, Number 1, was an excerpt of an address delivered by New York horticulturist William Wilson to the New York Horticultural Society in 1821. Wilson gave an overview of his grape-growing efforts since 1801, detailing site selection, ideal soil types, and pruning cycles. He also described training grapes on fruit trees throughout his larger orchard: "I have cultivated grapes for more than 20 years, and for the last 10 years with success. . . . It is no unpleasant thing to see a cherry tree on one hand, a pear on the other, and a peach tree not far off, all ornamented with clusters of grapes."[33] *New-York Farmer*'s Volume 1, Number 3, included two articles on grape care and the journal's second-ever published image, illustrating various pruning methods for the first four years of a vine's cultivation (Fig. 3).[34] Reproduced from *Wilson's Economy of the Kitchen Garden*, the article encouraged enterprising grape culturists: "In fact a wide field lies open for the ingenious cultivator to exercise his skill in making improvements in the management of the grape vine. Various situations too, in the country, might be selected for their culture, perhaps more favorable for their success than any yet tried." At the conclusion of the excerpt, the editors of *New-York Farmer* remark, "As a general rule, it may with safety be asserted, that the Farmers of the United States, are yet to learn the immense productive power of a perfectly cultivated acre [of grapevines]."[35] Many journals through the 1860s showed similar attention to viticultural matters, although many grape images through the 1850s were simple line drawings (Fig. 4).[36] On the surface, little practical information is gained from the many large but simple drawings published, in which grape figures have no specific detail and are merely a mass of circular globules—even the stems have almost no distinguishing features. At the time, shape, rather than color, was believed to be a trustworthy characteristic determining type. Illustrations in most journals in the first half of the century thus did not hold much visual information. The continual presence of line drawings of grapes must have been in part a marker for people flipping through pages—a signal that yet another grape

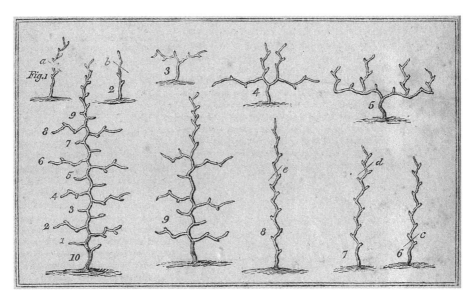

Figure 3. "Art. 48.—Grape Vines—extracted from *Wilson's Economy of the Kitchen Garden, Orchard, and Vinery*—just published by Anderson, Davis, & Co., New York," *New-York Farmer and Horticultural Repository* 1:3 (1828), image of grapevines on unnumbered pages between 56 and 57. Photo courtesy of the University of Minnesota Libraries.

had been successfully hybridized, a new technique mastered, and that grapes were a significant and paginated presence for the journal.

New-York Farmer continued for many years under the patronage of the New York Horticultural Society, and grapes continued their rhetorical and visual presence in it. Likewise, with increasing detail in later years, *The Horticulturist* (1846–75) represented the print world's fascination with grapes. Here the drawings became much more detailed, several of them on good-quality paper that folded out of the journal and presented grapes in near life-size (Fig. 5).[37] Many artists presented grapes with their leaves as a serving dish, creating a beautiful bed on which to display new breeds—and hinting at their ability to whet the appetite. Nearing mid-century, *The Horticulturist*'s grape became an increasingly aesthetic object, defined by its unceasing roundness and fullness: bunches, or clusters, of grapes signified abundance in all forms. The grape—in the garden, on the dining room table, the subject of much still-life painting, carved in furniture, embroidered in silk, and adorning the home, was at the center of a growing aesthetic of domestic cultivation.

Figure 4. Simple line drawing of
"Rebecca Grape," *The Horticulturist*
13 (January 1858), 14.

In several pictures throughout *The Horticulturist*, leaves explode from centered bunches of grapes, like feathers in a fancy cap, as if the final artistic
flourish of the lithograph symbolized the years it took to cultivate such refined delicacies.

Letters about grapes appear regularly in journal correspondence. Magazines devoted many pages to readers' letters each month, and included
numerous viticultural questions. A sampling from *The Horticulturist* is representative of reader interest:

July 1854: "Why are Grape vines that are trained on the ground to
propagate from, or for other purposes, freer from mildew than those

Figure 5. Life-size foldout of "The Anna," *The Horticulturist* 16 (June 1861), between pages 15 and 16. Photo courtesy of the University of Iowa.

trained on elevated frames? . . . An answer to the above is respectfully solicited, you shall be duly apprised.—Sandy Hill, Wash. Co., NY"

April 1861: "Dear Sir . . . We have some fine grape lands along the shore of Lake Erie . . . recently, attention to vineyard culture has been awakened. Isabella and Catawba are principally grown. . . . I would like to know if Diana requires any peculiar management. Does close pruning injure it? . . . Will you, Mr. Editor, please tell us all you know? (Editors must have no secrets.) We do want light on Grape culture in particular. Yours truly, A.S. Moss, Fredonia, NY"

November 1861: "Dear Sir . . . I think the 'Summer Grape' needs more attention: do not you? Its time is admirable. It has received no systematic treatment yet for seedlings, so far as I know; yet it has produced the chief American Grape. Yours, Aestivalis, New Bedford."[38]

Readers seemed to not just request, but demand, more and increasingly detailed information on grape culture from journal editors. Articles examining new methods of cultivation and reports on grape crops came from northern, southern, and western U.S. regions. In 1860, *American Agriculturist* (1842–1912) ran an article titled "Grape Mania," outlining the frenzied activities of grape enthusiasts and the dubious practices of some cultivators exploiting the craze to make a buck. Old vines were given new names and scandalously sold as "the latest thing." The author of the article warned his readers: "Let us not underrate the good old-fashioned things in our zeal for the new . . . let us be a little cautious . . . and if we must allow the mania to possess us a little, let us keep some sober friends by our side to guard us from too great indiscretions."[39] Fashion in grapes was as superheated, and as fickle, as fashion in ladies' dress design at mid-century.

American viticulture thus sought to establish itself on national, social, and economic planes through its mid-nineteenth-century print culture. Grape growers constantly patted each other on the back for their work. In January 1848, *The Horticulturist* interviewed several hybridizers about their trade. John Adlum was one of the many men with his hands in the engineering of the first wine grape to be easily grown in the United States. Numerous others had failed; until this point, viticulture was commercially unprofitable because grapes of value to winemakers—that is, European *vinifera*—would not grow in the United States. A journal editor quotes Adlum: "It appears Mr. Adlum had a proper appreciation of the value of the Catawba grape. In a letter to me, he remarks, 'In bringing this grape into public notice, I have rendered my country a greater service, than I would have done, had I paid the national debt.'"[40] The symbolic and monetary value of the grape he "invented" was lauded throughout the pages of journals and books in the 1840s, and weighed in terms of the United States' standing, comparing its natural productions and economy with those of other nations.

Editors of journals once again invoked a deep and wide historical stage in an attempt to establish a national history of viticulture over and against European wine practices in the 1860s. For example, in 1860, *American Agriculturist* ran an article entitled "American Grapes Two Centuries Ago." In it, editors develop the thesis that American grapes had been taken to Europe long ago and cross-bred with grapes there to create some of the popular wines of the past: "It appears that several of our native grapes were taken to England, about 1620, the date of the landing of the Pilgrims."[41] The story, which did not catch on, had a clear ideological thrust: growers wanted to claim that American grapes were part of the deep lineage of the highest-quality *vinifera* species in the world. While professional grape writers invoked these and other romantic tales when describing grapes, James Fenimore Cooper was the figure to coordinate a more coherent American grape mythos for an expanded audience.

Cooper's Vineyard Romance

James Fenimore Cooper, an author famous in his time and continually reckoned with in our own, is, according to Richard Slotkin, "the clarifier, codifier, and popularizer" of a basic American frontier mythology.[42] Cooper's *Leatherstocking* series has received much critical attention in this regard, and sections of it continue to pervade undergraduate anthologies of American literature. Among Cooper's dozens of other works is nearly a decade's worth of novels and nonfiction concerning European history and myth, as well as five European travelogues, the notes for which he recorded during his stint as U.S. consul in France from 1826 to 1833. It is difficult to overestimate Cooper's importance to an antebellum American audience.

Coexistent with Cooper's focus on various political and natural environments was the development of his formulae for American historical and frontier romances. First popularized by Sir Walter Scott, the historical romance was crafted for coordinated appeal to both fiction and history. The historical romance presents the sources of a nation's key traits and tropes through a romantic bedrock of archetypal characters, political moments, and natural spaces. Most works in this vein present sociopolitical contexts in microcosm, and as such the genre grew with the rise of European and U.S. nationalism. Cooper wrote many historical romances—indeed much of his fiction can be placed within this genre, including his *Leatherstocking* series—which are at once concerned with class legitimacy and racial status, developing democracies, speculation on and development of frontier lands, and moral regeneration.[43] Frontier romances have also been categorized as melodrama, one of the most popular forms in nineteenth-century American fiction and theater. Scholars define melodrama's many key features: stark battles between good and evil, stock characters (the virtuous young woman, noble hero, and satanic villain), familial dispersal and reunion, revelations of hidden actions and disguised identities, female sexual endangerment, hyperbole, and "vivid pictorial tableaux."[44] The frontier romance thus shares elements of seduction, threat, and thrill with many other genres, but most specifically here with the Greek myth of Bacchus. In Bacchanalian/Dionysian tales, order is questioned through alcoholic abandon, then civilization is restored—the basic plotline of almost all vineyard romances. Cooper popularized a third sort of romance throughout the 1830s—one coextensive with and sharing many of the properties of his historical melodrama and frontier romances—yet unique enough to necessitate articulation. Cooper's *vineyard* romance framed the details of this particular American subgenre so strongly that it continues to be imitated almost two centuries later in U.S. fiction and film.

Cooper wrote several works of fiction and European travel narratives in the 1830s in which grapes, vineyards, and wine figure significantly. Like many of his other works, his trilogy of European historical novels, published 1831 through 1833, comment on the sociopolitical context at home in the United States directly, or through analogy and metaphor.[45] The first book in this series, *The Bravo: A Tale* (1831), a sociopolitical thriller set in eighteenth-century Venice, focuses on corruption caused by aristocratic power and wealth in a seemingly egalitarian republic. Wine flows throughout the story, and wine sellers populate the minor characters. A central scene in *The Bravo* involves rare wine used as a ruse to capture two female characters. Although not the crux of the plot, wine culture infuses the narrative in an effort to provide cultural authenticity, mystery, and detail.

Similarly, Cooper's *The Heidenmauer; or, The Benedictines—A Story of the Rhine* (1832) is a sociopolitical novel set in the German Rhineland during the sixteenth-century Reformation. The conflict concerns the reigning aristocracy, the church, and a rising middle class. A single, but important, scene in *The Heidenmauer* centers on wine and a disputed vineyard. A count and an abbot both lay claim to the vine-laden property and decide that instead of resorting to violence, they will settle the dispute by means of a drinking contest: the man that drinks the most wine and can finally walk away will win the vineyard. The carousing begins, involving several subordinates, and continues through the night. Finally, a friend of the count is called in and begins to describe his devotion to the new doctrine of Martin Luther. The abbot, infuriated, gulps several goblets of wine and falls unconscious. The count, at this point unable to speak, nonetheless picks up the land title and staggers away, now the full owner of the vineyard. His power and prestige increase accordingly. While these two works include significant picturesque scenes full of local color and romantic vineyard and wine scenes, it was Cooper's next novel that laid the foundation for the basic, repeatable form of the vineyard romance.

Cooper's *The Headsman or, the Abbaye des Vignerons* (1833) established a fully articulated literary genre for viticulture, claiming long-standing European roots for nineteenth-century U.S. wine culture. As in many Cooper novels, characters in *The Headsman* are a motley group of travelers. Set in eighteenth-century Geneva, greater Switzerland, and the Alps, it exemplifies the landscape appreciation and overt melodrama typical of many antebellum novels. The book opens with passengers gathering on a ship sailing from Geneva to Vévey, worried about the rough weather they may encounter on Lake Leman, and wondering if rumors that the local headsman (an official executioner) will be joining them are true. After much fuss, the ship sets sail, and those aboard—including a sassy Neapolitan; a monk; a baron and his daughter, Adelheid; a Swiss soldier, Sigismund; a greedy merchant; a student; a few aristocratic passengers; and a few dogs—get to know one another. As foreshadowed, a violent tempest strikes the lake, and the passengers fight desperately for their lives. We find out later that Sigismund has saved multiple passengers from death and declared his love for Adelheid on board, but has not asked for her love in return. Once in safety, one of the travelers, Herr Müller, quietly reveals that he is Balthazar, the headsman.

Later, Adelheid takes a walk around Vévey's Blonay castle with her father, appreciating the landscape and talks of her love for Sigismund. The castle, surrounded by vineyards, holds "one of the most sublime and lovely views that ever greeted human eyes. Beneath it lay the undulating and teeming declivity, rich in vines, and carpeted with sward." The scene, along with most Swiss architecture, the narrator explains, is "generally inferior to our [Americans'] own; but the beauty and quaintness of the sites, the great variety of the surfaces, the hill-sides, and the purity of the atmosphere, supply charms."[46] The baron reminds Adelheid that Sigismund is without noble blood and should therefore not be considered a marriage prospect. Adelheid defies her father and declares her love to Sigismund, but the heroic soldier explains that marriage is impossible because he is of "ignoble, nameless origin"—and the son of Balthazar. Adelheid, should this romance continue, would be marrying the next headsman, and would plummet in caste. Her father and Sigismund in good conscience cannot allow it.

Meanwhile, preparations commence for the Abbaye des Vignerons, a Bacchanalian festival held every six years in Vévey. Throngs of visitors appear from all parts of Europe, and platforms for performances are built in the city square. The novel's central celebration is extravagantly woven throughout several chapters: vine-tenders, gardeners, mowers, reapers, shepherds, cowherds, and Bacchants make grand processions. Agricultural gods and goddesses all process with their retinues: Ceres, Flora, Pales, Bacchus, Silenus, and Hymen each carry their own songs and dancers. Bacchus, "the high-priest, robed in a sacrificial dress, with flowing beard, and head crowned with the vine, stood foremost, chanting in honor of the craft, of the vine-dresser."[47] The narrator explains why the details of the *abbaye* (company or festivities) of *vignerons* must be enumerated so explicitly: "The ceremonies which followed were of a peculiar character, and have an intimate connexion with the events of the tale. . . . [The point is] less that of sketching pictures of local usages, and of setting before the reader's imagination scenes of real or fancied antiquarian accuracy, than the exposition of a principle, and the wholesome moral which we have always flattered ourselves might, in a greater or less degree, follow from our labors."[48]

The essential work of the book is described, then, as not so much the (real and fictionalized) picturesque tourism within it, but the moral to be gained by the character play within its vineyards. This vineyard romance is above all didactic. Here, Cooper was transmuting Archibald Alison's *Essays on the Nature and Principles of Taste* (1790), a work intensely popular in the United States in the early decades of the nineteenth century. In it, Alison mounts the thesis that good taste relies not on perceiving nature's beauty, but in assigning human significance and value to it. Aesthetic appreciation of nature was thus fundamentally about communicating one's gentility. Cooper's daughter, Susan Fenimore Cooper, further embroidered the *abbaye* scene from *The Headsman* in her *Pages and Pictures from the Writings of James Fenimore Cooper* (1865). She reiterates her father's moralizing message about "this picturesque local festival":

> Mr. Cooper's fancy was pleased with the account of a holiday festival, celebrated at Vévey in past ages, and still kept up, at intervals, by the

good people of the borough. This is called the *Abbaye des Vignerons*—the great holiday of vine-dressers—a gay and motley scene, partaking largely of the carnival spirit; blended, however, with something of the better feeling of the harvest-home. . . . There were your aproned gardeners, armed with rake and spade—their sweethearts bearing on the head baskets filled with fruits and flowers. . . . There were reapers, mowers and gleaners, all in quaint and picturesque array. . . . The concluding scene of the procession was always a rustic wedding; the bride being dowered.[49]

Susan Fenimore Cooper is careful to say that the "gay and motley" carnival contained the "better feeling of the harvest-home," the quiet rounds of domestic life. "Sweethearts" process throughout the town, and their romance is refreshed, refocused, and legitimated with the festival's concluding wedding. Expectedly, there is no threat of Bacchanalian debauchery in Susan Fenimore Cooper's recounting.

In *The Headsman*'s fictionalized version of the festival, after the long processional, the crowd anxiously awaits the final activity of the day: a marriage of two young people in town, Sigismund's sister, Christine, to Jacques Colis. The bridegroom bears a single gold chain for his betrothed, a paltry gift in comparison to Christine's rather large dowry. Just as the marriage procession begins, drunken revelers and escaped prisoners create a commotion. They are caught and brought to the town square, where the marriage is about to take place. One of the prisoners abruptly identifies Christine as the headsman's daughter. Jacques tears up the marriage certificate, and the wedding is canceled. Adelheid comforts Christine and invites her to Italy, where she, the baron, Sigismund, and a larger party are traveling the next morning. On the trail, bad weather strikes the travelers again. (Nature is gloriously beautiful but also a continuous threat in this, as most, of Cooper's novels.)[50] A snowstorm descends upon the travelers, and the party is in danger of freezing to death. They are saved, but they find that Jacques was murdered during the night. Balthazar, the father of the jilted bride-to-be, is immediately arrested for the murder but soon acquitted. At the trial, Balthazar shares the shocking information, unknown to everyone else, that Sigismund is not in fact his real son, but adopted: Sigismund was left to Balthazar and his wife when their own son died in infancy. Sigismund's real name was Gaetano, his real father was an Italian noble, and the boy was left with a substantial sum in gold. Expectedly, Adelheid's father gives immediate consent for the marriage of Sigismund and

Adelheid, and they are wed. The storyline of *The Headsman* bears a striking resemblance to not only Cooper's other major works but several other later novels by Americans in which vineyards are a central setting.

The Headsman's plot and character play parallel the questions that Americans and Europeans had about the quality of U.S. grapes and landscape through the nineteenth century. Grapes in the United States were assumed to be of lower quality, indeed not of the same vegetable "bloodline" as European *Vitis vinifera*. In *The Headsman*, Cooper presents exotic Old World customs of vignerons and festive, romantic gatherings of Swiss and Italian travelers, yet throughout the novel he continuously plays down the beauty of foreign vineyards in comparison to U.S. vistas. Here, Cooper was up to some rather hefty cultural work. As the book's narrator describes, the point was not to fill readers' heads with local beauty or real knowledge of Swiss and Italian wine making. Instead, a "wholesome moral" should follow from the tale. The moral that rises to the fore is clear: questionable bloodlines, if one is honest and brave, eventually uncover themselves. Sigismund's real blood was aristocratic, cementing the necessity of his good stock for marriage to Adelheid. The aristocrat, here presented as deserving, ultimately receives his due, especially after a lifetime of hard work and thoughtful, heroic acts. As in many of Cooper's novels, the republican ideal is given lip service, but ultimately the cultivation of good, free people is dependent on a continuous revitalization of aristocratic bloodlines.

Yet perhaps the reader gains other morals from the novel. For one, Cooper's suggestion that agricultural landscapes in Europe, however beautiful, are "generally inferior" to those in the United States establishes the possibility for American grape production and picturesque scenery that could outstrip Europe's wine industry. Additionally, the exotic and beautiful processionals seen in Vévey could seemingly flourish in the United States: the characters in the parade, and indeed the entire Abbaye des Vignerons, are not marked as distinctly European, but are rather a timeless procession of civilization's stock laborers. Cooper presents Bacchus and company as repeatable actors in an ever-moving tableau of harvest time—suggesting that one need only tap into a long line of semipagan characters in celebrations of the harvest to establish cultural legitimacy. Lastly, among the nonspecific, reproducible, yet well-tended vineyards, the narrator explains that "morals . . . follow from our labors." Labor in the vineyard, for male and female authors, was described as a civilizing act, one that connected its practitioners to a long tradition in human history. Vineyards, like aristocrats, may have questionable bloodlines but can be put right with honor and care. Cooper, in the very title of the book, conflates the two issues: the central plot concerns the paternity of both the human characters (the headsman) and, for a viticulturally interested U.S. audience, also concerns the paternity and biological and cultural conditioning of vine culture (the Abbaye des Vignerons). Within the context of constant comparisons of European and American landscapes and labors, Cooper implies that vine culture would next migrate to the United States.

Beyond Cooper's fictional, symbolic forays into European wine culture, in the later 1830s he published several nonfiction picturesque tourist guides in which he stated his views on European and American wine culture rather plainly. Having been roundly critiqued by the Whig press for his previous three novels, by the mid-1830s Cooper's general opinion of Americans was low: he called people back home "matter-of-fact, utility-loving, and picturesque-despising."[51] In his travelogues, Cooper wrote for American connoisseurs of picturesque scenery and attempted to lure a wider audience into its wiles. Cooper published five picturesque travel books from 1836 to 1838, crafted from the notes and letters he had written while on European tours of Switzerland, the Rhineland, France, England, and Italy from 1826 to 1833. Although Cooper references vineyards and winemaking in each of these works, they figure most heavily in his first two travelogues: *Gleanings in Europe: Switzerland* and *Gleanings in Europe: The Rhine*.[52]

In *Gleanings: Switzerland* (1836), Cooper remains ambivalent about the beauty of European vineyards. Early in the narrative, his family travels from Avallon, France, to Switzerland. To Cooper this trip "was the first really beautiful bit of natural scenery. . . . [It contained] the temporary disappearance of vineyards; for the vine, though so high-sounding and oriental in the pages of a book, like the olive, invariably lessens the beauty of a country."[53] Early on, Cooper is resoundingly negative about the artistic merits of vines in the landscape. But elsewhere in the book vines are decorative, romantic, and even gothic. Traveling to Rapperschwyl, Cooper describes a Sunday in August: "Peasants and their wives were hurrying past, in rustic finery. Most of the men wore flowers and vine-leaves in their hats," and at Zolliken, he is astonished by Swiss sentimentalism in a five-hundred-year-old vineyard where a young American traveler was memorialized after drowning in the nearby lake.[54] Finally, he describes the magical trip through Vévey, the "most exquisite" scenery he had encountered yet. He expresses the party's approach: "Fully a mile of rapid descent lay before us, and nearly the whole distance was lined with vineyards, propped in terraces." The Coopers' driver continuously "filled their laps with delicious grapes," and the family found that it was "altogether a fairy scene!" An example of the "finest natural scenery" in Europe, this "magical little district" enchanted the entire group. In Vévey, Cooper finds "the luxurious repose of everything connected to the earth, the sublimity of nature." More precisely, "through this fairy land" in town, "The vintage had commenced, and, in addition to the raptures of such a scene, and the luxury of such a day, we had the satisfaction of beholding and of sympathizing in the feeling of plenty and merriment that the season always produces. We constantly met wagons bearing tubs of grapes, and men and women were staggering through the vines, all around us, under burdens in which the luscious fruit was piled above the baskets." This was the memorable day upon which he crafted *The Headsman*'s Abbaye des Vignerons chapters five years later. Cooper's language in the scene is ecstatic, but he explains that the party's feeling was not so much "touzy-mouzy . . . as one of calm and delighted satisfaction."[55] Through many of his travel narratives, Cooper's social vignettes (peasants in vine-leaved hats, women staggering under the weight of luscious fruit) seem to be just as picturesque as, and sometimes more so, than his descriptions of grand landscapes. For as much as Cooper critiques the aesthetic of vineyards in *Switzerland*'s opening pages, by the book's close, wine country and Swiss seasonal vine culture have been one of the most memorable and important experiences of the trip. In his next travelogue, *The Rhine,* he encourages friends "who intend to pass a summer . . . who have need of a house, to choose their station somewhere on the shores of the Leman," his favorite area of European wine country.[56]

In *Gleanings in Europe: The Rhine*, Cooper takes a somewhat different tack through European vine culture. In his descriptions of European greenscapes, Cooper reveals facets of the U.S. national character. For example, Cooper describes the spare hand applied to the landscaping of the U.S. White House grounds as reflecting "obliquity" and vulgarity in American culture, an egalitarianism gone too far, compared with what he found in the Rhine. Conversely for Cooper, French gardens and French government prove the opposite, each being tyrannical and "elaborate monstrosities."[57] Like gardens, vineyards are another nature-turned-culture human landscape that reveal much about a country and its people.

About halfway through their travels in *The Rhine*, Cooper's party approaches the German Rheingau, "in the heart of the richest wine region in Europe, perhaps in the world." Cooper samples several wines of the region and makes suggestions for Americans: the "Redesheimer Hinterhausen. . . .

I feel very persuaded it is the very article for our market. . . . It has body to bear the voyage, without being the fiery compound that we drink under the names of Madeira and Sherry."[58] Cooper then takes it upon himself to instruct Americans in what he understands to be the difference between European and American wine drinking: in the United States, wine is a luxury; in Europe, a necessity. This difference, Cooper believed, made for less alcoholism in the Rhineland. But again, by the later chapters in the book, he rescinds his original idea, because he witnessed much drunkenness in Paris. Explaining that he sees public intoxication as "peculiarly the soldier's and the sailor's vice," he does not blame wine for this offense but instead argues that "in reasonable quantities, [wine] is not injurious at all." Indeed, back in Vévey he is elated, saying, "We are looking eagerly forward to the season of grapes, which is drawing near, and which everybody says makes those who are perfectly well, infinitely better."

One chapter of Cooper's *The Rhine* is dedicated solely to a discussion of wine, vineyards, and drunkenness in the United States and Europe. He states that "vineyards abound all over the American continent," yet his reliability as a narrator is put in question with the remarkably inaccurate statement that "we have been in possession of the country [United States] for two centuries, without making a cask of wine. If this not be literally true, it is so nearly true, as to render it not less a leading fact." Here Cooper mimics many wine writers of the period. This overstatement about the general lack of American winemaking in the 1830s, like the Prince family's, was most certainly made in an effort to encourage fellow Americans along in the cause. Cooper also shares wine writers' belief that "the consequences of even total inebriety from wine, are not as bad as those which follow inebriety from whiskey or rum. . . . Nature is a better brewer than man, and the pure juice of the grape is less injurious that the mixed and fiery beverages that are used in America."[59] Cooper finally becomes a champion of wine, and throughout the rest of his travelogues makes the case that extensive wine growing could only bring good things to the United States.

Cooper also offers his views on various contemporary U.S. debates concerning wine growing. First, on the United States' meteorological adaptation to grape growing: "The idea that our winters are too severe can hardly be just. There may be mountainous districts where such is the fact, but, in a country that extends from the 27th to the 47th degrees of latitude, it is scarcely possibly to suppose the vine cannot flourish." Cooper stresses the example of Italian wine growing: vines are everywhere in Italy, in both the hottest and coldest parts of the country. He takes a stab at where he believes wine growing would flourish best in the United States: "This fact [of Italian wine growing] has induced me to think that we [Americans] may succeed better with the vine in the middle, and even in the eastern, than in the southern and western states."[60] Cooper's only concern about the landscape's aptitude for wine growing in the United States is that her soils may prove "too rich"—the great vineyards he had seen in Europe were composed of "thin, gravelly soils." Cooper closes the chapter by restating, "We have been too ambitious to obtain a fat soil. . . . A gravelly hill-side, in the interior, that has been well-stirred, and which has the proper exposure, I cannot but think would bring good wine, in all the low countries of the middle states." Like many other writers of the time, Cooper had visions of a vineyard-laden United States, its people growing more naturally inclined to temperance through increased wine drinking and diminished use of other forms of alcohol.

A more serious concern for U.S. wine growing was the American people's general temperament. On this point Cooper argues: "Time is indispensible to fine wines, and time is a thing that an American lives too fast to spare. . . . Patience, I conceive is the only obstacle to our becoming a great wine-growing and a great silk-growing country."[61] Attentive cultivation was all U.S. grapes needed to flourish. Indeed, "if one had a little patience to try the experiment, it would be found the common little American fox-grape, would in time bring a fine wine. It greatly resembles the grapes of some of the best vineyards here, and the fact of its not being a good eating grape is altogether in its favor." Cultivation of choice natural and local products, however disappointing currently, would undoubtedly bring U.S. civilization, symbolized through a more worldly grape culture, to further fruition.

As he and his family traveled through Europe, Cooper grew more and more enamored of continental wine culture. In *Gleanings in Europe: Italy* (1838), upon his visit to Florence, Cooper raves about the wine: "The wine of our palace is among the best of Tuscany, and I drink it with great satisfaction; the moreso because its cost is about four cents the bottle." Near Rome, they happened upon a grotto in a valley. Cooper searches for its provenance: "considering the proximity of the temple of Bacchus, the grotto is probably the remains of some Roman expedient to cool wine, and to drink it luxuriously. Religion may have been mixed up of old with these debauches, as we know politics and dinners go together in our own times. . . . This grotto and the temple of Bacchus, probably, had some allegorical connexion, the one being a place to carouse in, the other a temple to sanctify the rites."[62] Here

Cooper pointedly compares Roman religion, politics, and the trappings of its wine culture to contemporary American cultural rituals. This, like many other scenes, seems a stratagem for pulling wine culture out of ancient history and lodging it as an alluring possibility in U.S. readers' minds.

Later, Cooper evocatively sketches music and vineyards in a land of edible and visible Italian riches:

> The songs of Tuscany are often remarkable. . . . It is withal a little wild, and has a *la ral lal la* to it, that just suits the idea of heartiness, which is perhaps necessary, for the simplicity of such a thing may be hurt by too much sophistication. . . . I often hear it, as I sit in my belvedere, rising from among the vines or olives. . . . Walking to Bellosguardo, the other day, I heard it in a vineyard . . . and getting on a stone that overlooked the wall, I found it came from a beautiful young *contadina*, who was singing of love as she trimmed the vines: disturbed by my motions, she turned, blushed, laughed, hid her face, and ran among the leaves.[63]

Cooper reminds his audience that vine culture is not some aristocratic, heady enterprise but instead a practice of the people: country people, hearty and unsophisticated, not unlike those driving America's popular Jacksonian cultural tide. Rather, wine making is a simple, modest practice, a daily chore completed happily by beautiful young women. And importantly, Cooper catches this alluring but demure farmer-woman "singing of love" amid the vines. His travel narratives thus shaped the contours of his fictional treatments of the vineyard romance.

Cooper's vineyard romances recapitulated his historical and frontier romances in several ways, yet also pressed them into doing some additional cultural work. His frontier romances, much like Frederick Jackson Turner's frontier thesis decades later, focus on the positive characteristics of talent and virtue succeeding in the wilderness. Hard work and good-heartedness here rise to the fore without revolution, and usually without violence. Land speculation and ownership, along with decisions about marriage, are vexed but finally settled with white, noble descendants winning out in both cases. In the vineyard romance, this theme is the same, but instead of the pioneer, it is the winemaker and vinedresser that provide the positive stock characters who ensure that civilization will continue. The ownership of wine and vineyards may be in question through politically and religiously tumultuous times, as Cooper points out in *The Bravo* and *The Heidenmauer*. Ancient as well as developing democracies have their difficult moments, surely. But the natural beauty of the landscape, whether American or European, points to its recoverability, its good productions—at once natural, romantic, and political. Here and elsewhere, Cooper simultaneously lauds and hedges against what he calls Americans' "property patriotism"—a blind belief in the supremacy of the U.S. landscape.[64] He argues that it will take American society's characteristic hard work to truly move "luxurious" but "hearty" wine—and its symbolic trappings of egalitarian nationhood—to center stage.

Yet an implicit elitism complicates Cooper's overt celebration of egalitarianism, as both his later work and the work of subsequent vineyard romance authors reveal. Consistently throughout the Cooperian code, racially mixed and low-class characters die or disappear, whereas whites marry and continue their elite bloodlines. White womanhood is of a predictably pious piece; white manhood, while perhaps in question through the first scenes of his novels, passes the test and is strongly repositioned at the center of civilized society. Also similar to the typical Cooperian historical and frontier romance, the vineyard romance forwards various men-on-the-make threatening to rip apart the social and political fabric of society. Traditional forms of authority are first undermined, then put right by white marriage. Instead of the usual examples of the "new American"—the lone scout or hardworking pioneer— here moral regeneration is found through hewing to the traditional, timeless cultural trappings of wine making. And as the moment of the grape harvest is also the moment when young couples are expected to wed, the bounty of the land redoubles within expectations of marital happiness and fertility. Both are positioned at the center of a "natural" and stable state, a timeless reenactment of central tropes of civilization. This cultural code, Cooper argues, should not be abandoned, but continued with precision and vehemence on the "American continent." His call for further dedication to U.S. wine growing is thus not just made at the contemporary international level of political power and prestige, but is also addressed to America's contemporary social scene: grape culture through the ages brought luxury, "delighted satisfaction," temperance, and genteel romance to societies in turmoil. Wine culture offered a name to those of "ignoble, nameless origin": simultaneously the continent, its grapes, and its people. This cultivation of the self, landscape, and nation were themes American landscape designer, horticulturalist, and writer Andrew Jackson Downing attacked with great passion as well.

Gardens for Beauty, Profit, and Nation

Andrew Jackson Downing (1815–1852) picked up where Cooper left off in his attempts at the social adaptation of wine culture to American lifestyles. Known as both "the grandfather of landscape architecture" in the United States and the American "apostle of taste," Downing wrote several popular books on architecture, landscape design, and pomology. Like the Princes, Downing was a successful nurseryman in New York, and was known transatlantically for his work. Through his books and flagship journal *The Horticulturist,* Downing added a supercharged aesthetic element to the usual grapevine rhetoric. He also articulated a specific kind of materialist national consciousness that was in constant cultural—albeit artistic and "tasteful"—conflict with British, French, Italian, and Spanish national viticultural traditions. In *The Horticulturist*, Downing makes connections between a "cultured" garden and a "cultured" society, "between the order imposed by landscaping and the order imposed by civilization." In his writing on grapes, Downing's capitalist materialism was shot through with a grapevine aesthetic that legitimated not only civilized order and capitalist profit, but territorial expansion.[65]

The first issue of *The Horticulturist* appeared in 1846, just months before William Prince's appeal to the public concerning the cultivation of *vinifera*. *The Horticulturist*'s fruit of choice was the grape, and it relied in most issues on an aesthetic of curling, twining grapevines in the garden and the home. The grapevine was part of the magazine's aesthetic in varied ways. For years, the journal's cover displayed its title in block letters resembling rough wood-hewn logs, with grapevines twisting in and out of them (Fig. 6). Four bunches of grapes and large grape leaves intermix with other fruits and flowers, evoking a woodsy yet refined bounty. The magazine quickly grew to be the most popular journal of its kind. By 1849, the journal's circulation was "equal to that of any similar magazine in Europe, and far beyond any of its class hitherto attempted in America."[66] Over the years, *The Horticulturist* printed attractive plates of grapes and vines, from grapes in pots to staked and pruned grapes for small yards, to ornamental arbors covered in vines, to a full-color lithograph of the "Diana Grape" in 1857 (Fig. 7).[67] Taken together, the pictures evoke bounty in all shapes for all subscribers—from the professional vineyardist, to the backyard enthusiast, to the small indoor gardener. In 1862 and 1863, *The Horticulturist* devoted space usually reserved for the editor's notes and introductions to a monthly front-page column called "Hints on

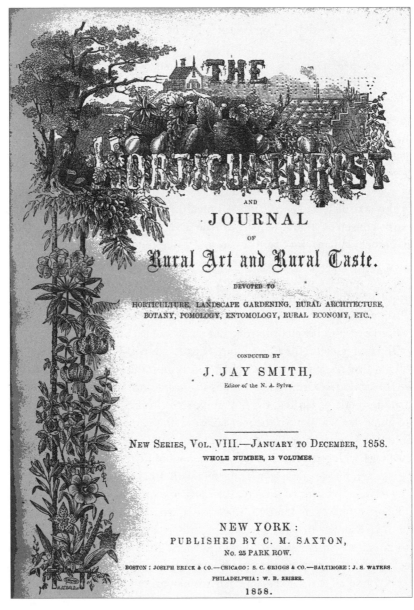

THE

JOURNAL

OF

Rural Art and Rural Taste.

DEVOTED TO

HORTICULTURE, LANDSCAPE GARDENING, RURAL ARCHITECTURE,
BOTANY, POMOLOGY, ENTOMOLOGY, RURAL ECONOMY, ETC.,

CONDUCTED BY

J. JAY SMITH,

Editor of the N. A. Sylva.

NEW SERIES, VOL. VIII.—JANUARY TO DECEMBER, 1858.

WHOLE NUMBER, 13 VOLUMES.

NEW YORK:
PUBLISHED BY C. M. SAXTON,
No. 25 PARK ROW.

BOSTON: JOSEPH BRECK & CO.—CHICAGO: S. C. GRIGGS & CO.—BALTIMORE: J. S. WATERS.
PHILADELPHIA: W. B. ZEIBER.

1858.

Figure 6. Title page of *The Horticulturist* 13 (1858).

Figure 7. Full-color lithograph of "The Diana Grape," *The Horticulturist* 12 (April 1857), frontispiece.

Grape Culture." For more than two years, the first several pages of the journal outlined new methods for caring for beds, trimming vines, cold storage,
building newfangled greenhouses, and every other aspect of growing grapes
imaginable. Counting the number of pages devoted to vine care alone, reports on viticultural practices in these years total nearly half the journal.

For Downing and others, the pomological arts (and especially viticulture) exuded domestic refinement and gentility. Downing consistently linked
"knowledge" of specific plants to rural aesthetics and "taste" in his journal
and books. Scientific knowledge and taste came intertwined for the "benefit
of the nation." Downing thus set domestic spaces within a nationalist scope:
"The love of country is inseparably connected with the *love of home*."[68] Advocates of the vine and wine described their mission to impart "taste" to their
readers and help them "settle down" into comfortable, respectable rural lifestyles. Downing's preface in his major work on landscape gardening, *A Treatise on the Theory and Practice of Landscape Gardening* (1852), evokes the
pioneer in the "far west . . . construct[ing] his rude hut of logs for a dwelling"
in opposition to "older portions of the Union," where people "are surrounded
by all the luxuries and refinements that belong to an old and long cultivated
country." This pioneer and his "restless spirit of emigration . . . form[s] part
of our national character . . . [and] to a certain extent [is] highly necessary
to our national prosperity." Other writers saw the frontier in opposition to
the vineyard as well. The frontiersman stood in stark contrast to his logical
follower, the cultivated vintner. The sequence offers a teleological narrative:
the landscape was once anarchic and savage, but with the cultivation of the
earth and production of wine, the United States will take its place among the
civilized nations of the world.

Downing was sure that another, more powerful relationship with the surrounding country was long overdue. His "strong attachment to natal soil"
and attention to soil embellishment methods were articulated within a consciously nationalist frame. He writes at length about the "evidences of the
growing wealth and prosperity of our citizens . . . the great increase of elegant
cottage and villa residences."[69] The preface in his *Treatise* uses popular mid-
century tropes that tied the landscape and character of the country together.
Although Downing initially defines the pioneer and landscape designer as
opposites, his preface essentially calls for a second wave of American pioneers, this time dressed as gardeners with Downing's book in hand, to further
subdue and control the land. In them, Downing hoped to prove to other (European) nations that with control and elegance came national power in the

United States. Elsewhere, Downing states, "When smiling lawns and tasteful cottages begin to embellish a country, we know that order and culture are established." He offered a Victorian overlay on the then-classic and nostalgic yeoman dream. Solidifying the United States' expansion and power was thus directly linked to landscape improvement for Downing. As the "arbiter of taste" and preeminent landscape designer, Downing gave gardening a national, capitalist, implicitly republican and imperial mission.

Downing advocated multiple uses for grapevines in the Victorian kitchen garden and in decorating the home landscape. In his 1845 tome *Fruits and Fruit Trees of America* (which sold 15,000 copies in less than eight years), almost 100 of its 590 pages are dedicated to viticulture. The book describes and evaluates nearly three hundred types of grapes using several criteria, among which a few are appearance, body, dependability, ease, and taste (off the vine and out of the bottle). He also includes a "Diary of the Vinery," comprising dozens of pages devoted to mapping the weather, the growth of grapes, the tools employed, new techniques of applying heat to vines, treating the soil, and dealing with diseases. His diary details the multiyear life spans of his vines, documenting the path of the grape from seed to bottled wine.

Grapevines were also an essential aspect of Downing's landscape and architectural design more generally. At mid-century, Downing's own home garden, Newburgh (fourteen miles north of New York City), or "Newburgh on the Hudson" as he liked to call it, was itself a symbolic space for gardeners because it was present in so many of Downing's writings in *The Horticulturist* and in other agricultural journals. Downing's four-acre garden, located at his home but constructed for experimentation and show purposes, further spurred the grape craze—half of it was devoted to grapevine experimentation by 1853, along with his signature use of "informal" coursing pathways and many types of shrubs (Fig. 8).[70] He considered naming his residence "Vinehall" and "Vinehome," but ever fearful of the temperance lobby, he and visiting Swedish friend Fredrika Bremer discarded the appellations because there was "something about the Winecellar in both." Bremer also suggested "Vinland," "Vineland," and "Vinehill" to Downing, explaining in a letter: "[My] forefathers gave this land [this name] on finding it full of fruit. And to me your Highland home has been a Vinland and I shall always think of it as my Vinland home."[71] Downing's house and the map of the grounds reveal his international training and yet overt sense of "American taste." The kitchen garden, orchard, and other utilitarian spaces are pushed to the edges of the property, in favor of more ornate, serpentine landscaping. The approximately

RESIDENCE OF THE LATE A.J. DOWNING. NEWBURGH ON THE HUDSON.

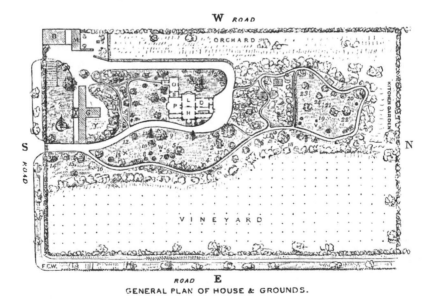

GENERAL PLAN OF HOUSE & GROUNDS.

Figure 8. Anonymous, "A Visit to the House and Garden of the Late A. J. Downing,"
The Horticulturist 8 (January 1853), frontispiece. The map of Downing's property was
drawn by Frederick C. Withers and engraved by Alexander Anderson.

two-acre vineyard, however, remains in full display, and half the total property is covered with vines.

The orderly geometric layout of Downing's vineyard was a complementary counterexample of landscape aesthetics—a scientific, experimental green grid against the homey, meandering walks around the rest of the estate. The vineyard held the popular native vines of the moment: "nearly a thousand vines, *Isabellas* and *Catawbas* . . . [and] a few other varieties scattered through the grounds; there is a fine specimen of the (native) *Elsinborough* near the office . . . none of the more delicate varieties that require artificial heat." Since 1852, one of his lawns also boasted a large imported French Borghese vase, decorated with Bacchanalian figures, similar to the vases Downing had chosen while he undertook a project landscaping the government grounds in Washington, D.C.[72] As trial gardens for his journal, Downing's home functioned as a model for readers, illustrating how readers' own homes and gardens could likewise stand as examples of design and productive experimentation. Taking cues from earlier English and French landscape designers, Downing found new meanings and uses for grapevines in the U.S. landscape. But by rejecting "delicate varieties" in his garden—that is, foreign *vinifera*, he only allowed thoroughly American vines into his landscape.

Downing describes the grape's aesthetic qualities in a section devoted to "Vines and Climbing Plants" in his *Treatise on the Theory and Practice of Landscape Gardening* (1852):

> In the American forests nothing adds more to the beauty of an occasional tree, than the tall canopy of verdure with which it is often crowned by the wild Grape vine. There its tall stems wind themselves about until they reach the very summit of the tree, where they cluster it over, and bask their broad bright green foliage in the sunbeams. As if not content with this, they often completely overhang the head of the tree, falling like ample drapery around on every side, until they sweep the ground. We have seen the very beautiful effects produced in this way by the grape in its wild state, and it may easily be imitated. . . . [It] winds itself very closely around the stem [of trees], however, and we have known it to strangle or compress the bodies of young trees so tightly as to put an end to their growth.[73]

Downing evokes the beautiful height of grapevines and, candidly, their deleterious effects on "bodies of young trees," strangled out of their native landscape.

The vine's ideal state is described in references to the gothic and romantic, but even more so through analogies to monarchy and power. Through the use of "crowned," "summit," "broad," and "sunbeams," Downing offers a somewhat guised reference to France's late seventeenth- and early eighteenth-century "Sun King," Louis XIV, and his gardens at Versailles. Such a reference was neither overwrought nor out of context for Downing. His *Treatise* opens with "Historical Sketches" of major world gardens, in which Versailles, "in its glories" as a "Royal garden," was the "most superb of all geometric gardens."[74] At first glance, seventeenth- and eighteenth-century French garden aesthetics—with flat parterres, astounding lengths of view, and rigid geometry—might seem to have very little to do with the aesthetic nature of wild grapevines, as well as Downing's own interests in "informal" taste making for Americans. But in this context, Downing calls upon a centuries-old notion of horticultural power: Versailles, since its construction, has been among the world's most famous imperial gardens. Versailles was constructed as a laboratory for, and a demonstration of, the French capacity to control global politics and landscapes. French leaders' material domination of nature was constructed as a theater of cultural and technical achievement—as nature made miraculous. Downing apparently learned much through the example of Versailles, where the state and nature were conjoined through grand landscape design. More precisely, the lesson Downing took from Versailles was that the state's power became naturalized through the strength and savvy it showed in remaking the physical geography of nature.[75] Although there are no pictures of strangling grapevines in Downing's book, a full-page picture of a "Gigantic Grape Vine" scrambling over trees in Burlington County, New Jersey, was included in an issue of *The Horticulturist* in 1858. He had first made note of the same "Enormous Grape Vine" eleven years earlier in the first volume of *The Horticulturist*.[76] As a reference to European precursors, Downing's grapevines at mid-century often evoked the beauty, power, and horror ("to strangle or compress the bodies . . .") of French monarchic and garden history. Within context, it seems a short stop for Downing's contemporary audience in remembering the horror and power of the American revolution and continuing U.S. imperialism against Native peoples across the West and against Mexico. Through this and other subtle methods, *The Horticulturist* gave further horticultural endorsement for colonization, imperialism, and the annexation of Native American lands.

Downing's description of the wild grapevine was also a metaphor for colonization in an American context. Other vines in this section of Downing's

Treatise, including ivies, the Virginia Creeper, clematis, wisteria, and honey-suckle, are discussed for their effects of color, contrast, and harmonization in the landscape, but not for their drastic height, and never with any reference to colonization or to the damage they could inflict on other plants. Downing ultimately warns readers to not carry this vine aesthetic to excess, nor "desire to see every tree . . . overhung with fantastic vines." Instead, in nature only "one in one hundred" trees is festooned in this manner, "and the very rarity of the example imparts additional beauty . . . when it appears."[77] As a trope for U.S. empire, the tree colonized with grapevines asserted its own entangle-ment with aggression and violence.

Downing's writings on domestic architecture include many related refer-ences to grapevines. He describes his preference for vines on small cottages: "How different such edifices, however humble, become when the porch is overhung with climbing plants . . . the ripe purple clusters of the grape hang down about the eaves."[78] Vines were central elements for assisting "humble" cottages in gaining airs of refinement. In his *Victorian Cottage Residences,* the designs for a "Suburban Cottage for the Small Family," "Cottage in the Eng-lish or Rural Gothic Style," and the "Cottage for a Country Clergyman," three among the fifteen original designs, include directions on growing grapevines on verandas and trellises, "for an air of rural refinement and poetry . . . with-out expense,"[79] and far more than that—thirteen designs total—show vines growing on walls (Fig. 9).

Beyond landscape design, grapes were an essential part of the garden, and fashionable trends in grapes were always changing. Different grape varieties were added to preferred lists in subsequent editions of the book, for each year a different grape proved "more in favor now." Determining a vine for every occasion, Downing set the grapevine within the classic and popular aesthetics of the time. Introducing a section on adorning homes, he waxes that "vines and climbing plants are objects full of interest . . . for they seem endowed with the characteristics of the graceful, the beautiful, and the picturesque, in their luxuriant and ever-varying forms."[80] For Downing, vines held both popular and traditional aesthetic principles—the "beautiful" and "picturesque" were at the height of their aesthetic popularity at mid-century in the United States. The picturesque in particular was an aesthetic middle ground, a "domesti-cated sublime," with endless occasions for entertainment. Visually located between "beautiful" and "sublime," the picturesque had elements of the fine, small, and smooth, as well as of dramatic terror and fright. This artistic trope has varyingly been described as the aesthetic of democracy and an expanding

Figure 9. "A Plain House" with vines, Andrew Jackson Downing, *Victorian Cottage Residences* (1842), 186. Image courtesy of Dover Publications.

economy. The picturesque generally presents vistas as settlement narratives, with civilization, domestication, and refinement at the center. In this way, the picturesque and Downing's use of it negotiated and helped absolve America's transformation into an industrial landscape and a rigidified class system.[81] Indeed, grapes were already artistic—horticulturists repeated that they had internal beauty and a developable character. Through Downing's writings and images, the "wild Grape vine" migrated picturesquely between savage and civilized states, naturally and autonomously holding these aesthetic elements. Downing pursued the grape in its wild, savage state and domesticated it in his home gardens, continuously pulling nature into culture.

At a time when the kitchen garden was utilitarian in design and purpose and usually screened from view in middle-class residences, gardens attached to the Victorian cottages in Downing's books often had central walks "covered by an arbor for grapes."[82] Downing's rhetoric spread as other authors picked up on his central use of the grape for fruit, drink, and aesthetic purposes, while also applying it to more humble sites. John Fisk Allen's *A Practical Treatise on the Culture and Treatment of the Grape Vine* (1847) presents a more synthetic idea of the home and garden, based on Downing's earlier writings. His section on the "culture of the grape" discusses the architecture and placement of houses for both vignerons and lay people. Allen weaves together Downing's and Prince's writings in a quiet call for Victorians to utilize their backyard spaces for both aesthetic and utilitarian purposes.[83]

The Horticulturist was published through 1875, continuing long after Downing died. He drowned while still in his thirties in the 1852 *Henry Clay* steamboat accident on the Hudson River. Downing's death was mourned within the pages of the journal for years. The other editors wrote his eulogy in September 1852, including a valuation of Downing's work and the work of all horticulturists on the international stage:

> We cannot, with safety, appropriate the result of horticultural labors in other countries. Our tastes and wants are peculiarly our own, and must be fostered and satisfied with American talent and research. Knowledge in the abstract may satisfy the German mind; the desire of supremacy may stimulate English energy; the vain-glorious pride of excelling in rare and beautiful products, may induce the Frenchman to exertion, but different motives urge us, as American citizens, to beautify our country, and increase its cultivation. We want the ornamental and the useful together—we require facts as well as theories . . . we cultivate gardens for profit, as well as beauty.[84]

Downing and other businessmen-horticulturists of mid-century used the trope of the grape not only to describe their nationalist dreams, but also to provide natural examples of national character and national landscape. For them, the American grape, like the U.S. body politic, was struggling to find its true "character" in the midst of the history of European imperial "supremacy" and "vain-glorious pride."

The propagation of grapes for "pure and unadulterated wines" is the final point William R. Prince made in his 1847 diatribe on the lackluster nature of

U.S. viticulture. In his "consideration of the influence the vine culture would have on society," he argued that "the pure juice of the grape is an innocent beverage . . . and if its use in its natural state would not be beneficial, it is scarcely rational to suppose that the Deity would have scattered vines so profusely throughout our country."[85] The wild grape's presence was proof enough for future cultivation of a strong wine culture. With the coming Civil War, the country would soon battle over the economic and ethical character of American culture and society. It would do so on similar rhetorical terms as the viticultural press, as questions of morality, cultivation, labor, and the links between national and local identity populated both discourses.

Horticultural publishing, nurseries, and landscape design were highly significant and overlapping economic and cultural industries in the nineteenth-century United States. Advancements in each of several developing fields—printing technologies, building technologies, gardening, and grape fever—were strikingly contemporaneous. But, even as the Empire State dominated the horticultural stage, its status as the premier U.S. horticultural center was increasingly contested through the antebellum period. Through the spread of viticultural literature, several more places of grape culture emerged at once. Though New York was crucial to the publishing and nursery arm of viticulture, with astonishing rapidity, other locations such as the Ohio Valley and California quickly surpassed New York in terms of producing marketable grapes and wine. In viticulture we thus find more specific nationalist pursuits blooming through an "imagined community" of reader-gardeners.[86] Each region's sense of place would be aided by its grape culture, which offered a new language and new aesthetic tropes for legitimating America's imagined significance.

The Prince family, James Fenimore Cooper, Andrew Jackson Downing, and their followers illustrated the ways in which domestic and horticultural spaces at mid-century were imbued with romantic imperial dreams, and these dreams of Roman civilization, Linnaean global scientific knowledge, and U.S. expansion were increasingly rooted in the urban bourgeois estate and the suburban home. The implications of this cultural work were numerous and significant. First and foremost, viticultural enthusiasts like the Princes, Cooper, and Downing offered the nineteenth-century national public material and ideological coherence against the perceived cultural and political incoherence of a young nation: viticulturists battled Europe's international stature and its wines' continuing prestige, and they took up the vexing task of cultivating a unique American national "genius." Second, through invocations of agricultural Edens, grape growing allayed accelerating fears about the Industrial Revolution. And finally, by mid-century, viticulturists were skilled at sidestepping the growing national strife over nationalizing markets, agricultural labor, and racial unrest. Viticulture promised a way into a rooted American identity—a native and natural, yet carefully cultivated society. Viticulture's promise of America's assuming a new place in a long line of grape-centered empires may be the most important message grape growers spread to the growing nation.

2

Propagating Empire

THROUGHOUT THE MID-NINETEENTH century, the international horticultural press highlighted grapes as a specific and significant fruit for American gardens. Many horticultural handbooks devoted much more space to grapes than to other fruits, describing the various grapevines' use and material and social value. An example of this is found in Thomas Bridgeman's *Young Gardener's Assistant,* a book sold to instruct gardeners in their plant-related purchases—and one reprinted many times from 1833 to 1865. The popular book was sold at nurseries and seed shops across the East and Midwest, from Boston to New Orleans, from Cincinnati to Washington, D.C. As was becoming common, it detailed grapes and their cultural and geographic history differently and more expansively than for other fruits and vegetables.[1] Bridgeman referenced the regions of the world most foodstuffs came from (for instance, "mulberry is commonly cultivated in Spain and Persia"), but he does not spend much narrative space on other plants' historical legacy nor fitness for American gardens. Technique and horticultural skill are important in all entries, but in his text the grapevine takes on an added historical and environmental meaning. Bridgeman writes, "Pliny speaks of a vine which had existed six hundred years . . . vines in Burgundy are upwards of four hundred years of age," and in Italy, England, Syria, and Spain, the case is the same. While offering just a few paragraphs for most other fruits, the *Young Gardener's Assistant* included fourteen pages of grape history. Bridgeman argues that "the vine is greatly the child of local circumstances," and that the "character" of the grape depended on regional differences, a rhetoric and reasoning in part stemming from grape histories expressed since Greek and Roman antiquity.[2] He then details various vineyards and their owners' techniques in New York, Pennsylvania, Delaware, and other sites. Interestingly, while the "character" of particular grapes was emphasized, as was the long imperial history grapes had enjoyed, the many new technologies needed for popular cultivation of wine grapes in America were not. In this text and many others, grapes continued to be a special crop, singled out and put on a national stage. Perhaps surprisingly, the grape enjoyed the same treatment from the U.S. federal government at mid-century.

In addition to antebellum horticulturists and handbook authors, the federal government was keen to present viticultural investment as an indicator of national power. There is perhaps no better example of this interest than a seemingly obscure federal entity, the United States Propagating Garden in Washington, D.C. Constructed in 1858—years before the U.S. Department of Agriculture was formed—the garden was built and maintained by the U.S. Patent Office. Located on a plot in the middle of the capital city, the five-acre garden and the vines that grew there provided much of the grape-related information published by the Patent Office in its many lengthy reports at mid-century. Here, the collection and dissemination of "information regarding the vine" took on new national status.

The Propagating Garden provided much of the data for the annual Patent Office *Reports* in Agriculture for 1858 and 1859, and was also the subject of most of the technical illustrations accompanying the publication of the *Report* in 1858, including a ground-level view of the garden (Fig. 10), a map of the grounds (Fig. 11), drainage schematics, greenhouse dimensions, as well as a drawing detailing how to cut grape wood for cultivation (Fig. 12).[3] The image of the garden at ground level mixes botanical, aesthetic, and architectural elements popular at mid-century. Balanced lateral framing of greenhouses reveal their claim to neoclassical stately elegance, a symbol of the continued reliance on Enlightenment ideals and aesthetics that pervaded horticulture for a much longer period than other commercial pursuits. An ornamental gazebo at the center contains occidental and oriental architectural styles, a signal that many cultural productions could flourish in America. Trees and shrubs of different types and heights line the foreground and background, illustrating their various states of cultivation. The fountain and gazebo provide a focal point, but also again mark the garden as a space of fluid national hybridity. Its trellis in back and rows of grapes in front provided an orderly yet natural structure, undergirding the placement of the technologically enhanced glass greenhouses that flanked its sides. The trellis, the *Report* explains, was used exclusively for training native grapevines, while

Figure 10. Ground-level view of the U.S. Propagating Garden. *Report of the Commissioner of Patents for the Year 1858: Agriculture.* U.S. House of Representatives, 35th Congress, Second Session, Executive Document Number 105 (Washington, DC: James B. Steedman, Printer, 1859).

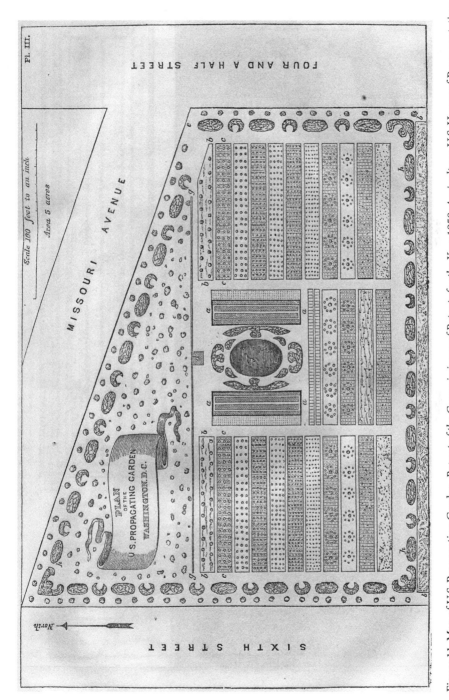

Figure 11. Map of U.S. Propagating Garden. *Report of the Commissioner of Patents for the Year 1858: Agriculture*. U.S. House of Representatives, 35th Congress, Second Session, Executive Document Number 105 (Washington, DC: James B. Steedman, Printer, 1859).

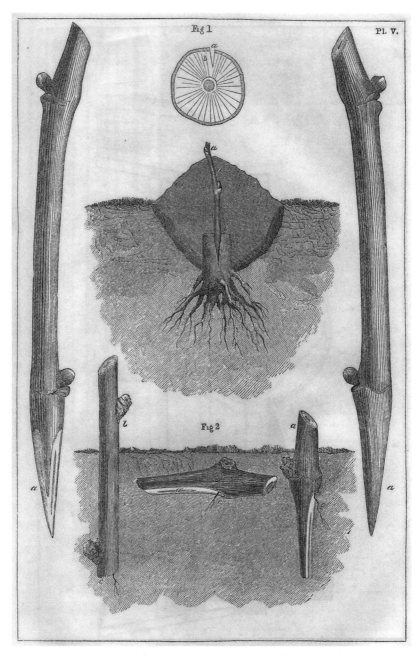

Figure 12. "Propagation of the Grape-Vine." *Report of the Commissioner of Patents for the Year 1858: Agriculture.* U.S. House of Representatives, 35th Congress, Second Session, Executive Document Number 105 (Washington, DC: James B. Steedman, Printer, 1859).

the greenhouses displayed hybrids and other "nationalities" of vines, such as those from Hungary, France, Germany, and Egypt.[4] In all, more than fifty varieties of native and foreign vines were grown on site. The image makes clear that the natural base from which all vines would grow was one of native heritage, but that all types of vines would ultimately flourish.

With overtones of cultivation and nationalism, the picture of the garden also contains obvious themes of domesticity and Christianity. A well-dressed family looks on, evaluating the scene, as a gardener waters the vines. A woman with an ornate hat in the foreground beckons the viewer—she springs from the bushes, and the shrub at her front takes on the appearance of a large bell-shaped dress. Her gesture and clothing highlight an ornamental overlapping of nature and culture, a progression from the uncultivated greenery in the foreground to the highly ordered bowery of grapevines at her back. Here, style and propriety in women's fashions are conflated with a natural decorative order: both the woman and the shrub are natural, yet both are refined. In this Edenic garden, instead of a fig leaf covering Eve's privy parts, a full ball gown and petticoat of greenery enswathes her. The artist seemed obviously aware of the sexual double entendre inherent in this national "Propagating Garden," and here took steps to defuse its lascivious message. The Propagating Garden is instead proper and chaste, a moral statement against sexual transgressions implied by the book of Genesis. Overall, the picture begs the viewer to compare the negative biblical sexual narrative of the Garden of Eden with the new, productive, and family-centered Garden of the United States. In the Propagating Garden, vinetending had all the markers of a proper nationalist and familial activity; it was not decadent, nor morally depraved.

The Propagating Garden realized a "national vineyard" within the nineteenth-century middle-class social scene—a homey yet stately space, "operating to a charm" and bursting with 25,000 vines by 1859.[5] As with those of the businessmen-botanists, state-sponsored images of grape culture relied on strategies of representation that implied American grape growing was a powerful, imperial act, but one that was legitimate because it was aesthetically beautiful, morally acceptable, and above all, natural in its claim to power. Growers long knew that wine grapes of a certain quality, the European *Vitis vinifera*, were very difficult to grow in America. Therefore, most *Vitis vinifera* brought to the United States could be coaxed to grow only through significant technological alteration of grape-growing environments. Despite several growers' ideological stances against the mechanization of agriculture, most viticulturists welcomed various new methods and tools that enhanced every aspect of grapevines' life cycles. The Patent Office's efforts at spreading horticulture, its patented technologies, many publications' aestheticizing and moralizing rhetoric, and a wider visual technics of the grape coalesced at mid-century. While firmly entrenched in agri-technological improvements— including heated greenhouses, new methods of vine hybridization, pest management, and fertilization, as well as new modes of transportation and industrial printing methods that generated a boom in horticultural books and journals—the Patent Office and viticulture authors nonetheless presented grape culture as a non-mechanized, natural, moral, and classically pastoral practice. It was a template for American viticulture to come.

The Technical World of Grapes

The Propagating Garden's glass and metal vineries were just one wave in a growing tide of horticultural hothouses popular at mid-century. Raising vines and increasing grape yields in antebellum America demanded a sophisticated knowledge of new horticultural techniques. In this way, enterprising grape cultivation depended on growers' use of technology. In addition to using advancements in soil science and hybridization, grape culturists utilized new technologies that enhanced urban horticultural production and the visual consumption of grapes.

Several scholars have theorized the extent to which ideology, national and individual identities, and technology are co-formative at any time in history. That is, social processes, ideological constructs, and technological innovation work hand-in-hand to create a cultural worldview and produce its material culture. Lewis Mumford first theorized this socio-technological matrix in his landmark *Technics and Civilization* (1934). Technics, as he termed it, is a cultural process whereby a society's dreams and habits are constructed along with its technological processes and inventions. Most basically, built environments and technologies, a society's physical tools, are formed in a close dialectic with a cultural worldview.[6] Frieda Knobloch, for example, describes how the moldboard plow, probably the most powerful and ubiquitous agricultural implement of the nineteenth century, was also an important cultural artifact. The plow was not just an example of new technological innovation; it supported the domestication of thousands of animals and brought about an "emphasis on commodity rather than food production . . . an ideology of improvement, [and] a language of cultivation. . . . An entire colonial technics is embodied in the plow."[7] The plow changed the structure of farms and of labor, as well as the American worldview about farming. Several indispensable tools for grape experimentation likewise reveal that symbolic, ideological, and economic technics were operating for viticulturists as well.

Throughout the nineteenth century, horticulturists argued that as nature was destroyed and divorced from city life through the Industrial Revolution, people practiced horticulture in order to reclaim that nature. By this logic, the most urbanized places would also have the most gardens, or at minimum, a significant public interested in horticulture. But how can we account for the millennia of horticultural practice and popular interest in gardens before the explosive growth of cities in the nineteenth century? A different scene emerges when the developments of nineteenth-century technologies such as vineries and greenhouses are taken into account, as they made it possible, as well as aesthetically alluring and socially rewarding, to propagate exotic plant species. Such improvements made gardening easier and more attractive, to a degree unmatched in previous times. In this light, the greenhouse and grapery in the nineteenth-century city—as spaces of botanical mastery, visual display, and changing economic relationships—are important markers of a significant change in middle-class culture and technology overall.

While on its face viticulture did not seem industrial or technological, mid-century grape growers used the highly technological "vinery" or "grapery" for propagating vines. Designed much like a greenhouse, a grapery was a space set aside from all other horticultural tasks to grow experimental grapevines in a controlled atmosphere. Numerous "cold vineries" and "warm vineries" were built and sold throughout mid-century, touted as the best spaces for encouraging exotic "little green shoots" in northern climes. Agricultural journals document that New York alone had more than forty glass vineries focused on grapevine experimentation during the 1850s; Connecticut also had dozens by 1854.[8] Vineries were far more prevalent and necessary in northern U.S. climates than southern, as most of the popular imported grape varieties came from Mediterranean regions and thus required climactic alteration to grow and mature in the northern United States. Grapery size and technological enhancement were important topics of discussion at annual meetings of the American Pomological Society in the 1850s and 1860s. These vineries could be "cold," "warm," or "hot," depending on the type, or "nationality," of grape with which the grower wanted to experiment. Early on, growers attempted dangerous methods of warming cold northern hothouses, including open flames, resulting in several vinery infernos. Various devices controlled temperature and humidity, and cut down on mildew and bugs. The most basic vineries were assembled in a lean-to style, with glass on top to allow for the sun's rays and trap its warmth for colder nights. More advanced vineries approximated greenhouses in their form and function, and had arched walls to create one continuous brace that grapevines could climb (Fig. 13). Illustrations reveal that the vineries were sometimes set apart from other spaces in urban gardens or country farms. Like little sparkling cathedrals, images of vineries in journals were often set in an unbroken plane of untamed greenery and passing clouds, in lovely contrast to their curved, ordered internal geometry.[9]

Vineries, and all glass houses of the nineteenth century, showcased three improved building technologies—efficient heat, iron production, and sheet glass manufacture—in all of their newfound power, beauty, and utility. Iron was a widely utilized building material by the 1830s, and sheet glass, which came in a variety of thicknesses, transparencies, and curvatures, became much cheaper in the 1850s.[10] Steam heat, the invention that revolutionized

Figure 13. "The Vinery at Medary, Near Philadelphia," *The Horticulturist* 6 (March 1851), 147. Photo courtesy of the University of Iowa.

the factory system and likely the single most important technological impetus for the Industrial Revolution, was both showcased and physically experienced in greenhouses of all types. Many factory owners in Europe and America used the same engines to pipe steam not only to factory floors, but into greenhouses, often constructed right next door. For example, in 1842 General William Paulding, former mayor of New York, built a wood-frame glass house on his Lyndhurst estate near Tarrytown. It burned down a few years later, and the next owner, railroad magnate Jay Gould, rebuilt it with glass and iron in 1870. This time the structure had a significant amount of space devoted to graperies. The conservatory boasted a large glass tower and was connected to several of Gould's company offices.[11] Many such large winter greenhouses were run in conjunction with factories—not surprisingly, the glass house had bloomed as a technologically improved building type at the same moment as functioning assembly plants. The horticultural hothouse was thus made possible through, and spread to a larger public by, the steel and glass technologies produced and used in industry. Indeed, the indoor garden was not a delayed emotional response to urbanization; horticulture actually grew in tandem with the city and perhaps even helped naturalize Americans' growing contact with machines.

In this light, the newly ubiquitous vinery was part of the infatuation with iron and glass architecture that pervaded, and altered, nineteenth-century public life.[12] The early nineteenth-century hothouse was a space of growth, storage, and display, as well as a gathering place and a location that beautifully and transparently marked social status. The large, public, glass-enclosed atriums—in effect, shopping greenhouses—provided for timeless, seasonless urban zones where nature and weather were marketable commodities. Here the greenhouse also serves as an architectural type predating the arcades and the Crystal Palaces of world's expositions—and as an unsung precedent for the department store. Two "Crystal Palaces" were constructed: the first in London for the Great Exhibition of 1851, and the second in New York City for the Exhibition of the Industry of All Nations held in 1853. These are just two examples of thousands of glass buildings that employed the greenhouse aesthetic and would further set the tone for the glass rage in architecture to come.[13] Joseph Paxton's design for London's Crystal Palace in Hyde Park was essentially a scaled-up version of greenhouses he had designed for the Duke of Devonshire at Chatsworth in Derbyshire. His largest private greenhouses spanned 300 feet in length; his Crystal Palace was 1,848 feet by 408 feet wide and more than 100 feet high, containing more than 293,000 panes of glass.

By many accounts, the unusually large greenhouse worked too well in letting light into interior spaces, as blinds and tents were added to protect fabrics and materials, roosting birds became an annoyance, and plants quickly outgrew their settings.

Through the practice and aesthetics of viticulture, grapevines and their new architectural technologies became a symbol of aesthetic beauty, the reach of commerce, and even the technological power of the nation. In vineries, not only the grapevines and grapes but the elements of the structure itself were on display, and hence part of the aesthetic effect. Among other similar architectural and artistic expenses, the vinery was perhaps most closely allied with collecting a personal gallery of art. In the vinery, a gardener could cultivate a growing still-life scene and present to friends a personally staged and directed "theater of nature." The grapery, the key tool propelling grape culture in America, was thus part of the aestheticized experience of the consumption of both grapes and wine. The grapery could even signify as a personal Garden of Eden, in which the gardener was the master of the collection of greenery gathered within. Here, the upper-middle-class gardener's space and plant collections stood in beautiful addition to, not in "showy contrast with" the artistic collections in the house.[14] Grape technology was always hidden in full view and embedded in aesthetic discourses that legitimated an increasing general reliance upon agricultural technology in nineteenth-century America. But viticulturists easily glossed over their technological dependence—they were, after all, working in see-through gardens that were crystalline and clean— while relying on these highly sophisticated greenhouses and tools for grapes' propagation. Greenhouses and other viticultural tools, specially constructed for grapes, were aestheticized as beautiful luxury items and constructed in the most conspicuous locations.

Graperies were thus a mark of distinction, a site to see and in which to be seen, by both city inhabitants and grape experts. *Woodward's Graperies and Horticultural Buildings*, published in New York for a local and national readership in 1865, marked that the first cold grapery was erected "on the Hudson" in New York in the early 1840s. Woodward offers dozens of collected designs for graperies, from the "moderate" size to larger "cold graperies for city lots." On the grand scale, one model included two hot graperies totaling 1,400 square feet, a cold grapery of 1,220 square feet, a forcing house of 690 square feet, not to mention the potting shed and camellia house (Fig. 14). Additionally, a "medium-size grapery," filling an entire city lot, is described as one of the first built in New York, designed and constructed by Woodward's

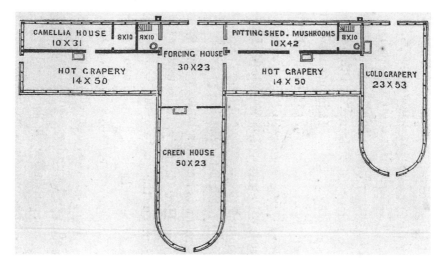

Figure 14. Ground plan of large grapery. Geo. E. & F. W. Woodward, *Woodward's Graperies and Horticultural Buildings* (New York: Stephen Hallet, 1865/1867), 125. Photo courtesy of the University of Iowa.

friend John Sherwood (Fig. 15). His large three-arched grapery was ideally "centrally located in the aristocratic portion of a city noted for its wealth, taste and influence." What was more, "these Graperies will be carefully watched as an index of what the future may do in the increased demand for houses on city lots for Horticultural purposes."[15] As a mark of wealth and as a built environment of grape technology, the grapery was itself on display in the city. City graperies were built taller than normal graperies, intentionally and for effect: "These houses are purposely built higher than is now usual, to give a finer effect from the drawing-room windows." The grapery owner's drawing-room windows took in the large glass structure, as would his neighbors', so that all could gawk and appreciate the luxury of an artificially heated indoor garden.

Indeed, for Woodward and Sherwood, it was better to be a city viticulturist than a country gardener, for the former utilized the latest technology for his pleasure: "Unlike the garden of a country gentleman that blossoms and fruits and passes away in a season, the horticultural building properly heated is a perpetual pleasure, a garden year round; vegetables and fruit and flowers follow each other without intermission." Other journals detailed the healthful effects of spending time in grape conservatories and educating one's children under its "crystal roof" in winter.[16] In the grapery, one could almost cheat the

Figure 15. "Medium-Size Grapery," Geo. E. & F. W. Woodward, *Woodward's Graperies and Horticultural Buildings* (New York: Stephen Hallet, 1865/1867), 124. Photo courtesy of the University of Iowa.

seasons and engineer a green paradise, without ever leaving the convenience of the city. The effect must have been quite grand upon peering into or entering vineries like this. A separate, spectacular universe of exotic vines climbed up around the viticulturist and his visitors, as bunches of grapes dangled down, in the coldest months of the year. For example, a conservatory and graperies designed by William Chorlton had "early" and "cold" graperies in the wings for propagating vines, but a main, taller conservatory in the center was reserved for displaying them. The technical work of growing the vines, along with all the tools needed for this labor, was done offstage; the main hall showcased vines without reference to their mechanical needs. Graperies thus helped naturalize and negate gardeners' contact with the machine in mid-century cities. Glass houses expressed a delicate mastery over both country and city, not in sequence or in response to urbanization, but in tandem with it. Vineries aestheticized agriculture as well as the city itself—they were an elegant conjoining of timeless nature with industrializing culture.

As Bridgeman emphasized in the *Young Gardener's Assistant*, in addition to connecting city with country, graperies helped horticulturists explore and establish international connections. The vinery was a space for experimenting with and ultimately controlling an exotic world of foreign vines, all the while seeking to propagate strong American species. Scottish master landscape designer and greenhouse designer John Claudius Loudon, famous for his work in Europe and the United States during the antebellum period, explains that the hothouse "gives man so proud a command over Nature, and renders a skillful practitioner in such requisition among the opulent, [that he] would receive an early attention from societies."[17] Loudon reveals here that the presentation of exotic plants was perhaps not so much about the plants, but about class and control, about attaining genteel social standing through mastery of horticultural productions. Indeed, the vinery and other tools associated with growing exotic grapes in northern climates reemphasized grape growers' participation in a national technics of agriculture. An elite horticultural crowd, determined to prove themselves in worldwide botanical adaptation and outclass their international competitors in grape innovation, placed high priorities on improvement, commodity, and cultivation. Nineteenth-century viticulturists, while discussing the technologies of viticulture, also negotiated issues of nationalist botanical control and social standing.

If one could not afford a greenhouse, there were plenty of other possibilities for displaying grapes in the city. Popular grape handbook author Peter Mead devotes most of his book to illustrating both aesthetic and efficient systems of growing and displaying grapes.[18] Published in New York in 1867, *Mead's Grape Culture* luxuriated in a large trim size and gilt lettering on the cover and spine. The title encircled a large golden grape leaf, offering up the book as much more than a handy grape-grower's manual. It was clearly also intended as a parlor book, to be flipped through and appreciated for its artistry as well as its usefulness. Addressing his text to the amateur and the professional vineyardist, Mead offers dozens of geometric designs for maximizing precious space in both the urban and country vineyard. In the book, a city townhouse and estate each grow grapes covering an entire wall, and multiple pictures show enthusiasts how to best train grapes (Fig. 16). Mead includes a few figures of bare canes to illustrate exactly how to train vines, but most of the pictures, like the one here, are abundant with leaves and grapes. Their profusion signaled a kind of urban wealth and lavishness claimed through private botanical and agricultural domestication.

Grape growers also invested in other glass implements for their vineyards. One distinctly beautiful technology was glass bells, which were set around bunches of unripened grapes on the vine (Fig. 17). Introduced in the 1840s, these crystalline "grape hats" focused sunlight on the grapes by day

Figure 16. Grapes trained on townhouse. Peter Mead, *An Elementary Treatise on American Grape Culture* (1867), 136. Photo courtesy of the University of Iowa.

and increased heat retention at night. "Vitis," the author of an 1846 article in *The Horticulturist,* explains, "These bell-glasses can be blown at our glass-works, and afforded at low prices by the dozen."[19] The particular bell-glass described in the article was imported from Holland, another northern country keen to "mature and attain an excellent flavor" from its experiments with exotic Mediterranean grapes. Thus, in addition to graperies being constructed of glass, the grape bunches themselves were often set behind glass—much like new shopping windows and displays made items shine a little brighter in department stores. Here, both glass and grapes were offered up for delicate social display and consumption.

New technology, effort, expense, and aestheticizing rhetoric were all required to encourage grape growing in America. A separate universe of spatial conditions and technologies was often required, demonstrating the extent to which horticultural activity was often at base a status symbol. As machines for growing grapes, perhaps better described as horticultural-technological landscapes, graperies claimed and expressed a sense of identity and location for their urban bourgeois owners. Vineries were clean, tasteful, fetishized,

Figure 17. Glass "grape hat," Vitis, "New Mode of Ripening Foreign Grapes," *The Horticulturist* 1 (August 1846), 70. Photo courtesy of the University of Iowa.

orderly, mechanical, and yet "natural." The grapery, as a techno-cultural artifact and as built space, helped construct an urban horticultural scene and sense of place that ran counter to ideas about the nineteenth-century city being a place of sheer industry. This sense of place was distinctly technological and urban, but also undeniably botanical and aesthetic. Many people lived in, or experienced, these close, overlapping spaces, dedicated at once to the technics of pastoral cultivation and urban sophistication. Indeed, the rage for graperies grew before most major urban parks projects or grand shopping palaces were constructed. New York City's Central Park, America's first major urban park, for example, did not begin construction until the late 1850s, and was not fully open for public use until the 1870s. Horticultural appreciation via new grape technologies was present as early as the 1840s; grape culture was industrializing along with everything else. These processes reveal that the grape's presence in many urban landscapes in America was perhaps not "natural" at all, and yet was an important tool for negotiating and negating widespread industrial change.

Changing Agriculture, Changing Culture

Of course, glass houses weren't the only new inventions remaking American agriculture. In a wider frame, by mid-century, mechanization and urbanization had altered the structure of farming at large. Agriculture in the United States had fundamentally changed after 1790: the decades between 1790 and 1860 were ones of expansion and reorganization. The days of carrying surplus goods to market for direct sale ended, and the farmer instead became dependent upon the commercialization of the market and its ensuing profit structure. Increased land investment was well begun in New York and other large cities by 1840, and technologically intensive farming ended farming by "extension," the practice of merely using more and more land to produce crops. Proof of agricultural worth and power underwent a paradigm shift in the minds of farmers by the 1860s: value was assessed in the early century through total acres worked, while later in the century the amount and quality of goods produced per acre became more important.[20] Agriculture, as well as the fruit trade specifically, was indeed growing in volume: the value of garden produce grown in U.S. gardens, orchards, and nurseries in 1847 was almost $460 million.[21] Increasing farm productivity also freed up labor for factories, and industrialism's higher production rates and improved transportation made getting goods and people to market much easier. As industrialization and urbanization picked up steam, an American working class emerged, and class distinctions solidified through the separation of labor and growth of capital in the 1840s.[22] Several new techniques made agricultural endeavors ever more efficient and lucrative throughout the nineteenth century. Advancements included the first serious chemical study of soils by Justus Liebig, whose findings were first published in 1840. Guano and other organic and inorganic matter were soon sold as fertilizers. Commercial fertilizers were available to antebellum farmers in the North, while farmers in western states, such as Utah, began irrigating crops.[23] Crop rotation came into general practice in the 1840s and 1850s, but was adopted earlier in some eastern locations. Before the adoption of crop rotation, farmers in general felt they had no need to rotate crops due to the availability of cheap "virgin" land. Previously, working the soil and minding its efficacy was thought to be a waste of time.[24]

Grape growers also developed techniques specific to grape culture. New soil layering techniques enhanced plants' root structures, and a flood of books and journals offered advice and hundreds of new methods, explaining how deep grapevine roots should be planted, why and how one should lay gravel in beds, and how to layer new soil additives, such as bone dust, lime, potash, gypsum, and sulfur. Sulfur and other chemical dusts were increasingly applied to vines to mitigate rampant "grape rot" in humid climates. Farmers and nurserymen also developed methods of keeping grape pollen viable over long periods of time and further distances. They then refined techniques in applying pollen to vines for best fertilization, which aided hybridization and vine strength. Grapes now also ripened early for urban markets through various new methods of "forcing."

The original reticence about—but ultimate acceptance of—new technology in grape growing, and competition with European states for the world's best wine, was constructed by several overlapping images of the ideal vineyard. The image of the classic western European vineyard implied a rootedness in the land, and buttressed a belief in the identity of the cultivated republican farmer, as vineyards were generally much smaller in scale than other crops, and vines required long-term tending. Because of these attributes, work in vineyards was thought to be less physical and technological, and more mental and scientific. Vinegrowers had to practice "book farming" just as much as "dirt farming" in order to keep up with the number of vines found and hybridized each year, in addition to the constant improvements being made in soil science. Book farming, an act of basic and sustained communication with national and international experts and experimenters, was crucial for the growth of grape culture.

Since grapevines only begin to produce grapes in the third year after planting, and vines were believed to produce in high volume and consistent quality for ten to one hundred years, investing in a vineyard's soil quality was a more long-term enterprise than investing in a wheat field or corn field. The fact that grapevines are a perennial fruit—and that the plant produces the same quality of grapes over much of the life of the vine—makes their care different from that of other agricultural staples. Corn, wheat, and most other agricultural commodities are annual crops, meaning the crop lives its entire life cycle (from seed, to plant, to maturity, to new seed) in a single year. A farmer must remove spent annual crops each year, not just for harvest but for soil rest, fertilization, and planting for the next year. Economically important annual crops, such as grains, were thus more mobile than vineyards and required less initial investment. Unlike annual crops, grapes are better left alone from year to year, and therefore carefully planning the vineyard, and setting the subsoil with all necessary amendments, is essential to the life of the vine and its terroir. Indeed, the "character" of the grapevine, its potential fruit and further value, was in large part thought to be determined by the quality of care a viticulturist gave to his vines in setting the soil and designing the vineyard, years before vines began to produce fruit. Early investment in one's vineyard promised profitable grape yields and success. Viticulture was thus suited to, and helped continually create, bourgeois sensibilities and an international market because of the physical, mental, financial, and emotional investments demanded by vineyards. The very act of grape growing was "refined" in that it was a long-term investment, not a fleeting crop. Although just as invested in new techniques for the care of their vines as other farmers with their crops, grape culturists clung to a conservative, fairly antiquated, and yeoman vision of the craft, one believed to be in a class different from other crops.

With the growth of early industrial agriculture, the federal government actively pursued information-gathering and regulation between 1839 and 1862. An act passed in 1839 assigned the U.S. Patent Office the job of collecting and publishing statistics about farming.[25] Henry Ellsworth, first Patent Commissioner, had several qualifications that helped land him the job, and which explain the office's early interest in agriculture. He had been mayor of Hartford, Connecticut, and president of a large insurance company, not to mention having been one of the twin sons of Supreme Court Chief Justice Oliver Ellsworth. Although the younger Ellsworth's Patent Office work was mostly organizational and administrative, his previous work as Chief Commissioner of Indian Affairs framed his approach to overseeing U.S. inventions and agriculture. As Commissioner of Indian Affairs, he administered the Indian tribes in the Arkansas area and made several trips to the Rocky

Mountains. In the 1840s and 1850s, with his previous experience in the West and growing knowledge of American inventions, he voiced a prophecy that the continent would soon be cultivated by steam plows (a vision that would unfortunately later be presented in the probate of his will to illustrate he was of unsound mind).[26] Under Ellsworth's direction, the U.S. Patent Office encouraged industrial invention as well as the agricultural possibilities in the West. At the same time, Ellsworth assisted horticulture's domestication and aestheticization in genteel urban centers in the East.

Federal support for grape cultivation began decades before the construction of the Propagating Garden. In 1839, Ellsworth convinced Congress to appropriate to his office $1,000 for use in "collecting and distributing seeds, prosecuting agricultural investigations, and procuring agricultural statistics." It was the first federal government aid, in monetary form, applied to any agricultural endeavor in the United States. Ellsworth spent much of the money on grapes, a seemingly unessential crop at that point to the national economy. While colonial governments had favored grape culture in the past, by not taxing wine and by granting large tracts of land to viticulturists in Virginia and South Carolina, and later along the Ohio, this first agricultural subsidy signaled a turn in U.S. policy. Ellsworth, behind the scenes, had been distributing plants and seeds to farmers as early as 1836. Grape experimentation would be a sustained priority for the Patent Office and larger U.S. government for decades.[27]

By 1857, the Patent Office mounted two exploratory grape expeditions. One was sent to explore Indian Territory (now Oklahoma and northern Texas). This trip, headed by agent H. C. Williams, was extended into what is now New Mexico and the Rio Grande Valley. The second expedition, led by agent John F. Weber, collected grapes and information in the New England and mid-Atlantic states.[28] Through these tours, government agents had a strong hand in encouraging grape research and experimentation in the antebellum period. In them, the United States was repeating a pattern set by colonial European powers, which had used scientific exploration as an "instrument of expansion" since the eighteenth century. International botanical prowess served to enhance leading countries' "contacts with the imperial frontier," and scientific knowledge retrieved from new territories helped solidify colonial land claims.[29] While several other national exploratory missions had been launched in the service of botanical research and land acquisition by the 1850s, dispatching government officials to collect commercial agricultural goods and information was relatively new.

The Patent Office was perennially interested in new market possibilities for goods generated by its technological and agricultural endeavors. Ellsworth oversaw a rapid increase in the number of patents for domestic and agricultural implements as early as 1837, which, by the 1860s, among hundreds of other inventions, included patents for an electric railway, an improved sewing machine, an adapted reel lawn mower, a hand-turned dishwasher, and a mechanical reaper. At the same time, Ellsworth began plans for a national seed house that would collect, select, and nationally distribute choice grains and seeds, including grape seeds and cuttings, to farmers. As part of this project, the Patent Office printed a separate agricultural report of several hundred pages for each year between 1849 and 1861. There were hundreds of thousands of copies of each report distributed annually.[30] To fill them, Patent Office officials asked naval officers and diplomats, or anyone of rank visiting other lands, to collect and send back useful seeds and plants they might find in their travels. The *Report of 1859*, along with Propagating Garden details, registered vine grafts sent from the U.S. consul in Switzerland and seeds transferred from the Minister of War to France, as well as seeds received from Algiers, China, Jerusalem, Japan, and Quito. Other registrations included receipt of Australian wheat; cotton, coffee, and sugar from Brazil; bulbs and grasses from the Cape of Good Hope; tobacco from Havana; beans from Spain; and nuts from Guatemala. In addition, grape cuttings, seeds, and dried grapes came in from Texas, Virginia, New Hampshire, California, New Mexico, and Massachusetts. Ellsworth, a decade earlier, was a key player in organizing a selection of Indian corn strains that promised increased crop yields in the northern states. The new "Baden" corn Ellsworth helped introduce also portended a 50 percent increased yield of corn in the Mississippi Valley. By 1840, the Patent Office was distributing 30,000 seed packages per year of all varieties of agricultural goods to interested U.S. farmers and horticulturists.[31] By collecting new tools and seeds for domestic and agricultural enterprise, the Patent Office also served as a clearinghouse for information and horticultural goods. Clearly at the forefront of agricultural colonization, the Patent Office thus proved very efficient in taking the resources of the land from the newly "removed" Indians, as well as goods from its international explorations, and distributing them to growing domestic markets.

Ellsworth never relented in his effort to rally support for U.S. agriculture, of which grapes were a central and symbolically resonant part. In his Patent Office *Annual Report of 1840,* submitted to Congress, Ellsworth outlined a number of agricultural statistics (mostly acres under production and bushels

sold) for corn, wheat, barley, oats, rye, potatoes, hay, flax, silk, and the obligatory cotton, tobacco, sugar, and wine. In a rhetorical move that would become familiar as the century wore on, only in the grape section of the *Report*
did he expound on the possibilities of national investment in agriculture. In
the grape section of the *Report*, the United States was agriculturally productive and hospitable, and above all, unique: "Probably no country can be found
on the face of the globe, exhibiting a more desirable variety of the products of
the soil, contributing to the sustenance and comfort of its inhabitants. From
the Gulf of Mexico to our Northern boundary, from the Atlantic to the far
West, the peculiarities of climate, soil, and products, are great and valuable."
Ellsworth then estimates the potential of U.S. wine production and compares
it to that of Europe, making a stupendous claim that American wine would
ultimately outstrip Europe by a factor of ten. He ends the *Report* with the rep-
etition of his praise of U.S. bounty, but takes the implications a step further:

> The diversities of her climate the vagaries of her soil, her particular
> combination of population, her mineral, animal, agricultural, me-
> chanical, and commercial wealth, developed as they may be by a right-
> ful regard to her necessities, might thus place her at last in a situation
> as enviable for her political and moral influence, as for the physical
> energies she had called into life and action. Our republic needs, in-
> deed, only to prove her own strength, and wisely direct her energies,
> to become, more than she has ever been, the point on which the eye
> of all Europe is fixed, as home of plenty for the destitute, and a field
> where enterprise reaps its sure and appropriate award.[32]

In the longer section, Ellsworth conflates "enterprise's reward" with "strength"
and "political influence" over Europe and in the larger world under the banner of U.S. agricultural "energies." An adamant opponent of European imports, he had earlier entreated readers that the "daily importation of goods"
was growing at an alarming rate, especially agricultural goods, "two-thirds
of which are on foreign account, to be paid for in specie or its equivalent!"[33]
Here, anything bought from another country was an inevitable waste, in that
it would support foreign agriculture, manufactures, and trade above U.S.
goods—American money was disappearing into European pockets many
times over. Ellsworth's other writings reveal a desire for far more than simply
improving America's trade balance; like others struggling to exhibit a strong
American cultural and economic nationalism, he wanted the United States

to gain the genteel world's attention and respect.[34] Ellsworth resigned from the Patent Office in 1845 and became U.S. Land Commissioner in Lafayette, Indiana, where he was one of the largest landowners, and most technologically up-to-date farmers, in the state. Ellsworth had set the tone for the Patent Office's interest in grapes and agricultural expansion for decades to come.

After Ellsworth's resignation, the Patent Office continued to apply funds and human resources to grape growing for a brief period in 1847. But its interest in agriculture then waned in the late 1840s and early 1850s, due to its efforts in telegraph construction as well as its responsibility for negotiating patent law for new U.S. territories (most significantly, the new state of Texas). But by 1857, under a new commissioner, the Patent Office had laid new plans for a large-scale effort to "collect and study native vines to learn which were best for table and wine" (among other crops such as tea), and construction of the Propagating Garden commenced.

By 1859, after almost twenty years of distributing seeds and vines, the Patent Office ceased distribution of domestic plantstuffs, because seed stores and nurseries were filling the public's need for them more than adequately. In 1862, the evident scale and importance of U.S. agriculture called for the formation of a separate department devoted to its needs. That year, the U.S. Department of Agriculture was formed out of the Patent Office to further shape the theory and practice of farming, and better manage its economy and products.[35] Until Prohibition in 1920, the department followed Ellsworth's policies of encouraging viticulture, which for decades remained, along with other fruits, cotton, corn, and wheat, one of its central concerns. As the Propagating Garden image shows, this national investment in grapes was inseparable from the idealized space of the vineyard, buttressed with an array of horticultural advancements, worked to legitimate viticulturists' contact with new technologies, and did much to promote the grape trade.

Technology Meets Morality

In this moment of accelerating agricultural expansion, then, horticulture and viticulture were active means of navigating wider trends in national mechanization and the transportation revolution. Wholesale changes in commercial agriculture prompted many people to find a moral attachment to smaller-scale horticulture. Thus, the image of an urban Victorian family at ease in the Propagating Garden was no small symbol. By the 1870s, tending a garden, an act loaded with the positive meanings of "goodness, virtue, and ever-renewing life," was seen as a prescient antidote to the Industrial Revolution's exhausting effects on a hard-working middle class. But many of the same men in New York, Philadelphia, and Boston who identified themselves with all things rural and agrarian were also responsible for altering early America's economy from a farming to a commercial and industrial base.[36] By the 1850s, public men of horticulture in urban centers, such as nurserymen, Patent Office workers, and consultants, were a different sort of professional than the weekend "country gentleman." Men like Patent Office employees were in the business of professional horticulture for their livelihoods, and in the case of nurserymen, for profit. Likewise, jobs at the Patent Office, and later the Department of Agriculture, were coveted as high-profile government offices. Both careers held prestige and power. At mid-century, professionals with the title of nurseryman, seedsman, or florist increased with every decade. In 1850, they totaled 8,479; there were 21,788 in 1860; the number increased to 32,520 in 1870; and by 1880, there were 56,032 nurserymen and seedsmen in America. New York agricultural historian U. P. Hedrick writes that indeed "every farmer and every city dweller with a yard was an amateur fruit grower" by the mid-nineteenth century.[37]

Viticultural experimenters could be found throughout the antebellum United States, but as seen in Chapter 1, grape culture's most avid and vocal supporters were largely white northerners. Through the 1850s, grape growing straddled the divide between the private garden and an emerging commercial wine-making industry. As we have seen, the transition from semi-subsistence farming to market-oriented commercial agriculture was aided in the North by machinery and animal power, while much of the South's market-oriented agriculture still relied on slave labor. Grape cultivation was more popular in the North than South for several reasons—for one, grapes were so closely allied with the Patent Office and Department of Agriculture. Furthermore, the South was generally opposed to the idea of a national Department of Agriculture. Since the Revolution, the republican vision of the expanding United States cultivated by free yeomen had largely rested on criticism of the immorality of Southern slavery.[38]

Although primarily a commercial activity after 1850, grape and fruit cultivation grew in concert with a new national and local place-consciousness, and was advertised as a "powerful antidote to the 'spirit of unrest'" horticulturists observed all around them.[39] The horticultural press believed that tending grapevines could soothe growing class conflict by training the lower sort to have middle-class morals through cultivating and displaying higher cultural tastes and skills. Cultivating grapes also had the added benefit of promoting and producing wine over "rougher" sorts of alcohol.[40] What can only be described as "garden mania" swept through larger national periodicals in the 1850s and 1860s.[41] Love of small personal gardens grew in tandem with nineteenth-century industrial and agricultural innovation and urban growth, in part because of the perceived moral, or "positive effects," of gardens on society. Horticulturists in America claimed they built a life of "utility and refinement" by continuing the "ancient virtue" of gardening and viticulture. While a product of many contemporary improvements, grape culture was nonetheless seen by most horticulturists as a natural, moral, domestic, and non-mechanized practice.

Moral literature and horticultural journals constantly advocated gardening for all ages, all classes, and both genders. The rhetoric about the positive effects of the country garden was easily imported to the city, because of horticulture's perceived ability to ameliorate, and perhaps reverse, a mechanizing civilization. In the urban East, this moralistic horticulture was a predominantly middle-class enterprise, a respite for the work-weary, and a specific antidote to commercial activities. Farmers and laboring men, many who worked twelve hours a day, six days a week, did not have time for ornamental gardening, and likely had "no patience with armchair gardeners who proclaimed it to be healthful and morally uplifting." But the bourgeois enclaves of urban centers in the East saw gardening as a great alleviator of all their urban woes. The Maryland Society for Promoting the Culture of the Vine, a group of enthusiastic grape cultivators, organized themselves in 1829, while the national American Pomological Society was founded in 1840. Internationally, the "rage for fruit" spanned the first fifty years of the century in the United States, England, and France. By then the Department of Agriculture was a little late on the scene in promoting a new, nationalistic agrarian lifestyle, for by 1860 there were already at least forty heavily circulated papers and magazines devoted exclusively to agriculture.[42] It was Jeffersonian agrarianism lite for the antebellum urban-suburban set, a flowery reconciliation of a still-virtuous republic with its emerging industrial empire.

Horticulture piqued other moral issues, too. Grape culture sometimes also entailed a retooling of the public's concept of nature. In 1867, this new relationship with nature was defined as one "of contract," wrote Peter Mead. He argued in his lushly illustrated *Mead's Grape Culture* that "Nature is a business partner . . . the head of the firm," and cautioned his readers to treat her as such: follow her lead, yield to her demands, but make as much money off the relationship as possible.[43] Additionally, at the American Pomological Society's national meeting that year, President Wilder "repeat[ed] and reinforce[d] [his] conviction, that the shortest and surest road to improvement of fruits is by hybridization and cross-breeding." To assure those collected at the meeting, he told a story of how one experimenter crossed two grapes, each having positive and negative qualities. The resulting forty-five seedlings "united the most valuable qualities of their parents . . . not one was found possessing only the inferior qualities of the mother plant." He went on to exclaim, "How forcibly does this illustrate the beneficence of the Creator! How strongly does it encourage us to persevere in this good work!" God wanted grape growers to improve grape plants via hybridization, Wilder argued; in fact, it was as important as improving themselves as Americans and as men. Later, when describing the "Characteristics of a Good Tree or Good Fruit," he argued, "A good constitution for a tree is as essential as a good constitution for a man." To be desirable for cultivation and for sale, and ultimately to carry the society's stamp of approval as a "recommended variety" for the general population, members decided that a certain number of characteristics were required of any fruit. Listed in order of descending importance, the key attributes were: health, hardiness, fertility, persistency of fruit, vigor of growth, persistency of foliage, and good growth habit.[44] Thus, the hybridization of plants and their successful adaptation to various U.S. regions was a matter of similarly enviable human traits that also connected strongly with definitions of state vigor and economic success. In other horticultural fields, as Bruce Weber and Charles Van Ravenswaay write, the adaptability, variety, and size of apples came to be a matter of national pride in the nineteenth century.[45] And as much as hybridization debates reflected anxieties about the purity of national identity and proof of America's natural moral and technical prowess, so did viticultural technologies resonate with other discourses that constructed a nationalist and genteel identity in these decades.

Mead's Grape Culture also situated moral attention to developing men-through-grapes within popular mid-century tropes of American manifest destiny. Manifest destiny, to Mead, had made itself apparent not only in men and the land, but in the land's produce and grapes' specific ability to be refined into a globally valued cultural good. The author offers his assessment: "Our taste for grapes really began in the woods, and it is surprising how many still seek its gratification there, unsatisfying as it must be, while the good is so plainly in sight. But a movement has begun; the masses are turning their faces to the light; a number have already reached the outskirts of the woods, and some may be seen wending their way up the fair hill of culture, rosy with excitement of their new-found pleasure."[46] For Mead, viticulture carried with it the Enlightenment's emancipatory mission. "The masses" would never be fully out of the woods and wending their way up the teleological hill of cultural consciousness until the skills of grape growing were imparted to them. The ability to distinguish between grapes and wine and "those nice shades and degrees of flavor which give a distinctive character" was important to any cultured adult. It was the duty of those "already enlightened" to show others the way to the new paragon of civilization, necessarily on U.S. soil, through American technological ingenuity.

Mead, forever an enthusiast of uplift through grapes, states in his final pages: "Be assured that all labor that tends to the improvement of public taste by placing the good within its knowledge and reach will meet its appropriate reward, not alone in that which makes rich, but also in that exalted consciousness of well-doing which riches can neither purchase nor take away. Attune yourself to the 'key-note' that runs through this book, '*Good grapes for all*,' and do your part to hasten the day when its vibrations shall be heard and felt in every dwelling in the land."[47]

Mead declared his vision of "good grapes for all" and meant for this dream to resonate individually, societally, and nationally. "Every dwelling in the land" was to be constructed with this double-entendre sense of the "cultivated" bourgeois, or a knowledge of nature, culture, and the quiet acceptance of horticultural refinement's genteel monetary benefits. The grape culture developed in the middle decades of the nineteenth century was thus a system of social and scientific principles creating a set of mores that linked individual horticultural practices to national enterprise. Manifest destiny's promise of ownership of the land and identity through such ownership would come to fruition with the assistance of citizen-vintners as they expanded their cadre of tools and technologies. The American vineyard was a site for propounding ideological beliefs about national and personal morality, the enhanced production of vines offering up a cultivated middle-class American character of "taste."

The Rhetoric of Vines

In the mid-nineteenth century, other significant advancements in grape technics included the print technologies that allowed grape information to spread. In particular, advancements in print imagery, such as the invention of lithography, led to new detail with which vine care was illustrated, as well as a growth in grape culture's potential audience. Seed catalogs with thorough cultivation instructions had been widely available since 1835.[48] These changes led to increased sharing of information, in turn spurring excitement about new products horticulturists could grow and build. In addition, national networks of communication, trade, finance, and transportation came together with new printing, binding, and illustration techniques to create larger audiences and deliver to them more materials. The printed word defined a specific horticultural lexicon and community across great distances.

In the 1840s, the act of experimentation alone was enough to garner praise in industry journals. An 1847 *Horticulturist* lauded a failed experimenter: "That gentleman, full of zeal in vine culture, collected every known variety from our woods, and cultivated them in his garden, manuring, stimulating and pruning them with great care, in the hope of changing and ameliorating their character."[49] Specific words like "character" were often employed in selling grape culture. The cultivation of the grape's "character" was arguably the most important aspect of tending grapes for future generations of Americans. Even uncertain experiments were therefore lauded. Indeed, the phrase "the character of American grapes" was on the lips of every grape writer in the antebellum period. Extendedly, character was of great importance in mid-century capitalist culture at large. All types of professional agencies constantly expressed concerns with the development of individual persons' and the collective nation's "character" in the antebellum United States. Character in people, ultimately a matter of personal self-control and self-reliance, was about developing a solid life narrative and habits of independence. "Self-made men" were moral pillars in a sea of confidence men and seemingly assured corruption; men of character were laws unto themselves, beyond the cheapening and evil influences of market capitalism. As Thomas Augst has argued, this central quality that middle-class Americans sought to develop in themselves was thus a multivalenced meditation on the nation and on self-representation. Americans sought security in character within a crisis of moral authority as the Industrial Revolution took hold.[50]

Character and horticulture ran hand in hand, as well. Andrew Jackson Downing repeated the sentiment in his journal *The Horticulturist*: "Horticulture and its kindred arts, tend strongly to fix the habits, and elevate the character of our whole rural population."[51] This also fit viticulturists' beliefs that they were at the apex of the agricultural crop-handler hierarchy. Fruit crops were allied with tea, silk manufacture, and a few other specialty crops, in that they were elegant, beautiful goods that could be cultivated by small-scale, skilled country gentlemen, or their urban brethren. Issues of self-reliance translated easily into the vineyard, as U.S. grape growers were intent on developing their own viticulture, separate from and better than European methods and wine grapes. Grapes in this way were an essential component to the mid-century obsession with the "civilizing process," the multipronged efforts in the "refinement of America."[52] Grapes assisted Americans in the performance of gentility, in drinking fine wine and developing elevated social tastes and skills. One therefore practiced horticulture not only on plants, but on one's self, in an era of industrial capitalism and social transformation.

"Character" could be found not only in the practice of horticulture, but even in plants themselves. Character in plants had a similarly multifold meaning: many nineteenth-century horticulturists believed that plants had specific virtues and somewhat fixed traits, and that they could be coaxed to outwardly demonstrate those traits differently in varying climates. For some hybridizers, American grapes needed only cultivation, a little "good breeding" of their own. Botanical descriptions of native grapes in America were thus sure to describe each type's positive "character." A vine's true worth lay not in where it was found or what it looked like, but in its potential, in what it could be made to do. In a trope popular since the beginning of grape publishing in America, "training grapes" was a metaphor for cultivating men. As one horticulturist put it in 1819: "Since all vines were once wild, like all men and other animals, it must be presumed, that it is our interest to cultivate all our wild grape vines."[53] In such tropes, the grapevine and its body of fruit parallel the larger national body. The parallelism was most potent within the contexts of the civilizing process undergone by both grapes and their growers. Only conscious attention to advanced cultivation would produce the best character in grapes and men. Failure in wine making was not, at first, the ultimate worry; rather, it was the character of the grapevine. Vineyardists were initially concerned with proving the sheer abundance of native vines, and only later their profitability and taste. The struggle to breed better local stock as a means of developing character was the first key in establishing viticultural legitimacy.

Along with the rhetoric of character, abundance, and magnitude that accompanied print descriptions of the grapevines in the United States, agricultural journal writers for decades used more specific language to describe their beloved native grapevines. Typical agricultural journal writers waxed poetic, with statements like "the [grapevine] fields were luxuriant," and "the grape . . . it soon envelops with its luxurious festoons."[54] The often-deployed words *luxuriant* and *luxurious,* though sharing the same root word, have quite different meanings. *Luxuriant* is a quality of being: a luxuriant vine is lush, vigorous, and profuse in nature. However, *luxurious* means opulent, rich. Only in the second sense does the changed ending to the root word invoke class status, where that which is "luxurious" involves extravagant, indulgent expense. The technically improper use of *luxurious* to describe the way grapevines roister upon the ground, or affect a scene of repose, belied Victorian middle-class intentions and hinted at an underlying sensuality, the risk of overcivilization, and even sexual promiscuity. The *Farmer & Gardener* of 1838 tellingly declared that "the vine is of very luxurious growth on any ordinary soil."[55] These words appeared in journals for decades, variously describing grapes, vines, their subsequent wine, and families' pleasures in growing them.[56]

The slippage between *luxurious* and *luxuriant* also reveals how the grapevine functioned as a domestic and nationalist trope. Grapevines described as "luxurious festoons" were part of a specific early Victorian romantic vocabulary, revealing a constant and public yearning for the finest things. These descriptions at the same time point to a consciousness of class status. Yet the continued substitution of one word for the other, *luxuriant* for *luxurious* and vice versa, also revealed the inherent promise of "luxury" found in the "luxuriant" natural world. Vines accompanied a luxurious life, one conscious of the finer things, with money enough for acquisition and control. But because luxury was not a necessity, it was suspect and was to be avoided according to earlier Puritan, republican, and Jeffersonian worldviews.[57] Its constant use in grape writing thus reveals how a horticultural consciousness was part of the negotiation of Jeffersonian ideals of yeoman husbandry in transition to a larger market economy.

Crucial to this connection is the way that both terms also referenced and even created a desire for national stature from the turn of the century through the 1850s. Grapevines were "luxuriant"—lush, profuse, prolific, easily propagated, and actively spreading their tendrils across the land—much like the Jacksonian-era public described its country to be expanding. Americans believed in the superiority of the rural agricultural existence, as it was the best example of the tempered life many believed existed between "savage" Native American lifeways and overly "sophisticated" cultures of Europe. Grapevines successfully combined the two extreme ends of the scale of cultivation: the savage and the sophisticated were accessed simultaneously through grape culture. While growing vines, one could flirt with untamed and abundant nature, while also courting lush and sensuous culture. Viticulturists promised early Victorians rampant and naturally abundant grapevines; mid-century tables were graced with opulent upper-bourgeois niceties, as well. In combining romantic excess and "native" spontaneity with economic value, managed self-cultivation, and improved class status, the grapevine was not only a telling trope for Victorian art and taste, it was an overdetermined symbol of Victorian values. The key terms used in discussing grape culture, *character* and *luxury,* signal the extent to which grape culture functioned as a bridge between predominant cultural worldviews. They also remind us that grape culture was dependent on—even inseparable from—grapes in print.

Herman Melville captured the relationship between the industrial paper manufacturing and horticultural worlds in "The Paradise of Bachelors and the Tartarus of Maids" (1855). The story is written in two parts and depicts two locations: the "paradise" of fine foods and comfort enjoyed by an urban cohort of bachelors, and the hell of an industrial paper factory, equipped with laboring, "blank," unmarried female drudges. The story's narrator is a professional horticulturist, for he had "embarked on a large scale in the seeds-man's business (so extensively and broadcast, indeed, that at length my seeds were distributed through all the Eastern and Northern States and even fell into the far soil of Missouri and the Carolinas)." The need for paper is a driving force of the story; as Melville writes, "The demand for paper at my place became so great, that the expenditure soon amounted to a most important item in the general account . . . of these small envelopes I used an incredible quantity—several hundreds of thousands in a year." The narrator needed the paper for envelopes to house and send seeds, and for orders and correspondence. He explains, "These are mostly made of yellowish paper, folded square; and when filled, are all but flat, and being stamped, and superscribed with the nature of the seeds contained, assume not a little the appearance of business-letters ready for the mail."[58] Looking for a way to economize, the seedsman travels to the paper mill sixty miles away to place an order for envelopes.

Business was good, and Melville's seedsman utilized the benefits of the factory system to fulfill his large orders "at wholesale prices," which relied upon a stark division of labor and sex. But the seedsman's own horticultural business does not take on the appearance of the sexually and socially "dirty" industry upon which he relies. On the contrary, the narrator metaphorically travels between the refinement of high society in town (the "paradise of bachelors") and the "savage wild" forest and paper mill miles away (the "tartarus of maids"). His paper seed envelopes avoid the corruption of both the "high" and the "low," and are cleanly middle class. Moreover, the narrator's seeds travel through one of industrial America's important new creations—mass-produced paper envelopes sent through new channels of transportation. The 1850s marked the most rapid expansion of the railroad in U.S. history. In ten years, total trackage grew by more than 20,000 miles.[59] The narrator uses these industrial channels to grow his horticultural business, while simultaneously helping his clients propagate nature. He as seedsman is the unimpeachable go-between for nature and culture.

With its social and agricultural technologies, viticulture was thus an important nexus for constructing bourgeois urban and national identity for Americans in the decades of superheated manifest destiny, an identity increasingly underwritten by technological innovation and the early U.S. Patent Office. New grape technologies, interest and funds from the federal government, and descriptions of horticulture as a moral act illustrated how mid-century viticultural activities were part of the social negotiation of Jeffersonian pastoral ideals in transition to a larger national market economy. Urban viticulturists, while discussing the technologies of viticulture through their sparkling glass houses, also articulated a new nationalism and growing class-stratified identities. Yet the regularly socially and politically vexed divide between urban life and the agricultural world found its amelioration in grape culture in quaint and grand ways. Grape growers seemed to succeed in navigating the new market economy with their morals enhanced, not denigrated. In America, nationalism and white middle-class identities would continue to be articulated through the cultivated technologies of viticulture.

3

Landscapes of Fruit and Profit

ALTHOUGH QUITE COMMON in the nineteenth century throughout all regions of the growing nation, fruit speculators have not received the same scrutiny as the traders, capitalists, and real estate men who more frequently populate the history of U.S. territorial and market expansion.[1] Nicholas Longworth (1782–1863), the "father of American wine" who made his millions in real estate in Cincinnati, is an ideal example of this type of horticultural cynosure. In romanticized mid-century fashion, Longworth's family described his methods of wealth accumulation in verse in 1857. A poem written on the occasion of Longworth's golden wedding anniversary described the early Cincinnati viticulturist's tactics:

> And all he saves, invests in land—
> Invests in land, with faith sincere
> The town will grow from year to year,
> To be a city rich and grand
> And all the Western World command.
> He thinks 'twill do him little harm,
> In such a case, to own a farm
> Or two, outside the rising village,
> Used now for pasturage and tillage,
> And hold on tightly for a rise—
> Perhaps the plan is very wise.[2]

Similarly, in his 1858 portrait, "Old Nick" stands among the things that brought him wealth: hundreds of acres of land surrounding Cincinnati, Ohio, and his grapes (Fig. 18). Viticulturists had known for decades that the most

Figure 18. Robert Duncanson, *Portrait of Nicholas Longworth*, 1858, oil on canvas. Collection of the University of Cincinnati. Photo courtesy of the Taft Museum of Art.

popular European winegrapes (*Vitis vinifera* like Cabernet Sauvignon and Chardonnay) would not grow well in North America under normal circumstances, but Longworth was convinced he could develop the Ohio River Valley into a great American wine-growing region. The cultural importance of finding a "native" American wine, as well as improving the quality and taste of America's antebellum vinous productions, are at the heart of Longworth's accepted life story. His other popular monikers—the "Western Bacchus," referring to the lesser Roman god associated with wine and revelry, and the "Croesus of Cincinnati," referring to an ancient Greek king synonymous with wealth in the nineteenth century—signal that for many, Longworth was assisting the United States in its quest for classical imperial significance.[3]

As the creator of the first commercially successful American champagne, Longworth has, perhaps erroneously, also been celebrated as the harbinger of an ideal democratic agrarian republic.[4] In fact, Longworth was a fruit entrepreneur who altered the Ohio landscape, brought a new type of alcohol to the new West, and continued a national interest in fruit culture in the growing regional center. Yet as an investor, Longworth also sought to capitalize on his fruit, and as the poem suggests, on the resale of the "improved" land the fruit grew upon, as well as the margin of profit that could be added by hired immigrant labor. Specifically, behind the Longworth horticultural egalitarian myth is a story of wealth made through land speculation and, crucially, decades of tenant labor that has been obscured by the democratic mythos of U.S. fruit production and fruit tourism. Known today as little more than "Cincinnati's first millionaire," Longworth was at one time the second-wealthiest man in the United States.[5] The "Croesus of Cincinnati" deserves a more prominent place within the history of the market revolution and early capitalist development of western agriculture, yet his story should not be a hagiographic one. Nineteenth-century pomology provided an excusable, even commendable, framework for turning public property into private property and for hiding any questionably exploitative dealings in the shade of its fruitful bowers in several regions. Ohio, in this regard, also should have a higher profile in the history of fruit- and grape-growing, alongside the better-known centers of New York and California. Claiming a kind of passive, utilitarian, scientific, and benevolent role in the landscape and society, viticulture and fruit-growing functioned to deny the realities of land speculation, agricultural imperialism, and the labor that were key ingredients of the business as it was practiced in the Cincinnati area.[6]

Dreaming a Vineland in Ohio

Early to mid-nineteenth-century Ohio has a unique place in the history of the Old Northwest, although it was a part of the larger market transformation happening throughout the antebellum West and upper South. Since the late 1700s, national policies distributed land to farmers and encouraged farm expansion from east to west, achieving the goal of nation-building through settlement by white migrants. Upon statehood in 1803, military lands were opened for sale in Ohio; before 1814, pioneers could also use squatters' laws to claim land. Through mid-century, investors leased school and military lands very cheaply, for terms as long as ninety-nine years. The Homestead Act of 1841 further opened lands in the Midwest to sale and farming.[7] While the proportion of all Americans living outside cities was still five out of six in 1860, new means of communication and transportation that linked country with metropole were booming. The Ohio River, in addition to its utility in commerce, at this time developed as a symbolic boundary between freedom and slavery. As "far western country," a kind of first stop "across the mountains," Ohio was an ideological borderland—a sharp line of division between slave territory and free—yet it was also an artery, linking the nation from east to west and north to south.[8]

Popular opinion held that one major city would eventually dominate the interior of the continent, and Cincinnati emerged as the early regional leader.[9] Charles Cist, an early booster, claimed in 1841 that "within one hundred years . . . Cincinnati will be the greatest city in America; and by the year of our Lord two thousand, the greatest city in the world." In his 1851 popular guidebook and who's-who list for the city (reprinted every few years for decades), he linked "Cincinnati—Its Destiny" with "the law of gravitation or centralization . . . known to be one of the laws of nature": "New York had been made so before . . . [but] Cincinnati is the grand centre of the United States, not geographically, perhaps, but the centre of the forces and influences, which, when readjusted after the introduction of the great disturbing cause, the railroad, must settle and determine the destiny and relative position of various cities or centres, which are now struggling for supreme ascendancy on this continent."[10] Cist's hyperbole, humorous today, was not entirely unfounded. In 1820 Cincinnati was nearly twice as large as its nearest midwestern competitor (St. Louis), and it increased that margin throughout the 1840s. With river commerce development in the 1830s, Cincinnati became the most diversified metropolis west of the Alleghenies; in the same decade, it grew from a few hundred residents to 50,000 people and to more than a mile in radius. The city thus acted as the spearhead of the antebellum capitalist frontier. Like many other cities at the time, Cincinnati often boasted that it had a central, riverine, "strategic," and "beautiful" setting—but it alone was able to make good on its boasts for at least two decades. Cist's booster-ism invokes the competitiveness that guided city-building in this period: he believed that the city's success through transportation and trade happened at the expense of its rivals.[11]

In addition to its importance in the river trade, Cincinnati experienced a remarkable cultural flowering in the three decades before the Civil War, when it was known as the singular "literary emporium of the West."[12] Due in large part to Longworth's dedicated patronage, many fine arts and hundreds of cultural clubs emerged. Longworth's interest and funds propelled many significant artists' careers, including that of sculptor Hiram Powers, as well as that of Longworth's portraitist, African American Hudson River School painter Robert Duncanson. A cultural self-awareness grew in this new space that identified as "not-East" as well as "not-South," as Cincinnatians wanted their city to be "living proof that civilization and refinement could flourish in the former wilderness."[13]

The city-building rhetoric and visual arts of mid-century Cincinnati il-lustrate the city's will to prominence. Fontayne and Porter's daguerreotype of Cincinnati in 1848 (Fig. 19) shows the city's waterfront and Mount Ad-ams's sloping hills behind, a bucolic landscape mixed with symbols of trade, with the Cincinnati Observatory peering down from above. As a river port, Cincinnati saw more than 4,000 steamboat arrivals in 1847. Similarly, in Eh-rgott and Forbriger's lithograph in the frontispiece to Cist's *Cincinnati in 1859* (Fig. 20), viewers were positioned to read the picture as proof of Cincinnati's claim to midwestern urban centrality.[14] Forbriger's piece is mapped in the classic artist's genre of prospect painting. Both documents present Cincinnati through a long, panoramic landscape with a gently twisting river, offering the city's beauty and riches to the viewer, and promise visual power over the land-scape. Cincinnati is ringed by green sloping hills—a city nestled in the curve of the river and its naturally abundant surroundings. Cincinnati took several names in the antebellum years: "Porkopolis," for its meatpacking industry, as well as her more elegant monikers, the "Athens of the West" and the "Queen City," as illustrated by Forbriger and Fontayne.

But Cincinnati was more than a lovely "city among cities" in the interior of

Figure 19. Cincinnati riverfront in 1848, Mount Adams and the Cincinnati Observatory in background, the *Ohio Belle* and *Cincinnatus* in foreground. Charles Fontayne and William S. Porter, "Cincinnati Panorama of 1848, Plate 6," daguerreotype. From the Collection of the Public Library of Cincinnati and Hamilton County.

the continent; it was also a center of the mid-century capitalist frontier.[15] Against the arcadian visual images of the city, Alexis de Tocqueville, in his trip through the United States and its territories in 1831, said of Cincinnati that "everything there is in violent contrast, exaggerated." Like a child's large-print schoolbook full of opposites, he saw that "all that there is of good or of bad in American society is to be found there."[16] Cincinnati in the early 1800s was surely incoherent to many eyes: muddy streets, slipshod downtown construction, frontier speculation, and a population of hard-drinking residents and German-speaking immigrants. The rivers often flowed red from the blood of hundreds of thousands of hogs slaughtered annually, and residents felt "enveloped in black smoke"

Figure 20. Ehrgott and Forbriger's 1859 lithograph of Cincinnati. Charles Cist, *Sketches and Statistics of Cincinnati in 1859* (Cincinnati: n.p., 1859), frontispiece.

billowing from its foundries. Longworth's family crafted a poem in 1857 describing Cincinnati as Longworth first knew it in 1803:

> The place was quite in embryo,
> Only a thousand folk, or so,
> To build a town did there begin,
> Which even now is not fenced in.
> A *Roman* name its founder gave it,
> But not a Roman name could save it
> From being chiefly noted for
> Its campaigns in the porcine war—
> For vending lard in cask and jar,
> And hams and shoulders, pork and oil,
> And other greasy things and vile.
> Wherefore, since wonders never cease,
> It's now a famous town of *grease*.[17]

Porcine war notwithstanding, Cincinnati's founding history was soon re-tooled as a progressive tale of capital accumulation and agricultural bounty, as it grew quickly from a small frontier outpost to a prosperous city. Longworth was dedicated to ensuring that Cincinnati would eventually live up to its illustrious Roman name, through arts patronage and horticultural refinements.

Cincinnati's efforts at such civilization and refinement were demonstrated in part through expert local wine production. New York agricultural journals such as *The Horticulturist* had for years called for further cultivation of the "far western lands" of the Ohio Valley.[18] New York horticulturists Andrew Jackson Downing and William Prince, who sustained the popular mythology of country gentlemen in their horticultural publications and nursery businesses, projected a neo-yeoman dream into the Ohio Valley. Both Downing and Prince repeatedly encouraged viticulturists to move west and the government to sponsor grape-growing experimentation there. In an 1848 report in Downing's *The Horticulturist* on "The Vineyards of Ohio," frontier civilization is manifest through domesticating grapevines:

> If we take a retrospective glance of fifty or sixty years . . . when the unexplored wilds of Ohio—the now *indeed* beautiful Ohio—were penetrated by a few hardy adventurers . . . encountering at every step the shrieks of wild beasts, and their little but less ferocious companion, the Red Man. . . . The great abundance of the wild grape, found indigenous in the forest, and the luxuriancy of their growth, towering and spreading over the tops of the tallest trees, abundantly loaded with fruit, justifies the idea that the better and finer sorts will flourish here also.[19]

The author, A. H. Ernst, links grape growing with natural abundance and a northern Anglo-American pastoral ideal: nature was *already* a vineyard in Ohio. This narrative—of an America that was once lush with greenery but now truly beautiful due to vineyards spreading through the Ohio Valley and beyond—was popular in the mid-nineteenth century. The scene reveals a continuing belief in fruit and garden cultivation as a key to civilization and the nation's future. Other narratives with viticultural overlays are apparent in Ernst's full text: that the land was wild and filled with savage men waiting to be tamed and taught a proper way of life; that the abundant agricultural riches were a gift from God for those with the moral and technical means to develop them; and that destiny was sealed from the second the first white foot was planted on American soil. "Wild" and "indigenous" as well as "better and finer" varietals could be enhanced and cultivated to produce the classic drink of civilization. The potency and "luxuriancy" of vines in their natural state would naturally be brought to their full potential when under the influence of commerce and social mores. This vinous vision of manifest destiny was especially important for a culture that needed to make the case that just as the nation should easily spread everywhere across North America, so should its number-one claim to refinement and bourgeois culture: wine.[20]

The Ohioan vision of cultural and national prominence through viticulture was also spread via horticulturists' contextualized appropriation of a biblical parable from 1 Kings 4:25. *The Horticulturist* and *Ohio Cultivator* both published an article detailing progress in "the vineyards of the West": "To sit under our own vine and fig tree, with no one to make us afraid, is the most ancient and sacred idea of a life of security, contentment and peace. In a national sense, we think we may begin to lay claim to this species of comfort. . . . There is no longer any doubt regarding the fact that the valley of the Ohio, with its vine-clad hills, will soon afford a resting place for millions of cultivators, who may sit down beneath the shadow of their own vines, with none to make them afraid."[21] "Under one's own vine and fig tree," a biblical allusion to individual peace and prosperity, is here re-envisioned "in a national sense" for cultivators in the Ohio Valley. It becomes a statement about nationalist dominion over the land, its pacific tone a paradoxical call to arms against those who would "make them afraid"—namely, the removed American Indians—and the reigning European wine producers. Beyond wine's traditional place in religious history and temperance movements, *The Horticulturist* and *Ohio Cultivator* helped instill Ohio grape culture within the nationalism that shaped so many expansionist frontier narratives.

Cincinnati was at the center of the West's pomological manifest destiny because, in addition to its "strategic" setting and cultural prominence, it was the largest and most productive wine region in the nation for two decades before the Civil War. Cincinnati growers exclaimed for decades that the area was ideal for wine growing. An 1840s Cincinnati viticulturist wrote, "The soil most congenial to the growth of the Vine, and the perfection of its fruit, is a rich, light, calcareous loam, with a dry, stony, or rocky bottom. . . . In soil and climate, our surrounding hills are not surpassed in advantages for producing good wine, by the best wine districts of France or Spain. . . . With a good natural soil, fair exposure, favorable climate, and a free and untaxed people, many of whom have been educated for the cultivation of the vine, there is no reason why we should not become as rich in wines as either of the above countries, after a few years' experience."[22] Still today, hillsides and river valleys are much prized in winemaking. Rivers, over thousands of years, carve their valleys, eroding some soil types and accumulating others. River valleys like the Ohio, with varied soils and microclimactic variations, had the complex, rocky terrain that winegrowers sought. Valleys also signaled relatively high water tables, and large rivers generally moderated their surrounding landscapes from cold and drought.[23] Cincinnati's landscape thus seemed well set for wine experimentation. The climate, however, was another matter. For better or worse, Cincinnati had extreme cold and hot temperatures, as well as wet summers, which often led to the growth of harmful fungi on most vine types. Scientific viticulture, as practiced in the nineteenth and twentieth centuries and today, operated on the belief that careful site selection and vine management could overcome many of the difficulties endemic to an area's climate. Cincinnati's dedicated growers were keen to try almost anything to transform their region into America's Rhineland.

Regional growers sought to share knowledge and capitalize on their collective prestige by organizing the Cincinnati Horticultural Society. Founded in 1843 by local businessmen-growers, the society was an active group of urban boosters, several of whom were also leading winemakers (Fig. 21). In the society's founding portrait, members gather around their edible riches. Grapes are draped upon and around other fruits at the table, illustrating the society's investment in viticulture. With weekly meetings, the group shared "correspondence with distinguished horticulturalists in different parts of the Union; new fruits were thus brought to light, and seeds and scions of superior varieties were exchanged and disseminated." They quickly acted on plans for a grand rural cemetery (Spring Grove), and held semiannual flower and fruit exhibitions. Membership swelled to 700 by 1851 and to almost 900 in 1859.[24] The society's charter outlined their goal to further "adorn our green hills and beautiful valleys, scattering far and wide her floral and pomonal riches."[25]

Under the society's guidance, wine making flourished. A period of major expansion of the Cincinnati wine industry marked the decades after 1842, the year in which Longworth stumbled onto his formula for "sparkling Catawba," a much more palatable and popular beverage than his previous "Cincinnati hock." In 1845, one of the society's charter members, Melzer Flagg (also Longworth's employee and son-in-law) collected statistics on vineyards in Hamilton County, supporting Cincinnati's braggadocio with geographical data. He found that eighty-three vineyards covered 250 acres in the Cincinnati area,

Figure 21. Cincinnati Horticultural Society, 1843. Longworth is seated at right. Courtesy Cincinnati Museum Center.

producing 23,000 gallons of wine per annum.[26] Five years later, the society increased its statistical scope to include any vineyard within twenty miles of the city, reflecting the Cincinnati area's growing dominance as a national wine region. Seven hundred and fifty acres of grapevines were then being tended, two-thirds of which were bearing fruit. By 1852, the acreage had increased to 1,200 acres, and more than 600 people were employed in wine making.[27] In 1853, the region's vintners produced 450,000 bottles of wine. The "Report from Ohio" at the American Pomological Society's national meeting in 1855 fairly burst with enumerated accomplishments: within twenty miles of Cincinnati, 1,400 acres of vines were planted, of which 800 were bearing. Society members claimed to be processing between 400 and 900 gallons of wine per acre. Labor costs ran $60 to $80 per acre, and wine was selling at $1 to $1.25 per gallon. The beaming committee summarized: "This culture is profitable, and vineyards are largely on the increase in the valley of the Ohio."[28]

By this point, Cincinnati's title as the "Rhine of America" had finally taken hold. *DeBow's Review, Ohio Cultivator,* and the *New York Journal of Commerce* all ran an article on "The Vineyards of the West": "Cincinnati is the centre of the wine region in the Ohio valley, and the Ohio river has not inaptly been called the 'Rhine of America.' . . . The 'vine-clad hills' already afford a pleasing variety in the scenery around this city, and the vintage is anticipated with interest and solicitude. It is a new feature in the harvest of this rich valley, and a product that must before long form an important branch of our national industry."[29] Cincinnati wine was clearly ascendant. In 1855, the viticultural area again grew to 1,500 acres, and these vineyards made up more than two-thirds of the total fruit acreage in the Ohio Valley. By the 1850s, Cincinnati's title as America's Rhineland was assured. The *Ohio Cultivator* was of course especially interested in spreading the "Rhine of America" designation for Cincinnati. It compared Cincinnati Catawba wine to Rhine wine in 1850: "The Catawba makes . . . a wine so much like the ordinary wines of the Rhine, that we could put three of the former bottles among a dozen of the latter, and it would puzzle the nicest connoisseur to select them either by color or flavor." Near the end of the decade, 35 percent of the nation's total wine crop came from the Cincinnati region, nearly double the percentage of the next most productive state, California. Some Cincinnati growers posted 40 percent profits by the mid-1850s.[30] The "Rhine of America" enjoyed its title and stature in fruit experimentation and production for more than twenty years, illustrating and crowning Cincinnati's claim to being the "Queen City" of the Great West.

Although motivated by high prices, grape growers experimented with new varieties. National journals published dozens of articles yearly about new native and hybrid grapes. Viticulturists, through regional and national meetings and public correspondence in journals, had generally settled the question of each U.S. wine-growing region's most favored and productive grape: for Ohio, it was the Catawba; for the South, the Scuppernong—and in the East, the Isabella, among others. Indeed, in the early 1850s in the Cincinnati region, likely as many as nineteen of every twenty vines were Catawbas.[31] But the dominance of this variety did not keep viticulturists from focusing a constant eye on new varieties, and devoting at least a few acres to experimentation. A partial list of "grapes raised and exhibited" by Nicholas Longworth in 1846 contained over twenty vines, their names evoking the grape's believed origins, the name of the breeder, or (more typical for other ornamental items like flowers) women's names.[32] Because of his wealth as well as his national reputation gained from successful grape experiments, Longworth (seated at the bottom right in Fig. 21) was the Cincinnati Horticultural Society's preeminent member. His leadership in and enthusiasm for the local grape trade, not to mention his bottomless pockets and many land investments, exemplified the society's ideals of agricultural beauty and industry through viticulture in Cincinnati into the 1860s.

Longworth, Entrepreneur of Fruit

At first glance, Nicholas Longworth's life history looks like a gilt recasting of the more down-home frontier icon Johnny Appleseed. Longworth's recorded life story is a classic rags-to-riches tale of an even-keeled, immensely hard-working, odd, and lucky frontier immigrant. Longworth came to Cincinnati from Newark, New Jersey, in 1803, at the age of twenty-one.[33] According to several early biographers, he was an impoverished but plucky lawyer, running away from an embarrassing family history—his parents had been Loyalists, and their estate was ruined after the Revolution. In his first case in Cincinnati, in which he defended an accused horse thief, Longworth reportedly received in payment two copper stills full of hard alcohol. With a keen early American capitalist's foresight, he immediately traded the appliances and liquor to a bartender for thirty-three acres of land on the town's outskirts. And in a typically mythic leap, most stories conclude that "by 1830 his lot was in the heart of the business district, and Longworth was one of the richest men in America."[34] According to the brief celebratory biographies, Longworth traded liquor stills for real estate assets that ultimately made him a multimillionaire.

The deeper details of Longworth's early years in Cincinnati reveal a less fortuitous, if more typical tale of a single young man fresh to the West. Letters to his mother are full of "gloomy reflections," a lonely man begging for his family to write him back. He wrote in 1806, "Even my brothers, amidst the hurry and bustle of the business, seem to have forgotten me—I mourn'd as I am in the wilds of the West, I stand in need of the correspondence of my friends, to cheer my gloomy hours, and make me contented with my situation. Willingly would I change it for the one which I deserted—But now it is too late to repine, and I must be content."[35] (A clue to family members' reluctance to write back may be found in a letter to Longworth's sister Mary in 1829. He spends half the letter critiquing her spelling!)[36] In his first four years in Cincinnati, Longworth also indulged in strong drink and a few too many hands of the card game euchre. As recalled in a family memorial album, one evening, the drunken young Longworth stumbled into the woods and passed out under a tree. There, a fairy landed on his shoulder, and, whispering messages into his ear, set him on the straight and narrow. He awoke with renewed dedication to his place in the West. By 1807, he was married to a woman of "many virtues . . . in the bloom of youth. . . . [She] is by the flattering world called hansome [*sic*]. I prize her . . . [for] her ingenious candid mind, and feeling heart." And by 1811, his letters home are altogether joyous: "I am as happy as I can be—I have two children."[37] Other authors have noted that throughout his life Longworth dressed strangely, spoke cryptically, had few close friends, and even in his extreme wealth lived a Spartan life. Having an odd carriage and lacking social graces, he was known to pin notes and to-do lists to his jacket cuffs every day—a detail recorded in his 1858 portrait (Fig. 18). What's more, Longworth so lived by the maxim "Do business first, and pleasure afterwards," that he was late to his own wedding. A family memorial poem recorded that in rushing to the ceremony from work, he hastily shaved, missing portions of his face, and that his wedding suit was too large: "He couldn't get entirely through / His wedding clothes, untried and new, / So rolled them up an inch or two."[38] Here, all quirky personal tics perhaps point to Longworth's obsessive business focus.

All biographies focus on Longworth's oddities, temperance, and pluck, but the real estate details and precision in business point to the more useful kernel of meaning in the Longworth myth. Henry Hobhouse has argued that vineyards have since the earliest times symbolized stable husbandry, a solid and expanding economic horizon, and security in civilization. Once planted with grapevines, the lands around Cincinnati produced the drink of an aspiring region. Longworth's grapes "tamed" and beautified the outlying lands and signaled permanent, cultured residence.[39] This foundational story of the first magnate of the West mirrored that of his growing home, the River City, which was then developing as a regional center for trade and several agricultural goods. Longworth's story served not only as a means of temperance-driven moral suasion—the monetary and moral benefits of wine over the stupidity and easy losses of hard alcohol—but as a story of Ohio's founding and promise as a nationally important space of cultivation and urban sophistication.

Beyond the myth, the years between Longworth's supposed sale of stills and his rise to wealth reveal much more was at work than a young American's pluck and luck. Having horticultural interests all his life, Longworth experimented with grape growing in 1813 but was not devoted to it until 1820, when he received his first vines from the Swiss colony in Vevey, Indiana, an earlier small-scale, but successful, wine enterprise. By 1820, Longworth was growing several types of grapes in vineyards just outside of town, and in 1823 he received the Catawba grape from a friend, renowned American viticulturist and handbook author Major John Adlum. In this way, Longworth's riches in real estate were accompanied by, if not in part driven by, his interest and promotion of the grape trade. He was a millionaire by 1825, and gave up his law practice three years later.[40]

Longworth's grape growing developed during these years from a tinkering interest to a serious investment of his surplus wealth. Like many real estate speculators in the period, he did not sit on one property, but was acquiring and selling dozens in any given year. The investor's method (one accurate piece of the Longworth myth) was simply to buy up all the land he could, as fast as he could. The 1838 Cincinnati tax list details over one hundred properties that Longworth owned, valued at over $115,000. This included land solely within the city limits, as well as only the land's assessed value, generally thought to be lower than the market price.[41]

Longworth knew that vineyards had a way of making previously unusable land profitable. No matter how "worthless" the land, or remote from the center of town, Longworth would buy it and begin planting vines. The vintner and others called this "waste land," "not worth shucks."[42] Especially surprising at the time, Longworth bought up hilly land, much of what was available in southern Ohio. Hills were beneficial when growing grapes, as opposed to the flat landscapes necessary for so many other crops.[43] Longworth's vineyards thus made previously "useless" land pay first through its rents and production of grapes, and second through its sale and repurposing in preparation for an expanding city. As Cincinnati grew, the city and private buyers bought back Longworth's land, then covered with vineyards, for continued grape growing or urban development.

He may have been an odd duck, but Longworth had prevenient skill in real estate marketing. Like later real estate entrepreneurs, Longworth understood the importance of language. Among other ventures, Longworth called his vineyards in Cincinnati's near east side, on Mount Adams, the "Garden of Eden" (today's Eden Park)—and later his family joked that Longworth and his wife were the city's Adam and Eve. On Cincinnati's east end, he bought Bald Hill in the 1830s, so named because it "had been deforested at an early date." By the 1840s, he had turned the barren hill into a Catawba vineyard and rechristened it "Mount Tusculum," a name borrowed from a "hill in ancient Rome where wealthy patricians had built their villas."[44] Acting as the fairy on Cincinnati's shoulder, Longworth had a gift for enswathing the inconvenient and unseemly in mythic grandeur.

Taking a page from his father-in-law's book, Melzer Flagg encouraged other Horticultural Society members to buy hilly land in his treatise "Remarks on the Culture of the Grape in the Western States" (1846): "The cultivation of the vine gives employment to a peculiar kind of labor, better suited to those rocky and hilly lands than any other; and it will establish a permanent value to vast tracts of lands that are too steep for the plough, which will sell for a price they would not bring under any other culture." He continues the argument on temperance grounds: "Would it not vastly improve our moral condition as a nation, to turn our rocky hills and waste lands into vineyards, from which we could supply all classes with a cheap and wholesome drink, than to continue to exhaust our richer bottom lands in making whiskey?"[45] A. A. Mullet, member of the Horticultural Society, in a report to the same, showed that others were having similar luck in the 1850s: "The successful culture of the grape is of vast importance to the country, when we take into consideration the number of hands and the capital employed, the value of the exports of Wine from this city, and the high eminence it has attained, to say nothing in the rise in the value of the lands devoted to its culture. Lands which could not be sold for ten dollars per acre, have, since the introduction of the vine, been sold for upward of seventy dollars. . . . The superiority of [Catawba] wine speaks for itself, and its merits are acknowledged through the length and the breadth of this vast Union."[46] New York socialist muckraker of the early twentieth century Gustavus Myers decried Longworth's "land fortune" made this way: "The growth [in antebellum Cincinnati] kept on increasingly. His land lay in the very center of the expanding city, in the busiest part of the business section and in the best portion of the residential districts." Longworth's resold land was the actual source of most of his wealth: by 1850, his original thirty-three acres was worth an estimated $2 million.[47]

Although far from his primary source of wealth, Longworth's revenue from his vineyards was also impressive. By 1844, Longworth had ninety-one acres of vineyards, yielding 20,000 gallons of wine annually. By the mid-1850s, he produced 100,000 bottles per year and advertised nationally. Viticulture for Longworth was no longer just a gentleman's pleasurable pursuit. In 1852, his wine alone was worth $64,000. What's more, Longworth's success was mirrored throughout the region—by 1859, there were 3,000 acres of vineyards between Cincinnati and Ripley (forty miles upstream), and those vineyards produced 570,000 gallons of wine annually, one-third of total U.S. wine production and still more than twice that of California.[48]

Nature into Culture

Longworth popularized his wine through the tourism he encouraged to his picturesque vineyards. After several less-than-profitable early attempts to sell wine, he created tourist sites in his country vineyards positioned 300 feet above the city, and built a tasting "Wine Garden" and "wine house" in the middle of downtown Cincinnati. Articles about and romanticized pictures of Longworth's vineyards ran in *Harper's Weekly* (Fig. 22) and other national magazines in the 1850s. The pictures include images of old-world vinetenders and their skilled handiwork juxtaposed to, yet in civilized comfort with, the modern technological advances of the railroad and steamboat. Part of the vineyards' allure and popularity lay in their proximity to the city, an aspect highlighted in Cincinnati tourist literature and included in *Longworth's Wine House*, a promotional pamphlet published in the 1860s. In a picture from this tourist literature (Fig. 23), a blissful scene unfolds as rows of vines nestle into the gently curving river below. Also appearing on the labels of his Sparkling Catawba bottles, Longworth's vineyards lay in an inviting "semi-circular arc that enclosed [Cincinnati's] natural amphitheater for twelve miles in circumference."[49]

Figure 22. "Mr. Longworth's vineyard, near Cincinnati." *Harper's Weekly*, July 24, 1858. Courtesy Harpweek.

Figure 23. Longworth's vineyards in Cincinnati. "Longworth's Wine House," 1866. Courtesy Jed Dannenbaum, *Drink and Disorder*.

A vineyard tour offered not only a leisurely stroll among the vines, but an elevated perspective on the growing city and region. Longworth's most prominent vineyards were quickly established as premier tourist attractions in antebellum Cincinnati. His house was described in *Harper's Weekly* as: "a plain but capacious and home-looking building, and its fine locality and beautiful garden and surrounding grounds render it the most popularly attractive spot in the city. As 'Mr. Longworth's Garden,' it is known throughout the Western country; and it is freely used, by citizens and strangers, as a place of visit and promenade. In it are several fine conservatories, well filled with exotic and rare plants, a grape-house for foreign vines, and an experimental forcing house."[50] Vineyard tourism added value to Longworth's real estate, and its views reinforced Cincinnati's status as a burgeoning empire city. Visitors to Longworth's vineyards and home could thus experience the best of old and new civilizations in a still-natural setting. From 1850 to 1852, Longworth hired Robert Duncanson to paint eight 9½- by 6-foot high murals lining his mansion's foyer (Fig. 24). The Hudson River School views, here evoking the Ohio Valley, were replete with smashed trees, river scenes, tumbledown

Figure 24. Robert S. Duncanson, *Landscape with Grand Estate and Aqueduct*, 1850–52, oil on plaster, 109 3/8 x 91 3/4 in. Painted for the foyer of Longworth's home. Courtesy the Taft Museum of Art, Cincinnati, Ohio. Photographer: Tony Walsh, Cincinnati, Ohio.

cabins, stone bridges, and early imperial city-states.[51] Pastoral elegance was lavish inside and outside of Longworth's home.

The pictures of Longworth's vineyards in Figures 22 and 23 reinforce a distinction between other agricultural crops (even other specialty fruit crops) and grapes, when placed on a scale of perceived "naturalness" in a landscape. Very often, vineyards were planted among stumps of felled trees left in the ground. Stumps often figure as signs of progress in nineteenth-century visual art—progress both necessary and violent.[52] But in Figure 23, in the foreground and amid the vines, stumps are not so much a scar as a naturalized part of the landscape, softened by their placement within the process of making a commodity of high culture. In these images, the vineyard keeps its neo-yeoman, "natural" feel—it is nature, but nature cleaned up, straightened out, made productive and beautifully civilized. In the vines covering the hillsides, nature and culture were inseparable. Winemakers worked hard to make Cincinnati's claim to civilization seemingly self-evident.

Cincinnati winegrowers established their vineyards as special places in the local tourist landscape, and in the larger regional and national consciousness. An eastern grape writer for *The Horticulturist*, Lewis F. Allen, reported in 1851 that he "spent a delightful week" in Cincinnati attending the fall Grand Horticultural Jubilee. During this "week of hospitality, of kindness, and polite attentions . . . we visited the finest and most extensive vineyards in the neighborhood, Mr. Longworth's, Mr. Buchanan's, Mr. Ernst's, Mr. Resor's, and others." He commented on the region's Isabella grapes, and waxed profusely about the "luscious, large, plump, and wonderfully developed fruit of the Catawba, then in their full ripeness." The Catawba, he went on, exceeded any outdoor native grapes he had ever seen, and was comparable to the "Black Hamburgh of a hot-house." Allen summed up his journey: "The numerous vineyards of the Catawba, dotting the hillsides and valleys . . . around the city, to an eastern man, were truly a luxury to look upon."[53] He delighted especially in the "Champagne Catawba of Cincinnati" (Longworth's Sparkling Catawba), which he was certain would continue to be drunk at the best public tables in the East and West, comparable in all respects to imported wines (Fig. 25). Likewise, tourists from Hungary Ferencz Aurelius and Theresa Pulszky in their two-volume set of travelers' notes, *White, Red, Black* (1853), wrote that Cincinnati was a collection of old and new worlds: "Thirty gigantic steamers are always to be seen here . . . heavy wagons throng the banks. . . . This place is one of the great markets of America." The couple then describe extensive storehouses packed with busy laborers much "like

Figure 25. Label of Longworth's wines, artist and year unknown. Courtesy Cincinnati Museum Center.

bee-hives." The busily industrializing city is tempered, however, by the vines covering the surrounding hills: "The villas and the country seats . . . on the heights, command a most beautiful view; gardens are laid out around them, and the houses, though nearly all of them frail wood structures, look very elegant."[54] These visitors to Cincinnati's vineyards highlighted exactly what winemakers packaged their region to be: a network of industrious but luxurious outdoor spaces, attractive to tourists seeking the picturesque experience.

Promoting tourism to Cincinnati, Longworth's Wine House published a circular in the 1860s that was distributed at their branch offices in New York. The ten-page advertisement contained a series of eleven images detailing the winemaking process at Longworth's "wine house" in Cincinnati. Figure 23 opens the circular, the riverine scene described as "a faithful representation of one of the Vineyards in the vicinity of Cincinnati, which has been rendered, by its advantages of soil and exposure, famous for its grapes."[55] Readers then progress to the door of the Wine House, the building made of brick and stone with an appropriately aged patina, of course enswathed in grapevines. The armchair tourist then quickly descends into various winemaking rooms: the wine press room, dry wine vaults, cold vaults, the bottling/corking/wiring room, and the lower fermentation cellar are all drawn in the advertisement. Smaller vignettes end the pamphlet, illustrating wine bottles stored "on point" (tilted downward to collect sediment), ready for disgorging, a male laborer working at the wine bottle finishing stand/disgorging station, and a large picture of the Wine House corking machine. Longworth's pamphlet described and pictorialized labor in Cincinnati wine cellars as well. Industrious men work in detailed shop environments, performing skilled tasks. The pamphlet is descriptive and prescriptive: a machine that introduces sweetening agents to wine is lauded as an "ingenious contrivance," and all bottles in the wine-making process must be kept "scrupulously clean."[56] Large machines, such as the wine press and the corking machine, figure prominently but are specifically shown to be run by manpower, not steam. Thus, Longworth's Wine House showcased new and sophisticated winemaking techniques, but also skilled Old World winemakers. The vineyards were a happy mark of progress for the West, yet winemaking technologies also simultaneously seemed centuries old. On Longworth's properties, visitors could experience the gentle art of winemaking, yet revel in Cincinnati's progress too.

Longworth grew into his role as one of the great arts patrons of the early West. He had long made gifts of fruit trees, brandy, and his wines to friends, artists, and business interests. While employing Duncanson as well as funding dozens of other Cincinnati artists in their work through his arts patronage, Longworth also found a venue for advertising his wines outside of the Ohio Valley. He was well known (and has been roundly critiqued) for sending generations of the city's best artists away to Europe for training and life experience. One such artist was sculptor Hiram Powers, who spent several years in Florence, Italy, with his large family in tow. Powers wrote to his benefactor in 1856:

A Friend of mine, The Marquiss Ponciattica (you will never pronounce his name) wants to know if you could send him some of your dry Catawba in the barrel, and what it would cost pr. bottle sent in that way. He is a good judge of wine, and says that *there is nothing better than yours*. I sent him a bottle and he speaks of it with enthusiasm. If you tell me what it would cost delivered for shipment in N. York I can estimate the rest. We got the wine you sent me so kindly, very cheaply through the Custom House here. Your namesake told them that it was "some *domestic* wine of America," and they allowed it to pass without examination; a few "crazie" was all he paid, but had they *tasted* it, these crazie would have been *francesconi*!

Power's "Marquiss" at least once ordered "50 bottles or so" of Longworth's dry Catawba (Fig. 26).[57] Through grape growing's links to tourism, real estate investment, and the arts, food and beverage production in Cincinnati was created by capitalist interests but also served to elide capitalism's noticeable presence. Horticultural elites served an interested bourgeois class exactly what they wanted—the promise of power, refinement, *and* nature's wonders, in the city no less.

Temperance Politics and the Labor in Grapes

Viticulture played a role in the debates over temperance in the nineteenth century, and Longworth was a key figure at the local level. By 1850 Cincinnati was among the top five national producers of whiskey, ale, and wine. As might be expected from its annual alcohol output, through the antebellum years, Cincinnati simultaneously served as a hotbed of prohibition reform politics.[58] Perceptions of drinking in America had changed rapidly between the Revolution and the Civil War. At the nation's founding, alcohol was seen as a liquid necessary for basic health. Between 1790 and 1830, Americans participated in the heaviest drinking era in the nation's history. Partaking of spirits before breakfast, in mid-morning and late afternoon, after dinner, as a nightcap, and with every meal, they "sipp[ed] a little at a time, but frequently," consuming about seven gallons of absolute alcohol per capita in 1830. America's growing ideology of individualism aided its flow of spirits: a solitary binge was often seen as a positive rejection of social restraints. Yet this wet-and-rugged individualism may have also reflected the increased stress Americans felt themselves under in a time of great promise and great change. Jacksonian men-on-the-make had big dreams, plans that were often risky and sometimes seemed impossible to force to fruition. Alcohol may have been a way of coping with early nineteenth-century America's many anxieties.[59]

Many things changed Americans' heavy drinking habits in a short span of time, and immigration was a primary factor. Two million Irish and almost one million Germans came to the United States between 1830 and 1860. Both groups brought their own traditional drinking habits, and new spirits,

Figure 26. Bottle of Longworth's Sparkling Catawba, in *Memorial of the Golden Wedding of Nicholas Longworth and Susan Longworth celebrated at Cincinnati on Christmas Eve, 1857* (Baltimore: Hunckel & Son, 1858). Courtesy of the Cincinnati Museum Center.

with them. Both groups also dealt with the stigma of being immigrants, and thus were targets for temperance advocates and other nativists. In Cincinnati, the immigrant German population had changed much over the first half of the century. In 1825 there were only about fifty Germans living in the city, and they were relatively well off. They had been careful to hide their accents and native customs in order to fit in with native-born, or otherwise English-speaking, neighbors. In 1827, upon the advice of friend Daniel Drake, Longworth began a campaign to advertise Cincinnati to Germans still in their home country. He hoped that with the growth of Cincinnati's population and business through immigration, his wealth would be "correspondingly increased." A census and historical sketch of Cincinnati had been recently published by Daniel Drake's nephew Benjamin. It outlined Cincinnati's "various resources of wealth, the soft and balmy climate, rich agricultural lands surrounding, the beautiful river," as well as the city's growing public institutions. Longworth paid to have the volume translated into German, printed several thousand copies, and then distributed them free across Germany. German newspapers reprinted excerpts from Longworth's "alluring little sketch-book." Soon, "freights of Teutons" came, and Longworth was ready for them. Temporary shelter was available, as was immediate employment in Cincinnati's vineyards, quarries, brick-making facilities, and in tenement construction.[60] By 1840, German immigrants made up almost 30 percent of Cincinnati's population—over 15,000 people—and changed the composition of the working class. The newly arrived Germans, *Dreissigern,* kept their foreign tongue and habits longer, lived with their own people in their own part of the city, and were generally poorer than earlier immigrants. Their love of drink and tendency to violate the Sabbath made them additionally suspect to the established white population. Germans made up almost 50 percent of the population of Cincinnati in 1850, and by 1860, there were 2,000 establishments in town serving alcohol.[61] The largest concentration of saloons, concert halls, and beer gardens was on Vine Street, in the German part of town called Over the Rhine. Although Cincinnati's premier citizen had invited them, alienation, antagonism, and all other conditions for constructing an ethnically "other" population were quickly and easily met in Cincinnati. Along with intemperance, Germans were regularly blamed for Cincinnati's unemployment and outbreaks of cholera. In 1855, a nativist mob attacked Over the Rhine, and were met with "gunfire of the well-armed and highly organized German American militia units and rifle clubs." Five hundred German Americans successfully barricaded and defended their turf for two days.[62]

The push for temperance was thus a product of the market revolution and changing ethnic composition of the United States. Before 1830, distillers were numerous and small, serving their local communities. After 1830, distilleries consolidated, a nationalizing grain industry more aggressively sought an outlet for its increased production, and relationships around the production of alcohol changed. Alcohol merchants found it profitable to ameliorate expensive foreign wine with cheap whiskey or other spirits, creating drinks often fortified with 20 to 30 percent alcohol. Watering down, fortification, and other adulterations were so common that Americans recorded drinking five times as much Madeira as was reported imported into the country. Temperance advocates capitalized on the fear of disorder—the changing patterns of immigration and market activity around alcohol—to further demonize alcohol and immigration.

Growing in many Americans' minds as (typically) a social problem, and (quite often) an outright evil, all spirits in the antebellum United States were attacked by growing temperance lobbies in one way or another. The American Society for the Promotion of Temperance formed in 1826 (later changing its name to the American Temperance Society). Early on, it adopted a moderate position: the measured use of alcohol. Winemakers often exploited this idea, arguing that wine, as a fermented but not distilled beverage, was instead "preventive of the ravages of intemperance." Marshall Wilder, president of the American Pomological Society through these decades, urged that fruit culture, and especially wine making, had positive "moral and social influences . . . it ministers to the comfort and happiness of the human race, not merely by gratifying the sense of taste, but that it strengthens local attachments, and multiplies the joys of home; promotes industrial happiness and the love of kindred and country; sweetens the social relations of life, and opens the heart to the study of nature in her most beautiful, bright, fascinating moods. . . . [It will] soothe and cheer in sickness and suffering."[63] Throughout the period, temperance was a distinctly middle-class issue; a vocal portion of the middle class quickly shunned wine as an aristocratic beverage, as well as "demon liquor," like every other. Often aligned with other urban uplift schemes (education, sanitation, women's rights, mental health), a full-borne temperance movement emerged in the 1840s, and quickly framed its cause as a major state and national political issue. In 1846 and 1851, Maine signed into law increasing restrictions on the sale of alcohol. The 1851 "Maine Law" was the country's first statewide prohibition statute, and many temperance advocates saw it as the first step in their ultimate goal of "preserving the republic." Soon,

Massachusetts went dry; versions of the Maine Law carried in Vermont, Minnesota Territory, and Rhode Island in 1852, Michigan in 1853, Connecticut in 1854, and Indiana, New Hampshire, Delaware, Illinois, Iowa, and New York in 1855. Similar laws carried in Pennsylvania, New Jersey, and Wisconsin (but in the last they met the governor's veto twice). During the 1850s, this translated into the lowest drinking rates in the nation's history, with annual consumption down to, per capita, three gallons of alcohol.

But the coming Civil War dislodged prohibition's chugging train from its tracks. Instead of national anti-tippling crusades, headlines by the late 1850s were dominated by Bleeding Kansas, the Dred Scott case, the Harper's Ferry raid, and Southern threats of secession. A number of European medical reports were also published, concluding that alcohol in moderation was not a threat to human health. By 1858, the Maine Law had again been changed, taking the teeth out of the original bill. When the first battles of the Civil War began in 1861, prohibitionist voices had quieted.[64]

Conventional wisdom about wine in the nineteenth century, especially exploited by wine sellers, was that its effects on the human body were far different from those of hard alcohol: one did not suffer from "roughness of character" when imbibing wine, nor would wine make a person drunk. Longworth was typical of winegrowers in that he was a longtime advocate of temperance: wine in moderation, rather than prohibition. Moreover, he, like other winegrowers, argued that wine was a good beverage because it was locally grown and "naturally fermented"—only when other elements were added in the distillation process (including sugar or other sweeteners) did alcohol become truly dangerous. He thus placed high importance on the "purity" of his wine over other drinks.[65]

The decades-long battle over prohibition took on an embittered class valence in Ohio during Longworth's lifetime. Until 1846, Longworth and other elite entrepreneurs' wine circulated almost solely among the highest society and the lowest German immigrant bars of Cincinnati. This made the high and low classes unlikely allies against the middle-class push for prohibition, awkward bedfellows in the struggle to keep wine consumption legal.[66] And here another symbolic layer of the images of Longworth's vineyards comes to light. Figures 22 and 23 include romanticized labor as part of the classic conception of the vineyard—yet the labor illustrated in them elided its real local conditions. In the classic vision of the vineyard, work was done by the owners: skilled, middle-class, white hands. But quite the contrary to the blissful, rather Mediterranean pictures here, Longworth essentially utilized shared tenants—German immigrants—throughout his wine business. The images, in promoting tourism and an ideal yeoman mythos of the vineyard, also functioned to erase the public perception of his dependence on German labor.

Fully considered, in this way Longworth's life story differs dramatically from recent "democratic" and celebratory accounts. As part of his *self*-crafted democratic and "yeoman" identity, Longworth always propounded a do-it-yourself ethic: "The cultivation of the grape for wine will be profitable where persons do their own work. It is seldom that any farming pays well where there is much hiring of hands."[67] This view of labor in the vineyard was in line with the perennial myths of wine production. Wine had long been prized by drinkers for being the essence of unalienated experience, in its claimed and believed processes of production and consumption. In brief, the logic over centuries has been this: "Great wines come only from fine grape varieties grown in great vineyards, which in turn require great labor and great expense." Thus "great wines" are produced from the world's premier varietals planted only in ideal locations that add to the grape's taste and the wine's expression of that taste (its *terroir*). Additionally, "great wines" are produced by highly skilled owner/winemakers who have an intimate knowledge of wine history, wine production, and their own land.[68] The yeoman farmer dream found within the romance of wine lived on unchecked in the image of the mid-nineteenth-century vineyard. It was the quintessential white, elite space, stocked with an ethic of independent natural production, epitomizing power and wealth. Longworth put a fine point on the myth of good wine and genius of elite wine production: "[A] poor man cannot make good wine." The reason is obvious. The rich man not only has more influence in obtaining favorable opinions, but he also uses more care and skill in the manufacture. The poor man must sell his wine as soon as made. The rich man retains it till it is improved by age, and never sells under his own name, but that which proves to be of superior quality."[69] Longworth was aware that as a "rich man," he benefited twice over from his name alone: first in his "influence," essentially the ability to buy "favorable opinions" of his wine, and second, in his ability to put his name on only the very best wines that his investments produced. Longworth had sufficient wealth to age his wine before selling; he could invest in it but not see a profit from it for years, also a crucial component to the elite wine business.

Longworth did not follow his own ethos or instructions regarding labor in the vineyard. There was no way he could, with over one hundred acres under cultivation. From the beginning, although he did not "hire hands" (that is, he did not hire white day laborers), he did contract German immigrants as tenants. He described his process thus:

> It has been usual to give a piece of land of say 15 to 20 acres, with a small house on it, to a German vine dresser, on a lease of 12 or 15 years, binding the tenant to put in a certain quantity in grapes each year in a proper manner—and at least five or six acres within as many years, he paying the proprietor one-half the proceeds of the vineyard annually after bearing. . . . I would recommend landlords to rent from 15 to 20 acres to Germans, for vineyards and orchards, on shares. . . . Land will be suitable for it, that is too rough for the plough, and eight to ten acres will give employment to a whole family.

Longworth practiced and advocated family tenancy for the production of grapes and wine. In his co-authored *Treatise on the Cultivation of the Grape* (1850), at the end of his description of employing German vinedressers, he promised his land-owning, grape-growing readership that "those who commence this business, and conduct it properly, will make fortunes by it."[70] Similarly, in a piece in the 1847 *Report of the Commissioner of Patents*, Longworth summarized: "An industrious German family will from their own labor and at idle seasons of the year, expend labor on them twenty times the cost of the land, and make it more profitable than our richest [agricultural] bottoms."[71] The focus in these writings was ultimately on not the grapes nor wine, but instead the profit to be made from German vine dressers' labor in enhancing landed investments.

Longworth sometimes capitalized on mid-century German immigrant alienation. He made regular inspections of his land and tenants' work, describing one visit:

> On the banks of the Ohio, two miles below our city, I yesterday [went to see] some Germans at work, trenching, banking, and walling one of the most steep, rugged, and stony hills in the country. To have hired the work done by the day, would have cost from $300 to $400 per acre. When completed, it will be a lovely spot. The cost . . . is a trifle . . . [and] they raise their own hominy and sour crout [*sic*]. . . . The greater part of the work in the vineyard is performed by their wives and daughters, without interfering with household affairs.[72]

Longworth economized by not hiring and paying single laborers, instead employing a method of family tenancy akin to sharecropping, making use of an entire German family's labor. His immigrants were not only industrious but thrifty, raising and eating their own foods. And, unlike mid-century middle-class genteel women, his male tenants' wives and daughters could labor in the vineyard, grow their own food, and continue their work about the house as part of their normal, hardworking, salt-of-the-earth routine. Longworth's ultimate motivation was also clear: the site, "when completed . . . will be a lovely spot." His attention to the vineyard as an improved aesthetic commodity suggests its value as a tourist site and a future real estate sale. Collectively, these examples point to Longworth's grape empire as an example of capitalist expansion through horticultural land speculation—and of the simultaneous erasure of economic exploitation through the mythos of neo-yeoman American wine production. Scenery in the vineyard, in other words, was sometimes just another word for real estate.

Longworth's arguably exploitative dealings were registered by the public at the time, mostly in the debates over prohibition. Due to his substantial wealth and his devotion to temperance, Longworth was known to the proponents of teetotalism as a member of the "wine-drinking aristocracy."[73] The Western Bacchus dug in against advocates of prohibition, tirelessly promoting wine and the wine industry, and battling teetotalers in newspapers and in public debates. One of Longworth's repeated arguments was that prohibition would ruin the wine industry and hurt the larger Cincinnati region economically. He was, on the surface, correct: prohibition would effectively have put nearly one thousand people in the local wine industry out of work. But lying beneath the surface of his arguments was also a consciousness about the way that the city's economy was diversified through its several productive landscapes: Longworth was aware that his investment in viticulture, tourism, and the land surrounding the city reinforced Cincinnati's image as a national economic and cultural center.

To Longworth's argument that prohibition would harm Cincinnati, Samuel Cary, leader of the prohibition movement, once responded: "We protest against that wealth and splendor which are secured by the miseries, tears and blood of society."[74] This was a serious charge. One assumes that Cary was describing how the "miseries, tears and blood" caused by the intemperate use of alcohol could befall anyone—"miseries" that the middle-class prohibition lobby fabricated to scare imbibers away from "demon liquor." But read with class status in mind and in light of Longworth's family tenancy system, this seems a bit more than political bravado—it was aimed at the real estate mogul on the hill who had invited lower-class Germans to town to work in his vineyards. Cary's charge is also important in light of Longworth's own claim, as well as that of his biographers, that he had "democratized" wine. As stated, in the early years, Longworth's flat wines (still wines, or "hocks") were sold nearly exclusively to taverns serving a poor German immigrant clientele—wines for which the same Germans had grown the grapes. Thus Cary perhaps had a point when he accused the "aristocracy" of extracting their wealth from the most "miserable" in society: Germans labored as tenants to grow the grapes for Longworth, and bought them back from him as wine. In other cases, the tenants made the wine themselves. Longworth writes in 1847: "I was at the vineyard of my tenant, Mr. Schneike, in the Garden of Eden, recently, and it is about seven weeks since he made his first wine. He made but two barrels, one of which he sold, the other was retained for me."[75] Longworth consistently countered his teetotaling opposition by maintaining that only through wine would the United States be a cultured, civilized country. But his vision of American culture and civilization hardly met its traditional democratic ideal.

Longworth's, and Cincinnati's, Horticultural Empire

Cincinnati's importance as a place of capitalist accumulation and urban transition are thus nicely encapsulated in the example of Longworth's mid-century wine empire. Vineyards in the region made previously "useless" land pay through its production of grapes, the rents collected from tenants, and in its later sale in preparation for an expanding city.[76] The wine that Longworth produced was made with the latest technology but was promoted nationally as a symbol of an agrarian, preindustrial past. Moreover, Longworth's wine was both local and regional—most grapes were fermented into wine within miles of where they were grown, but he also imported Scuppernong juice from North Carolina. Also, some vines were not indigenous, and for decades the wine bottles needed to be shipped in from the East Coast. Lastly, the vineyards encircling the city acted as a space of both agricultural and urban capitalist accumulation. Longworth built many vineyards, knowing the city would expand to engulf them, and that he would receive a premium for his improved parcels. The formula for capitalist exploitation of the countryside, tied to urban profit, could not be more clearly Cincinnatian. Thirty years later, and two thousand miles west, it would reappear in California.

Longworth died in 1863, and by that point, he was known as "the fifteen millionaire." His nickname underestimated his wealth: his city lots alone were worth that much. His property in the suburbs of Cincinnati, as well as Hamilton and Sandusky Counties, swelled the value of his estate to $20 million. The process of capitalist urbanization was unwittingly described in the *Ohio Farmer* in an 1867 eulogy for Longworth: "The growth of the city demands that very space [Longworth's vineyards] occupy, and another summer may see the excavations preparatory to the erection of splendid houses, where, for thirty years, this persevering vine student trained the canes, and led the tendrils upon his favorite grape trellises. Pioneer of Viticulture in the West, he has nobly opened the way—who will follow it?"[77] The newspaper celebrated Longworth as a noble pioneer, his experiments with viticulture wholly different from the "erection of splendid houses" and new growth of Cincinnati. Again, Longworth's pioneering pomological history is identified not as the direct precursor to capitalist urbanization, but instead its antithesis. The land baron was remembered as being concerned only with his fruit, not the immensely valuable land on which it was raised. Longworth successfully masked his fortune in real estate and family tenancy through fruit, and continued to be memorialized as a neo-yeoman pioneer who democratized wine and brought good health to the West.

The region's identification with its foremost fruit investor did not wane until long after Longworth's death. By 1860 the prohibition lobby had ceased to be a threat and remained dormant for a few decades thereafter. But throughout the 1850s and 1860s winemakers had a growing, and much bigger, problem on their hands: black rot and downy mildew were ravaging vines and destroying as much as three-quarters of the grape crop per year.[78] Robert Buchanan described the mounting situation in 1854: "Thousands of things are suggested as a cure for the maladie [vine disease], but not one has yet proved of any value. The disease, like the cholera, pursues its course with unrelenting severity, and no obstacles employed by vine-growers has abated its malignancy in the least."[79] Longworth was quick to blame his German vinedressers for grape difficulties in an 1858 open letter to the Horticultural Society: "Do not our foreign vine-dressers prune too short? They generally follow the rules of their "daddies" in Germany. . . . In our vineyards, in pruning, they generally pursue the German rule, and prune too short, as they did in Germany. As our vines here grow three times the length in a season that they do in Germany, common sense—a scarce article—would say, leave three times as much bearing wood, and plant your vines further apart than the rule in Europe."[80] Already long associated with cholera and Cincinnati's other ills, German tenant families were also blamed for the wine industry's lower yields in the 1850s. In light of the diseases rampaging through the Ohio industry, the focus on and investment in grapes quickly shifted further west. But the late-century meteoric rise in California's wine trade should not be read as inevitable. It was just as constructed by massive capital investments and just as plagued by boom and bust cycles. Even then, Cincinnati continued as an important wine producer and national horticultural space through the 1870s.

The Ohio region must be added to the national narrative of important horticultural locations in the nineteenth century. New York's agricultural empire was one largely constructed from paper (magazines, books, and persuasive pamphlets), individual plants, and through the popularity of domestic greenhouses. Ohio's form of horticultural power was constructed much more through the growth of its burgeoning "Queen City," and the added value its vineyards and wine gave both to real estate and to its status as an urban destination. Previous scholars have argued that New York's prominence in all horticultural fields began early in the nineteenth century and continued unabated until 1900, when California took the title of the nation's most important horticultural state.[81] The history of Cincinnati wine production instead confirms there was a long gestation period for national horticulture in the Midwest, between its inception on the East Coast and its fully fledged latter-century West Coast empire. In each site, horticulturally invested elites offered their region the promise of power, refinement, and the full fruition of nature's wonders. Vineyards functioned as holding spaces for surplus capital, for ennobling and displaying wealth, and for developing other forms of cultural capital. Cincinnati fruit investment and tourism is thus a crucial addition to a history that has sometimes denied the original Great West's importance in processes of capitalist urbanization and horticultural production. The extant histories of grape growing—which nearly all celebrate the "great men" of horticulture and focus on the "failure" of U.S. viticulture before it reached California—must be balanced by attention to the persistent capitalist and nationalist thrust of fruit culture in the early Midwest.

The crucial point that comes to light with the long gestation of the viticultural trade in Ohio is that the mid-century frontier was not a place of incremental development, nor was it in all places a Chicagoesque explosion of urbanization. A more accurate description of cultural and economic development, at least in the Midwestern and upper Southern states, must take into account the highly cultivated horticultural space of the vineyard, at that time also understood as highly cultured spaces between and connected to those of New York and California. Vineyards and orchards were markers of the development of towns into cities, emblems of class status, and scenes of labor exploitation, while also serving as tourist destinations. These horticultural spaces were important scenes for deploying ideologies linking manifest destiny, ethnicity, class, land use, and urbanization. They also worked to set standards for an ideal of ancient republican citizenship that linked pastoral cultivation with social refinement and restrained taste. In this way, the vineyards surrounding nineteenth-century cities were a not-so-veiled marker for capitalist development, perhaps as telling a marker as the "creative destruction"[82] constantly at work on Main Street.

4

Fear of Hybrid Grapes and Men

SURPRISINGLY OFTEN, THE world of professional grape growing served as a site for the construction of gentility—and race—in nineteenth-century America. *The Horticulturist* was one of the clearest publications, but far from the only one, to articulate the connection between grapes and the construction of race in the Civil War and Reconstruction era. An October 1865 article, by a contributor with the pen name "Gladiolus," detailed a recent excursion to the estate and vineries of a "gentleman of wealth and taste" in Orange, New Jersey. Gladiolus took seat with "two other friends (guests fresh from the land of Dixey)," and soon met with the "graceful manners of a true and cultivated country gentleman." The party "entered the fruit garden, and our eyes were regaled with a sight of luscious fruits of all kinds and in profuse abundance . . . native grapes in abundance, and representing the best new varieties." Gladiolus exhorted that in the garden, "all indicated a liberal and well-informed proprietor." The idyll was, however, shattered upon their entry into a vinery for delicate European varieties: "Picture to yourself, a fine structure got up in the best style . . . and filled with noble old vines with stalks as thick as your arm, each well loaded with bunches . . . just ripening, and the whole suddenly converted into a reeking mess of rottenness. Mildew—mildew—mildew—covering every leaf and bunch . . . the whole house reeking with a nauseating, stifling atmosphere." Seeking the cause of this calamity, the group surmised the vinery was like the Old South: "The plants were just in the condition favorable to the development of mildew which, when once began spread like wildfire, and the whole concern went up at once like the Southern Confederacy—one grand collapse." And although the bounty of the outdoor gardens had been attributed to their proprietor, a wealthy "country gentleman," the "wreck" in the vinery was wholly the fault of his hired gardener, who had created the "cruel, perfectly cruel" scene. Under the wayward gardener's "abominable neglect" and "morbidic influence," the Northerners and Southerners agreed, the death of the vines was certain.[1] Here, although good grapes were clearly grown by a laudable man, bad grapes were just as surely a mark of a bad individual.

Gladiolus's story is one of many nineteenth-century iterations of the axiom "as in the man, so in the plant," a phrase often used by professional white horticulturists. Like so many other mid-century character-building activities, this phrase was deployed by professional plantsmen to remind gardeners that the cultivation of plants would lead to the positive cultivation of themselves as effective citizens and businessmen. As we have seen, horticulture promised self-reliance, gentility, and respect—reminiscent of the high public stakes surrounding nineteenth-century fashion, funereal ritual, and professional comportment.[2] More than just picky grape growers obsessing over "quality" fruit, in history and fiction we find viticulture's constantly anthropomorphized discussion of grape breeding was also constructive of ideas about morality and taste.

Throughout such works of nineteenth-century horticultural literature, issues of human bloodline, class, and regionalism were constantly evoked in entries ostensibly about grape cultivation. Put together, the writings provide a paradigm for grapes' and white American bodies' believed natural adaptability and strength across varied regions of the United States. But against the assumed backdrop of the relative "whiteness" of American horticulture, Charles Chesnutt, one of the most famous African American authors of the Reconstruction period, wove several fictional tales that bring the construction of race through professional viticulture into high relief. For Chesnutt, other metaphorical similarities between plants and men stemmed from the "as in the man, so in the plant" aphorism: as his fiction reveals, many professional viticulturists throughout the century pondered issues of blood quantum and parentage in their treatment of grapes. In Chesnutt's hands, the axiom's more ominous references to miscegenation, scientific racism, and postwar carpetbaggery come to the fore. The grape-breeding debates that raged throughout the second half of the nineteenth century expand the contemporary canon's discussions of race and an everyday culture of empire in the United States.[3] Chesnutt, a gifted novelist, teaches us that grape culture fastidiously and methodically carried with it the continuing project of white racial dominance. More specifically, for Chesnutt and several popular horticultural handbook authors, a racialized grape culture mirrored larger themes of cultural nativism, white claims to land ownership, and rational business practice. Mapping several authors' grape-related choices helps unlock important themes in Chesnutt's work with new depth, and can teach us much about horticulture's defining interface with the nineteenth-century North-South racial economy.

Charles Chesnutt's Vineyard

Novelist Charles W. Chesnutt's (1858–1932) "The Goophered Grapevine," originally published in 1887, perhaps best illustrates the cultural knot of race and grape culture. "The Goophered Grapevine" is the foundation for all other works in his 1899 book of collected fiction, *The Conjure Woman and Other Conjure Tales*. The collection is centered around John, a white viticulturist from Ohio who has moved to North Carolina after the Civil War. Seeking a milder climate for his ailing wife, Annie, John is also "enough of a pioneer" to invest in postwar Southern land, which "could be bought for a mere song." Long "engaged . . . in grape-culture" in Cleveland, John sought expand his business.[4] In the (semifictional) Patesville, North Carolina, the couple acquire an old plantation and begin various improvements. John and Annie encounter Julius McAdoo, a mulatto ex-slave and plantation caretaker, whom they "promote" as their carriage driver. Throughout the collection, Julius narrates stories about the plantation's past. His tales contain several examples of "conjure" (goophering or bewitching), a sinister magic that black conjurers enact on local personalities and places for hire. Most of the stories begin with John asking Julius his advice on various plantation "improvements," like whether he should extend its vineyard. In "The Goophered Grapevine," Julius tells of an antebellum slave, Henry, who was bewitched into a physical connection with the plantation's Scuppernong vineyard—his body seasonally growing and withering with its vines. Without fail, Julius delivers a haunting tale of death and conjure, and advises against altering the plantation. At the close of many tales, John observes that Julius has had a personal stake in his recommendations, and John promises himself that next time he will be the wiser and stick to his rational Northern principles.

Chesnutt's biographical details provide deep context for his stories. Light-skinned but making a lifelong decision not to "pass" as white, he included the color line as a constant theme in his stories. More specifically, he broached miscegenation taboos in many works. Chesnutt was born in 1858 in Cleveland, Ohio, and when he was eight, his family moved to Fayetteville, North Carolina. There, Chesnutt was a dedicated student at the local Freedman's Bureau Howard School, and when the family finances necessitated that he work, Chesnutt began teaching at the institution. He continued teaching in Charlotte in 1872. By 1883, he had taught himself shorthand and moved to New York for a few months, but he moved back to Cleveland in 1884. Chesnutt had married in 1878, and he and his growing family lived in Cleveland the rest of his life. Chesnutt soon passed the Ohio bar and established a prosperous legal stenography firm, while also developing himself as a short story writer. By 1885, he was publishing stories in many major (and largely white) periodicals. "The Goophered Grapevine" was his breakthrough piece, the first short story published by an African American in the prestigious *Atlantic Monthly*. He then published a series of novels, receiving mixed reviews. Chesnutt was also a long-standing and active member of the National Association for the Advancement of Colored People (NAACP) of Cleveland. Through the "gritty optimism" shown in his stories, he was known as an impassioned political moderate in the African American community. He filled the role so well that there was "mutual respect between him and both Booker T. Washington and W.E.B. DuBois." In many works, he was known to ridicule the "fiction of 'Anglo-Saxon racial purity,'" a constant theme in his stories being characters pretending that they are something they are not, among other "missing persons, mistaken identities, purloined identities, mimicking, masquerades, [and] imposters."[5] Although creatively successful, Chesnutt was not thought central to the American literary canon until the late twentieth century. In his time, he had radically expanded the range of racial realism in American literature.

But why, in the largest sense, would Chesnutt have been interested in horticultural themes, and why would grape-raising professionals be so concerned with race in the postwar period? As we have seen, "hybrid" fruit have been an important topic throughout the history of horticulture, which by definition constantly probed the fissure between "wild" and "cultivated" fruit of varying vegetal "bloodlines." Put simply, growers working with cultivated plants spent a lot of time thinking about breeding those plants, and about improving the "next generation" of their fruit. "Race" and "breeding" were essential concerns in the profession. Additionally, the specific issue of race as brought to light through grape culture was also centrally about its historical context, specifically mirroring issues of cultural nativism and continuing white claims to land ownership. As we have seen, the beginning of an established commercialized grape industry was linked to the ideal of an expanding agricultural empire. And, just as the industry was taking hold in the postbellum era, a racialized grape rhetoric emerged alongside it. Grape culture proved to be an interestingly unstable site through which viticulturists discussed and understood racial identity in America. In a phrase, grape culture fastidiously and methodically carried with it the project of manifest destiny.

Since the earliest days of colonization, Americans were conscious of the international social hierarchies attached to wine. In the nineteenth century, the national stakes driving grape breeding were even higher. Within the "grape mania" of the 1850s and 1860s, the race for better U.S. wines intensified. Grape culture exploded simultaneously in the East, South, and Great West, with growers eager to develop the most productive and palatable crops for their region. A highly cultivated market crop, grapes altered their taste and growth habits upon being planted in different regions and soils. Linking agricultural and human adaptation in various new environments seemed to come naturally. Many horticulturists could not resist likening grapes' adaptation processes to those of human immigrants to and within the nation.[6] Chesnutt articulated these social hierarchies and adaptations in his fictional grapes and men.

Chesnutt's conjure fiction has received much attention in literary criticism.[7] Oddly, however, the scholarship has missed attending to the primary setting in the *Conjure* stories: the old McAdoo Scuppernong vineyard. Chesnutt gave significant space to viticulture on the plantation, and he details specific grape types (the Scuppernong and Catawba) in his stories. Much of what Chesnutt describes actually existed within grape culture's best-known mid-century personalities and practices. Among the voices at the heart of professional viticulture were Nicholas Longworth, mid-century Ohio millionaire grape grower and winemaker; Peter B. Mead, grape handbook author of the 1860s; and Wharton J. Green, proprietor of the Tokay Wine Company through the 1880s. Each propounded specific ideas about whiteness in the American vineyard.

Early on in "The Goophered Grapevine," Julius warns John that the vineyard the Northern interloper intends to buy in Patesville had been "goophered, cunju'd, bewitch'" before the Civil War. (Patesville is a fictional Fayetteville, but "pate," referring to the top of a person's head, or hair, is an important symbol for the story.)[8] The original owner, Mars Dugal, hires the local conjure woman, Aun' Peggy, to protect his ripening grapes, which were being eaten by his slaves. Aun' Peggy casts a spell on the grapevines and informs the slaves that anyone who eats the grapes will die within the year. The goopher takes, and Mars Dugal is heard laughing that the 1,500 gallons of wine he took that year was "good intrus'" on the ten dollars he paid Aun' Peggy for the conjure work. The next year, Mars buys a bald slave named Henry, who slips into the ripening vineyard and eats its grapes before anyone had informed him of its spell. Mars takes the ailing Henry to Aun' Peggy, who saves his life, and instructs him to rub the grapevine sap on his head each season to ensure his safety from its goopher. Soon hair begins to grow on Henry's bald head, "de bigges' head er ha'r on de plantation . . . reg'lar grapey ha'r . . . his head look des like a bunch er grapes."[9] With the springtime growth of the vines and Henry's now-luxuriant hair, Henry becomes a tireless worker, seemingly younger, more lithe. Mars, astonished at his labor output, sells Henry to a neighboring plantation for $1,500. Nearing fall, however, as the vines die back, Henry slows significantly, and becomes ill. Mars buys Henry back for a much-reduced price, and this cycle of buying and selling Henry with the seasons continues for more than five years. Mars is ultimately able to buy another plantation with the money garnered from the seasonal sale of Henry.

One year, a Yankee visits the plantation. He promises Mars he can make the grapevines bear twice as many grapes, and that the wine press he is selling will produce more than twice as many gallons of wine. Mars "'peared ter be bewitch' wid dat Yankee . . . [and] drunk it all in." The Yankee digs the soil away from the grape roots and applies a concoction of "lime en ashes en manyo." He also severely cuts back the established vine stock. In early spring, the vines "growed monst's fas'," but soon turn yellow, wither, and die completely. (The vines were "burned" by overfertilization.) Henry, who is one with the vines and their natural cycles, dies as well. Mars, "a monst'us brash man w'en he once git started," is so unhinged by the loss of Henry, his vineyards, and his gambling money, that he vows during the Civil War to "kill a Yankee fer eve'y dollar he los' 'long er dat grape-raisin' Yankee." Julius then adds, "En I 'spec' he would 'a' done it, too, ef de Yankees hadn' s'picioned sump'n, en killed him fus'."[10] The central storyline in "The Goophered Grapevine" hangs on vineyard ownership and the vineyard's slaves, emphasizing their linked development and decline. There are several nested layers of exploitation in the tale: Mars's dominance over his slaves and the land, the Yankee's bilking of Mars, and John's impending carpetbaggery over the postbellum plantation. Henry acts as allegory for the realization that exploitation through vineyard cultivation was at work in the South before and after the Civil War.

Chesnutt's fictional interest in the North-South grape trade stemmed from actual events following the Civil War. Just months after Lee's surrender at Appomattox, the July 1865 *American Agriculturist* ran an advertisement inviting interested parties to invest in a wine-growing scheme in North Carolina and Virginia. With slavery outlawed, Southern farmers suddenly needed crops that would be easier to manage than cotton or tobacco; in other words, crops that required fewer laborers, like vineyards had long promised. George Husmann (1827–1902), Missouri author of several popular grape cultivation articles and books, also encouraged agricultural immigration to the West and South. For 1865 and 1866 volumes of *The Horticulturist*, Husmann, then vice president of the Missouri State Board of Agriculture, penned a four-part series of essays titled "The New Era in Grape Culture," wherein he detailed a grape tenancy scheme modeled precisely on Longworth's Cincinnati plan: he contracted German tenants to live on and work his land, lay vineyards, and reap half the return. Husmann, a German immigrant himself who came to the United States at ten years old, ultimately employed dozens of fellow Germans in this manner. He asked the readers of the postwar *Horticulturist*, "Has there ever been a better opening for the poor industrious laborer than he can have in Missouri now? . . . I am ready and willing to welcome a dozen industrious families to go to work on [my new acreage]. . . . Now, that we have perfect peace and quiet again, we look forward to a flood of emigration, and it will come. It will not be long before land will rise to treble its value now." In closing, he writes directly to those prospectors interested in investing in Southern lands: "To those of our Eastern brethren, who wish to try their fortunes in the West, we offer a kind invitation to come and judge for themselves. They may rest assured of a hearty welcome."[11] (Husmann would later be lauded as one of America's greatest viticultural experts, move to California, and there become one of that state's most prominent grape boosters.)

Northern viticulturists were quick to answer these calls and visit warmer climates to assess their worth as possible investments. In the period immediately following the Civil War, between 20,000 and 50,000 Northerners moved to Southern states to try their hands at agriculture.[12] The majority of new winegrowers hailed from Ohio and New York. By the 1870s, large vineyards were laid, or rehabilitated, in many Southern locations, including Charlottesville, Ridgeway, Brinkleyville, Norfolk, Whiteville, Wilmington, and (importantly for Chesnutt) Fayetteville.

Fayetteville had proven to be a continuing locus of wine-growing activity: its largest vineyard was planted by M. T. "Jolly" Horne as early as the 1840s. By 1860, Horne had thirty acres in vines, "situated on a broad undulating

tableland on the Cape Fear River, [where] the eye takes in a semi-circular horizon of twenty odd miles in radius." Legend tells that Yankees hanged Horne
at the close of the Civil War because he would not relinquish the keys to
his prize wine cellar. His property passed to his nephew, Henry Horne, who,
in 1865 and with the help of professional vintners, improved the business.
Henry then sold the vineyard in 1879 to Wharton J. Green, who brought it to
fame as the Tokay Wine Company. (Tokay was originally the name of a sweet
Hungarian wine, repurposed in America as one of the names for Catawba
wine.) By 1885, Tokay Vineyard was a showplace. With 100 acres of vines, it
produced 20,000 to 35,000 gallons of wine per year. The wines won awards at
local and national wine tastings, as well as in Vienna and the Paris Exposition
of 1889. His vineyard compound also included a "fine peach orchard of some
eight acres, the fruit being mostly shipped North." As Longworth's vineyards
had been largely abandoned by the late 1880s, Tokay was believed to be the
"largest single vineyard this side of the Rockies, and all visitors have pro-
nounced it one of the loveliest spots on the continent." Press coverage gushed
about Green's "celebrated spot" that "nature has done much for it; art more."
Imperial fantasy was again a constant trope for media coverage of the vineyard. An author opined: "That vine-growing is destined at an early day to
assume the proportions which it has long maintained in the older world as its
leading industry, none can doubt."[13]

Like most winegrowers in North Carolina, Green specialized in Scuppernong wine, popularly called Virginia Dare. While he produced wine from
other native grapes, Green believed that the Scuppernong, a "grape prodigy,"
was especially valuable because its "discovery [had been] coeval with Caucasian rule on the continent." Virginia Dare, produced throughout Ohio and
the South, became the most popular American wine for decades before and
after Prohibition. Sold as the most healthful wine available, Scuppernong
wine was considered "pure" and "without adulteration or artificial flavoring."
Foreign wines were condemned as "impure and sophisticated abominations"
by the proprietor. Green was well known for his wines, as well as his bom-
bastic temperament and writings. In the 1880s, Green was an avid fan of (the
then-deceased) Nicholas Longworth, often citing him, along with Sir Walter Raleigh, Christopher Columbus, Hernando De Soto, and Daniel Boone,
as one of America's most important pioneers. Longworth also filled the roll
of America's most illustrious "public benefactor" and "hero" for Green. In
Green's 1880s promotional pamphlet for Tokay Vineyard, he imagined himself following in Longworth's venerated footsteps. Green was reported to have

kept his vineyards "as neat and trim as a lady's flower garden, all around be-
tokening a refined taste combined with practical judgment, well worth a long
journey to behold." He was lauded as "socially and politically one of North
Carolina's most distinguished men, as well as a leading industrial factor," and
soon won a seat as congressman. While Green was in many ways a South-
erner of the old school, like Longworth, his wine business and home had all
of the latest conveniences, including water pumped in by steam power and
gas lighting. Yet, press coverage highlighted the vineyard's Old World charm,
not its modern accoutrements. The *Wilmington Journal* wrote in 1883: "A
neat but modest cottage, resting on the brow of a gradually sloping hill, surrounded by well-kept grapevines. . . . It is one which might well be called
the ideal home of a poet; being beautifully located, and handsome in its surroundings, nestled as it is in the midst of the beautiful Tokay Vineyard, surrounded by almost innumerable trellised grape-vines of equal height, whose
verdure embraces every tint of spring's first harbinger of abundant yield. The
unpretentious cottage of our congressman is truly a beautiful oasis of peace
and tranquil repose in this ever progressive world."[14] Elements of Tokay Vineyard's long history—its amenable location, its first owner's personality and
death at the hands of Yankees during the Civil War, the purity of its wine
production for white drinkers, its modern conveniences—ring throughout
Chesnutt's stories. The fiction author seems to have modeled additional wine-
growing details on the man whom Green deemed the "true father of American wine," Nicholas Longworth.

Although remembered as a "noble pioneer" and democratizer of wine,
as we have seen, Longworth was up to other typical mid-nineteenth-century
"frontier" business as well. Beyond the larger expansionist horticultural
mythos that Longworth helped promulgate in America, his story is one set
within a specific regional horticultural context, one with which Chesnutt
was also familiar. Both men spent significant portions of their lives in Ohio,
as well as in North Carolina. What is more, significant events in American
grape history evolved out of the connections between these two states. North
Carolina was the place of origin for the Catawba—early Ohio's most popular and profitable wine grape, a natural hybrid of American and European
vines. Major John Adlum, a grape writer in Washington, D.C., came upon
a Catawba vine growing beside an inn in Montgomery County, Maryland.
The inn's owner had acquired the vine in North Carolina, where it was found
wild in 1802. Adlum took cuttings of the vine, grew them in his vineyard in
Washington, DC, and after first naming the grape Tokay, renamed the grape

Catawba after the North Carolina river and Catawba Indians. Adlum then supplied Longworth (his longtime friend) and other Ohio viticulturists with their first cuttings of the vine.[15]

In addition, Longworth had personal history linking him to North Carolina. He stayed with extended family there on his original trip west just after the turn of the century. While there he fell in love, but he ultimately separated from his sweetheart and continued to Ohio. Longworth and the woman's family had disagreed on the subject of slavery, Longworth being against it, and the family feeling that his opinions were simple "Northern interference."[16] Later, Longworth claimed that he was the inspiration for the beneficent rich white Cincinnati family in one of the most dramatic scenes in Harriet Beecher Stowe's *Uncle Tom's Cabin* (1852). In the story, Eliza and her son, both slaves in Kentucky, bolt from slave catchers and bloodhounds and make their way across the Ohio River's broken ice blocks to Cincinnati. Longworth's account is quite different: he claimed to save a single male slave, Harvey Young, from slave catchers, by buying his freedom.[17] Longworth accounted for the difference in the stories by explaining that it was Stowe's dramatic fictionalization of events, not his own. Longworth's Yankee "Northern interference" in slave matters seems all the more significant, given that the main character in "The Goophered Grapevine," John, is a viticulturist from Ohio. Like most Northern planters who moved South, John regularly imagines himself opposed to, and far removed from, the local history of human bondage. For Northern capitalists like Longworth and the fictional John, "material and moral developments [for the South] were but two sides of the same coin."[18] Growers believed there would be enough prosperity to go around, given a proper investment in Northern-style viticulture. Longworth propagated the ideal of a vinous republican citizenship that linked pastoral cultivation with yeoman freedom, white refinement, and restrained taste.

Ohio grape culture was thus founded upon North Carolina vines and Longworth's Northern moralism, which denounced slavery but argued the benefits of what was essentially tenant labor of new immigrants and ex-slaves. The connection between Ohio and North Carolina was further strengthened throughout the 1850s and 1860s, when viticulturists in the Carolinas imported thousands of Catawba cuttings *back* from the booming Cincinnati area to establish new vineyards alongside their old vines. Southerners also exported Scuppernong juice to Longworth and other Ohio growers "to impart a flavor and a *bouquet* not otherwise obtainable, to [their] celebrated Cincinnati wines."[19] Clearly, as Longworth, Chesnutt, and others reveal, Northern viticulture prospered through its Southern grape trade. Chesnutt was aware that viticulture had provided easy justification for turning public property into private property, legitimating family tenancy and cheap land sale, and dismissing local networks of knowledge.

Chesnutt focuses on the Scuppernong on his stories—a variety of the muscadine vine also native to North Carolina—that was said to be unlike any other grape. Greenish-bronze, white, black, or red in color, the Scuppernong grew in clusters (instead of bunches), each berry as large as a cherry. One Scuppernong vine could cover an acre of ground and produce a ton of fruit, usually equivalent to five barrels of wine. Its taste was also unique: similar to fresh plums, with a musky aroma. The name Scuppernong was derived from the Southern Algonquian word *askuponong*, meaning "in the place of the magnolia swamp." The Scuppernong has had many other significantly co-lonial names, including the Sir Walter Raleigh Vine, the Roanoke—and per-haps most commonly—the White Grape, Big White Grape, and Great White Grape.[20] (It is unknown whether this was for the color of the grape, or, as Green put it, the grape's "coevol[ution] with Caucasian rule.") Importantly, the Scuppernong is the American parent grape of the Catawba, the grape Longworth brought to national fame. The Catawba's suspected spontane-ous hybrid lineage is believed to include *Vitis rotundifolia* (Scuppernong), *Vitis labrusca* (another native U.S. variety), and/or *Vitis vinifera* (European grapes). (As mentioned previously, Tokay, the name of the largest vineyard in postbellum Fayetteville, is also one of many synonyms for the Catawba grape.) The Scuppernong was a hot topic at the American Pomological So-ciety's 1858 meeting, growers having declared that they were "just now get-ting into a 'grape mania' in the South." They found the South to be the "true home" of the Scuppernong and its descendants, as each vine grew "with a luxuriance, and produce[d] fruit in such abundance as is seen in no other part of the Union." Scuppernong grapes were regularly suggested for South-ern planters who had "worn out" their land on cotton and corn. The society predicted that "the time is not very far distant when the culture of Grapes and Wine making will be second in importance only to the growth of Cotton."[21] Grapes were here forecast as the crop that would not only buttress, but would ultimately save, the antebellum cotton economy.

Chesnutt's use of the name Scuppernong in his stories—not Big White—is telling. It suggests, like in the case of the Catawba, an effort to accentuate the deeper heritage of the grape—acknowledging its native appellations, not its colonial ones. Naming grapes this way was nostalgic, but simultaneously aware of the continuing benefits of dispossessed native fruits. Through this naming, Chesnutt reveals the larger economic motivation behind the professional viticultural trade and provides a counterpoint to Longworth's well-tilled life story as a beneficent Northern grape grower. Grape culture was not, for Chesnutt (unlike Longworth's claims), a local yeoman enterprise. It was instead an industry dependent on, and sometimes destroyed by, alien investors (John and the Yankee). Read against Longworth's dominant narrative, that grapes made worthless land "pay" and invested surplus capital in a productive, civilized fashion, Chesnutt's *Conjure Tales* argues that fruit growing, alcohol production, real estate investment, and questionable labor practices were not-so-strange bedfellows in both Northern and Southern grape culture. Seen through the lens of regional grape culture, Chesnutt performs several other deep critiques of the postbellum racial economy.

Of Grapes, Land, and Race

Throughout "The Goophered Grapevine," John, the Yankee, and Mars Dugal see the plantation landscape as a rational machine, and devise ways to extract as much capital from it as possible. As Lawrence Powell argues, most Northern planters that had come South during Reconstruction "intended to make the freedmen more reliable workers by inculcating in them the bourgeois ethic of sobriety, responsibility, and above all else, steady industry."[22] Progress for the South, as with progress for the old McAdoo plantation, was a function of rationalization and hard labor. Chesnutt's story is also, then, about shifts in Northern and Southern, white and black, forms of land use and ownership. Chesnutt illustrates the continuance of a master-slave relationship between white and black people on the plantation after the Civil War: the freed Julius even calls John "marster" at the end of the tale.

If perhaps a mix of both Green and Longworth, the character John in "The Goophered Grapevine" could have also been based upon the narrative voice that Peter Mead adopts in his popular viticultural guidebook, *Mead's Grape Culture* (1867). Mead was at the center of the New York grape-growing and publishing circle that dominated the trade in the postbellum years. He details grape growing from his experiences in the East, but generalizes for other regions. In Chesnutt's story, John is always conscious of the state of his Scuppernong grapes: "The luscious scuppernong holds first rank among our grapes, though we cultivate a great many other varieties, and our income from grapes packed and shipped to the Northern markets is quite consider-able."[23] The Scuppernong turns a nice profit for John—he often talks of clear-ing more land to plant more vineyards. John also pays attention to technical developments in the field. Similarly, Mead assures his readers, "There are few material interests that at present claim a larger share of public attention than the culture of the grape. This is true, whether we regard the grape as some-thing that ministers to our enjoyments, or fills our pockets with gold." But throughout Mead's book and for John, means and ends are ones of unfailing rationality applied to grapes. Instead of "joy" or even "riches," the point is rationality in and of itself.

Mead and his fictional counterpart both evoke conscious Northern ap-proaches to the vineyard and thoroughly rational tactics of organization and profit. Mead makes a literal comparison of a man's worth to his vineyard. In a chapter on planning vineyards, titled "Laying Out the Vineyard," he argues: "'Let everything be well ordered' will apply to the vineyard. . . . A man's na-ture and habits may be seen in the smallest matters of everyday life; a man of refinement and taste may be as readily recognized by the arrangement of his trees and vines as by the neatness of his dress or orderly disposition of the contents of his library or parlor. It may not enhance the value, but it clearly adds to the beauty of the vineyard."[24] Following this paragraph, Mead outlines hundreds of ways to espalier grapevines into precise geometric designs (Figs. 27 and 28). Against these positive grapevine aesthetics, Mead offers a negative example of an untrained vine: "The whole arrangement is rude . . . left to take care of itself." Significantly, Mead provides examples of how one might train grapevines for order's sake alone, not for improved yield or better-quality grapes. "System and order have now made their appearance in the vineyard," he states, "let us hope, to abide there; for it is a good place for them." Hus-mann, too, in a later installment of "The New Era in Grape Culture," empha-sized (seemingly ironically) that "extreme neatness and thorough work can be combined, with a great saving of labor."[25] Northern rationality dictated that the vineyard be not only profitable, but aesthetically refined and visually pleasing—"as in the man, so in the plant" is here a marker of the viticulturist's white bourgeois status.

John is like both the Yankee and like Mars (who makes 1,500 gallons of wine a year prior to the Civil War), when he applies fetishized "order" to the vineyard in the way Mead describes. In fact, both John and Mars are well past seeing their investments rationally, or clearly. John evaluates that the estate has been under "shiftless cultivation [that] had well-nigh exhausted the soil,"

Figure 27. Country house with grapes trained on wall. Peter B. Mead, *An Elementary Treatise on American Grape Culture and Wine Making* (New York: Harper & Bros., 1867), 140. Photo courtesy of the University of Iowa.

while in the same paragraph he describes grapevines that "grew in wild and unpruned luxuriance," a contradiction, as grapes could not grow in "luxuriance" if the soil was completely "exhausted."[26] Regularly unable to read the social and physical landscape he has inserted himself into, John views the land in terms of the improvements he can make to the plantation, not in terms of its actual state of natural abundance, nor its worth beyond its strict beauty or current dollar value in Northern markets.

Even more to the point, Mead expounds, "Fruit growing is like a business, . . . and, like other kinds of business, has its laws, which cannot be disregarded with impunity; but, unlike other kinds of business, it must be conducted as a partnership, Nature always being one of the partners. She, indeed, is 'the head of the firm.' . . . She opens her great Book of Laws . . . and then says, with an encouraging smile, 'Obey these, and you shall partake of our pleasures and profits: Otherwise, not.'" Much like Aun' Peggy, the vineyard sorceress, Mother Nature in the passage above is an alluring, demanding woman, and rational in her own right. She is also ultimately used for the

Figure 28. Precision-grown grapes. Peter B. Mead, *An Elementary Treatise on American Grape Culture and Wine Making* (New York: Harper & Bros., 1867), 77. Photo courtesy of the University of Iowa.

owner's profit. Describing "her" as simply one of the business partners, yet one that must be understood and finessed before she "opens her great Book," denies that the land, grapes, and slaves have any variation or history. Clearly, Mead's logic is rational to a deep fault. However, Mead's rationality, like John's and Mars's, had one key purpose in antebellum and postbellum America— that of keeping both the races and land title strictly separate, or unmixed. The strict lines of color, labor, and land inheritance are ones that Chesnutt's stories constantly work to blur and critique, through both the metaphor of grapes and the contemporary knowledge of grape breeding circulating in popular published texts.

Julius tells John and Annie a second tale concerning land title in "The Dumb Witness." The story is set on the neighboring Murchinson estate and centers on its troubled family history. Malcolm Murchinson lives on his family's dilapidated plantation with Viney, his house slave and blood relative. Due to extreme avarice, Malcolm has lived as a bachelor for most of his life, but at one point, a rich white widow agrees to marry him. In a fit of jealousy or rage, Viney tells the widow an (unrevealed) story so as to make her break her engagement with Malcolm. Infuriated, Malcolm cuts Viney's tongue, so that she may not "dip [her] tongue where [she] is not concerned." The next day, Malcolm receives word that his uncle died, but that he has been left "several notes, and mortgages securing them, on plantations in the neighborhood . . . and some bonds and other securities of value and your grandmother's diamond necklace."[27] The uncle also explains that only Viney knows the location of these assets. Malcolm demands that Viney tell him where the papers are, but she is dumb with her damaged tongue, and has never been taught to write. After years of battling, the two are driven insane by their constant hollering at one another, Viney responding to Malcolm in a "meaningless cacophony" of sounds. Finally, Malcolm dies, and Viney, suddenly able to speak in perfect English, shows another relative where the papers are—in Malcolm's old rocking chair on the piazza, the seat from which he oversaw the plantation, and often hollered at Viney. In this way, even through her abuse, Viney stays connected to the family land throughout its trials of ownership. Her name, evoking the tendrils of Scuppernong grapevines from previous stories, represents her ability to stay grounded there—even as the white owners change and all the other slaves are sold. In keeping the papers hidden, she prevents the land from becoming an alienated commodity of a hateful relative, and secures her claim to the land by natural right.

Julius and Viney, as well as virtually all black characters in Chesnutt's conjure tales, have deep links with the landscapes around them. But Julius and Viney share another personal detail: they are both of mixed blood. Julius "was not entirely black . . . [he had] a slight strain of other than negro blood," while Viney was a Murchinson by blood, and indeed looked like Malcolm, but with a "strong infusion of darker blood . . . a tall, comely quadroon . . . [she had a] passionate strain of mixed blood in her veins." Mulattos and miscegenation taboos appear in Chesnutt's other stories, including *The Wife of My Youth*, "The Sheriff's Children," *The House Behind the Cedars*, and *The Marrow of Tradition*. As several scholars have pointed out, Chesnutt makes a larger sociohistorical point by frequently including characters of mixed race in his fiction. In the *Conjure Tales*, Chesnutt stakes a new claim in the long lineage of American literature concerned with blood quantum and property, a field in his time populated by William Dean Howells, Mark Twain, George W. Cable, and James Fenimore Cooper.[28]

In the plant-breeding world, historian Philip Pauly has argued that midcentury horticulturists' ideas about race were formed before 1800, under the late Enlightenment writings of the French Comte de Buffon, Belgian J. B. Van Mons, and English Thomas Andrew Knight. These scholars developed theories about the natural "degeneracy" of most people of color, as well as cultivated fruits—especially those humans and biota found in America. Continuing for more than a generation, these debates often boiled down to the relative commodiousness of the European versus American continents, and set the stage for nationalist grandstanding through the next century.

While Enlightenment debates in fruit culture remained central into the 1820s, by the 1830s, and increasingly after the Civil War, other ideas about race and "degeneration" were in circulation about American fruits. Indeed, explicit white racial prejudice toward Native Americans, blacks, and Mexicans was an eminent characteristic of 1830s Jacksonian culture. By the 1840s, "race prejudice was national" and a core concept propelling manifest destiny. Between 1830 and 1850, racial types were codified in American discussions of race, and a superior "Anglo-Saxon race" permeated discussions of American progress. The concept of "racial destiny" inflected white and black social discourse.[29] White Americans' growing nativism bridged into their murky articulation of the concept of "native" fruits and people. What constituted nineteenth-century native fruits was often ambiguous; grape men were seldom positive which plants were American, which were European, and which were hybrids. Sometimes "native" simply meant "local," or more generally, indigenous to North America. Often, plants were considered naturalized natives if they had grown on the new continent from imported seed. Pomologists' preference for "native" apples also complemented the anti-Irish nativism of 1840s America. Americans feared that apples were going through a process of creolization in the 1830s and 1840s. Under pressure from temperance agents and struggling in a declining farming culture, New Englanders abandoned their orchards, leaving uncultivated seedlings to sprout in the fields.[30] Horticulturists believed that the American apple was declining through its too-profligate crossbreeding with local varieties, and not enough attention to its proper cultivation. The 1844 national election further focused anti-immigrant momentum, as Americans were determined to deny newcomers the rights of native-borns. Ultimately, horticulturists believed "Yankees were unquestionably native Americans, but not all foreigners were automatically naturalizable. Possibilities for ordinary usage [of the word "native" in fruit growing] flowed from those core convictions."[31] Further illustrating the confusion over who and what qualified as "native," the most popular wine made from the Scuppernong/Big White Grape, the Virginia Dare, was named after the first child born to white settlers in North Carolina.[32]

Racial issues continued to overlap with agricultural ones when James K. Polk, president from 1845 to 1849 and an expansionist Democrat, in the face of Eastern farm abandonment, argued that democracy could survive only if the United States remained a strongly agrarian nation. Through the late 1840s, he re-enlivened the Jeffersonian mythos of the white American yeoman planter and projected its promise onto the bleeding edges of America's imperial contact zones. Mid-century expansionists like Polk held two principal objectives: to "acquire land in order to augment the nation's wealth, power, and security," and to "ensure racial and cultural homogeneity within their expanding empire." In the 1840s, expansionists melded "simplistic ideas of race, culture, and nationality into a single self-serving concept of empire," as Enlightenment ideals "faded and disappeared."[33] By 1850, most Euro-descended Americans believed it was scientific fact that the "Anglo-Saxon branch of the Caucasian race" was innately superior to all other races. Believing in their status as God's and Europe's "noblest offspring," they held that the essential core of human civilization had passed from "Asia Minor to Greece, to Rome, to England," and finally, to the United States. Ideas about the scientific superiority of the "Caucasian race" grew in horticulture in the 1850s as well, as fruits were sold as having identifiable racial characteristics. The Concord grape, especially, was "a native grape with a decidedly Yankee character."[34]

Another important scientific advancement to revolutionize American grape growing was vine hybridization, and here, too, grape cultivators had to walk a fine moral line. Since the late seventeenth century, horticulturists knew that cross-fertilizing grapes would lead to new varieties, and this technical process was further developed in the eighteenth century. American grape breeders in the early nineteenth century—Bernard MacMahon in Philadelphia, the Prince family in New York, Professor Thomas Nuttall of Harvard University, Samuel Pond of Massachusetts, Dr. William Valk of New York, and John Fisk Allen of Massachusetts, among others—began haphazard experiments with crosses, after time and again finding that the most popular European *vinifera* would not flourish in the eastern United States' weather and soil conditions. Although the (native) Scuppernong and (natural hybrid) Isabella grapes were grown with success in many states, most grape men believed that only through combining two or more varieties of grapes of American and European origin could commercially useful wine grapes actually be grown in the United States.

The popular dedication to searching for new vines and experimenting with hybridization was invigorated after Edward Staniford Rogers, a Salem merchant's son, first made successful crosses in 1851. It was a particular achievement because crossing grapes, as with most fruits, was a long, tedious, and usually unrewarding process. In any given cross, hundreds of new but useless varieties were formed. To see if a given cross was useful, hybridizers had to wait three to four years for vines to mature and produce grapes. The president of the American Pomological Society, Marshall Wilder, lauded Rogers on his hybrid: "You have achieved a conquest over nature and your efforts will constitute a new era in American grape culture." Concurrently, one of the most famous grape propagators was Ephraim Bull of Massachusetts. His Concord grape, a chance seedling found in his garden in 1849 and exhibited at the Massachusetts Horticultural Society in 1853, became the iconic American table grape. In the fifty years following the introduction of Rogers's and Bull's hybrids, 2,000 more American hybrids were propagated and made public.[35] Yet throughout the discovery of these hybrids, the morality of the scientific management of nature and America's most important fruits was hotly contested. In the broader context, Darwin's *On the Origin of Species* was published in 1859; professional biologists and others in nearby fields in the United States read it with great interest and debate into the 1880s. Even with Bull's Concord triumph, not until the 1870s did hybridization gain a metered social acceptance.

By the third quarter of the nineteenth century, the physical U.S. borders, the U.S. population, and a larger American worldview about race had changed rather radically. Fruit growers had bridged the early national goals of material and philosophical "improvement" of their foodstuffs with a latter-day, more aggressive white nativism. Clearly, hybrid varieties entailed the crossbreeding of European *vinifera* with "sturdier" native U.S. vines, and symbolized a threat to genteel Euro-centered identities. Herein, viticulturists expressed their own identities through their fruit, and applied their more latent prejudices through grapes' social and biological culture. In this reactionary context, intensely conservative ideas about fruit cultivation solidified.

Fears of race mixing were most prescient in professional viticulturists' practices during the "grape mania" of the 1850s and 1860s. The term *miscegenation*—coined during the 1864 presidential campaign by Democrats who believed Republican policies "threatened literally to establish a 'miscegen' nation"—was deployed as epithet and threat, and soon came into widespread use. Race mixing, to party naysayers, was an "unnatural theory" that would invite "a war of the races." They wrote that miscegenation, "the evil . . . would make the manumission of slaves the means of infusing their blood into our whole [American] system. . . . The cultivators of the soil must then become a hybrid race, and our government a hybrid government, ending, as all such unnatural combinations have ever done, in degraded, if not abortive, generations."[36] For Democrats, abolition meant racial and governmental "amalgamation" and decline, most especially for America's traditionally virtuous white yeoman farmers.

Compare this language—the terms *infusing, blood, hybrid, unnatural, evil,* and *degraded*—to those used in popular grape manuals of the period. In his 1867 text, Mead discusses several popular modes of propagating grapes, including cuttings (a grapevine cane that is cut and set in soil to grow new roots), layering (a cut portion of a grapevine is placed in the ground while still attached to the mother plant), grafting (the propagating vine is attached to different root stock), and hybridizing (crossbreeding the pollen of two different grapes to produce new seed and new stock). Cuttings, layering, and grafting are all described in similar, technical terms. One slices, attaches, and/or plants the original grape cane to make genetically identical stock, because the original grapevine is coaxed to keep growing, just on a separate host rootstock. When Mead approaches the topic of hybridizing, though, the tone and word choice change. He describes hybridizing grapes in clearly personified and racialized terms:

> It has been thought by some that we should look chiefly to hybrids between the native and the foreign grape for any marked improvement in the quality of the former, while others have doubted the possibility of getting a hybrid between them. . . . We are by no means convinced that it is desirable, or that we shall gain what we wish. . . . Is it wise, then, to seek an infusion of blood from a source that has been proved to be constitutionally unfitted to our wants? Can we produce a hybrid that will not possess this constitutional failing? We think not. It must appear, more or less, in the whole race produced this way. If we get enough of the goodness of the foreign grape to make itself apparent in the seedling, we shall just as certainly get enough of the evil to make the goodness of little or no use to us.[37]

For Mead, hybridizing grapes entailed an "infusion of blood" that would introduce an "evil" as well as a "constitutional failing" in "the whole race" of the next generation of grapes. Mead is certain that there would be "enough of the evil" in this new hybrid to outweigh the good.

As we see here, grafting and hybridizing, in particular, carried specific social and sexual references. Several accounts document that many horticulturists would not crossbreed fruits; they would only graft them, because of religious and moral misgivings. Biblical injunctions against crossing cattle were one of the sources of this prejudice, as well as a more general fear of interfering with God's divine plan.[38] However, grafting, a different horticultural process, creates well-adapted, but true-to-the-original fruit subjects: grafting is the hands-on technique of slicing, placing, and tying foreign vinestock to native rootstock. This process allows the chosen vine to grow unchanged, supported by the native stock's hardier root system, but with none of its indigenous "unemeliorated" qualities. Grafting was not the sexually profligate practice of cross-pollination—often described as the magical, even godlike production of new flora. Grafting was the apex of a particular type of intensive cultivation: clean, asexual, specific, and local, it depended on craft and literal handiwork for every vine. To step away from grafting and adopt hybridization through pollination was to risk the creation of a whole new plant: for better or worse, it would be a random synthesis of its parent vines. Fear of the mulatto, half-breed, and mixed-blood throughout the period informed such thinking: for Mead as well as other viticulturists, seemingly rational scientific experimentation was trumped by postbellum racial fright. It was these fearful connections between the fruit and human worlds that Chesnutt deploys—and devastatingly critiques—in "The Goophered Grapevine" and other writings.

Chesnutt made plain his critique of the Euro-American obsession with blood quantum in "The Future American," a series of nonfiction essays he published in the *Boston Evening Transcript* in 1900. He describes with biting sarcasm whites' attempts at race improvement: "This perfection of type—no good American could for a moment doubt that it will be as perfect as everything else American—is to be brought about by a combination of all the best characteristics of all the different European races, and the elimination, by some strange alchemy, of all their undesirable traits—for even a good American will admit that European races, now and then, have some undesirable traits when they first come over."[39] Chesnutt was known to mimic contemporaries' voices in his prose—especially those with whom he did not agree.[40] In the second installment of "The Future American," subtitled "A Stream of Dark Blood in the Veins of the Southern Whites," Chesnutt details precisely how white and black blood became mixed. He writes, "Slavery was a rich soil for the production of a mixed race, and one need only to read the literature and laws of the past two generations to see how steadily, albeit slowly and insidiously, the stream of dark blood has insinuated itself into the veins of the dominant, or, as a Southern critic recently described it . . . the 'domineering' race."[41] Although the action is placed on "black blood" in the sentence, Chesnutt strongly implies that the systematic rape of black slaves by white owners was the "rich soil" from which hybrid Americans grew. In the natural metaphors in "The Future American," Chesnutt channels decades of hybridization debates regarding race and agricultural products. For the author, horticultural fiction revealed Southern fact.

Scandalous and/or unwanted sex scurries beneath many of Chesnutt's writings. The author drew upon common folklore as fodder for several of his *Conjure Tales*, folklore that contained obvious sexual innuendo. "The Goophered Grapevine" was culled from an older story that is similar to Chesnutt's rendering, except for one detail: instead of Henry's hair growing lushly each spring, his penis does. Yet, the exploitative cycle stays the same: his master advertises that Henry can "beat any man in bed and make any woman cry for him to stop."[42] Here, Chesnutt's asexual adaptation of the story, from focusing on Henry's penis to Henry's pate, has several effects. If a metaphor for a grapevine's sexual cycle, Henry's penis signifies a grapevine that was a source of "pollination" for some other vine. Instead, Henry's hair grows, an analogy more similar to grafting or cutting—encouraging the same vine to grow in a new host environment. By this change in the story, Chesnutt signals that grape culture, a metaphor for slave culture, had not fundamentally altered—grapevines, as symbolized through Henry's body, were not altered through the sexual regeneration (his penis/pollen) of the original story, but by reinvigorating the growth of the old vines (his hair). This was a loaded metaphor, considering Chesnutt's thoughts on the South and the plantation upon which the grapes grew: although there was quite a bit of crossbreeding, or intermixing, of various sorts of vines and people on the surrounding plantations in his *Tales*, miscegenation was not dealt with openly, and no person of "negro blood" could lay claim to plantation property, no matter their genealogy. Instead, the old antebellum ways of abusing vines and people under slavery were, during Reconstruction, dressed up and fertilized with fresh manure—so much so that they ultimately again burned and withered. Ownership of the plantation changes hands, but simply from old white hands to new white hands. Chesnutt knew that popular Victorian propriety would have been offended in several ways, had he left the details of the gargantuan penis intact. First, it would have been unthinkable, in a Victorian magazine, that a story focus on a man's sexual member; second, the threat of the sexually profligate (and potentially fruitful outcome) of that black penis put to use on several women of undiscerned race would have been untenable in the 1880s; and third, hybridization was hotly debated in scientific and moral circles—like Mead, several grape writers had long argued the sexual hybridization of grapes would incur bad consequences for the American wine industry. So while Chesnutt couldn't have left Henry's privy parts in the story, in changing them, he made major themes in his story resonate all the more deeply.

Racialized rhetoric was widespread in the general discussion of fruit hybridization throughout the North and South at mid-century. Thomas Volney Munson, a well-known Southern grape writer of the period, linked fruit hybridizing with race mixing, warning viticulturists to not make large leaps into poor mule/mulatto varieties, but take small steps when crossing vines.[43] As well, *The Horticulturist*, in an 1852 article "On the Improvement of Vegetable Races," conflates white Americans' mastery of the land with the cultivation of fruit:

> Every person interested in horticulture, must stumble upon facts almost daily, that teach us how much may be done by a new race or generation, in plants as well as men, that is utterly out of the question for the old race to accomplish. Compare, in the Western States, the success of a colony of foreign emigrants in subduing the wilderness and mastering the land, with that of another company of our own race—say of New-Englanders. The one has to contend with all his old-world prejudices, habits of labor, modes of working; the other being "to the manor-born," &c., seizes the Yankee axe, and the forest, for the first time, acknowledges its master. While the old-countryman is endeavoring to settle himself snugly, and make a little neighborhood comfortable, the American husbandman has cleared and harvested a whole state.[44]

The "New-Englander"/"Yankee"/"American husbandman" has evolved to be the best "race" in two worlds: he is both master of *wilderness* and the *wildness* of native fruit. Since transplantation in America, his bloodline, with roots in European stock, has improved through contact with American soil. He has also adapted his methods of cultivation. *The Horticulturist* continues:

> As in the man, so in the plant. A race should be adapted to the soil by being produced upon it, of the best possible materials. The latter is as

indispensable as the first—as it will not wholly suffice that a man or tree should be indigenous—or the American Indians, or our Chickasaw Plums, would never have given place to either the Caucasian race, or the luscious "Jefferson" [plum]. . . .The same thing is true of the foreign grape. Millions of roots of the foreign grapes have been planted in the United States. Hardly one can be pointed to that actually "succeeds" in the open air culture—not from want of heat or light—for we have the greatest abundance of both; but from the want of constitutional adaptation . . . [we must] raise seedlings here.[45]

The Horticulturist contends that although being born on American soil was of benefit to the cultivator and the cultivated, being of truly indigenous stock was decidedly less beneficial. The journal's nativism soon turned into outright ethnic intolerance. Two months later, *The Horticulturist's* editor, Andrew Jackson Downing, decried the degeneracy of ever-arriving Irish gardeners. He fretted that foreign gardeners were unable to adapt to American horticulture, and he lectured his readers against planting exotic trees like the ones of the "Tartars" or "petted Chinaman"—instead advising them to stick to "clean natives."[46] These poor cultivars and cultivators were set against the fruit and people that had *"American constitutions,* adapted to the American climate"—namely, the "Caucasian race" and the Jefferson plum. Horticulture here helped justify the removal of American Indians, at the same time legitimating a "native sort" of white race and Euro-American grapevine. Downing models the mid-century conflation of Enlightenment and Polkian era approaches to ethnic hybridity: he argues the "Caucasian race" proved itself adapted to the continent in a way that neither the indigenous native, nor the effete European, could have been. The "rightness" of the plant or man to place was demonstrated by its thriving in that place. Here Downing repeats the Lockean and colonial Puritan argument that the New American was to know the land was his because his family and vegetable produce would thrive in ways it did not for previous societies. Downing and his contemporaries saw the land and its plants as ultimately justifying their racism, as they believed their environment had naturally chosen one race over the other. This horticultural racism was also key in defending viticulturists from their own envy of popular foreign wines: there were several varieties that they could not yet grow in the United States, but it was thought that with the right amount of cultivation, America's wines would be as unique and tasty as her many other successful fruits.

By extension, this logic fed into a vision of America as the next leading horticultural nation: "The United States . . . is probably as good a fruit country as can be found in the world," Downing wrote.[47] Nicholas Longworth, years earlier, agreed: "The day is not far distant, when the banks of the Ohio, will rival the rivers of France and Germany, in the quantity and quality of their wines. But after an experience of twenty-five years, and a waste of time and money in the cultivation of a great variety of foreign grapes, I concluded that we must confine ourselves to American varieties, and the producing of new varieties from seed."[48] This vision, taken on the whole, is one of the United States taking the lead in horticulture and new nationalist land development. The development of "vegetable productions," and of racial betterment, would grow into world leadership in these arenas. Although Longworth ultimately favored hybridization, not grafting, his was still a classically imperial vision: a nationalist project to be accomplished not just through Americans' white racialized prowess, but also the cultivation of her native fruit stock.

Part of this nationalist racialized rhetoric was also a concentration on grape and wine purity. On this topic, Peter Mead was one of the more restrained voices: "It is not claimed that we will make better wines than those of Europe; but we can and shall make them purer than most of those sent to us."[49] Technically, "purity" was retained in a wine only if no sweeteners (usually cane sugar or other alcohols) were ever added. Wine purity was the topic of decades' worth of journal letters and articles. For example, *The Horticulturist* in 1863 compares the faulty practices of "European wine-makers" to the American dedication of focusing on the "*pure* juice of the grape . . . [closing the door on] all manner of adulterations." Yet, the American dedication to the "purity" of recent vintages was also constructed against the believed miscegenation of grapes. Purity in American wine was a conscious effort at combatting a past lower-class history of "Yankee ingenuity . . . [where they] get something out of corn and potatoes, and call it wine,"[50] as well as a feared future of racial mixing. The indiscriminate use of all types of natural ingredients was frowned upon; "purity" of juice and process would lift the masses through developed skills in correct grape cultivation and cooperage.

The focus on a new American wine culture took on class and ethnic overtones. "Yankee ingenuity" only got Americans so far, they intoned; it was time to settle down and refine their grapes and themselves through advanced, and "purer," viticultural technologies. These debates arose nearly contemporaneously with arguments regarding the preservation of racial "purity" of American Anglo-Saxons. Perhaps the most influential writer on the subject (although by no means its only author), Josiah C. Nott expounded the pressing need to preserve the superior white race's "purity." He published books, journals, and pamphlets on the topic, and his diatribes appeared many times in the *Southern Quarterly Review* and *De Bow's Review* (both popular Southern periodicals) in the 1840s and 1850s. Utilizing work in phrenology and other "scientific" studies of the differences in human bodies, Nott ultimately believed that if the white race was not kept pure, it would lose its talents to "rule and control other races." To support his desires of racial separatism, Nott also went so far as to cite rare horticultural studies and ultimately manufacture much of his own evidence, which stressed that "hybrids" produced by racial crossing tended to produce infertile offspring. He found it a sign from God that hybridizing across races was untenable, even an abomination. Any mixing, any declension in purity, would weaken the elite stock.[51] Decades later, Chesnutt was still battling this view in his nonfiction essays: "There are no natural obstacles to such an amalgamation [of the black and white races]. The unity of the race is not only conceded but demonstrated by actual crossing. Any theory of sterility due to race crossing may as well be abandoned; it is founded mainly on prejudice and cannot be proved by the facts. . . . My own observation is that in a majority of cases people of mixed blood are very prolific and very long-lived."[52] Indeed, the "hybrid vigor" (as we now call it when applied to agricultural foodstuffs and animals) of Chesnutt's friends of mixed blood may have been exactly what Nott was afraid of. In Chesnutt's nonfiction, as well as fiction, then, hybridity was not only to be embraced, but foreseen as the ineluctable future of America.

The mid-century vineyard was the horticulturist's template for experimentation, for consciously and unconsciously cultivating nineteenth-century American landscape and society. Because of their location between urban and frontier worlds, horticultural pursuits in Ohio, as in New York—two of the most self-consciously "imperial" cities in the nineteenth century—are important indexes to imperial expansion. When we extend the view to the South, however, horticulture reveals gardeners' worldviews and practices concerning race and land ownership with special clarity. The debates over viticultural bloodline informed ideas of race in this period because the two discussions were so essentially about the constant processes of cultivation and hybridization, in all of their philosophical and tangible manifestations. The old horticultural saw "as in the man, so in the plant," for many during Reconstruction, now shed a rather terrifying light on the fear of past and future racial mixture. The discussion of fruit culture was thus informed by, and indeed helped produce, nineteenth-century racialized constructions of the "indigenous . . . American Indians," and other "hybrids"/"mulattos" found (in person or in symbol) on Southern plantations and in Northern vineyards. Of course, like other forms of scientific racism, theorists' "prejudices helped shape their research, and their research helped give society the justifications it needed for its actions."[53]

In reframing the core issues of grape culture around racial identity and Northern colonialism, Charles Chesnutt's *Conjure Tales* should have proved very troubling to nineteenth-century viticulturists' dreams of yeoman farmerhood. It was not virgin land that "pioneering" (or rather, "domineering") white families made a living from, but a black community and its horrifying history that had been infiltrated and put to work in only slightly different ways. Interestingly, although neither Chesnutt nor anyone else knew it, the North's most profitable vine, the Catawba, once believed to be native, was actually a hybrid of European and native American (Scuppernong) grapes—in human terms, its racially different parents had conceived a mixed-race offspring. In "The Goophered Grapevine," Julius had warned John not to buy the vineyard, "'caze de goopher's on it yit, [and although the old vines] . . . did 'pear ter die, but a few un 'em come out ag'in, en is mixed in 'mongs de yuthers." Vines of various legacies were intermixed on this Southern plantation: the conjure yet stood on John's, as well as his real-life contemporaries', vineyards. John denied his new land's bewitchment, and instead found the grape trade he developed there a rational and "striking illustration of the opportunities open to Northern capital in the development of Southern industries."[54] In his portrait of a goophered and racialized grape culture, Chesnutt found many ways to subvert the romanticized South.

5

California Wine Meets Its "Destiny"

IN THE SUMMER of 1857, *The Horticulturist*, published in New York, ran an article on the California State Agricultural Society's Third Annual Fair, Cattle Show, and Industrial Exhibition, held in San Jose the previous fall. Suspicious but intrigued, the author titled the piece "The Way They Talk in California," listing the reported behemoth size of California's vegetables and fruits, its acres under cultivation, and its general promise as an agricultural region. The journal also tied California's agricultural abundance to the American people's own racialized, expansionist vitality: "A whole new country, falling from the hands of an inert race into the possession of a new and energetic people, has been transformed; the results of energy are here pointed out in most energetic language, and in a spirit that has already swept the lazy Spaniard from the soil; we hear no more of him than of the red Indian." The references to the "energy" of whites and their language is juxtaposed to the "laziness" of the Spaniard and Indian, land and country "falling" from one set of hands to the next. A few sentences later, the author (with no sense of irony) recounts that in most farms and vineyards, "most of the labor is performed by Indians." As in the past, the growth of fruit meant the decline of Native populations, as well as their (literal or nonliteral) enslavement for fruits' cultivation. In northern California, there were two races replaced by the arrival of whites and their agriculture—the "Spaniard" and the "red Indian"—but the grape's power to evoke scenes of racist regional and nationalist place-making remained unchanged. The author adds that one grower "has eighty varieties of grapes, whose thrift and luxuriance afford strong evidence that they could not have found a more genial climate." Grapes, like their white growers, were energetic, thrifty, and fecund, naturally fated for greatness.

The author ends the article: "California seems destined to stand first

among wine producing States. . . . We *are* a wonderful go-ahead people, and
it is only surprising we do not yet own Cuba, and the right of way to the
placers."[1] Here, viticultural growth and abundance legitimated not only the
removal of Native Americans and Mexicans, but blessed the imperialist campaign for Cuba, as well as the rest of the unsecured "right of way" to "the placers," or gold mines, of the West. The author relies on one other nationalist and
Californian trope: that of the region's "destiny" as the nation's premier wine
state, and other incredible agricultural riches. This description of California
had earlier origins, and certainly continues in today's popular understanding
of the state. But the centrality of grapes to this California dream was a product of the later nineteenth and early twentieth centuries.

California's wine history has often been sold as an epic tale of foreordained glory—something about the Californian terroir was better, more
magical than all other viticultural regions.[2] But California's unquestioned
dominance in agricultural production, especially in wine growing, did not
suddenly materialize. It took decades to develop in the national imaginary
about the Golden State, as well as manifest on the ground. California viticulturists battled both the East and the Midwest for horticultural dominance,
not just in terms of what could grow in each region, but for the public's belief
in the one region that would prove to be the most profitable—and whose
land would ultimately reign as the metaphorical fruit basket of America. This
vision of California as an imperial "land of plenty" was a rhetorical and visual construction, on par with previous efforts by horticulturists in New York
and Ohio who had made the same basic claim. In all regions, of course, fruit
growers and others in the trade had a stake in constituting a vinous Garden of
Eden for future investments. In addition, each of these regions tied its urban
imperial dreams tightly with the semi-wild, semi-domesticated spaces of horticulture. While the types of wine being produced changed, and the scale of
production increased immensely, much of the material practice and ideology
underlying the growth of Californian viticulture were direct results of previous wine-growing attempts.

In California, much like in New York and Ohio before, viticulture acted
as an idyllic cover for industrialized agriculture and capital accumulation—a
way of mediating the machinery of industry and naturalizing imperialist activities. California grapes and vineyards, like those in the East and Midwest,
evoked ideal conceptions of civilization and restored Eden. Put another way,
grape culture was a widely used cloak for the massive "land banking" so essential to urban capitalist growth. Vineyards in California, as with vineyards

in locations past, became the standard for agricultural beauty in the late nineteenth century, all the while functioning as key resources for enhancing social and material capital.[3] Though occurring farther west and later in the century, California's wine tale is far more similar to the previous narratives and locations of U.S. wine growing than scholars have allowed. In achieving their "destiny," California winegrowers relied on the twin narratives of venerated pastoral elegance and white racial succession, both normalized through grape culture. These narratives positioned California as the heir to age-old European and Spanish colonial wine knowledge, masking winegrowers' dependence on biological circumstance, technological innovation, astounding investment, and a fabulous publicity machine. Agricultural colonization had no better vanguard than the grape in California.

The Grape Arrives

The first cultivated grapes for wine in California were planted by Franciscan friars along *el Camino Real*, California's colonial mission path. Wine was invaluable for the celebration of mass, as an everyday table beverage, and as an important item for trade with explorers and settlers.[4] From Mission San Diego to San Francisco de Solano, grape growing assisted and legitimated California's colonization as the Franciscans traveled north. The Mission grape, which was to become the colonial Californian standard, was likely first cultivated in the Americas in Baja California, by Father Juan Ugarte at Mission Nuestra Señora de Loreto in 1697. Most sources agree that Father Junípero Serra brought the first cuttings of the Mission grape to California in 1769; other sources question Serra's direct hand in viticulture, arguing the vine could not have arrived in Alta California until 1778, and the first local wine was not produced until 1782–84.[5] Beginning in 1834, California's twenty-one Spanish missions were secularized by the Mexican government. As church property became government property, the missions' orchards and vineyards fell into neglect, and in some cases, also fell under the axes of infuriated padres.[6] By the 1830s, tensions were growing between the U.S. and Mexican governments for ownership of Alta California and Texas. Twice, in 1835 and 1845, the U.S. government offered to buy half of Mexico's lands. Mexican leaders declined the United States' offers, and did not recognize Texas's declared independence from Mexico after the Texas Revolution of 1836. When elected in 1845, President Polk then sought to expand U.S. boundaries by provoking Mexico into war. Tens of thousands died on each side in the protracted, multiple-front war from 1846 to 1848. After the Mexican-American War and the cession of Mexican territory through the Treaty of Guadalupe Hidalgo, and under a flood of gold seekers, California became a state in 1850. The treaty was signed in 1848 by men who were arguably not the legal representatives of Mexico, but the United States nonetheless gained the current states of California, Texas, Nevada, Utah, and Arizona. The U.S. government's formal and aggressive Mexican land grab took place as many other Euro-American methods of de facto land ownership were already in place. Los Angeles, by that time, was known as the "city of vineyards," and the Gold Rush in northern California was on.[7]

The pervasive presence of racist laws in the period—including the Fugitive Slave Act, Chinese exclusion laws, and legal techniques of dispossessing *Californios* and Indians from their lands—is an important context through which to view Californian grape history, laws whose ideological tenor was closely connected with other cultural practices. For example, in an article for an 1859 issue of *California Farmer*, the editors urged vineyardists to grow only "foreign" (Western European) varieties. He argued that the future marketability of California wines depended upon a better wine than her "native" and "lower" Mission grape could produce.[8] Belief in the superiority of European grapes extended to local racial politics. While earlier debates in the East had promoted the use of the "native" grape against ethnicized European imports, "native" took on another connotation in California in these decades. In this instance, the Mission grape was still linked with its traditional Spanish (Catholic and feudal) roots, a product of the "lazy" races viticulturists so gleefully claimed they had swept away through their industrious vineyards—race removal being an added benefit of their "industry" as horticulturists. This confluence in California of a bias toward newer, "better" French varietals, as well as the perennial nationalist attempts to produce and claim the products of the "highest" civilizations, in tandem with the scientific racism of the period, was a way for viticulturists to identify with their newly conquered land, while at the same time, and in no uncertain terms, dispossess others from it. Grape culture laid a "natural" base for these cultural assaults.

In this racialized context, as a national commercial endeavor, wine growing had its roots in the east-to-west Anglo regional explosions of grape culture. The eastern seaboard's scientific experimentation with and commercialization of grapes was also practiced in the Los Angeles area. Immigrant Frenchman Jean Luis Vignes bought and expanded a vineyard close to Los Angeles in the 1830s.[9] Vignes soon developed the Los Angeles cottage wine culture into a commercial industry. He imported European varietals and grew to operate a hundred-acre vineyard. William Wolfskill, a Kentuckian by way of Missouri, also developed a successful 145-acre vineyard and orchard in 1830s Los Angeles. English, Scottish, American, and Irish winegrowers then joined them. A map of Los Angeles in 1849 illustrates the extent to which the city was ringed with grapes: the dotted lands between the town and river were all planted with grapevines (Fig. 29).[10] Prior to the Gold Rush, grape growing for profit was largely confined to the Los Angeles area. The hot, dry character

Figure 29. *Plan de la Cuidad de Los Angeles*, map surveyed and drawn by Edward Ord, 1849. This item is reproduced by permission of The Huntington Library, San Marino, California.

of much of southern California seemed well suited to grape growing, developing good sugars in the fruit. But vineyards in Los Angeles were too far inland to benefit from the cooling effects of the sea—the proximity of temperate bodies of water being a hallmark of other successful wine regions. In the region's long periods of heat, sugars developed, but acids fell, making the wine imperfect to many palates. Los Angeles's lack of water was also troublesome for growers who needed crop irrigation. After the great push for placer (that is, gold) in 1849, however, miners' consumption of alcohol ensured that grape growing remained the most profitable form of agricultural cultivation in California throughout the 1850s.

For these initial reasons, there was great interest, speculation, and experimentation in viticulture in California, in concert with practice nationwide. Sources recount that soon "nearly every farmer and small landowner . . . caught the vine fever" along the California coast.[11] In 1855, there were approximately one million vines in California; by 1860, there were eight million; and by 1870, 28 million vines were planted and 40,000 acres were under cultivation, one-fourth of them in the Los Angeles area. To give some perspective on the economic importance of the wine market, the 1870 census showed the total livestock value of the Los Angeles area at $1,398,556. At the same time, wine production was valued at about $1,063,000 (just $335,000 less than cattle)—and this figure did not include the fresh grape and brandy value. Grape production was a major economic force in the Los Angeles area for decades.[12]

However, by the 1870s, Los Angeles lost its centrality in the statewide wine trade. From 1850 to 1870, Los Angeles was making a little more than half of the total wine in the state; by 1890, it produced less than one-tenth of the total grapes in the state. Early viticulturists in Los Angeles by that time had largely given up on wine growing. Many moved on to citrus, a second Californian glamor crop, to avoid the grape competition growing in the north. After the Gold Rush, northern California wine growing flourished. With the populations of San Francisco and Sacramento quickly outstripping that of Los Angeles, a major advantage for northern California vineyards was their proximity to a much larger urban wine-drinking public. Some geographic areas of northern California were particularly well endowed for growing top-quality wine: coastal fog tempered extremes in weather; soils were varied and adaptable; there were nicely scattered hills and mountains; rains came largely in the winter, providing a sufficient water table that grapes could draw upon without threat of rot from summer rain; and sunshine and heat generally resulted in ideal balances of sugar and acid in the grapes.[13] The decline in southern Californian wine growing is illustrated through the relative presence of viticultural topics covered by southern California horticultural journals in succeeding decades. Throughout the 1870s, *Semi-Tropic California and Southern California Horticulturist*, published in Los Angeles, reserved a large section of the journal for viticulture each month. In many issues, nearly half the magazine was devoted to grape culture. The journal then consolidated and changed its name to *Rural Californian* in 1882.[14] By 1898, there was a precipitous drop in attention to viticultural matters, in favor of other horticultural interests, including smaller fruit crops, chickens, and flowers. From 1870 to 1890, viticulture had become big business, moved north, and was developing outside of the world of "rural" readers. Wine aficionados today might reiterate northern California's terroir as the major—perhaps only—factor propelling wine's success in the region. While climate and soil quality are of course crucial factors in any agricultural endeavor, it took far more than an ideal natural mix of sunshine, water, and soil to create northern California's wine legend.

California's Biological "Destiny"

California did not emerge as a major wine producer until several significant factors coalesced. Nicholas Longworth's death in 1863 further weakened an industry that was also blighted by vine-killing diseases. With widespread wine-grape monoculture popular throughout western Europe and the United States by mid-century, there were a number of grape diseases and blights that vintners were forced to combat. In the 1840s, the fungal disease *oidium* spread from the United States to Europe in vine and grape shipments. Oidium is a white powdery mildew that grows on the surface of the grape's leaves, stems, and fruit. Attacked portions of a vine dry up, die, and fall off. The fruit remains dwarfed and acidic, never reaching maturity. Oidium's spores were carried by the wind and rain, and spread easily.[15] Though controlled through the use of sulfur and other topical chemical dressings, it remained an annoying presence in vineyards through the rest of the century.

In the late nineteenth century, French vineyardists imported American grapevines with a higher degree of resistance to oidium in the hopes of producing stronger hybrid varieties. Inadvertently, they also imported *Phylloxera vastatrix*, a far more devastating infestation. A miniscule root louse with a complex life cycle, phylloxera destroyed millions of acres of vineyards in Europe through the final three decades of the century. The spread of phylloxera was greatly increased after the advent of speedier railroads, steamships, and expanded viticultural trade in the 1860s. Infested cuttings from the United States were delivered for planting in European vineyards a few weeks after being removed from the ground, and the root louse was primed for infestation. The insect traveled above ground and underground in various stages of its life cycle, so further infestation was swift. The louse damaged a grapevine by sucking its roots, thereby weakening the plant, which allowed secondary diseases purchase on the vine, and finally the plant became starved of nutrients. Phylloxera also produced galls on the leaves of growing vines, essentially attacking every method of energy production. The late nineteenth-century international infestation still ranks high as one of "the most destructive plant-disease epidemic[s] of all time."[16]

As phylloxera hit western Europe (particularly France) with ferocity during the 1870s, growers noticed that certain vines native to the United States, including popular varieties such as the Scuppernong and Concord, were fairly resistant to its effects. At first, French winemakers tried various methods of chemical sprays and additives to save their vineyards. They flooded their vines and used other drastic measures to attempt to control the bug, sometimes killing their vines outright. Dozens of methods for control were offered to French congresses convened to combat phylloxera, but two schools of pest mitigation emerged: those that believed chemical means could quell phylloxera, and those who thought only the use of some type of American vine, as hybridizing stock, or as rootstock, would ultimately solve the problem. By the early 1880s the sides were drawn, the opponents having distilled their beliefs into one-word teams: translated from the French, it was the "Chemists" versus the "Americanists."

The debates about which method to use were laced with social Darwinist ideas about each nation's "natural" strengths and their grapes' "bodily constitution." A French professor of botany suggested hybridization (crossbreeding American and French vines to create an entirely new vine) as an answer to the phylloxera problem. He asked, "Must it be that by giving our varieties sufficient 'American blood' to make them invulnerable to the various plagues which their delicate constitutions cannot withstand, some of their qualities are lost in the crossing? I am certain they will not—our wines will retain their principal character."[17] Wine culture worldwide was consumed with their beverages' ideal national "character" and "constitution." While U.S. grapevines

had introduced the disease, cuttings of American grapevines would ultimately save the global industry as well. And French "Americanists" promised
that the French character of wines, their most important attributes, would be
left unchanged.

After years of debate and trials with various methods, most agreed that
the only way to save European *Vitis vinifera* vinestocks was to graft them
onto American *Vitis riparia* or *Vitis rupesteris* rootstocks, digging out native European winegrapes and replacing them with grafted varieties. This
proved an enormous task in two ways: first, in convincing French (and other
European) winegrowers and the public that it was necessary, even vital, to
replace nearly all native grapevines with ones whose rootstocks came from
the United States. France, having a rich wine-growing heritage that had been
a point of national pride for centuries, had enormous difficulties accepting
the infiltration of American grapes, and the ultimate remaking of the most
essential aspect of their vineyards' prized terroir. But, it was evident that phylloxera had devastated the French wine industry, with the worst years being
the late 1880s: French wine sales had previously averaged in the thousands of
millions of francs; by then sales were reduced to around 800 million francs,
about half the value of the previous sales.[18] There were any number of additional fears about U.S. stock, from the central issue of national pride, to
whether grafted vines would affect the taste of the wine.

France had a long moment of national crisis over American pest and
vinestock infiltration, likely because the issue cut so deep into French articles
of faith regarding nature and culture. Not only were prized French vineyards
destroyed, but vines that had been hand-cultivated for generations were uprooted. The country's most prized national commodity was under threat of
total annihilation, or perhaps worse, utter transformation at the hands of the
greenhorn New World. French practice, French pride, and their deepest to-
kens of national identity were at stake. Upstart United States wine growing
was no longer a joke; it was a nightmare. But if France wanted to continue
making any kind of wine, it had to turn to American stock to do so.

Second, the task of actually performing the grafting and replanting of a
nation's worth of grapevines was a grand undertaking. In 1880, in France
alone, more than 11 million grapevines were planted. To make a new grapevine that could defend itself against phylloxera, twenty-five to thirty-five cen-
timeters of resistant grapevine rootstock was needed per plant. This meant
that thousands of kilometers of grape wood were needed, at the very least;
unfortunately, not all cuttings would take, and several in any batch would

need to be grafted a second or third time. The potential French market for American cuttings could have thus been as much as 2,760 trillion francs. As the phylloxera situation grew serious, growers in Missouri initially came to the world's rescue as the source of hearty rootstock. George Husmann, the well-known Missouri viticulturist, took the lead in furnishing rootstalks. In this and in his later roles as California wine delegate to several world's fairs, as well as acting as the most important international promoter of U.S. wine, Husmann was a force in the field for decades. He wrote in 1880: "Millions upon millions of American cuttings and vines have already been shipped to France, and are growing there now, and the French *vignerons*, who, but a few years ago, trembled for the very existence of their beloved calling, now concede that the only remedy, applicable everywhere, is the cultivation of American varieties, either as stocks to graft upon, or to furnish grapes direct."[19] Although this situation would seem to have been an economic boon for U.S. vineyardists with valuable phylloxera-resistant rootstocks, after the initial Missouri infusion, most of the American rootstocks were eventually propagated and distributed by the French government. French viticultural leadership insisted on controlling distribution and ultimately checked the entrance of any further diseases into the country. In rare instances, some French vineyardists were so desperate for stock that they contacted United States growers directly through black-market means. But through the help of the French government, growers were soon able to propagate their own American rootstocks.[20]

In the midst of this international wine industry turmoil, California not only survived, but expanded. In 1856, there were more than 1.5 million vines in California; by 1858, there were almost four million. In 1863 alone, 12 million more vines were planted in California. By 1870, there were 139 wineries in the state, but by 1880, the number fell to 45 due to overproduction and market consolidation. In 1900, there were more than 90 million vines in California; by 1909, this meant 250,000 acres were devoted to viticulture. Although these figures seem large, the United States only ranked eleventh in world wine production in 1911. Italy and France far surpassed the rest of the world, each producing more than one billion gallons of wine; Spain, Algeria, Austria, and Hungary all produced hundreds of millions of gallons of wine; and Portugal, Bulgaria, and Russia all produced at least 60 million gallons of wine, coming in ahead of the United States' total of 50 million gallons.

Yet during the phylloxera crisis, California drastically increased its production. In 1870, 3.8 million gallons of California wine were recorded, and by 1880, the total was 10.2 million gallons. Output of California wine had "quadrupled between 1866–69 and 1883–86, doubling again by 1898–1901." By 1911, California was producing almost 90 percent of the United States' total 50 million gallons that year.[21] In 1914, the State Board of Viticultural Commissioners estimated that "15,000 heads of families were directly engaged" in some branch of California viticulture. The state's meteoric rise in winemaking accompanied the stumbling of many other wineries, across the nation and in western Europe. California was not totally untouched by phylloxera, but outbreaks were localized and slow to spread in the 1880s. Partly because the French wine sold in U.S. markets was often adulterated, and partly because of increased taxes on imported wines, East Coast merchants grew more interested in California wines through the final two decades of the century. With California's rise, this moment also marks the shift in viticulture to a new level of a globally networked industrialized marketplace. While wine had traveled the world for centuries, California's ascent underlined a new, more competitive phase in world grape cultivation. It was clear that California would soon be a contender for the world's best wine.

Ultimately, millions of acres of European vineyards were torn up and replanted with American rootstock. In the fifty years before 1915, phylloxera destroyed more than two million acres of grapevines in France alone—almost 40 percent of its vines and fruit—at a total loss of about one billion dollars.[22] It was perhaps the first, and definitely the most significant, economic example of historian Alfred Crosby's definition of "ecological imperialism" working in reverse in the late nineteenth century. Crosby explains that Europeans consciously and unconsciously exported all types of threatening biological materials since their earliest colonizing trips to the New World.[23] The phylloxera crisis updates Crosby's argument for the latter nineteenth-century United States' growth as a global power: as the country extended its agricultural and economic power, it was assisted by the country's various biota. It was no coincidence, then, that in the wake of the phylloxera crisis, California also became a "leader in creating scientific and administrative infrastructures to protect its crops"; the state was reacting to a series of diseases and insects blighting many new commercial monocrops.[24] In addition to ultimately illustrating U.S. vines' "strength," as well as the U.S. wine industry's potential power, phylloxera thus helped American wine growing, and its new star, California, appear to be destined for greatness. This, by the last decades of the century, along with California wines' emergence as a blue-ribbon presence at world's fairs, signaled in rather brutal, as well as majestic ways, that California wine had *arrived*.

Capitalists and Their Wine

Perhaps the linchpin for the glamor of the early California wine industry, and fodder for the argument that although viticulture pictured itself outside of capitalist endeavors it was indeed thoroughly wrapped up in them, was that many major nineteenth-century railroad men and other industry magnates were also wine-growing champions. The five decades after the Civil War saw the nation's 35,000 miles of railroad track grow sevenfold, to 242,000 miles.[25] In the California context, "Big Four" railroad member Leland Stanford, as well as mill owner and land and gold investors John Sutter and James Marshall, all fancied themselves winegrowers. In addition, George Hearst, as well as fur magnate Gustave Niebaum, Comstock millionaire E. J. "Lucky" Baldwin, and borax magnate Julius Paul Smith all owned major vineyards or wine cellars.[26] Thus several vineyardists were among the most elite men in California from 1870 to 1890. Captains of other industries had vested interest in the success and prestige of California wine.

Leland Stanford, "man of many careers," fancied himself a farm boy throughout his life. Although known more for his activities in building the Central Pacific Railroad and serving as president of the Southern Pacific lines, as well as his time as governor of California, a U.S. senator, and university founder, Stanford found time for a few glamorous agricultural endeavors as well. A large, beefy man, he loved high society and was meticulous in appearance and speech. The consummate power politician, he traveled widely throughout Europe with his wife and spent much time in grand cities. By the 1880s, he held many arguably urban accomplishments. In that decade, when working on railroad business from his New York office, editors of the *New York City Directory* asked what they should list as his profession. Stanford replied, "Put me down as a farmer." Although he had experience on farms as a child and had invested in a few high-profile agriculturally related endeavors, given the minimal hours per week he was putting into those endeavors (as opposed to railroading and politicking), Stanford was arguably no farmer. His statement seems a crafted misrepresentation, intent on tapping into the late nineteenth-century romanticization of all things agrarian. A power politician and industry captain, he instead chose to play up his agrarian interests for the public.

It was true that in addition to his investments in a world-class cattle ranch and interest in breeding expensive racehorses, Stanford wished to create high-quality table wine, and sell it internationally.[27] Stanford began amassing land for the project in Vina, a northern California town, in 1881. In 1882, his employees set 1,000 acres in vines in Vina's hot, dry climate; in 1883, they added 1,500 more acres, and in 1888, another 1,000 acres. His vineyards and winery at his Great Vina Ranch in Tehama County, California (located north of Sacramento near Redding), quickly grew to one of the biggest in the world. His rows of vines were placed next to the Sacramento River and along the railroad line running through his land.[28]

Stanford's railroad and vineyards running parallel proved an apt symbol for the consolidated way he ran his large-scale businesses. Stanford employed about two hundred permanent workers on the Vina Ranch, and although he expressed a "preference for Caucasians," most of his staff were single Chinese men. For seasonal work, as many as 1,000 more hands were hired, generally boys from San Francisco. By 1891, an editorial in *Pacific Wine and Spirit Review* wrote that Stanford was "the largest vineyardist in all the world."[29] (Although Stanford indeed grew more rotund with each passing year, we must assume the author was referring to the vineyard, not the man.) The Stanfords had planned to build a million-dollar mansion on the Tehama County site, but their only son died as a teenager. In their depression, the couple canceled their plans, never living on-site, instead staying at the foreman's house when they visited.

Beyond his vineyards, Stanford's winery and wine vaults were of rather astonishing size: the winery was 120 by 270 feet, two stories high on the ends, and three stories in the middle. It held two steam grape crushers, each with a capacity of twenty tons an hour, as well as an automated grape stemmer. Powered by a hydraulic ram and steam pump, they required 60,000 gallons of water a day. In a separate 105- by 157-foot fermenting house, various rooms were dedicated to red and white wines, with a capacity of 400 tons of wine every twenty-four hours. Hand and steam pumps were used in the fermenting rooms: the juice was "pressed out by a hydraulic press driven by water power. . . . It [was] conveyed from the fermenting house to the still by means of tubes." In yet another separate building, the distillery ran on a fifty-horsepower Corliss engine pump, able to process 1,376 gallons of brandy a day. The facilities had incandescent lighting by the late 1880s, their power produced by the use of a dynamo, with "sufficient power to run 150 lights." Finally, the storage vaults alone covered nearly two acres of land, and held five hundred 2,000-gallon ovals, as well as four hundred 1,600-gallon ovals, for an on-site capacity of nearly two million gallons of wine and brandy.[30]

Yet despite the operation's size, and all the cutting-edge technology, Stanford followed winemaking's traditional stable of imagery in advertising his ranch and wine. Rather than illustrating its distinction through its immensity and machinery, coverage of Stanford's ranch in an 1889 *City Argus* focuses on cattle relaxing under a large oak, as well as Stanford's ponies and "famous milkers," evoking the classic image of a pastoral rancho (Fig. 30). The images, especially the top center "noontide siesta," seem designed in conscious contrast to the unflattering nickname author-humorist Ambrose Bierce gave him: "Stealand Landford."[31]

Stanford's wines were generally thought to be of low quality. Stanford had planted the wrong types of grapes for the hot, dry northern Californian valley climate: Burger, Charbono, Malvoisie, and Catawba, among others. Soon, he turned to brandy, in effect distilling his bad wine into marketable hard alcohol. The ranch proved a small success, though his wine quality was "proportional neither to the size of the plant nor the effort and cost invested."[32] By 1888, on business trips to London primarily concerning the railroad, Stanford took his brandy along for sale (Fig. 31). By 1890, his ranch was over 55,000 acres, 3,825 of it in vineyards, with a yearly production of 1.7 million gallons of alcohol, far less than its possible capacity. Most of it was shipped to and sold in New York.[33] Hubert Bancroft wrote in his 1888 biography of Stanford that the ranch's size, and the vineyard's 2.9 million vines, made it "by far the largest vineyard in the world, and, as some assert, larger than any three vineyards in the world combined." Stanford's Vina Ranch was dismantled rather quickly upon his death in 1893. His wife and the university felt the land could be put to better use, and prohibitionists were raising a fuss about Stanford's embarrassing interests in alcohol, even if he claimed they were "medicinal." A final, much reduced vintage was taken in 1915, and the vines were uprooted.[34] Although the Vina Ranch example is not typical of California wine growing, its size and intent are of note. As Stanford's career shows, California's power in viticulture was far from preordained: it was produced through incredible investment, required an increasing reliance on industrial monoculture—and it often failed even then.

Many of California's capitalists-turned-vintners also benefited from several major agricultural shifts in the state at this time. Fruit growing in general exploded in California from 1880 to 1930, with an increasing emphasis on one-crop farming. Farmers adopted methods of intensive cultivation (getting more fruit out of land already under cultivation) over previously popular methods of extensive cultivation (plowing more land to produce more

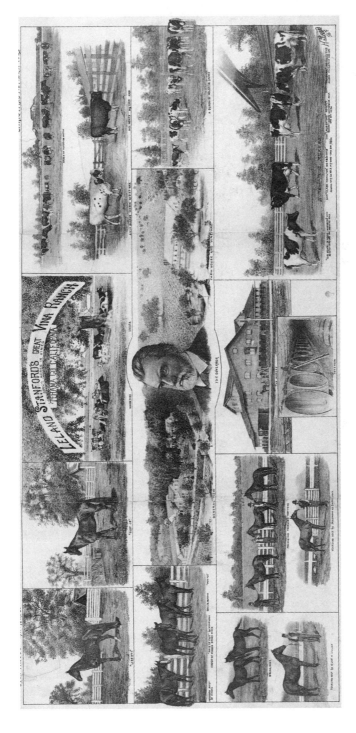

Figure 30. Leland Stanford's Great Vina Ranch, "3500 acres in vines." *City Argus* (San Francisco, CA: Christmas, 1889). Courtesy of the California History Room, California State Library, Sacramento, California.

Figure 31. Senator Leland Stanford's "Pure Grape Brandy," c. 1888. Courtesy of the California History Room, California State Library, Sacramento, California.

crops). Fruit monoculture "became the very engine of industrial agriculture in California," and fruit growers were among the most elite agriculturists in the state, in social and economic terms.[35]

And yet there was also a rather marked difference between viticulturists and the larger group of horticulturists. Although grape growers were central players in a larger capitalist fruit industry in these years, they always thought of themselves as slightly different from their counterparts, and outsiders reinforced this.[36] Grape growers insisted on being called "vineyardists" or "viticulturists." They imagined themselves in a "higher order of agriculture"—at the very top of the heap of (white, often upper-class) men concerned with agriculture in the nineteenth century. One step down from vineyardists were the rest of the fruit "growers" (an elite class themselves), and then came mere "farmers" who tended every other crop, each successively lower on the agricultural hierarchy. In addition, vineyardists held separate meetings, thought of the vineyard as a separate space, and developed different horticultural methods and trade journals throughout the period. They also had to constantly combat prohibitionists, an ideological battle most other growers never faced. Grape culture was a thoroughly commercial business, but through various means continued to represent itself as a pastoral and non-industrial pastime, and an unfairly attacked one at that.

The confluence of the capitalist speculation endemic to the California wine scene, and the major wine parties' ultimate denial of that speculation, was made clear in the popular magazine *The Californian*, published in January 1880. Arguing for the "Physical and Moral Influence of the Vine," Charles Wetmore, a successful vineyardist himself, encouraged the growth of the California wine industry through every conceivable method. He assured his readers that only when winemakers flooded the market with wine would new wine drinkers be found, as well as raise the price of wine. (He was wrong on both counts.) The aptly named Wetmore also believed that fresh grapes would only sell back east through overstocking the market with growers' fresh, sweet Western product. He began the article by painting a *rich* picture, associating viticulture with the Gold Rush: "Surely there is no danger of over-production. Our people will soon realize this, and the rush of the Argonauts in 1849 will be distanced by the rush to the shrine of the wine-god in the near future. The results which this agricultural development will show in our industrial and commercial life will be amazing. The gold of the Sierra did not build cities as surely as will the vines of its foothills."[37] Indeed, vineyards were the key to not only moral values, but urban prosperity: "The vine makes home in the country attractive, and develops village growth. Already we see this tendency in our new State. Los Angeles, San Gabriel, Anaheim, Sonoma, St. Helena, Mission San Jose—how beautifully they grow!" Hart Hyatt, editor of *California Rural Home Journal*, in his widely read *Hyatt's Hand-Book of Grape Culture* (1867), also tied the legacy of gold mining to wine's potential: "Say what we may of the rich mineral resources of California, and they do, indeed, seem inexhaustible, we confidently believe and predict that long ere the close of this century, the grape growing and wine making interests of California will far outstrip every other." For Wetmore and Hyatt, viticulturists were not only latter-day Forty-Niners, but genteel captains of city growth. Wetmore was also here modeling his importance as the organizer and cheerleader he would later become for the wine displays at the 1915 San Francisco World's Fair. In addition to "creating patriots" and "saving marriages," he argued that viticulture ironically "inspires men with the spirit of industry and blesses them with contentment; it will check the feverish spirit of speculation."[38] Once again, viticulture was an activity set at the height of capitalist denial: the article placed grape-growing at the very crux of speculation, through gold-digging and in city building, yet denied its very creation through such speculation. To this end, Wetmore offered a final directive: "The vine will build up our state. . . . [The] moral: plant vines, and make a home; drink wine, and become a gentleman."[39] The use of the land through viticulture, as well as the power offered through its social cachet, led to not only "the moral" of gentility, but the economic circumstances and land ownership one needed to ultimately "become a gentleman." Many in California sought viticulture as a means to achieve just that. Viticulturists presented California grape growing as a means for creating beautiful landscapes and practicing a type of refinement that distinguished grape growers from their more "commercial" counterparts.

Despite high hopes and a climate conducive to grape culture, of course winemakers in California did not have an unencumbered trail to industry success and status. They too were vulnerable to capitalist forces and biological diseases. The industry expanded too quickly during the 1880s, leading to a decline in profitability and eventually to a "wine depression" in 1889. In 1893, the national economic downturn threw wine markets into disarray as phylloxera attacks grew in the wine-growing counties of Napa, Sonoma, Alameda, and Santa Clara. In an attempt to strengthen the industry against these forces, seven of the most powerful wine firms joined together in 1894 to create the California Wine Association (CWA). An instantaneous near-monopoly, it dominated local as well as national markets. Wine was now technically big business: it enjoyed a growing percentage of the state's economy, with all of the positive and negative repercussions a trust had in terms of market control.[40]

By 1906, the CWA formally controlled half the wine in San Francisco. Soon, with the closely associated firms of Italian-Swiss Colony and Lachman & Jacobi winemakers, the CWA had direct or indirect control of at least 15 million gallons—three-quarters of the commercial wine market—held in cellars in the Bay Area.[41] The earthquake and fire that struck San Francisco in April 1906 destroyed most of that stocked wine. But the consolidated wine industry was able to bounce back quickly, and it enjoyed growing profits through the next decade and a half until Prohibition. This focus on production and trade took a new interest in exports at the turn of the century. Like other agricultural businesses, the U.S. wine industry was now annually creating wine in excess of what it could sell domestically. Connected to this, scholars have pointed out that since the 1880s, the growth of the U.S. naval fleet was tied with national desires to expand trade, especially for U.S. agricultural goods.[42] The use of the military extended Americans' sense of manifest destiny, and cleared the way to new markets. By the 1890s, Teddy Roosevelt's "new Manifest Destiny" was reborn through his aggressive reliance on the Monroe Doctrine. The U.S. cavalry had been dispatched to Cuba, and the annexation of Guam, Puerto Rico, and the Philippines had begun. Displaying and legitimating these imperial activities to a wider public was one of the major functions of world's fairs throughout the nineteenth century and into the twentieth. Not coincidentally, grapes figured as a growing presence in these fairs, culminating in 1915 at the Panama-Pacific International Exposition held in San Francisco.

California viticulturists were at the heart of an imperialist agricultural ethos in the late nineteenth century because of their claim to certain natural advantages. Many argued that wine's trek across the country had been only natural, that California had natural gifts in agriculture, and that its centrality in various regional agricultural landscapes had merely followed the best natural conditions for the vines. Here we trace another genealogy of California's claim to viticultural destiny: biological circumstance, big money, a deeply racialized context, and the massive advertising campaigns of world's fairs, especially the 1915 Pan-Pacific Expo. Continuing its pastoral mythos, the moment when winemaking was most industrial, through wine trusts, mechanized wine presses, alienated ethnic labor, and market control, was the moment when it was most draped in yeoman pastoral elegance.

California Wine on Stage

Through various aesthetics of imperial abundance, a public culture of flow, and the vineyard's importance in the popular neo-colonial Californian Mission aesthetic, the San Francisco exposition was the ultimate example of wine's mythos coming to maturity in California. Winegrowers utilized cultural tropes of tributary flow and neo-colonial nostalgia to identify their land as unique and distinctly Californian, while at the same time developing methods of dispossessing others from their new Eden of wine production.

World's fairs have been understood as sites of unmatched "imperial abundance." As scholars have argued, fairs promised material bounty of all kinds, but that promise of abundance was "contingent on the acquisition, maintenance, and growth of empire." All types of displays (mechanical, human, and artistic) thus equated abundance with empire, as well as the conquering of "savage" populations and ways of life. Since London's Crystal Palace exhibition in 1851, world's fairs had been hard at work glorifying and domesticating empire. World's fairs were one example of how, rather paradoxically, as the United States became the most aggressively expansionist society in the world at the end of the nineteenth century, its artistic domestic and pastoral ideal also grew.[43]

Agricultural displays at world's fairs often showcased imperial designs and an imperial reach. Of course, the objects of most importance in agricultural competitions were the medal winners, highlighting that competition and hierarchy were of central importance in modern capitalist society—and often reiterating the belief that sheer natural abundance was crucial to American strength. Moreover, the country's ever-adaptable and improving technological gadgetry on display at the fairs were the means by which to create and secure wealth, sometimes at the expense of colonized people and land. Advertisers incorporated this "ethos of imperial abundance" in their copy and designs for ads as well, carrying these tropes from world's fair displays into a larger world of salable goods. Although each fair was only experienced by the public for six months on average, the world's fairs in Chicago, St. Louis, San Francisco, and other cities had a far wider grip on everyday life. Perhaps most significantly, they helped "translate imperial dreams into daily practice."[44] Fin-de-siècle viticultural exhibitions at world's fairs reveal the desires of viticulturists to represent and solidify U.S. agriculture as a colonizing project. For the powerful California Wine Association, the fair expressed and solidified its grip on the state, and the nation, and made claims upon several specific international spaces as well.

Californian grapes and wine had a significant presence at most world's fairs since 1876. That year, they were displayed at the Paris and Philadelphia fairs. At the Paris fair, U.S. wines won two awards.[45] By the 1885 New Orleans World Fair, the California State Board of Viticultural Commissioners put together an advertising pamphlet for distribution and stocked a booth. The pamphlet detailed the history of the vine in California, and its crucial role in "all civilization." The pamphlet also summarized the costs and profits of viticulture in California. Wine growing in France was its constant source of comparison.[46] Viticulturists had booths and displays through the rest of the century: in Paris in 1889, Chicago in 1893, and St. Louis in 1904. Grape growers also created elaborate booths at large regional fairs, including San

Francisco's Midwinter Fair in 1894, as well as the California Land Show in San Francisco in 1913. All of this was precursor to the largest and most impressive display of wine at a major exposition, the Pan-Pacific Expo of 1915.

Displaying grapes in order to impart a pastoral yet imperial image of California winelands at U.S. fairs was nothing new in 1915. Indeed, at the 1876 Centennial Exposition in Philadelphia, a massive Mission grapevine from Santa Barbara, California, was the subject of many articles about the fair (Fig. 32).[47] In the midst of a wine bust, the industry did not do much else to

Figure 32. W. N. Tuttle, "Old Mammoth Grapevine," photographic print, Santa Barbara, California, 1875. Courtesy of the California History Room, California State Library, Sacramento, California.

promote wine at the fair. The exhibit and its wine were the products of private individuals, and most visitors believed the wine displayed was of poor quality.[48] The Mammoth Grapevine, however, was a "great center of attraction."[49] The vine had been dug up, cut into labeled sections, shipped to Philadelphia, and reassembled near the center of the Agricultural Hall. Displayers called it the largest grapevine in the world, making sure to also note that it beat out the previous holder of the title, the Black Hamburg vine at Hampton Court in England. (And by cutting it down, they ironically made the Hampton Court vine number one again.)

By the time of the Philadelphia fair, significant lore had already been published about the Mammoth Santa Barbara vine. In the *Overland Monthly* a decade earlier, a story was published of a Californio, José Dominguez, who gave the vine to his betrothed, Doña Maria Marcelina, in 1775 for its domestic use and as a living memorial to himself.[50] The vine symbolically represented the familial bond and vineyard romance that had nurtured it in its productive, pastoral California landscape. Planted just one year before the nation's founding, and displayed in 1876 at the Centennial Exposition in Philadelphia, the vine symbolized a celebration of the founding of the United States and its victorious appropriation of Mexico's heritage and lands in the Southwest. In this case, the message presented about viticulture in California was not a simple replaying of the imperial grape cultures of New York and Ohio. Instead, California grape culture was rooted in U.S. independence but finally solidified in the violence and triumph of the Mexican War in 1848. California winelands continued their "connections" with Old World domestic wine cultures, but practiced them under a new and thoroughly Caucasian flag.

Several Philadelphia fairgoers wrote about the Mammoth Vine in their published accounts. One boy described the setting: "The mammoth grapevine that came from California is very large. Around it is a stand where they sell pictures and a good many other things. There is a stuffed bear, moose . . . and a good many other animals in a glass case."[51] Although the Mammoth Vine was situated in the Agricultural Hall, its placement was not simply for sheer agricultural illustration. This account describes it sitting as the centerpiece for other pictures and objects advertising California—a distinctively wild California, with a bear and moose also placed around the display. But as the illustration of the vine in *Lippincott's Magazine* suggests, the vine was also draped over a refined pergola at which visitors could sample or buy wine (Fig. 33).[52] In this image, well-dressed ladies and gentlemen linger and chat at the bar, the vine's many canes reaching delicately above them. The Mammoth

Figure 33. Fairgoers enjoying wine samples underneath the "Mammoth Grapevine, From California." *Lippincott's Magazine of Popular Literature and Science* 18 (November 1876), 527. Courtesy of the Steenbock Memorial Library, University of Wisconsin–Madison.

Vine was thus at the center of a display that implicitly described that the highest forms of civilization were present in California. Although California wine was perhaps not yet at its peak, the soil could nevertheless produce remarkably large products. The vine, so indicative of agriculture and bourgeois development in California, served a similar, if smaller-scale purpose at the Philadelphia fair. Under its branches was a respite from the peripheral wildness of California. In this space was a comfortable and refined vantage point from which to survey the rest of the fair and the other objects brought in from the Californian countryside. It offered assurance that agricultural colonization was succeeding beautifully in California.

At the next two world's fairs, California wine displays grew in size, opulence, and prestige. At the Paris Exposition of 1889, the United States received three dozen medals and four honorable mentions for its wines. Thirty-four medals went to California wines, including four gold and twelve silver; other

winning U.S. states included Florida, New Jersey, New York, North Carolina, Ohio, Virginia, and Washington, D.C.[53] George Husmann, previously a
supplier of phylloxera-resistant Missouri vinestock to France, had moved to
California in 1881, and he served as a delegate for collecting California wines
for the Paris Exposition. By this time, he was the State Statistical Agent for
California, and an agent for the U.S. Department of Agriculture. He received
a gold medal himself for acting as the California wine collaborator and promoter at the Paris Expo. He played these roles again at the 1893 Chicago Columbian Exposition. Through these charges in the various fairs, he positioned
himself as the most important international promoter of U.S. wine.[54]

At the Chicago Exposition, the grape and wine displays grew immensely,
and there are differing reports on record as to their success. Grapes abounded
in the California state exhibit in general: the primary entrance into the California building was "guarded by plaster casts of California bears . . . the sides
of each pedestal being festooned with casts of vines loaded with grapes." Also,
just within the gateway, there were "four urns higher than one's head, filled
as if to overflowing with bronzed clusters of grapes." Under the north "sky-
roof, on a pedestal . . . [was the] majestic 'Statue of California.' The figure was
that of a young girl. . . . At her feet lay a grizzly bear . . . [as well as] grapes,
and California fruits, symbolizing plenty." Many fairgoers wrote that the California exhibit was the most impressive state exhibit they had ever seen. A
reporter for the *Salt Lake Tribune* wrote, "California on Admission Day was
making herself felt from one end of the globe to the other. . . . Carload after
carload of fruit was thrown out in the vast throng gathered in front of the
building. . . . People by the thousands carried away bunches of grapes." Indeed, fair organizers had packed half a dozen train cars with fresh fruit from
California, and furnished 300,000 visitors with samples. The *Chicago Herald*
proclaimed, "California has fairly outdone all the States, and her big building heaped with barrels of sparkling wine, tons of delicious fruit, grain, and
vegetables, is a never-failing source of delight to exposition sight-seers." Leland Stanford mounted a display showcasing his Vina Ranch, which included
two ornamental fountains, one jetting with wine, the other with Stanford's
brandy: imperial plenty aplenty.[55]

Yet many viticulturists believed that several factors still held the California wine industry back from sufficiently promoting its wines through imperial exhibition. For the Chicago fair, California winemakers had again put
booths together cooperatively. But the displays were privately described as
"confusing" by the State Board of Viticultural Commissioners, and the wine

concession at the fair was limited to one man who hocked cheap French wine. The judging was also fraught with controversy, and it seemed every party was upset at the close of the fair.[56] But the displays did send the valuable message that the United States and the world should be aware of California grapes and the state's growing viticultural and enological talent.

In the years before the Pan-Pacific Expo, the *Pacific Wine, Brewing & Spirit Review* (*PWBSR*) was an unflagging cheerleader for the California Viticultural Exhibit Association as it made its plans for the exposition.[57] In a May 1913 article, the *PWBSR* announced some of the plans for the fair, and included photos of previous wine exhibits at World's Fairs. The magazine touted that the upcoming California exhibit "promise[d] to set a new standard for such displays."[58] The article included photographs from the California Wine Exhibits at Chicago in 1893, San Francisco's Midwinter Fair in 1894, and St. Louis in 1904. The illustrations reveal the evolution of display design, each display growing more dramatic (Figs. 34, 35, and 36). The journal thus encapsulated previous fairs' displays as minor prologues to their upcoming exposition.

The California Wine Exhibit at Chicago in 1893 (Fig. 34) is a study in geometrically stacked wine bottles. On a central "octagon pyramid," the display was replete with American flags, and the classic symbols of California were again on display, with the golden bear, flags, and wine bottles of all types stacked high. Upon the pyramid's shelves were "vintages of California winegrowers and producers. There were dark and light colored wines, champagnes, brandies, etc., to the number of six hundred bottles, fifty-three exhibitors displaying three hundred and one types of wines, and thirty-three distinct types." At the top of the center display was "a beautiful plaster cast of Hebe, who, in classical mythology, was the cup-bearer of Jupiter." Yet, Hebe was "represented as a typical California girl, standing erect with garlands of grapes entwined around her head and a bunch of grapes in her left hand . . . while in her right hand, lifted gracefully upward, was a tiny goblet."[59] The 1894 San Francisco Midwinter Fair exhibit (Fig. 35) again grew in opulence: bowers of grapevines were draped from the ceiling and urns and fancy pilasters formed every endcap; elements of high Victorian artistic profusion adorned the walls. At the St. Louis World's Fair ten years later (Fig. 36), the emphasis centered on a display of gigantic obelisks with leering Grecian faces. The wine shelves were lined with drooping vines and capped with wood, hewn in a wave pattern. Vines were draped from the center obelisk, evoking a merry-go-round or ancient carnival. The room's ceiling and walls, made of geometric

Figure 34. "California Wine Exhibit, Columbian Exposition, Chicago [1893]." Anonymous, "California's 1915 Wine Exhibit," *Pacific Wine, Brewing & Spirit Review* (May 31, 1913), 13. Courtesy of Special Collections, University of California Library, Davis.

trusses, contrasted with the graceful arches of the bowers and human faces. They were balanced with the straight, symmetrical rows of wine bottles, as well as with their contrasting white labels on dark bottles.[60] The displays combined country elegance and imperial abundance, a theme that would remain popular through later world's fairs. They repeated what winegrowers had sold as their image for so long: wine appreciation was an elegant, pastoral, even feminine pastime, reminiscent of the splendors of ancient Greece but also as homey as an overstuffed Victorian parlor.

The California Land Show, held in San Francisco in October 1913, gave viticulturists the opportunity for further dress rehearsals of displays of their grapes and wines for the 1915 International Exposition. The State Board of Viticultural Commissioners commended this feat of advertising, and encouraged more exhibits in the upcoming international fair. The board made recommendations for the types of display, and for the best use of grapes and new technologies in each season. The Land Show exhibit was "housed in an attractive rustic pergola booth decorated with trailing vines," a model for future

Figure 35. "California Wine Exhibit, Midwinter Fair, San Francisco, California [1894]." Anonymous, "California's 1915 Wine Exhibit," *Pacific Wine, Brewing & Spirit Review* (May 31, 1913), 13. Courtesy of Special Collections, University of California Library, Davis.

displays. For future fairs, the board urged Californians to take advantage of "improved methods of packing and transportation" and to make use of fresh berries "from July through Christmas." During the rest of the year, buyers were to be tempted by displays of "processed grapes in attractive jars, photographs of vineyards and the various products of the vine." The goal of these displays was, of course, to educate consumers on "the matter of the grape," but also to educate them on the size and scale of California viticulture. The commissioners boasted that "such exhibits would prove a revelation, because only a comparatively few people outside the borders of California realize that our grape acreage is twice that of all the other states in the Union combined and that . . . we are able to grow over one thousand varieties of [grapes]."[61]

The commissioners' attention to matters of display illustrates how crucial shows and fairs were in constructing California wine's claim to imperial dominance and pastoral elegance. They were not only places to display commercial products, attract customers, and compete for vinous prizes, but

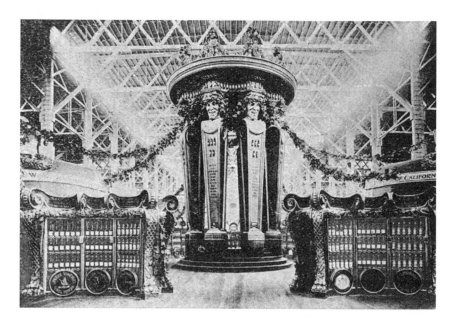

Figure 36. "California Wine Exhibit, Saint Louis World's Fair [1904]." Anonymous, "California's 1915 Wine Exhibit," *Pacific Wine, Brewing & Spirit Review* (May 31, 1913), 13. Courtesy of Special Collections, University of California Library, Davis.

also spaces to prove California's new and central role as the United States' premier wine region to the public. The California displays at national and international fairs bridged a fairly major gap in the American imagination of manifest destiny: they seemed to prove that old agricultural lifestyles could, be made new again, but without reference to the vexing industrial machines and ethnic labor they relied upon. California wine, its vines, and its industry were here simply and graciously abundant—highly organized but naturally, fantastically effusive.

A Temple of Grapes

Wine growing in California continued to expand through the turn of the century. The U.S. Census of 1890 reported a total grape acreage in the United States of 401,261 acres; 213,230 acres, more than half, were in California.[62] In 1914, on the eve of the exposition, the State Board of Viticultural Commissioners published a report of California grape statistics and directives for its readers. It detailed that 330,000 acres of land in California were planted with grapes (170,000 acres in wine grapes, 110,000 in raisin grapes, and 50,000 acres in table grapes). The commissioners' conservative estimate for the value of this land was $66 million; the additional infrastructure and equipment added to this figure for a total viticultural investment of $150 million. For this investment to truly pay, however, the board believed that "no favorable opportunity should be lost in the matter of displaying the viticultural products of California" at all large state, regional, national, and international fairs.[63]

The success of the wine displays at previous fairs, coupled with the promise of easier access to world markets in wine through the opening of the Panama Canal, convinced the CWA and the state board to help San Francisco in its bid to host the planned 1915 Pan-Pacific Expo. In April 1910, winemakers attended San Francisco's exposition bid fundraiser at the San Francisco Merchant's Exchange, helping raise $5 million in two hours. In coming weeks, organizers quickly raised more than $17 million. Soon, the national competition for which city would host the Pan-Pacific Expo had narrowed to New Orleans and San Francisco. Lobbyists from the West Coast city launched a massive public relations campaign in Washington, D.C., and arrived in the east well stocked with gifts, including crates of northern California wine. The San Francisco delegation at this time also assured Congress that no national funds would be needed should the fair be held in their city. Congress soon selected San Francisco, and by 1912, the wine industry had formed the California Viticultural Exhibit Association, with dozens of directors. Smaller regional committees assembled all over the state, and the California wine pump and its advertisers were primed for action at its own international exposition.[64]

The Pan-Pacific Expo covered 635 acres next to San Francisco Bay, and more than 18.8 million people attended the fair.[65] The grape and wine display was mounted in the Food Products Palace, organized into four parts around a domesticated Mission theme. The California Wine Exhibit, quickly nicknamed the "Grape Temple," was 270 feet by 65 feet, and held forty-two booths, circling the outer edge of the display room (Fig. 37). The room was dressed "with an enclosure like a trellis of vines supported by columns formed of casks painted white, with gilt hoops. Everywhere were garlanded casks and clambering vines."[66] Wine casks formed the pillars for the room, and pictures and Victorian furniture were set among the dangling vines, evoking domestic elegance. At the center of the room was a twenty- by forty-foot

Figure 37. The Grape Temple, Panama-Pacific International Exposition, San Francisco, California, 1915, "Splendid Collective Wine Display," *Pacific Wine, Brewing & Spirit Review* (March 1915), 12. Courtesy of Special Collections, University of California Library, Davis.

viticultural map of California, with all exhibiting wineries modeled in miniature upon it, each illuminated with electric lights. To one side of the map was the Historical Room, and on the other, the Moving Pictures Room, with seating for one hundred people. The film room showed 15,000 feet of film every day. Said to be about seven hours long, its topic, of course, was wine growing in California. The film's primary subjects were the vineyards and wineries of the fair's exhibitors.[67] Two pergolas and fountains stood to each side of the map (Fig. 38). Everywhere there were "multi-colored grapes, rare vintages . . . wine temples and famous California wineries reproduced in facsimile." The statues and pictures spotlighted the obligatory Bacchus and Pan, raising their wineglasses. Women and children were also pictured, festooned in vines and crushing grapes with an old-fashioned hand press—nothing like

Figure 38. Map of the Grape Temple. Anonymous, "California's 1915 Wine Exhibit," *Pacific Wine, Brewing & Spirit Review* (May 31, 1913), 12. Courtesy of Special Collections, University of California Library, Davis.

the steam-powered presses winegrowers used at the time.[68] The displays were designed and funded by the all-male Viticultural Exhibit Association, but men in vineyards (other than Greek gods in statues and pictures) were conspicuously absent from the display. The picture of the Italian-Swiss Colony booth within the California Wine Exhibit also reveals that the wine on display at the fair was set within a domestic, feminine atmosphere (Fig. 39). Such displays forwarded the feminine pastoral ideal surrounding grape cultivation, an aesthetic similar to much high-Victorian homemaking. Positioning wine as a beverage used in moderation with meals in the home perhaps helped dislodge it from association with beer and spirits in saloons. This domestic context seems an effort to further separate wine from other forms of alcohol in a time of growing prohibitionist fervor.

The entire wine display was constructed on a Mission theme, with an open court, and forty-foot towers at four corners. The Grape Temple was thus something of a miniature of the larger fair itself, which included several buildings in the Spanish Colonial Revival, or Mission Revival, style on the grounds. Popular between 1890 and 1929, the Mission Revival style was known for its white plaster walls, rough-hewn exposed beams, heavy masonry fixtures, and low-pitched red clay tile roofs. Some architects have since critiqued this style as a "wrong turn" in California building history, indeed even an "art of deception." They explain that "affluent gringos generated the myth of an indigenous California architecture based on 'Spanish Roots' . . . a cultural legend that was useful in selling property to Eastern investors and Midwest settlers."[69]

Figure 39. Italian-Swiss Colony Booth, Panama-Pacific International Exposition, San Francisco, California, 1915, "Splendid Collective Wine Display," *Pacific Wine, Brewing & Spirit Review* (March 1915), 13. Courtesy of Special Collections, University of California Library, Davis.

Mission Revival architecture and California grape culture had in fact been brought into the national public eye through identical venues. Helen Hunt Jackson's picturesque Spanish novel *Ramona* (1884) was the earliest popular work set within California missions, idealizing its vineyard spaces and colonial past. In addition, Leland Stanford's Stanford University was built in 1888 on Mission and Romanesque themes, with much praise and coverage in popular periodicals and professional journals. Late nineteenth- and early twentieth-century culture was once again imbued with old republican fears that U.S. society had become overcivilized, effete in its arts and popular lifestyles. Mission architecture, in its seemingly organic, historical, strong, and sturdy construction—and always sporting a quaint vineyard—fit a regional and national psychological niche, complementing a continuing mythos of American grape production nicely.

Likewise, at the 1893 Columbian Exposition in Chicago, the California and Texas Buildings had been much acclaimed for their "Mission-Moorish style." The Macon, Georgia, *Telegraph* wrote: "The immense California Building looked in every detail what it was meant to represent—and old Spanish mission—and in that quiet time, when the odor of its many flowers floated faintly in the still air, it was easy to imagine one's self in the old Spanish garden and among the riotous semi-tropical growths which embowered the old California missions."[70] The aesthetic was quickly further popularized: the Cotton Palace in Waco, Texas, was built in 1894 in tribute to the Chicago Fair's architecture.[71] The trend continued through competitions for the California Building for the San Francisco Midwinter Fair of 1894, as well as California's structure at the Louisiana Purchase Exposition in St. Louis in 1904. By 1915 in San Francisco, the style was all over the fairgrounds. But more than a strict architectural style, the Mission craze extended into the home and garden as well. The rough-hewn oak wine barrels and straight rows of grapevines extended this type of architecture into a sort of exoticized experience, aesthetic lifestyle, and advertising ploy.

The Mission aesthetic also proved the perfect frame for the other items of imperial abundance that were organized within it at the 1915 fair. The Mission theme's rustic but grand qualities revealed a particular reliance on a pastoral Californian past that archaicized and glorified Spanish pre-national history in the state. Used throughout the 1915 fair, the aesthetic at once obviated the violence and glorified the outcome of the Mexican-American War, transforming this architectural style into a celebration of Californian statehood as a crowning moment in national and imperial expansion. In a prospectus written for the fair, a planner wrote, "California has treasured the missions long. . . . The soldiers and the adventurers are remembered. The priest-civilizer still lives."[72] Set within the specific context of the fair, the architecture seemed to erase the violence of the Mexican-American War via clean, simple arches and open breezeways. Mission architecture here also normalized and further legitimated the U.S. presence in Latin American sites in the period, including Cuba and the Panama Canal zone. The Mission aesthetic ultimately focused California's previous and contemporary colonization through wine growing. California wine had been able to step away from its European influence and develop its own nationalist identity through claiming its innocuous architecture.

The image of a rich harvest of wine and grapes was spread throughout the fairgrounds, in its building design and in the color palette used across the site. The fair's richer burgundies and oranges were a marked departure from the traditionally white fairgrounds of Chicago and St. Louis. Additionally, another commissioned statue of Bacchus, "with his grapes and wineskin," was placed outside of Festival Hall, the great central auditorium of the Exposition.[73] The California Building, built entirely in the Mission style, was the largest of the state buildings ever erected at an exposition. Its "commanding tower" held a large statue of Father Serra, overlooking a replica of the garden at Mission Santa Barbara.[74] California's first colonial father and fabled bringer of wine was chosen as the herald of the exposition's flagship state building.

Wine, grapes, and the Mission aesthetic were central to the later memorialization of the larger fair as well. A commemorative poem about the exposition was published in *Sunset* magazine and separately in a book in 1916 with nine colored "illustrations after photographs" of the grounds. Titled "The Evanescent City," the poem used multiple metaphors of winemaking to evoke rich scenes of the fairgrounds. The poem opens:

> Great on the west, darkness crush her domes,
> Wine-red the city of the sunset lies.
> Below her courts the mournful ocean foams;
> Above, no foam of cloud is in the skies.

Other terms also evoke the wine press: the use of the color "crimson" and evocations of liquid continue through the piece. This memorial poem envisions the San Francisco fairgrounds as both an "evanescent city," and as a winepress, producing a "fleeting beauty" of temporary experience—but rich memories.[75] Wine, the poem illustrates, was inherent to the showpiece city, and framed the way the fair was to be recollected. Redolent and romantic, winemaking and the city itself are feminized here. San Francisco's earthquake, fire, capitalists, and laborers were forgotten in its autumn wash. San Francisco is instead pictured as a place of wine appreciation—a genteel, "evanescent" activity enjoyed over countless sunsets. No longer imperially white, San Francisco and its fair harkened to its colorful—but now controlled—regional pastoral mythos.

On July 12, 13, and 14, 1915, a newly formed International Congress of Viticulturists gathered at the fair for their first annual meeting. They discussed wine history, grapevine diseases, regional differences in grapes, and new chemical products for vine care. World War I prevented many Europeans from attending, but the Congress still met with over three hundred delegates and their wives in attendance, with twenty-five nations represented in all.[76]

Leading up to the official meetings, national and foreign delegates were taken on a grand tour of viticulture in California. Arriving in Los Angeles on July 7, they attended banquets in their honor nearly every night of the trip. The delegates attended the San Diego Exposition for a day, then visited wineries in Riverside County. Next they traveled to Fresno, visiting vineyards, packing houses for raisins, and wineries. By July 11, they reached San Francisco and were shown Winehaven, the CWA's great wine plant and storage facility.[77] The delegates were impressed by the size and scope of winemaking in California, and the coordinated flow of their nonstop tour through the state's thousands of acres of vineyards. The trip was a cooperative orchestration by California winemakers and grape growers to showcase their state as a new and grand wine region, on par with the French wine regions of Bordeaux, Alsace, and the Rhone, and far surpassing the faltering U.S. Midwest. The grand tour of California's vineyards with several hundred international delegates, as well as the California winemaking film shown in the Grape Temple, presented a comprehensive, connected picture of the strength and international promise of California wine. The tour proved that California already had a fully operational and impressively systematic wine industry—and all of her international visitors were led as eager, pampered tourists through its beautiful script. The railroad and other industrial conveniences may have assisted their journey, but California's friendly pastoral elegance night after night was presented as more indicative of her burgeoning wine culture. Here, Old World was staged with New World, and was key to California's burgeoning agricultural dominance.

Several rather new technologies at the 1915 fair helped winegrowers with their displays. The popular use of "moving-picture machines" across the fairgrounds was cited by many fairgoers as a major difference from fairs past.[78] A cataloger of the Pan-Pacific Expo wrote that films ran in the majority of buildings on site, "everywhere showing industrial processes." In fact, no fewer than fifty-four different films ran across the exposition grounds.[79] The subjects of the films differentiated the wine exhibits from the larger exhibits of food and industry, however. The larger Palace of Agriculture held films of "threshing machines, harvesting machines, reapers, [and] sowers," the emphasis being on the machinery, not the crops themselves. Mechanical adaptation and the industrial production of crops were featured throughout the building. Much the opposite, the Californian grape growers' displays and films showed the simple vine-clad countryside and its vineyard families. In the Grape Temple's film, winemaking was not industrial—it was rural,

domestic, and quaint. Commissioned by wine industry leader, assistant secretary to the International Congress of Viticulture, and secretary of the Grape
Protective Association H. F. Stoll, the grape film was displayed as "plain, un-
varnished facts," and several attendees requested that some portion of the
film be shared with schools and interest groups across the country (see Fig.
38 for the Grape Temple's "Moving Pictures" room). Scenes from the Vintage Festival in Napa Valley's St. Helena township and the process of making
champagne were among the film's main subjects. Viewers described the film's
beauty and educational qualities, but also requested that it be shared nationwide as proof to prohibitionists that viticulturists' jobs, lives, and landscapes
were clean and simple, and that the wine they made should not be outlawed.[80]
What was more, the California wine film did not highlight a central subtext
found in much of the rest of the fair—that of San Francisco rising from its
own ashes from the Great Quake and fires just a few years earlier. Instead,
the films emphasized small, family-style production of wine, in traditionally
pastoral settings, framed within the Mission aesthetic.[81] In all, an estimated
more than 100,000 people viewed all or part of the seven hours and 15,000
feet of film, illustrating "the beautiful wine country of California, with all the
scenes of cultivation and the vintage," as well as the "diversity of California's
topography."[82] The film and exhibit relied on a narrative of historical continu-
ation, not of change; it held fast to unchanging tradition, to pre-industrial
pastoralism, to the myth of an idyllic pre-CWA wine trust life.

Another impressive novelty was presented at the fair: a five-acre moving, working model of the Panama Canal, "on so extensive a scale that visitors seated in comfortable theatre chairs [were] carried along the route of the
canal upon a moveable platform."[83] Water and fluidity were apt metaphors
for the larger fair itself, as it was centrally a celebration of the opening of
the Panama Canal, a waterway that held untold promise for industry and
travel. This ride helped visualize and normalize the canal as a crucial item of
U.S. "imperial prosthesis," domesticating the international mechanical feat
of engineering.[84] But when tied with wine's constant presence at the fair, the
canal, perhaps even more than a symbol of technological prowess and brute
strength, also represented a new sense of imperial flow. Visitors drifted above
the coursing model of the canal, their sense of flow doubled from the canal's
motion beneath them and their own movement atop it. The canal, its ride at
the fair, and the exposition itself perhaps deftly illustrated imperial fluidity
to fairgoers.

This new, comprehensive experience of perception and flow was popularized to a much greater degree at the Pan-Pacific Expo than anywhere before. Geddes Smith, a reporter for the *Independent*, commented on the "staggering amount of motion at the Fair. . . . The curious mixture of everything, dissolved in the flowing stream of visitors from everywhere, is a new creation, no matter how familiar its elements."[85] The wine displays accentuated this fascination with "flowing stream[s]." Fountains were made to look as if they flowed with wine: "splashing electric fountains, emblematic of the juice of grape, will show streams of water reflecting all the brilliant colors of the season."[86] Draped grapevines and flowing fountains of wine were primary material examples of how grapes fit into both new and classic visions of high culture—an elite lifestyle that was fluid, elegant, elite, and easy. The Grape Temple's impressively long-running film on the vineyards of California accentuated this theme. What is more, samples of wine "flowed freely" to visitors, its salubrious effects on the human body long explained as loosening the nervous and circulatory systems for optimal health.[87] Free wine punch was served at the Grape Temple for the duration of the fair, and it was offered up across the entire fairgrounds on the exposition's official "Wine Day" on July 14, marking the final day of the International Wine Congress. Wine punch and souvenirs were given out on Wine Day by "practically every state and foreign pavilion . . . wine punch was on tap in the Grape Temple in the Palace of Food Products, and in the booths of Napa, Alameda, Fresno, Sacramento, Santa Clara and Sonoma counties in the California Building." More than 10,000 people were served wine punch in the Grape Temple alone.[88] Additionally, on the mezzanine floor of the exhibit hall, while enjoying their "refreshing sample of California wines," visitors could also "look into the adjacent booths or watch the constantly moving procession of spectators in the aisles beyond."[89] The new imperial vision of tributary processes was elevated, graceful, and effortless; a culture of flow, with wine at its employ, could act as though its empire had been naturally foreordained. The culture of the grape had, not coincidentally, been claiming this all along, ever since the use of tributary tropes and technologies that legitimated and distributed viticultural products from New York and Cincinnati. Flowing streams of media thus matched nicely with the flowing alcohol and fluid motion of a new, liquid imperial space of commerce in the Americas found through the Panama Canal.

Viticulturists were quite accustomed to discussing "flow" long before the emergence of canal technology at the 1915 fair, however. Liquid motion was prevalent in the literature of grape industry specialists. For example, one of the most studied techniques in vine care for decades was the issue of when

and how to prune grapevines. Grapes needed to be pruned every year to ensure a vigorous and abundant crop, and one of the issues in pruning grapes
was the amount of "sap flow" the grape grower would encounter in his vines at
different times of the year. Pruning and sap flow was the subject of one of the
major papers presented to the International Congress of Viticulture at the fair
on July 12 and 13. Viticulturists understood that the most sap flowed through
grapevines with the rush of spring growth, and this flow continued through
harvest. Conversely, the least sap flowed in grapevines from fall through the
beginning of spring. But vineyardists debated how much sap flow was most
beneficial for the cut vine; some believed more sap flow would mean some of
the vigor and "life-energy" of the vine would drain out of the plant, but more
sap could also better cover the wound made by the cut. F. E. Gladwin's paper
at the Pan-Pacific Expo argued for early pruning, thereby not affecting the
heaviest, healthiest flows of sap from their natural course through the vines in
spring and summer. He argued for pruning during the vine's dormancy, well
before spring, because "there is a considerable sap flow within the vine even
before there are external evidences of it."[90] The grapevine was constituted of
flowing liquids, external and internal, visible and invisible, and the best approach was to impede its movement as little as possible. Noticing and following the grapevines' liquid lines was well ingrained in viticultural technique
before the Pan-Pacific Expo, but the fair clearly accentuated this culture of
flow through attention to perennial agricultural seasons, flowing wine, moving rides, and moving pictures.

   This imperial culture of flow was in viticultural exhibits through the display of essential agricultural crops of "imperial abundance," which implicitly
argued that grape culture functioned as a natural and anti-imperial force.
Coleman's Rural World ran an article by Charles Stevenson in 1914 titled
"Value of Exposition to Agriculture: What the Panama-Pacific Exposition
Will Do for Farmers of the World." The article claimed to expound the value
of the fair for agriculture the world over, while detailing the numerous ways in
which U.S. agriculture could be spread around the globe—especially through
the fair and the profit to be taken from its impressive advertising campaigns.
"All wealth is based on agriculture," the author argued, ". . . [it is of] supreme
importance as a factor in order and stability in life. The acquisition of domain
has ever been a prolific source of war—wars of aggression and conquest. But
the Exposition, by making agriculture a means of ample sustenance and more
abundant life, renders unnecessary aggression and conquest of territory."[91]
Both agriculture and the fair itself rendered aggressive national expansion of

territory unnecessary, Charles Stevenson explained, because they produced, extracted, and displayed goods from foreign lands through seemingly non-violent means. Benign but still immensely profitable, new agricultural techniques presented at fairs were more than just a source of profit; they enhanced nations in their own twentieth-century form of Mary Louise Pratt's definition of "anti-conquest."[92] As Stevenson wrote, "Agriculture at an International and Universal Exposition is in reality a promoter of good government and human happiness far and away beyond even increasing products and values."[93] The fair, rather ironically, highlighted itself as the benefactor of many streams of imperialism, while at the same time grandly reinventing the widely accepted pastoral cover story of its brand of expansionism.

The perception of flow and the archaicizing Mission aesthetic presented the grape as natural and "native" in ways that could claim a romantic colonial past, and conveniently continue to mask the violence of 1848 and contemporary forms of ethnic removal embodied in new Californian law and wealth. At the height of California's colonial, imperial, and industrial aggression, winemakers forwarded a pastoral, feminine front. Stanford was a "first of all a farmer"; architects selected the most beautiful architecture and garden habits from its rustic past and combined them with eastern elegance; race removal was seemingly finished and paying off in the ease of flow of new bourgeois lifestyles. In later decades, after Prohibition ended, the industry developed other successful advertising outlets: works of fiction and film, as well as alluring on-site tourism at California's burgeoning wineries. Authors and films highlighted specific elements of vineyard life, combining Old World aesthetics with the grit of fabled Western pioneers. In romantic vineyard fiction, vineyards continued to act as stages for the threat of racial and social mixing—a mixing by the end of each book or film that was cleanly reorganized and sealed. In this chapter and the next, the wall separating nature and culture in American viticultural practice has often appeared as permeable and as fraught as the thin skin of *vinifera* varietals that arguably still make the world's best wine. The many tendrils of California's "destiny" flowed seemingly organically from a main trunk in its grape culture.

6

The Danger of a Vineyard Romance

"TODAY'S WINEGROWERS ON the North American continent are modern pioneers," observes Barbara Ensrud at the beginning of her coffee-table book *American Vineyards* (1988). Indeed, she writes, "The sweep of human history is perhaps at its most powerful in the saga of the pioneers." Sidestepping the "history of politics" in wine, she wrote her book of vineyards to map the "life and culture of those who crossed the continent, who settled the country and chiseled its destiny out of the earth." But more than crafting history, Ensrud asks that when readers visit vineyards, they ponder what life was like when "the country was being explored and settled." More than pioneer homemaking, anywhere grapes are grown is modern cowboy country: "Today grapevines grow where the cattle and buffalo once roamed, and although you do not need a six-gun or a lariat to round up grapes, tending them there is still a gritty task."[1] Ensrud continues her homage to "our pioneer forerunners" and their "destiny" throughout the lushly illustrated tour of contemporary North American vineyards.

Similarly, Ryan Page and Christopher Pomerenke's film *Blood into Wine* (2010), a documentary about rock star Maynard James Keenan's vineyards in northern Arizona, relies on a frontier mythology. The film opens with references to the Wild West (dusty highways, cactus, characteristic whistling), as its theme song repeats, "A cowboy's work is never done." Keenan and his winemakers remark throughout the narrative, "We really are on the frontier. We don't know what's around the next bend," and "Not only are we on kind of a frontier in regards to Arizona, we're on a frontier with viticulture and the idea of expressing this place." Here, the rough-and-tumble mythical world of ranch hands and cattle wrestling has evolved to cast winegrowers as the contemporary West's key adventurers. A winemaker adds, "Pioneers are going to take the brunt of the setbacks and mistakes, but we also have the opportunity to take all the notoriety." Throughout the film, Keenan is anxious to separate his rock-and-roll life from his work in the vineyard, and frame the vineyard as a space of authenticity and groundedness. He explains that the life and friends of a rock star are uncouth in a vineyard—his celebrity a fun diversion, perhaps, but merely an act, and one that is inappropriate in his simple, unassuming "vineyard . . . in dirt." Later, Keenan sums up his philosophy of vineyard authenticity: "Here I am making wine. It's a much more grounded experience than being in a bus [on tour], surrounded by decadence."[2]

With aerial views of vineyards, evocative pictures of stone cellars and antique wine presses, brimming tables of local food, rustic hand tools, and perfectly manicured estates, both the book and the film present winemaking as an enviable profession. Ensrud writes of destiny fulfilled: "And in the fertile valleys of California, land of promise and dreams fulfilled, one sees the triumph of the vine as it covers whole valleys end to end."[3] Vineyards are presented as ideal tourist sites, places to connect with swashbuckling tales of America's past and present founders and fortune-hunters. Yet they are also sites of supreme authenticity, where nothing is an act, and nature determines one's comportment. But why is the contemporary winemaking process so often one of romanticized "settlement" and "pioneering"? Why are the continued comparisons of vineyards to the frontier, and vintners to cowboys, so culturally resonant? And why is winemaking still so often framed as the process of colonization itself in the twenty-first century?

Part of the answer lies in that the contemporary romantic vineyard trope continues to hearken back to Greek myth in an ancient attempt to bridge nature and culture. In tourism, advertising, and fiction, vineyards are still spaces for marking natural and human seasons, exploring mystic nature and then reasserting pragmatic self-control, for setting and crossing boundaries, and ultimately advancing a perceived line of civilization. Additionally, vineyard romances work to cement venerated histories with current lifeways. In vineyards, wine writers insist, the country's "destiny" continues to be "chiseled out of the earth," the land just waiting for the right hands to pick up the right tools, and continue their exalted work. Although the grand sweep of history is always evoked, there is no sense of reality to (or remorse for) continental expansion, indigenous depopulation, or environmental degradation in Ensrud's book; there is no irony in Keenan's cowboyhood. Likening wine growing to exploration and settlement, in these texts and others winemakers and tourists relive the past in a genteel fashion, forgetting the bloodshed and destruction, and instead focus on the rustic fineries of age-old winecraft. Here the past is made attractive, rooted in "local" history and place—as packaged, as aged, and as palatable as fine wine.

In the longer view of fictional vineyard romances, going back almost two hundred years, in addition to frontierism and authenticity, one more constituent theme makes itself clear: a consistent reliance on removing unworthy characters—almost always coded as ethnic and/or low class—from the story and symbolic inheritance of the vineyard. Although *American Vineyards* and *Blood into Wine* are egregious examples of the genre, they frame the larger cultural work of the vineyard romance and tourist experience perfectly. Put together, the three themes present in contemporary wine culture—frontierism, authenticity, and race removal—constitute a conscious and unconscious grappling with America's perennial troubles with expansion and colonization.

Contemporary wine enthusiast magazines, tourism, and advertising strongly and obviously rely on the first two themes, while we must look to fiction and film for wine culture's development of the third. Ostensibly, industry magazines like *Wine Spectator*, *Wine Enthusiast*, and *Wine & Spirits* discuss and promote great wines. The glossy, large-trim monthlies and semimonthlies present information on the current science of wine, recent wine rankings, and in-depth studies of famous and lesser-known wine regions the world over. They often educate readers in how to pair wine with gourmet food prepared by expert chefs. As such, the magazines sell the contemporary good life—and in that stead, they provide ample space and context for lush wine advertising. The November 2011 issue of *Wine Spectator* ran a full-page advertisement from Bridlewood Estate Winery. It reads: "Thirty miles north of Santa Barbara, along California's Central Coast, sits Bridlewood Estate Winery. A picturesque destination all its own, Bridlewood blends modern artistry with rustic, Spanish-style architecture. Our critically acclaimed wines tell the colorful story of the Central Coast: the adventurous spirit, the relaxed lifestyle, and the incredible vineyards."[4] With pictures of Spanish architecture, the coastline, and their wine, Bridlewood here sells vineyard tourism as much as they sell wine. At Bridlewood, wines are the medium of California history, telling a "colorful," nonthreatening story of "picturesque" adventure. With visual and textual themes of place-making, authenticity, and oblique references to cultures past, it's imperialism lite, ever-so-elegantly framed. The set of tropes is the same for a December 2011 Beringer Knights Valley wine advertisement. The tagline reads, "Rugged—Dramatic—Undiscovered," and the text continues, "When Thomas Knight's wagon broke down crossing the California terrain in 1845, it was in a very dramatic place. Before him lay the undiscovered valley that was beautiful but wildly rugged, characteristics that still define the area today. . . . Beringer crafts an iconic wine like no other. . . . The tradition continues with the 2009 Knights Valley Cabernet Sauvignon."[5] Fairly shocking in its denial of the hundreds of thousands of Native peoples that lived in Alta California before statehood, Beringer draws an equation between an early white "pioneer" and their current-day "undiscovered" vintage.

Often using phrases like "pioneering winery owners," *Wine Spectator*'s articles, not just its advertisers, also often rely on a frontier theme. A March 2012 profile of Amador County viticulturist Ann Kraemer begins, "In the nineteenth century, the foothills of the Sierra Nevadas were home to California's Gold Rush, making a few prospectors rich, but leaving many others empty-handed. It's been much the same story for winemakers. Boasting some of the oldest vines in the Golden State, the region's winemaking history runs deep. . . . The nearest town [to Kraemer's vineyard] is Sutter Creek, a bustling mining camp 100 years ago whose main street still looks like a set for a Western."[6] The Wild West, it seems, lives on in top-quality wine. One might argue that this type of promotion is harmless, even cute, on the individual craft winery scale. Yet the mythic revelry rife in contemporary wine culture functions to deny particular portions of the United States' (here specifically California's) actual history—a continued dismissal, justification, and whitewashing of its often violent and exploitative past.

Fictional Grapes

Throughout his fiction and travelogues, James Fenimore Cooper proved a cheerleader for European and U.S. viticulture and was the progenitor of the vineyard romance for an American audience throughout the 1830s. But beyond Cooper, dozens of such formulaic vineyard romances filled nineteenth- and early twentieth-century journal pages. Nathaniel Hawthorne's 1828 *Fanshawe* was deeply embedded in wine culture, while magazines *The Ladies Companion, Casket, The Critic*, and *Harper's Bazaar* all frequently ran short works of romantic fiction with vineyard, grape, and wine themes. Many of these pieces hearkened back to the "Old World" of wine, set in the exotic and dreamy locales of Greece, France, and Italy.[7]

But increasingly throughout the later nineteenth century, the vineyard romance was set closer to home—in the "precapitalist" California of just a few years prior. After the Gold Rush, California's literary and cultural production relied upon pastoral visions that often included scenes of vineyard maintenance and wine production. As had been the case in New York and Ohio, California winegrowers were presented as ideal yeoman farmers, if just a bit more ruggedly Western and "pioneering." While actual wine growing relied on biological circumstance and big money, advertising and fictionalized accounts promoted the vineyard as an uncorrupted space and winemaking as a wholesome practice of the independent, small-scale wine family. These first vineyard romances served to establish the grape's status as a "glamor" or "specialty" crop in California, which continued through Prohibition and into the later twentieth century. The vineyard romance has been largely confined to California, I believe, because the state so quickly outstripped all others in terms of wine production, and still constitutes 90 percent of all U.S. wine made. In addition, since the 1970s, California has been the state most effective in making wine culture an essential part of its tourism machine.

Helen Hunt Jackson's extremely popular *Ramona* (1884) set the tone for this adapted regional genre. The novel is set in southern California, at the rancho of a deceased Mexican general's widow. The rancho extended forty miles west of the San Fernando mountains to the sea. There, "on either hand stretched away other orchards . . . and beyond these, vineyards. . . . A wide straight walk shaded by a trellis so knotted and twisted with grapevines that little was to be seen of the trellis wood-work."[8] It is vintage season throughout the book, and vintners use Old World methods: "There were several vineyards which had not been touched; every hand on the place was hard at work, picking the grapes, treading them out in tubs, emptying the juice into stretched raw-hides swung from cross-beams in a long shed . . . everywhere were to be seen large, flat baskets of grapes drying in the sun. Old women and children were turning these."[9] The grape harvest framed life on the rancho, and every task was completed by hand by the community. The novel romanticizes Spanish colonial life, in which vineyards are central, and against which all other white forms of land use and labor are baldly capitalist and dishonorable. Still, the novel has been described as holding a "racialized nation-building logic," for it focuses on *criollo* elites and encroaching whites.[10] Californios and Yankee developers are both oppressive to indigenous cultures, and there is no imagined future for people of other ethnicities. Characters that fall outside of the competitive racial hierarchy of Californios and whites are ultimately banished to Mexico. *Ramona* was a bestseller for five decades and set a picture of the idealized California vineyard in the minds of many readers.

Similarly, Maria Amparo Ruiz de Burton's *The Squatter and the Don* (1885) constructs the vineyard as a safe, productive place of virtue in the face of threatening interests. Within its agriculturally abundant setting, the novel posits romantic love as the way out of mounting U.S.-Californio conflict and violence. The Alamars, a family of Californio aristocratic planters, are under threat of losing their San Diego–area land to eastern white squatters, the Darrell family. After horning in on the Alamars, Clarence Darrell offers to buy the land to assuage his conscience. At the same time, he falls in love with Mercedes Alamar and proposes. Clarence's father William finds out about the land sale and the wedding, and cancels both. The Alamars are then confronted with their own diminishing wealth, the growing industrialization of the landscape, accelerating westward expansion, and the demands of the impending larger market economy.[11] Don Mariano pleads with local ranchers, "This county is, and has been, and will be always . . . the very best for fruit-raising on the face of the earth. God intended it should be. Why, then, not devote your time, your labor and your money to raising vineyards, fruits and cattle, instead of trusting to the uncertain rains to give you grain crops?" Vineyards, he posits, could be the productive link between the previous and future economies. Mercedes and Clarence wed (there are multiple marriages between Californios and white settlers), and the "happy ending" that Ruiz de Burton offers readers has been described as an effort at imagining a course of racial accommodation in California. This happy ending redoubles in terms of vineyard interests: businessmen come around to the idea of planting grapes in San Diego. Mr. Holman, a rancher, discusses southern California's agricultural potential with his associates: "We have no capital to make large plantations of vineyards or trees, but what has been done proves, conclusively, that for grapes, olives, figs, and in fact all semi-tropical fruits, there is no better country in the world."[12] Ruiz de Burton presents grapes as a thrifty and reliable crop for small planters as well as larger operations in California, and the marriage of Mercedes to Clarence highlights the novel's theme of natural-cum-cultural fecundity. Their union also accentuates the symbolic significance of the "accommodation" of one culture into another—and one economy into another.[13] For *The Squatter and the Don*, the vineyard serves as sacred space for building an authentic life, and as palimpsest for grand, if always elite, historical transitions.

Frank Norris's *The Octopus* (1901) further spread this colonial mythos of California viticulture. The opening pages establish a lovely, pastoral, and feminized Spanish colonial vineyard, set against the big-business ranches of grain and the presence of the railroad in 1880s California. A local centenarian describes the past:

> "De La Cuesta held the grant of Los Muertos in those days. . . . There was no thought of wheat then, you may believe. . . . There was always plenty to eat, and clothes enough for all, and wine, ah, yes, by the vat . . . and also a vineyard, all on Mission grounds. . . . The vine; the Fathers planted those, to provide the elements of the Holy Sacrament. . . . Ah, those were the days. That was the gay life." . . . "This"—he made a comprehensive gesture with his left hand [to the grain and railroads]—"this is stupid."[14]

Several characters in *The Octopus* romanticize wine growing as the opposite of industrial wheat farming, as in *Ramona* and *The Squatter and the Don*. Yet, Norris's novel is set in a moment when wine growing was actually a major agricultural industry in California—a highly networked machine of wealth. In 1889, the value of wheat in California, and of slaughtered cattle and sheep, were $32 million each. Gold and silver totaled $17.5 million, while fruit (excluding wine) ran $16 million, and barley $9 million. Wine and brandy were valued at $8 million, rounding out the top five agricultural products in California, even during a wine depression.[15] Indeed, it was at the turn of the century that the industry matured, patterning itself upon the big-business practices of the Gilded Age. Focusing on vertical and horizontal integration, California wine growing expanded quickly, soon producing 88 percent of American wine.[16] Not coincidentally, these novels set all vineyards' highest work as assuaging difficult historical transitions, legitimating worthy people and their romantic unions, and finally as evidence of a culture and economy in the right. All three novels have enjoyed much recent deeper scholarly attention, and it need not be reiterated here.[17]

By the twentieth century, the typical vineyard romance was strongly reframed around conflicts within vineyards and concerning winemakers. Here, the vineyard romance formula is found to be doing some specific and rather insidious cultural work. Many vineyard romances of the era present their central conflict as a threatened falling away from the ideal vineyard as a space of ultimate virtue. With themes of racial mixing, capitalist debasement, and the struggle to maintain traditional social hierarchies, the vineyard at first reads as a space of threatening historical transitions, a space of possible ethnic mixing. These threats are always calmed, and outliers finally punished. Ultimately, few stories in the subgenre have broken its didactic, strikingly colonial, racist, and reactionary nineteenth-century mold. Put together, they constitute the lasting mythos of Californian grape production.

Several constituent details and plotlines define the twentieth-century vineyard romance. Stories include some combination of six key elements: long moments of vineyard landscape appreciation and love for the aesthetics of healthy grapevines; attempts at translating perceived Old World vineyard and wine customs for a contemporary American audience; attention to the naming and categorization of vines, wines, vineyard lands, and the people that work them; validation of heterosexual romance in vineyards, leading to assumed marriage; inclusion, then marked unmasking, dismissal, or death of characters of low class and/or ethnic minorities; and emphasis on secured land title of vineyards, continued proper yeoman winemaking techniques, and romantic fulfillment for white middle- and upper-class characters. There is no evidence to suggest that vineyard romance writers have simply copied each other's plot points. Instead, the link between the narratives is found deep at the root of what animates grape culture—the importance of tradition and naming, land management, and producing "authentic" wines.

Strikingly, even advocates of Prohibition followed the romantic vineyard code. Nathan Hoyt Sheppard's *Lucile of the Vineyard: A Temperance Romance* (1915), for example, used its melodramatic structure to highlight "the curse" of rum and wine on California. Sheppard states in the introduction that he "sincerely prays [the novel] will, in a small degree, be to the poor slave of drink what *Ramona* was to the fear-enslaved Red Man and what *Uncle Tom's Cabin* was to the legally-enslaved Black Man."[18] Although it was a story written to convince Californians to vote in favor of Prohibition, many of its elements mimic the subgenre's standard formula. In *Lucile of the Vineyard*, northern California valleys are just as beautiful as they are in other vineyard romances: "a level plain, as fair as Paradise, caught the eye, entrancing it with the sight of thousands of golden, luscious grapes," and fall harvest festivals ensue.[19] Yet throughout the novel, prohibitionists rage against those sympathetic to wine. The book attempts to reconcile wine controversy perspectives through the figure of Rector Newhall, an English clergyman, who at first acts in favor of moderate wine drinking and in support of local wine families. Rector Newhall asks prohibitionists, "What shall we do with our neighbors' wineries? . . . Look out upon this beautiful paradise Valley, the holy field of man, the vast vineyard of the Lord. Shall we wreck his wineries, root up and despoil its sweet harvest of luxuriant grapes? Nothing can be grown upon this soil in their stead."[20] Yet soon, the minister's family and other characters are carried away by drink: his daughter Lucile is ravished, major wine families are ruined and their patriarchs crushed, and Newhall resigns from the ministry. Newhall later buys a small house attached to a vineyard. He manages the vineyard and cares for the widow of a great winemaker, soon realizing that the

> wine-business of man that had ended in tragedy and death would, in future years, be the food-business of God. . . . He began immediately a thorough investigation in to the commercial products, other than fermented wine, that could be profitably made from the grape crop of this great vineyard. . . . Not only could this vast field of grape-vines, by proper treatment in grafting and otherwise, be made to produce the most enticing table grapes and the best and sweetest raisin food, but that the pure, unfermented grape juice extracted for these luscious grapes was in demand. . . . Profits from this sale would far exceed the profits from the sale of fermented wine.[21]

Newhall soon sets the community at work "cultivating, grafting, rooting out the old and replanting new varieties." The former rector uses the profits from his newly replanted vineyards to begin ministering again, this time in the "hot-bed of the world's great cauldron of evil, San Francisco . . . [proceeding to assist] the lost souls in the slums of the wicked Bay City nearby." Newhall's daughter Lucile marries a new minister in town, Reverend Cecil Manning, and they also move to San Francisco, taking up ministering in the slums: "Here, Black and Yellow, Red and White, old and young, male and female intermingled indiscriminately, like wriggling, crawling worms in a reeking cess-pool of black, nauseating corruption. . . . What a hideous scene of wild Bacchanalian revelry! Here were the pandemonium of mad delirium, the vortex of darkest hell."[22] Although the Manning and Newhall families labor in San Francisco, they are still "workers in the Lord's vineyard," and seek total ethnic separation. The families then take a trip to Europe. While they are traveling, San Francisco suffers a devastating earthquake. Lucile and Cecil return to redevelop the destroyed "city by the Gate of Gold [into] the New Paradise on Earth."[23] Thus, God's righteousness wreaks havoc on San Francisco, "the vortex of darkest hell," but opens a space for ministry by devoted followers who have stepped away from alcohol.

In addition to the physical city of San Francisco, also destroyed by the end of the novel are all wine-producing grapes in California's valleys, as well as all racially diverse spaces of "Bacchanalian revelry" in the city. Wine drinking here is clearly a harbinger of racial and social "corruption," and both the wine drinking and racial mixing occurring in San Francisco are set to be eradicated by the now-pious (and white) central characters. Agricultural landscapes are finally purified through their happy replanting by sober, industrious families of English, Scotch-Irish, and French extraction. Although the very presence of "Black, Yellow, and Red" souls in San Francisco is clearly disconcerting to the narrator and characters in the story, the racial mixing (indeed, like "wriggling, crawling worms") that it assumes redoubles the threat of American civilization's decline. While Sheppard aligns his book with the far more racially sympathetic *Ramona* and *Uncle Tom's Cabin,* bloodline and separation of human and viticultural "stocks" are key in *Lucile of the Vineyard,* as in other vineyard romances. The novel finally shows that the dream of the American vineyard as a positively capitalist, perfectly productive horticultural space was perpetuated across contemporary ideological divisions, with or without the presence of wine. As the grape in the late nineteenth and early twentieth centuries was sustaining and growing its place as one of the most profitable crops in California, vineyards were also the site of sweeping melodramatic romance, laying claim to a preindustrial vision of northern European, white, heteronormative life and labor.

While the previous Spanish colonial romances had been set in vineyards, later California vineyard romances such as Sheppard's increasingly became *about* the vineyard. These stories focus on vineyards as contested spaces—spaces in which ideal American national identity and white landed investments are at risk. Vineyard ownership problems here are a microcosm for the larger cultural dangers of national expansion. Unknown people, disputed landscapes, foreign flora, and alien property rights abound. Tellingly, the growing number of vineyard romances paralleled the growth of California vineyard tourism, which developed throughout the late nineteenth century and exploded in the postwar period.

Land Possession in the Vineyard Romance

At the turn of the century, San Francisco Hearst newspaper columnist Frona Eunice Wait (later Frona Eunice Wait Colburn) was a prime mover of the vineyard romance. Also a fiction writer and socialite, Wait initially galvanized California wine tourism in her *Wines and Vines of California, or a Treatise on the Ethics of Wine Drinking* (1889). Her 215-page illustrated guide covered the art of winemaking, the history of the industry, wine-drinking etiquette, wine as a "temperance agent," and "enterprising and prominent" wine men in California. The wine culture manual was also a tour book: it included chapters on the "banner wine making counties" of Napa, Sonoma, the Livermore District, Los Angeles, Santa Anita, Fresno, as well as "lesser" wine counties. Wait's book was thus concerned with the twin practices of educating the Anglo public in wine appreciation and growing California wine tourism, and provides a detailed map of the growth of the transplanted Euro-American wine experience across California. The book had no true predecessor, and it took decades for anything similar to appear. Wait was soon one of the most prominent wine writers of the Gilded Age.[24]

Similar, specific themes emerge in both Wait's fiction and nonfiction, themes repeated throughout much vineyard romance literature. In *Wines and Vines*, Wait deliberately compares new grape stock to immigrant human stock: "Some of these conditions [in California] of climate and soil and altitude favor France and Italy, some Germany and Greece. . . . So, to a great extent, the result here will be a new one, like the individuality of a new race of human beings; but, when science and skill have been exhausted in the preparation of the juices, we shall make good enough wines and have a new nomenclature, and our ranches, with their pretty Spanish names, may sound as sweetly in the ears of the connoisseur of the next generation as do Roussillon or Amontillado now in our own."[25] The issue of naming—of people, land, and wines—is central to Wait's work, as in the vineyard romances before and after it. Wait is interested in keeping the "pretty Spanish names" of vineyards but believes that only northern European vines, science, skill, and laborers of northern European extraction will make them flourish. This adaptation of wines and people ultimately demanded a new "nomenclature" for California viticultural land as well. The new vines and wines, of pure western European (French, Italian, German, Grecian) stock but planted in colonial Spanish soil, here naturally mimic the identities of their human cultivators.

In addition to her famously successful nonfiction wine travel guide, Wait's novel *In Old Vintage Days* (1937) epitomizes the fictional vineyard romance. The story includes requisite scenes of bringing in the harvest, fall harvest parades, dinners, wine pressing, and other ritual viticultural activities. Set in the "gay nineties," the novel takes place in a Napa vineyard and focuses on its changing ownership, wine trade politics, two unrequited love stories, and the threat of racial mixing. A waif of Hispanic and Indian descent, Chonita Tiburcio, is the granddaughter of a "proud Don" with fading family ties to local vineyards. Chonita is duped into a false common-law marriage with a wine business scoundrel, JJ Simeon. There is public speculation that JJ has "Hebrew ancestry": "JJ has a yellow streak in his make-up. Harry Sanger declares that JJ told him that he is not a Jew. He claims to be an Armenian and that no one knows his right name."[26] Other characters are unnerved by JJ's temper, ruthless business practice, his looseness with women and guns, but most of all, his questionable ethnic identity. Yet Chonita worships JJ, the "miserable cur," and has an illegitimate son by him.[27] JJ keeps house with Chonita but soon proceeds to woo a lovely wine tester of German ancestry, Inga Hertzen. Inga has a gifted palate and professionally blends most of the wines in the valley. Her family owns Hertzen Cellars, though shakily, and Inga, while retaining traditional Old World values and style of dress ("blonde braids wound around her head"),[28] has lived in California at Hertzen Cellars all her life. JJ soon proposes to Inga; Chonita eventually confronts Inga with the facts, and Inga calls off the engagement. Chonita, intemperate and disconsolate as the typically racialized and helpless woman, is so heartbroken that she drowns herself in the sea and leaves her mixed-race and "nameless" child in her aging, impoverished parents' care.

Enter the "true Yankee," a somewhat rigid New Englander, John Iverson. Very wealthy and in his late twenties, John is in love with Inga but can not let her know until she gets over JJ. The scoundrel, after attempting to burn down Hertzen Cellars and kill one of the workers, gets his comeuppance and goes to prison for many years. Finally John and Inga are united, and their marriage saves Hertzen Cellars: John's fortunes buy the vineyards outright, and he has special skills in maintaining vineyard agriculture. With Inga's skills in tasting and blending, they run the operation together, producing small vintages of high purity and quality, never selling to big firms, nor transporting their grapes to New Orleans or New York to be blended with other "nameless," questionable crops. Chonita's body is never found, and John and Inga decide to give Chonita's illegitimate Hispanic-Armenian child "a name" and "provide for his future."[29] Inga and John thereby erase the potential namelessness of both their wine and a local child. Yet significantly, John and Inga do not promise to love Chonita's child or fully accept him into the family—he will not be the vineyard's future proprietor.

As in most vineyard romances, the larger agenda of *In Old Vintage Days* seems to be battles concerning vineyard ownership and moments detailing wine production and enjoyment. Clearly, the novel's moral stems from the positive actions taken by good, noble, pure-blooded characters; they battle industry scoundrels who look for profit through strong-arming simple vineyard families. The story thus reiterates the genre's fetish for hardworking white wine families and the terroir to which they are tied. Yet, a more disturbing narrative is also propagated widely throughout the California vineyard romance. *In Old Vintage Days* ends with many disappearances: evil capitalists recede, as do the Hispanic, Indian, and Chinese families and workers, who all fade into the distance. JJ is unmasked as a cur, in classic Dionysian mythic fashion. Ethnic characters of all types have no place in the vineyard's future. Meanwhile, the proud, white, heterosexual couple of German and New England descent come to the fore and are assured of continuous vineyard ownership. Inga and John sustain a now-idyllic and totally white Californian vineyard, through a classically gendered division of labor, no less. Like many other novels of the period whose stories include ethnic communities, Wait's characters of color and ethnic diversity "appear to disappear" in the storyline in light of new white, pure, and efficient ownership and viticultural expertise.[30] Note that their labor is noncapitalistic: their wines are made in small batches, only of the highest quality and purity, like their secured future bloodline.

In the story, JJ, Chonita, and her elder family members die or disappear. As in many other vineyard romances, they did not exhibit the requisite rationality and restraint for citizenship or vineyard ownership.[31] Chonita's son assumedly assimilates to white life in Napa Valley, "named" by the new owners. The issue of naming, in terms of both namelessness and name development, weaves throughout these stories as a trope for grape stock, ownership of the land, and a method by which people become more rooted to the soil. Naming here is a process of development, of a culture's becoming naturalized through generations of action in a particular place. The land's identity through being named, as well as people's development of their titles, sets up for Californian grape culture a seemingly "natural" distinctiveness and standing that is also forever seeking further proper social cultivation.

The trope of naming and hierarchy points back to the thrust of the original American historical romance, or Cooperian code. Here we have attempts at establishing a literature and landscape that legitimized American civilization in Old and New World contexts. As a melodramatic text, *In Old Vintage Days* continues the goal of the genre to "confirm the necessity of order, continuity,

and rationality."[32] Moral instruction is offered to the audience through a series of appropriate, and inappropriate, examples of social behavior in the
vineyard. Making a good marriage is often the ultimate example of positive
social behavior. Again elaborating on the idea of vines being metaphors for
the people who plant them, *In Old Vintage Days* broaches the topic of wine
blending resembling a marriage. Inga has a conversation with another cellar
worker:

> "Don't the French celebrate the marriage of wines, when they happen
> to have a noteworthy vintage year?"
> "If these new juices don't blend properly we could call that a viti-
> cultural divorce with you acting as judge."
> "I solemnly promise to sever the bonds in each and every case,"
> laughed Inga.[33]

Marriage, as a major western naming ceremony and social contract, is reiter-
ated and celebrated with seasonal wine creation. A popular ritual in France,
here it is broached as a possible new rite for Anglo-derived Californian wine
culture. Wait's specific attention to the names (and thereby assumed lineages
and proven quality of wines) makes overt and constant the attention to name
and status in matters of marriage. Heterosexual love and marriage, along with
wine growing, are here models for national consensus, landed wealth, and
social power. The redemptive value of white women's bodies—once safely
married and landed—suggests the patriarchal white family as a template for
future social control. As in the classic myth of Bacchus, women "yoked" to
civilization through marriage are no longer a threat to society. Their "natural"
predilection for danger, especially through Dionysian release, ceases to be a
threat. Ultimately, women fulfilling their maternal roles in these novels further the solidification of territorial conquest.[34] The consolidation and control
of good white Euro-American families, good wine, and good white-owned
landscapes takes place across several symbolic national and cultural registers.

Critic Amy Kaplan has called this stockpiling of the themes of marriage, domesticity, whiteness, and land acquisition in American melodrama the trope of "manifest domesticity." Domesticity was central to not
only late-century imperial discourses of "improvement" but real, landed
nation-building practices. Indeed, the discourses of domesticity and nation-
building in fact reinforced one another.[35] In the vineyard romance, domestic
life—a set of civilizing aesthetics and practices, and a way to confirm land

ownership—rewrites national norms as ones of healthy housekeeping and communal celebration around harvests. Whiteness and white land ownership are challenged, but ultimately win out. Manifest domesticity thus stems directly from the classic construction of manifest destiny: the moral, economic, racial, and spatial dimensions of manifest destiny are all fulfilled by the vineyard romance subgenre, with shockingly little change over time.

In this vein, the vital cultural work that vineyard melodrama often performs is that of legitimating white territorial expansion. The (at first troubled, but in the end strikingly clear) formation of white families is codified into a template for an idealized white California and nation through several texts. In *Ramona*, Mercedes marries Clarence and secures her family's white status; in *Lucile of the Vineyard*, Lucile marries Cecil and they set to work cleaning up the "cess-pool of black, nauseating corruption" of ethnic mingling; in *In Old Vintage Days*, Inga marries John and the family vineyard is saved, while JJ and Chonita disappear. The necessary excising of Chonita from *In Old Vintage Days* (and other characters of color from later vineyard stories) is written as civilization's doing away with shifty—now defined as extranational and questionable—bodies and interests. Inga rises over Chonita; the land and the living to be made from it are finally wrested from colonial Spanish dons by new, thoroughly Anglo "true Yankee[s]." Elite white identity and land ownership are affirmed in every case. Later vineyard romances follow these plot arcs remarkably similarly, even though the wine industry was in rapid transformation throughout the century.

With the end of national Prohibition in 1933, winegrowers attempted to pick up where they had left off in growing California's wine economy. Focusing on vertical and horizontal integration, in 1934, California grape businessmen formed the Wine Producers Association, an organization much like the previous California Wine Association, which had been a near-monopoly at the turn of the century. Within a few years, growers and vintners also formed cohesive marketing organizations: the Wine Institute and the Wine Advisory Board. The following decades were marked by multiple market consolidations. Suppliers united with distillers, and large Eastern liquor companies— including Seagram's, Schenley, and National—made major investments in California wineries. Increasingly through the 1960s, large distillers controlled half of the commercial wine production in the nation, and "big wine" continued its expansion. At the same time, postwar prosperity led to gains for smaller California wine families. Starting in the 1950s, there was a dramatic rise in table wine sales in California, with other states following through the next decade. A larger American middle class, increasingly on the move in automobiles, was spending more of its growing disposable income on short trips to family farms in California's newly codified "wine country."[36]

In this context, Alice Hobart's *The Cup and the Sword* (1942) sticks close to the standard vineyard romance script yet seems almost conscious of the crippling weight of its increasingly problematic local racial trajectory. Set in Napa Valley during and after Prohibition, the novel centers on the extended family of Jean-Philippe Rambeau, an aging Catholic Frenchman whose vineyards and wines were among the most respected in the state during the high times of the 1880s and 1890s. As patriarch, he oversees three generations of Rambeaus, who have aggressively intermarried with the Fairons, another powerful California wine family. Several years into Prohibition, the vintners are struggling to keep their empires intact. While waiting out the national dry spell, they sell small amounts of legal wine for religious and medicinal purposes, and seek to grow their table grape and grape juice trade. While the novel opens as a fairly standard vineyard romance, with many scenes in mysterious vine-laden gardens at night, stolen kisses in barrel rooms and behind the winery, and picnics in the vineyards, by the end of the book, only one marriage in four is happy. These families' marriages have secured land rights and formally continued the Rambeau legacy, but in the end the main characters are dissatisfied with each other and with their life choices. They yearn for other things and lead rather loveless existences.

The narrative centers on Elizabeth Rambeau, in her early twenties and the granddaughter of Jean-Philippe. Raised English, Elizabeth moves to California after a disappointing and embarrassing affair. As a new and beautiful family member, she is immediately presented with three possibilities for marriage: John Rambeau, a feisty, racist, but physically alluring first cousin training to be a vintner; Andrew Fairon, a quiet, loving, hardworking first cousin training to be a viticulturist; and Henri de Swanaña, the stepson of one of Elizabeth's aunts and a deceased Spanish don. Henri is a "lazy" and "ugly" but rich heir to his family's colonial Spanish vineyard. Family members attempt to engineer the marriage of Elizabeth to Henri to grow their fortunes, but Elizabeth finds his "Spanish blood" distasteful: "Elizabeth glanced at Henri. His long wide nostrils were pulsing. She felt repelled . . . [he was not] healthy, normal."[37] In an effort to escape both Henri's and John's advances, she elopes with Andrew. Their marriage is one of four in the novel: Henri soon marries Elizabeth's French stepsister; Buz Dietrick, an ethnic German girl impregnated by John Rambeau, seeks security and a father for her child by marrying

Luigi, a recent Italian immigrant; and John's sister, Monica Rambeau, marries Jewish Nathan Frostner for love, initially to the serious dismay of her family. Among these marriages, only Monica and Nathan's is happy: they produce several children and become the center of the family for the future generation. Henri and his wife disappear for several years to tour Europe, returning when Henri concocts a plan to cripple the Rambeau estate in order to buy it for a pittance. Buz and Luigi's relationship is tempestuous in the early years, as Luigi finds out that John is the father of Buz's child. He explodes in rage one night and shoots John, who becomes lame but is not killed. Buz and Luigi escape to Mexico and through the years are transients throughout Mexico and California, running from what they imagine to be John's wrath and their possible arrest. They live a mean existence, but end up somewhat content, especially when their relationship is compared to others in the novel.

The novel's racial hierarchy is made clear through these marriages and in the understanding that French, English, and old-stock German families have all easily become "American" and righteously defend their status in vineyard land sales and wine deals. Italians, Armenians, Spanish Californios, and recently arrived German Russians are far from white ethnic inclusion and are generally distasteful to the now "American" stock. When the older, powerful families disagree with the business decisions of the new immigrant houses, their first resort is intimidation. John leads a group of self-defined "Americans," calling themselves the "night riders," who don masks to terrorize newly arrived families by tying the male heads of households to the rear fenders of cars and dragging the men through the valley. Violence, as John's friend explains, is indeed "the only way to make good Americans out of foreigners. They don't understand anything but force."[38] This brutality is chastised within the course of the novel—John, as the leader of the night riders, is found out, cut off from family inheritance, and does not snare Elizabeth as his bride. Yet he does ultimately rise to prominence and respect in the developing California Wine Consortium (a thinly veiled CWA). John and Elizabeth share a continuing attraction—he pleads with her later in life to leave Andrew and run away with him, arguing that they are "from the same stock" physically and mentally. But John's racism, night raids, bootlegging, arson, price fixing, and efforts to control railway cars distributing the family's grapes, not to mention his generally sour demeanor, make him unable to form lasting bonds with anyone.

Over the years, Elizabeth and Andrew grow increasingly alienated from one another. Andrew loves Elizabeth desperately, yet he never lives up to her cosmopolitan needs. Due to her constant neglect, he is driven to abandon her before the birth of their second son, and he wanders Europe for many years. Elizabeth is forced to tend the vineyards herself and learns several difficult lessons. When she attempts to smoke in the barrel rooms, a hired German foreman knocks the cigarette from her hand: "'You are dumb. Wine iss—how shall I say? I tell you it iss living. It takes a breath. You smoke. It breathes in the smoke.'... The incident fixed itself in Elizabeth's mind. Fritz, old Philippe, and Andrew, too, did not see these rare dry wines just as a commodity out of which to make money. Until now she had seen them only commercially."[39] Through her labor in the vineyards and wine rooms, Elizabeth comes to appreciate the deeper sense of wine culture imparted through her family lineage. She learns patience with and devotion to wines and people. She writes several times to her estranged husband, who finally ventures home after being seriously wounded in the Spanish Civil War. At the end of the novel, she and Andrew have patched together a life in their vineyards. The land, the labor, and the process of making wine have "settled" her into being a good mother and wife, and finally bound her to the family's future, but she remains deeply unfulfilled.

The Cup and the Sword thus adheres to the landed aspects of the typical vineyard romance: good land and good wines are the only way to legitimate a family's fortune and standing in America. The novel ends with the looming threat of a second world war, yet the war also draws the family back together in ways they had not been close for many years. In all the surrounding ethnic and familial strife, the Rambeaus' central struggle is keeping their land intact: "Land!... If he [Philippe] could not live on in his family, it suddenly seemed he could live on in the land. Whatever his sons and grandsons might do, there would be the land. Some day this region he had developed might be the greatest wine-producing district of the world, his name immortalized in the Rambeau vineyards."[40] In the landed aspect of the vineyard romance, then, the characters and novel proclaim success.

Success in the social and marital realm is far more difficult and ultimately in question, however. *The Cup and the Sword* sets many social problems in the path of the typical vineyard romance and its characters: first, the national strife of Prohibition and multiple wars weaken the family and the business. Second, ethnic tensions are rife. Unworthy, common, and swarthy foreign winemakers populate the fringes of the narrative, and main characters' loathsome violent attacks on the defenseless blight the novel's central "American" families. Third, however much the extended Rambeau-Fairon family originally desired multiple intermarriages between their second- and third-generation offspring, most marriages in the book are ultimately unhappy. Indeed, all the unions but one are dejected in the grandchildren's generation. In their parents' generation, one Rambeau sister's husband had a multi-year affair with a Rambeau brother's wife, which, unbeknownst to anyone but them, produced Monica, the one granddaughter who goes on to have a happy marriage. This marriage and the satisfaction it represents is particularly striking, as it is the only marriage in the third generation of the Rambeau-Fairon family that does not include a blood relative—instead, Monica marries Jewish Nathan Foster. Andrew and Elizabeth, among the most central characters, marry "within the third degree of blood kinship without permission,"[41] and while this marriage preserves and extends the Rambeau name and land, its obvious incest, one-sided love, and final crippling of one of the few redeeming male characters ultimately bring a bitter harvest.

Throughout *The Cup and the Sword*, Hobart seems to be reconstructing the early twentieth-century vineyard romance as its own endgame: families here feel compelled to keep their vineyards within their own (white, American, and now quite inbred) ranks. Indeed, within the novel, there are no real alternatives, as marrying a more recent ethnic immigrant—whose speech is poor, pockets empty, and morals loose—is untenable. The possibility of Elizabeth's marrying the repugnant and avaricious son of a Spanish don is set up to be dismissed: she is "repulsed" by him, and he is the most evil figure in a novel full of unfriendly and manipulative relations. Although the Rambeaus at first will the union of Elizabeth and Henri, and Henri ultimately marries Elizabeth's stepsister, the marriage does not produce children and so is also symbolically failed. Henri's angry retribution reigns over their union throughout the course of the novel. Elizabeth must protect herself from Henri's primary romantic assault, and finally his economic and landed attacks on her inherited vineyards. Driven by a scorned sexual predator's fury, greed, an unattractive mien, and mixed blood, Henri embodies the threat of the evil ethnic "other." While ethnic "others" populate the entire book, its specter is found nowhere so deep and total as in the figure of the elite Californio. The happy ending of romantic race relations through vine culture penned by Ruiz de Burton in 1885 is here, in 1942, preposterous. Under Henri's unwanted advances, the once-worldly Elizabeth is forced deep into the arms of her dissolving family and has to make a hasty decision between an alluring but disturbed and violently racist cousin or a cousin that has dedication, fortitude, and love, but no other appeal to her.

The Cup and the Sword finally points to the brittle reality of other stories in its genre. John's entreaty to Elizabeth that they are "from the same stock," in a novel concerned with the health of grapevines and the best choices in rootstock and hybrid grape varieties, rings as distressing and wrong, as do most of the marital unions in the family. The characters are stuck between very few options—at once crying out for "new stock" while at the same time discarding all recently arrived and otherwise colonially landed options. In the end, after Prohibition, the Rambeau name and lands are indeed intact publicly, their land and their wine defended, and they are once again set to prosper. But privately the family disintegrates, caught in an eddy of pain and bad decisions. There is no final, magical unmasking or revelation of love that can fix this ultimately debilitated vineyard romance. Instead, following the code, the novel finally buckles under its own racist weight. Depressing though the novel was, Universal International Pictures made *The Cup and the Sword* into a film in 1959. With a simplified and further romanticized plot, and retitled *This Earth Is Mine,* the film starred Rock Hudson and Jean Simmons. Like other works in the genre, a key phrase recurs throughout the film: as good vines are blended to make good wines, "good bloods are blended to make a good family." *This Earth Is Mine* received mixed critical reviews, with some critics stating that the details of Napa winemaking were its best feature. The film otherwise "grossed $30-$40 million" and enjoyed box-office success. Its beautiful cinematography marked a new chapter in the popular imagination about life in California vineyards.[42]

The Contemporary Vineyard Romance

California wine grew increasingly glamorous during the last four decades of the twentieth century. Wineries big and small began paying more attention to architectural amenities for tourists, incorporating gardens, elite restaurants, well-appointed tasting rooms, and gift shops into their estates. By the mid-1970s, sales of California table wine outpaced previously popular fortified wines; in ten years, table wine production had grown by 200 million gallons, three times what it was a decade earlier. California also gained more than one hundred wineries in the decade after 1965, constituting a "wine boom" in the late 1960s and early 1970s. In Napa County alone from 1965 to 1979, sixty-nine new wineries were established. The national wine industry in these years was also expanding 10 to 15 percent annually, and wine consumption grew nearly on pace, at 58 percent. Constituting a new California "gold rush," investors of all kinds flocked to California wine and its growing tourist trade.[43] Large wine businesses continued their well-worn pattern of consolidation into the late 1980s. Large acquisitions marked the 1970s: Nestlé bought Beringer, Guild Wineries bought Glen Alden, and Coca-Cola bought Sterling Vineyards. In the 1980s, Schenley purchased Rodney Strong, Nabisco bought Heublein, and Seagram's bought Sterling.[44] California wine grew larger, and seemingly more dazzling, each passing year.

The literary romantic dreamscape of California wine kept up with real industry growth. A number of epic vineyard romances were published in 1980, and the majority worked within the standard conventions of the genre, while seemingly conscious of the twentieth-century need for its revision. Anita Clay Kornfeld's *The Vintage* tells the story of three generations of a Napa Valley Italian wine family, the Donatis, spanning the late 1890s to the 1960s, the patriarchs of each seeking their fortunes in the northern California grape and wine trade. Building and sustaining the Donati family's Spring Mountain estate and securing good human stock in the Donati family line remains the basic premise, as in most romances. Yet the novel consciously confronts the racism family members encountered in the late nineteenth century, sympathizing with California's newcomers. They deal with overt threats of violence from the Ku Klux Klan and understated prejudices from local families in Napa's high society. Adam Donati, the novel's central patriarch, seeks to marry the rich young Napa socialite Sara Reynolds. Violence and family stonewalling prevent them from marrying for several years, in which time Sara has Adam's son out of wedlock, and Adam has two other sons with another woman. Eventually, Sara and Adam are wed. Theirs is a happy marriage, but their three boys do not get along. David, Sara's biological son, is the only son to stay in Napa Valley and inherits Spring Mountain.

David marries Lilliana, a poor Italian girl from town. While Sara and Adam approve of the union, many notice that Lilliana cannot "keep up" with Spring Mountain society and her household chores the way a middle-class woman would. Regardless, David and Lilliana are happy and raise three girls. Their third daughter attends the University of California at Davis to become a winemaker and inherit Spring Mountain. This third daughter, Victoria, soon falls in love with a "wetback"—Jerrod James, whose mother was Mexican and whose white Texan father disowned him before he was born. David finds Jerrod hiding out on the Spring Mountain property, and desperately in need of a good laborer, David tells Jerrod he will hire him if he changes his name to Carlo Carducci and acts the part of a distant cousin. David explains that Jerrod/Carlo looks more Italian than Mexican anyway, and Carlo "passes" easily in Napa Valley. David senses the attraction between Carlo and Victoria, however, and ensures that they are never in the same place for too long: he sends Carlo to do business in other towns, and Victoria is sent to finishing school, and then to UC Davis for her winemaking degree. When they can catch moments together, Carlo and Victoria have a torrid love affair. After many years of their relationship remaining undetected, David comes around to the idea of Victoria and Carlo creating a family, but it is finally Victoria that cannot come to grips with Carlo's true identity, and spurns his advances. One night, Carlo again seeks out Victoria on Spring Mountain to propose, and to warn her that grape workers' union roughs have been planning violent and destructive trouble in the area. Victoria brushes Carlo off once again, and later that night finds her estate on fire. As she rushes to put out the flames, she hears Carlo calling for help—he had been stabbed in the back and is near death. Victoria rushes him to the hospital, and through his weeks of surgery and recovery, she realizes she does love him. He will not see her, however, and after his recovery, he slips away to escape embarrassment. The novel ends with Victoria disappointed, but hopeful that Carlo will return for the fall crush, as he had many times before.

The Vintage thus includes most of the stock attributes of the typical vineyard romance, yet is a bit more conscious of their role as plot devices in its attempt to overturn the racism enacted upon Italian immigrants. But the same courtesy is not paid to characters of Mexican ancestry. Jerrod Jones, a Mexican American, is forced to don the mask of Carlo Carducci to associate with second- and third-generation, and now considered white, Italian Americans in postwar America. Rather ironically, Hispanic wine growing traditions in early Alta California are nowhere referenced in the novel: Jerrod is simply a "wetback," a foreigner in a space and with a people that have actively forgotten the land's contested history. Although the novel narrates the discrimination against Italians, and eventually triumphs in an Italian family's rise to vineyard success, it repeats a similar racism against a different group just one generation later. The narrative voice, while sympathetic to Jerrod's plight, is clearly still not sure that Jerrod is worthy of the vineyard and its family. For example, one of the motivations attracting Jerrod/Carlo to Victoria is his base desire to take part in his own estranged white father's wealth: "I asked myself if I'm loving you, dreaming about you, wanting you every day of my life just so I think I can be inside that big house of my father's."[45] Jerrod is possibly using Victoria as a stepping stone to higher racial status, and thus has not earned rightful entry into the family line, and does not comprehend the depth of white "heritage" upon which he trods. This is the same type of racism that haunted Victoria's grandfather, Adam, as he attempted to woo Sara. Sara's mother wrote to Adam: "You do not apparently understand that in this country, heritage means a great deal to some of us; we do not accept just anyone who steps off the boat and decides he is free to marry whom he so chooses!"[46] The novel does not find a resolution as to whether a Mexican American will finally be accepted into the Donati family, take ownership of Spring Mountain, or produce heirs of mixed heritage. There may be hope, but Jerrod is left out as the novel takes its final stock.

The many elements of the vineyard romance—landscape appreciation; the translation of Old World agricultural and cultural traditions into the New World; the issues of naming and combining vines, land, and people; and the vineyard's imperturbably yeoman and authentic place within a debased capitalist system—all remain hallmarks of the subgenre into the twenty-first century. The racism and class prejudice endemic to most vineyard romances also continues; characters of color are still regularly dismissed from romantic possibility with whites. Furthermore, the narrative disallowal of ownership and proprietorship of future vineyards by racial minorities continues as well. This veiled racism and class prejudice remains alive and well in the twenty-first century vineyard romance, as evidenced in the acclaimed films *Sideways* and *Bottle Shock*.

Sideways (2004) at first presents itself as a modern-day vineyard anti-romance.[47] Miles (Paul Giamatti), a shlubby, divorced, alcoholic eighth-grade English teacher and frustrated writer from San Diego, treats his friend Jack (Thomas Hayden Church), a semi-failed actor, to a week in Santa Barbara wine country for a final fling as a bachelor. Jack is engaged to be married to Christine, a rich, thin Armenian American woman whose father is offering Jack entry into his "property business" and will "provide some stability" to Jack's life and finances. While Miles's intention is to have a relaxing week sampling wines and playing golf, Jack's goal is to "get my nut on this trip . . . get laid before I get married on Saturday. . . . We're here to fuckin' party, man!" They meet Maya (Virginia Madsen), a blonde, curvy, articulate waitress studying for her master's in horticulture, and Stephanie (Sandra Oh), a sommelier at a small winery, with dark hair and Asian features. Jack easily falls in with Stephanie for a raucous weekend fling: Stephanie for Jack is "not uptight or controlling, she's just cool." While Miles has a bit more trouble with Maya, they have an enviable time in wine country for a few days.

Sideways initially upends some traditional approaches to vineyard narratives. Miles, a constantly lying alcoholic, is the central character, while Jack's sexual deception grows throughout the film. This lack of groundedness and authenticity in the film's central protagonists is striking, when for centuries winemaking and wine drinking have, without fail, been presented in fiction as an authentic expression of the landscape and its (yeoman, trustworthy) people. While many wineries in *Sideways* are presented as deeply authentic natural extensions of local wine-growing processes, one example—Miles's and Jack's stop at Frass Canyon—is presented instead as a "joke." In the parking lot, wine is poured through a large hose into a tanker on a semi's tractor-trailer; inside, there is an overflowing wine fountain and a kitschy mish-mash of pseudoclassical wine ornamentation; a flock of tourists suck down wine that tastes to Miles "rancid, like the back of an L.A. school bus" and paw through overstuffed displays of branded merchandise. Here, wine is an alienated commodity and the vineyard is a disingenuous tourist space, a setting for Miles to experience another mental breakdown after receiving word that his novel has again failed to find a publisher. Similarly, both male characters have several moments when they are seen lying, stealing, or making choices that are not consistent with who they purport to be. These deceptions and Miles's depressing career as a junior-high teacher are contrasted with the seemingly genuine and fulfilling romantic experiences that he has with Maya in wine country. The question of authenticity, in wines and in human life choices, is thus central to the plot and is not cleanly resolved. We learn that winemaking and wine appreciation, like people's life choices, can be both authentic and debased—a marked contrast to other vineyard romances, wherein the authenticity of the landscape and its people is assumed and/or unquestioningly resolved by the story's close.

Yet there are several ways in which *Sideways* does conform to the standards of the subgenre. It continues the genre's classic anthropomorphizing of wines and landscapes as people and further judges characters' personas in wine terms. *Sideways* presents each character as having various appreciable wine characteristics: to Jack, Stephanie "smells different, she tastes different"—she is above all a new gustatory experience. And about Jack's escapades, Miles says, "this whole thing has gone sour," like an ill-tended vintage. Further, in one of the most romantic moments of the film, Miles and Maya share their deeply personal love of wine:

Maya: Can I ask you a personal question, Miles? Why are you so into
   Pinot? I mean, it's like a thing with you.

Miles: I don't know, it's a hard grape to grow, as you know, right? It's
   thin-skinned, temperamental, ripens early. You know, it's not
   a survivor like Cabernet, which can just grow anywhere, and
   um, thrive even when it's neglected. No, Pinot needs constant
   care and attention. You know, and in fact it can only grow in
   these really specific little tucked-away corners of the world. And
   only the most patient and nurturing of growers can do it, really.
   Only somebody who really takes the time to understand Pinot's
   potential can then coax it into its fullest expression. Then, I
   mean, its flavors—they're just the most haunting and brilliant
   and thrilling and subtle and ancient on the planet.

Maya's "personal question" for Miles reveals a description of Pinot in which
Maya is asked to understand the demands of Miles himself. Miles, so far in the
film, has been "thin-skinned, temperamental . . . not a survivor . . . need[ing]
constant care and attention." Here he clearly asks Maya to "understand [his]
potential," so that perhaps he can develop—or they can share something—
that is "haunting and brilliant and thrilling and subtle and ancient." In a wider
frame, Maya shares her love of wine through a metaphor of appreciation of
human life and death:

Maya: I originally got into wine through my ex-husband. You know,
   he had this big sort of show-off cellar. But then I discovered that
   I had a really sharp palate. And the more I drank, the more I
   liked what it made me think about.

Miles: Like what?

Maya: Like what a fraud he was [laughs]. . . . No, I like to think about
   the life of wine. How it's a living thing. I like to think about
   what was going on the year the grapes were growing. How the
   sun was shining, if it rained. I like to think about all the people
   who tended and picked the grapes, and if it's an old wine, how
   many of them must be dead by now. I like how wine continues
   to evolve, like if I opened a bottle of wine today, it would taste
   different than if I opened it on any other day, because a bottle
   of wine is actually alive, and it's constantly evolving and gaining

complexity. That is, until it peaks, like your '61. And then it begins its steady, inevitable decline. . . . And it tastes so fucking good.

For Maya, a growing appreciation of wine helped her excise what was inauthentic, a "fraud" in her life. Here, wine has life and character, and a life course much like that of a maturing human. Wine for Maya negotiates a path between grounded nature and human culture: it marks the natural environmental factors of a region over time, yet also assumes its own unique soul. Wine and people evolve, gain complexity, and die. Wine appreciation is used to reveal what is real, and what is inauthentic, about each character and space in the film.

Sideways thus includes several traditional vineyard romance elements and overturns others. There is near-constant attention to the beauty of vineyards, the harvest, and the pleasures of wine drinking, as well as special consideration of categorizing and naming wines and wineries. Yet the film departs from the standard form of the genre by presenting a rake in a primary romantic role: Jack is getting married at the end of the week but has flings with two women in wine country. Where *Sideways* finally and unequivocally tows the standard vineyard romance line is in the dismissal of the lower-class and ethnic character of Stephanie. Throughout the film, while Maya is marked as deeply worthy of Miles's attention, Stephanie is cast in a distinctly different light. Maya is described as a "cool smart chick, beautiful, with a lotta soul," while Stephanie is sexually provocative and described as "nasty, nasty" and simply "some wine pourer." Stephanie is also a single mother, coded in various ways as the lowest-class character in the film: her home is rather unkempt and threadbare; we meet Stephanie's adoptive white mother in a bowling alley; Stephanie parties loudly into the night as her daughter is trying to sleep; she drives a motorcycle. While there are signals that Jack perhaps loves Stephanie more than he does his fiancée, he leaves Stephanie for the white features and fortunes of Christine. Stephanie is finally dismissed as charming and sexy, but rather emotionally unstable—a character at last present for comedic shock value. Jack returns to San Diego with the broken nose that Stephanie gives him, realizing, "If I lose Christine, I'm nothing." He marries Christine, thereby securing access to the wealth and prestige that Christine's high-class, landed family represents. While Jack may not be romantically fulfilled and we are not sure that he has grown as a person, his status is undamaged. We are left with the possibility of white, middle-class Miles and Maya continuing their romance in wine country, and with *Sideways* mimicking a whole lot of romances in its line.[48]

Bottle Shock (2008) adheres even more forcefully to the original vineyard romance script, with the ownership of a family vineyard and winery at stake and the romantic happiness of several characters in question.[49] *Bottle Shock* purports to be "based on a true story," about the events leading to the 1976 Tasting of Paris, in which California wines won over French varietals and made their first twentieth-century international splash.[50] The narrative focuses on the family dynamics of Chateau Montelena and other Napa Valley winemakers seeking to gain respect in their trade. Again, the film includes marked landscape appreciation and many savory, romantic moments with wine; classic worshipful attention to wine culture marks many scenes. Jim Barrett (Bill Pullman), Chateau Montelena's beleaguered owner, in taking out his third loan on the property and business, tells the banker, "It's not about getting it done. It's about getting it done right. It's about making the best goddamn wine we can." Similarly, Steven Spurrier (Alan Rickman), the British owner of the French wine shop that holds the Tasting of Paris, states, "The smell of the vineyard, like inhaling birth. It awakens some ancestral . . . some primordial, anyway . . . some deeply imprinted and probably subconscious place, in my soul." And, on the labor of the vineyard, Sam Fulton, the comely young blonde intern (Rachael Taylor) summarizes, "from hardship comes enlightenment." Standard vineyard philosophy notwithstanding, *Bottle Shock*, somewhat like *Sideways*, first sells itself as a vineyard anti-romance through its opening scenes, directly tackling the issue of race that has been generally submerged within the genre.

In an early scene, Bo Barrett (Jim's long-haired, wayward, hippie son, played by Chris Pine), Sam (the "eager and willing intern"), and Gustavo (Jim's Mexican American wine blending employee, played by Freddy Rodriguez) walk through the nighttime streets of downtown Calistoga heading for a bar. A truck driver shouts out: "Hey, hey, boy, *chico!* Check my back, make sure it's clear." Gustavo bristles and demands, "Apologize. You should have said 'please.' You didn't say 'please' because you assume that I serve you, because you are a racist." Bo enters the mounting argument: "Hey man, my friend doesn't want to fight, but he also doesn't want to be addressed with disparaging colloquial expressions that imply some sort of genetic or cultural inferiority, or that are simply used out of some form of inappropriate ethnocentrism." Bo's overstatement of the obvious provides comic relief but also positions Bo (along with the larger film itself) as the close, racially enlightened white friend of Gustavo. The truck driver punches Bo, but the argument is soon defused by Sam and Gustavo. Later, at the bar, Bo compliments Gustavo on his wine-tasting abilities. Gustavo demurs, and Bo prods, "'Stavo, you're too modest." Gustavo offers back, under his breath, "Modesty is a virtue of slaves." Bo then waxes about his friend: "Gustavo Brambila was raised in the vineyards of northern California. He has our valley's grapes in his blood. If you pour this Mexican *hombre* a glass of wine, he can tell you how much Cabernet and how much Merlot is in it. He can even tell you the vintage. . . . He's the son of an immigrant field hand." Here, *Bottle Shock* tackles the racial history of Napa Valley directly. Gustavo's family lineage, soul, and ambition are contrasted with Bo's lack of focus throughout the film. In one scene, Bo has clearly had recent sexual relations with yet another anonymous woman, and is prodded by his father: "Do you have any ambition at all?" Bo quips back, "Uh, I dunno, to see The Dead live at the Cow Palace?" Jim then asks: "Which one were you with today?" "Shelly." "Shelly who?" Bo defends himself, "I dunno. I slept with a person, not a name." Bo's lack of attention to names is marked: the film is consumed with the specific varietals of wines and with "making a name" for Chateau Montelena and other struggling Napa Valley vintners. His father finally condescends, "Woodstock was seven years ago," questioning Bo's life choices, his appearance, his undiscriminating encounters with low women, and his lack of dedication to making great wine. Another local winemaker later tells Bo, "If I had been born with your privilege, I wouldn't have squandered it." Bo's central challenge, then—paralleling the challenge of Napa Valley in the 1970s—is to straighten up, develop respectability, and cultivate discerning tastes in several arenas.

Against Bo's wasted privilege, the film locates authenticity and hard work in the figure of Gustavo. With his winemaking ability and refined palate, Gustavo has been quietly blending wines of his own with his uncle off-site. Jim finds out and fires Gustavo for making the secret wine: "You're on your own now, kid. . . . I can't afford you anyway. . . . Your focus has been elsewhere for some time now." Gustavo replies:

You people, you think you can just buy your way into this. Take a few lessons, grow some grapes, make some good wine. You cannot do it that way. You have to have it in your blood. You have to grow up with the soil underneath your nails and the smell of the grape in the air that you breathe. The cultivation of the vine is an art form. The refinement

of its juice is a religion that requires pain and desire and sacrifice. . . .
My father knew that. He was a field hand, and he never had the opportunity to make his own wine. I know that, and I'm going to make
it happen one way or another.

Gustavo chastises Jim and family for not possessing the requisite groundedness to the land. He argues that in the winemaking process, nature becomes
culture through the human form: grapes and wine are said to be in Gustavo's
blood, and vineyard soil a part of his body. Gustavo claims, and Bo as well as
Jim later agree, that this is the only process by which distinguished wines are
made. Wine and identity here blend once again in what is constructed as an
authentic, organic art.

This appreciation for Gustavo's specifically Mexican American skill and
passion is taken up in the film's central romantic storyline as well. Sam negotiates sexual attraction to both Bo and Gustavo throughout *Bottle Shock*. In
a quiet moment with Gustavo, she offers the winemaker seductively, "Can I
try it, your wine? . . . [She toasts] To Gustavo Brambila, renegade, who worships the sanctity of the vine . . ." Gustavo finishes the sentence: ". . . and can't
afford a full tank of gas." They kiss and make love on a sunny afternoon in
her vineyard hilltop shack. At the same time, the mounting sexual tension
between Sam and Bo erupts. Bo is upset when he finds out Sam and Gustavo
have had sex. Sam immediately denies the significance of her encounter with
Gustavo: "C'mon Bo, it was just sex. People connect for all different sorts of
reasons. It didn't mean what you think it means. . . . It didn't mean anything."[51]
Sam's statement only emphasizes the film's already latent accepted reason for
her suddenly dropping Gustavo and seeking Bo romantically: Gustavo was a
momentary wine-soaked fling; Bo and his vineyard inheritance are her real
future. Sam and Bo soon engage romantically, sharing relations in the Chateau Montelena wine cellar. At the end of the film, Gustavo is hired back at
Chateau Montelena, continues making his own wine, and remains friends
with Bo. Authenticity and craft are still symbolically left in Gustavo's hands,
not Jim's or Bo's, and yet Chateau Montelena and Stags' Leap (white-owned
vineyards in Napa) win the Paris tasting. Although Gustavo has been treated
with far more respect than Californio characters in previous iterations of the
genre, the closing scenes remain the same. Gustavo's blending ability pulls
down Paris honors for his white employees, and Chateau Montelena is saved
for the Barretts. However, Gustavo's economic and romantic future is still in
question—and Bo, not Gustavo, gets the girl.

*   *   *

As we have seen, in addition to vineyard appreciation, the display and celebration of traditional winemaking techniques, and escapist pleasure, the primary cultural work that all vineyard romances perform is the careful sorting and hierarchizing of wine, wine regions, vines, and the people who grow them. On one level, vineyard romances have articulated a pointed cataloging of America's ethnic hierarchies over the past two centuries. Cooper's vision of an ideal American wine culture through the 1830s included only western Europeans of class. Ruiz de Burton's *The Squatter and the Don* extended that in the 1880s to include elite Californios. This racial (but not class) opening was quickly shut back down by Wait's *In Old Vintage Days* (1937), Hobart's *The Cup and the Sword* (1942), and the film *Bottle Shock* (2008). Sheppard's *Lucile of the Vineyard* (1915) and Hobart's *The Cup and the Sword* are the most virulently racist, jingoistic, and fear-mongering examples of the genre, and serve to lay bare what is essentially at stake in all vineyard romances—the reordering of indiscriminate "interminglings" in American society. *Sideways* symbolically counts Armenian Americans as white, an improvement over Hobart's exclusion of the group (along with Italians and German Russians) sixty years earlier, yet the film still marginalizes lower-class characters and, arguably, Asian Americans.[52] All this naming and hierarchizing is not insignificant or simply technical, since it is also deeply about sorting the identities of people who have the access and ability to control America's best wine lands. Although the definition of whiteness and the status of various ethnic and racial minorities have altered over the centuries, the focus on ethnic hierarchy and class status remains central to the genre.

The danger in the vineyard romance, then, is a thoroughly Americanized version of the danger of the ancient Greek myth of Bacchus broadcast onto California, one of the country's most contested contact zones. The American version repeatedly functions as a precautionary tale of the perils of immediate carnal pleasure over the long-term goals of white social standing and land control. The persistent thrill and danger of the vineyard romance is one that circles around the possibility of "going native": white characters flirt with lower-class characters of color but not so deeply that they lose control of their landscapes or lineages. The imagined dangerous release of Bacchanalian revelry in various works—San Francisco's wine-soaked wriggling sin in *Lucile of the Vineyard*, JJ's impregnating of Chonita in *Old Vintage Days*, John's impregnating of Buz and Elizabeth's forced flirtation with Henri in *The Cup and the Sword*, Jack's sexcapade with Stephanie in *Sideways*, and Sam's naked

afternoon with Gustavo in *Bottle Shock*—ends with each white character re-
treating to other white characters for long-term familial fulfillment and economic promise. The wine that is so alluring—and the bodies that are so easily
seduced through it—ride an edge of pleasure and threat that seems an endlessly productive formula for vineyard romance writers. That edge of pleasure
and threat, when summing up the conflicts encountered on winemaking's
"frontier," speaks of the vestiges of a colonizing project that still haunt the
California winemaking machine. Beyond the basic titillation of Bacchanalian
surrender, however, the true danger of the vineyard romance is that the future
still solely belongs to white characters of class.

An Empire of Wine

WELL BEFORE HE moved to California in 1881, grape scientist and promoter George Husmann published one of his most widely read books. Written from his home in Missouri, Husmann's *The Cultivation of the Native Grape and the Manufacture of American Wines* (1866) describes both East Coast and Midwestern wine-growing scenes: "I firmly believe that this continent is destined to be the greatest wine-producing country in the world, America will be, from the Atlantic to the Pacific, *one* smiling and happy *Wineland*, where each laborer shall sit under his own vine, and none will be too poor to enjoy the purest and most wholesome of all stimulants, good, cheap, native *wine*."[1] Spanning the East, Midwest, and West, Husmann's "happy Wineland" was predicated on many things: national mission, private property and real estate speculation, inexpensive labor, and the ideology of the sober, Protestant, bourgeois family home. His treatise suggests that only with proper training and the combined efforts of the inhabitants of the continent could all people prosper from wine's salubrious effects. And yet, writing in Missouri in 1866, Husmann was professing all of this fifteen years before he moved to California—illustrating the extent to which the state's grape culture was based on the rhetoric and practice from the East, as well as the extent to which its status as the fulfillment of the nation's destiny as a "smiling and happy Wineland" was embedded in nineteenth-century society.

Many academic and popular works forget that California was culturally constructed as a vast agricultural Eden long before it was lived out upon the ground. California's version of manifest destiny in the late nineteenth and early twentieth centuries was effectively deployed through grape culture, just as it previously had been in Eastern wine-growing regions. Although imbued with a fresh aesthetic, and with new types of grapes, the rhetoric and practice of nationalism and empire through grape culture was structurally similar from New York to Ohio and California. In this way, in each case, viticulture was a monoculture in denial of its industrial origins, and was a reusable, endlessly applicable tool of cultural imperialism. Winemaking and wine myth have long offered the country ideological coherence to powerful social groups. Viticulture has been a site for the expression—and often realization—of manifest destiny.

The crowning of a horticultural manifest destiny that had progressed from ancient Greece to contemporary California was dramatically illustrated in an 1869 advertisement for California wines sponsored by New York distributor Perkins, Stern & Company (Fig. 40).[2] In W. J. Linton's engraving of W. J. Hennessy's drawing, Silenus passes the thyrsus of winemaking to California's new wine God. In Greek mythology, Silenus was the tutor to Dionysus, the Greek God of wine and raucous behavior. Silenus was the most drunken, but also oldest and wisest of Dionysian followers, possessing prophetic powers and special knowledge of winemaking.[3] Here, supported by his entourage of satyrs, he passes the staff of wine production to the "new gods" of viticulture—a young Californian Adam and Eve in a wild garden of grapes. Bacchants follow in a flowing path behind him, traveling east to west, across the country and through the mountains, vines and grapes festooning the landscape. The title declares: "Bacchus in America—the *Old* Wine God and the *New*," and below, the caption doubles the parallelism between the old and new wine empires: "Pure California Wines, *Equal* to European." The clothing of the young Californians reveals the mix of impulses functioning within grape culture in the 1860s. A somber young woman, the "genius of America," is dressed in stoic garb made of stars and stripes fabric. As a viticultural precursor to the Statue of Liberty (not constructed until 1886), she dons a crown of stars, while other figures wear grape leaves on their heads. She is a classical but chaste overseer of the transfer of power to the new Californian Adam—a more virile, and also more industrious, version of Silenus. Here, the unkempt, wilder histories of grape culture are subsumed into an organized nationalist tableau of youth and beauty. "Old" Greek imagery and Bacchanalian rites are juxtaposed to the "new" Californian golden bear and the promise of heterosexual union in the figures on the left. The young Californians are sober and assiduous by comparison to the old Bacchanalian rites, ready to take their place at the helm of a new dominion of grapes. Silenus, it was said, could see the future: California here offers the ideal natural conditions for a new, chaste, and truly powerful international wine culture to take hold.

In this way, viticulture in the nineteenth century transformed landscapes

Figure 40. William James Linton, *Bacchus in America*, wood engraving, 1869. Courtesy of Minneapolis Institute of Arts, gift of Timothy Cole, August 1919.

and propagated a nationalist worldview of cultivation and control. The culture of the vine relied on strategies of representation that implied that U.S. grape growing was an imperial act, one legitimate because it was aesthetically beautiful and morally acceptable in its claim to natural, and national, power. In many cases, grape culture functioned as a trope for the nation: images and rhetoric constructed America's easy and natural imperial growth, like grapevines colonizing a hillside. It modeled an ideal pastoral republican empire for all who cared to tend a vineyard or drink of its fruits. Yet, fruit culture also had long ties with frontier speculation and urbanization. Through horticultural land speculation, grape culture often acted as the cutting edge of capitalist expansion—and yet conveniently served in its own erasure by also propagating a strongly middle-class and democratic mythos of American fruit production. In their writings and artistry, viticulturists' capitalist materialism was shot through with an aesthetic that legitimated not only civilized order and capitalist profit, but territorial expansion. Grape culture was thus performed at the crossroads of several difficult transitions in nineteenth-century life, and ensured for its practitioners an image of America as a virtuous pastoral republican empire.

Famous viticulturists in the United States claimed they had built a life of refinement and usefulness by practicing the ancient art of viticulture, yet grapes also lined their pocketbooks and steeled their social and international standing. Grape growing was thus a genteel cover for other activities in regional, national, and international trade. In addition, grape culture in its scientific and fictional forms was set within, and propounded, the racist ideologies present in many other expansionist discourses. But the ultimate gift of viticulturists' work was in making U.S. imperial culture look natural, even foreordained. The vineyard and its vines served as templates for experimentation—for consciously and unconsciously dreaming about, cultivating, and controlling the American landscape and society.

Later-century California boosters often reminded grape growers and the nation of California's "natural advantages" over grapes grown in other regions. Gustav Eisen, a raisin grower in the 1890s, wrote that "the safeguard of the raisin industry is to limit to the conditions under which the grapes can be grown and under which the raisins can be cured."[4] There was conscious choice in the matter of "limiting the conditions" under which the "best" grapes grew; grape growers narrowed their ideal climatological range by also limiting the "best" types of grapes to be grown. This was a way of manipulating the market for those grapes and their products, and of adding value to the shrinking lands that superior grapes could be grown upon. This sort of environmental determinism not only won these growers premier status in grape and wine markets, but also offered total control of those markets to the few people that owned land in its well-defined boundaries.

There are two larger points that recur throughout this book. First, the wine world has practiced this style of environmental determinism for centuries, primarily through its international cult of terroir, the sum total of the processes that go into making wine: the land and its soil content, slope, and sun; the weather, the water, the fertilizers, and even the expertise of the *vigneron* present to create a wine. The terroir of good wine thus authenticates everything else in its web: the land, the methods, the science, the growers, the region, and the nation. Grapes and the cult of terroir, by default and by necessity, literally root a nation's imperial sense of itself.

But far beyond location and a nation's "inherent" terroir, national economic interest and historical circumstances made wine a reality in nineteenth-century America. Much as any new nation goes through a brisk cultural reprogramming to convince its people that it was and will remain a natural and eternal political formation, nations remain constructed, socially determined spaces and ideas. A nation's wine and the "natural advantages" it relies upon are just as historically and culturally dependent. A strong ideology of terroir further strengthened U.S. winemaking in the twentieth century, and remains important to winemakers today, by linking their product with ideas about the nation and its power, as well as increasing the value of their wine through delimiting the lands upon which fine wines are grown.[5] The nineteenth-century fin-de-siècle California wine moment was able to capitalize on all of these constructions far better than previous U.S. regions. California became the lucky, but not predestined, benefactor of centuries of national and global attempts to build strong empires through cultivating its grapes.

This is not to say that terroir is unimportant, or a wholly unreal conceit of grape growing. Any gardener or farmer will tell you that climate and soil quality are absolutely indicative of plant performance, and of course, any fruit's taste. Winegrowers have long argued, and wine drinkers will agree, that the grape has a special ability to express the essence of place more than any other foodstuff. The soil, the site, the weather—all the physical elements that make up terroir—are undeniably important for the future chemical profile of the wine that is produced, as well as the beverage's perception on the palate. But perhaps most important, wine has an ability to hold and "express" its original location and growing conditions, the flavors of the moment for generations hence. It has been argued that "wine is tied to place more than any other form of agriculture, in the sense that the names of the place are on the bottle."[6] There is a symbolic *and* quite real ability of wine to link with the past in a specific location and time. Wine seems to have had a preternatural ability in bridging human groups' concepts of nature and culture for centuries.

Yet in *both* of these elements of terroir—the material and the cultural—we must remember the extent to which vineyards and wine culture have always been, and remain, socially constructed experiences. No matter how natural they claim to be, no vintner can deny that terroirs are deeply managed spaces—often minutely managed spaces. Soils, vines, water, fertilizer, and all other inputs are controlled to the utmost degree. The factors contributing to quality wine are in fact too numerous to engineer with reliable success each year. Again, however, the fact that terroir's constitution may be ambiguous does not necessarily mean that it is not real—it does, however, mean that it is constantly up for social manipulation.

This manipulation, throughout American history, has often occurred through language. The language of manifest destiny has mapped exceedingly well onto the language of terroir in America in part because the two lexicons have been so similarly overwrought for centuries. Henry Hobhouse describes that the language used to sell wine, as far back as Greek and Roman times, was already an "extravagant joke" at its ancient birth.[7] The language of manifest destiny in America has been similarly unrestrained. Wine's parlance has been grandiose for many centuries; the language of manifest destiny only two hundred years—and yet they have easily flowered together in each of the main sites of U.S. viticulture, and racialized U.S. national expansion, since their meeting.

Perhaps the racism found at the heart of the terroir issue in the United States persists because it is of a peculiarly plastic nature. Reginald Horsman has described many types of "racialism" that drove nineteenth-century Americans to perceive vast differences between people with different skin tones. "Scientific racialism" depended on differences scientists believed they could see in the human form: the size of the cranium, the bridge of the nose, the color of the eyes and skin. "Romantic racialism," in contrast, which speedily gained favor throughout the first half of the nineteenth century, sought to distinguish people upon their national identity and origins, historical uniqueness, and language.[8] Strikingly, the racism endemic to the vineyard mythos in the United States fits both of these types of key racializing processes: it has depended simultaneously on the science, and the romance, of terroir.

The cult of terroir thus continues to be a generative nexus where the mythos of American rural life and the realities of industrial agriculture still meet. American vineyards over the nineteenth century were constructed as virtuous places where historical progress could occur. Even today, the vineyard mythos is one still predicated on employing techniques and tools opposite those of industrial agriculture. Thus, terroir appears in nineteenth-, twentieth-, and twenty-first-century America as an essential component of a more cultivated sense of manifest destiny—the promise of ownership of the land, and of identity and power through such ownership.

The second larger point this book ends on, then, is how grape culture has rather deftly assisted Americans in their negotiation of two centuries of capitalist development. In the nineteenth century, the winemaking ethos was at heart an exercise in developing one's gentility. Andrew Jackson Downing, Nicholas Longworth, and others constantly argued that cultivating grapes was the best method of developing a genteel life. In fact, grape culture as a performance of one's gentility worked at multiple levels: by virtue of being constantly engaged in the question of social and physical cultivation, grape culture helped middle-class Americans obviate their fear of the changes to everyday life wrought by the accelerating Industrial Revolution and consumer capitalism. Many Americans were able to find a resolved gentility within capitalism through grape culture.

In the twenty-first century, the central narrative of American viticulture seems to have changed. In the past several decades of tourist literature and wine films, the experience of American winemaking has been framed not so much around the cultivation of gentility, but instead the search for authenticity. Each winemaker today portends to give consumers the "real" winemaking experience, with natural wines, age-old customs, and local foodways brimming out of their vineyards. In a Famille Perrin advertisement in the April 2012 *Wine Spectator,* for example, Robert Parker, a respected authority in wine, is quoted: "Purchasing a wine from this family is about as close to a guarantee of authenticity and high quality as one can expect." In *Spotlight's Wine Country Guide*, a current free booklet detailing events and wine tasting for tourists visiting Napa and Sonoma, the authors describe inhabitants of Sebastopol, a town in the southern Russian River Valley: "Sebastopol natives [are] friendly and welcoming if a bit quirky. Nonconformity is the norm among many locals in this unabashedly authentic and American small town." The *Wine Country Guide* offers tourists approachable, "authentic," and organic simplicity. The *Guide* includes details about Pope Valley Winery in

Napa: "Along a winding country road, up an unpaved drive and past Gus—a big, friendly, chocolate lab—you'll find one of the most unpretentious, down-to-earth tasting rooms around. . . . The winery itself is housed in the original historic barn built over a hand-dug cave."[9] Said more simply, a Rodney Strong Cabernet Sauvignon advertisement in the March 2012 *Wine Spectator* declares, "PLACE MATTERS. Sonoma County."

If advertisements are an indicator of wine buyers' latent desires, wine today, in addition to hewing to its specificity of place, must be made by unique people. In a January 2012 advertisement, Josh Cellars's winemaker, Joseph Carr, describes his wines as "bold and expressive, but unassuming and approachable. Just like my Dad."[10] Like in the latter-day versions of the vineyard romance, winegrowers here are ideally no longer gentlemen, but "pioneers" or mavericks, and their wine regions singular in the way their wines express their terroir. The wine produced is above all unique—an expression of one place, one moment, one grape, one vintner.

All of this in mind, the focus on wine's uniqueness and authenticity now seems designed to obviate the overwhelming homogenization of late capitalism. Wine sellers above all claim "authentic" experiences in barrel rooms and tasting rooms. Perhaps the best evidence of this shift in wine consciousness from a cult of gentility to a cult of authenticity is that U.S. winemakers did not use the word *terroir* in the nineteenth century, although they were influenced by all other French winemaking techniques and the French wine lexicon at large. Today, terroir, a specificity and authenticity of place, reigns over all winemaking. Wine has subtly and elegantly negotiated both the panic for gentility and the panic for authenticity for an American public for two hundred years—wine's romantic story has been malleable enough to translate easily and beautifully from century to century.

But wine culture's deep narratives of gentility and authenticity are also why a racialized cult of terroir has also been so continuously problematic for a multiracial America. Tomasik explains that within the cult of terroir, "only things with clear origins have value."[11] As we saw in California vineyard fiction, it is not just clear origins: it is finite origins, fetishized origins, ideal and unreal origins. In this context, it is striking that one of the old saws in wine growing, "you can't buy terroir," is at once so true and so false, and at the center of winemaking's perennial myth and obsession with preserving land for the winemaker's progeny.[12] Indeed, "You can't buy terroir," and yet well-managed terroirs are often seen as the crowning landscapes of the planet's most capitalist countries. As well, the near-constant battles over the

boundaries of particular American Viticultural Areas (AVAs) since their federal delineation in 1978 are particularly telling (the Napa area alone has fourteen of them). If a particular AVA has had success, or developed an enviable
cultural cachet, vineyard owners surrounding that AVA often "lobby vigor-
ously to be included." In this way, many AVAs have been altered due to economic and political interests, and often represent marketing initiative over
natural physical realties.[13] Sure, "you can't buy terroir," but you can definitely
sell it and its romantic products.

Of course, the transformation of organic life and land into alienable commodities has only accelerated in recent decades, and twenty-first-century patent law and activities have dwarfed the scale of the Patent Office's original
grapevine Propagating Garden. The Plant Patent Act, drafted and passed in
the 1930s, determined that plants could fall under monopoly ownership. This
was at first limited to horticultural and ornamental asexually reproducing
plants, for Congress did not want crops that were vital to the nation's economy and welfare (like potatoes and corn) to come under private ownership. In
1970, Congress then passed the Plant Variety Protection Act, which granted
plant breeders exclusive rights to several sexually reproducing plants for up
to twenty-five years. This law too, while taking another step into the privatiza-
tion of life, still preserved exemptions for researchers and farmers, who were
allowed to save and propagate their own seeds. Patent law was again irrevoca-
bly altered in 1980 in the case of *Diamond v. Chakrabarty,* which went so far
as to state that even life's genetics could be owned. In this case, oil-eating mi-
crobes, considered by most scientists and cosmologies to be *life,* were deemed
patentable.[14] This case opened the floodgates to companies being able to le-
gally own genetic material and the life that springs from it. Twinned with this
ability to own life in the late twentieth century were advancements in cellular
biotechnology that made life genetically manipulable. Although it would take
much more research to be sure, it seems to me that the patenting and selling
of life has trodden a contemporaneous cultural path with a twentieth-century
perception of a loss of authenticity—we can, and we have, been buying and
selling life, and authenticity, for decades now.

In 2007, Italian and French researchers mapped the genome of Pinot
Noir. It was the first grape, not to mention the first fruit, ever genetically
mapped. Since 2009, several thousand wild and domesticated vines have been
"fingerprinted," or had their genetic profiles recorded. Future genetic modification promises to make grapes more disease resistant, and wine crops more
reliably palatable. Genetic researchers indeed see the grape's gene sequencing

as "a model organism for fruit trees in general."[15] Although food scientists are likely still a long way from producing genetically modified wine, we are left to wonder what will happen to world wine culture when they do. In the United States, "nature's nation" and its grape culture depend in large part on a perception of nature that, on the one hand, has at its center a revitalizing relationship with "primitive wilderness," and on the other, celebrates the generations of intensive cultivation grapes have enjoyed. This tension between the "wild" and the "controlled" in wine has animated the Bacchus myth, visions of pastoral republican empire, and indeed much of wine culture's latter-day narratives, including the cult of terroir and the vineyard romance. But what happens to grape culture and a larger sense of national identity when genetic modification short-circuits both the nature and the culture of wine-making? Does grape culture continue on, perennially in denial of its technical and scientific remaking, or does it finally lose its claim to natural and national authenticity? Of course, the ability to engineer and control living beings is the subject of many other books and important debates. But the proprietary nature of patent law, and the government's willingness to enforce it with major industry backing, goes far beyond capitalism's inherent end-game of monopolistic land ownership, profit making, and the propagation of a hegemonic white identity. Indeed, at the turn of the twenty-first century in America, major corporate agribusiness executive leadership and the U.S. presidential cabinet have at times been utterly interchangeable.[16] It seems the stuff of science fiction, and yet such an outcome is invariably a culmination of the work of people like Ellsworth, Prince, Longworth, Downing, Mead, Husmann, and their fellow nineteenth-century viticulturists, who were engaged in a thoroughly nationalist, capitalist, expansionist grape culture. For the past two centuries, horticultural imperialism has meant owning and controlling both green and human life through the economic manipulation of nature and the seductive rhetoric of national power.

NOTES

Introduction

1. *The Cultivated Life: Thomas Jefferson and Wine*, dir. John Harrington (PBS, Madisonfilm, 2005).

2. "Methyl bromide is classified by the U.S. Environmental Protection Agency as a Category I toxic compound, a designation reserved for the most dangerous substances." Environmental Working Group, Friends of the Earth, Pesticide Action Network, "Pesticide Watch and Western Environmental Law Center Press Release," March 19, 1999, http://www.panna.org/legacy/panups/panup_19990322.dv.html, accessed March 11, 2013. See also Pesticide Action Network, "Pesticide Information," http://www.pesticideinfo.org/List_CA_Chem_Use.jsp?chk=385&cok=00&sk=00, accessed September 1, 2011. See also Paula Harris, "New Report Claims Pesticide Overuse in Sonoma County Vineyards," *Sonoma County Independent* (November 13-19, 1997), http://www.metroactive.com/papers/sonoma/11.13.97/news-9746.html, accessed August 27, 2011.

3. Mike Weiss, *A Very Good Year: The Journey of a California Wine from Vine to Table* (New York: Gotham Books, 2006), 92. See also James Liebman, "Rising Toxic Tide: Pesticide Use in California 1991–1995" (San Francisco: Californians for Pesticide Reform, 1997); Californians for Pesticide Reform, "Fields of Poison 2002: California Farmworkers and Pesticides,"http://www.pesticidereform.org/article.php?id=4, accessed March 11, 2013; Californians for Alternatives to Toxics, "Time for a Change: Pesticides and Winegrapes in Sonoma and Napa Counties" (1997), 1, http://www.alternatives2toxics.org/publications.htm, accessed March 11, 2013.

4. Patrick H. Mooney and Theo J. Majka, *Farmers' and Farm Workers' Movements: Social Protest in American Agriculture* (New York: Twayne, 1995), xxiv-xxv. Cesar Chavez, "The Wrath of Grapes" (May 1986), in *American Earth: Environmental Writing Since Thoreau*, ed. Bill McKibben (Washington, DC: Library of America, 2008), 690-695.

5. Weiss, *A Very Good Year,* 43.

6. The Wine Institute, "California Wine Profile 2010," http://www.wineinstitute.org, accessed August 12, 2011.

7. *Proceedings of the Seventh Session of the American Pomological Society, held in New York, 1858* (Brooklyn, NY: George C. Bennett, 1858), 12, 14, 23-24.

8. Among many more, see Julia Flynn Siler, *The House of Mondavi: The Rise and Fall of an American Wine Dynasty* (New York: Gotham Books, 2007); Charles L. Sullivan, *Zinfandel: A History of a Grape and Its Wine* (Berkeley: University of California Press, 2003); Paul Lukacs, *American Vintage: The Rise of American Wine* (Boston: Houghton Mifflin, 2000); Gary L. Peters, *American Winescapes: The Cultural Landscapes of America's Wine Country* (New York: Westview, 1997); Thomas Pinney, *A History of Wine in America: From the Beginning to Prohibition* (Berkeley: University of California Press, 1989); Leon D. Adams, *The Wines of America,* 3rd ed. (New York:

McGraw-Hill, 1985 [1973]); Robert C. Fuller, *Religion and Wine: A Cultural History of Wine Drinking in the United States* (Knoxville: University of Tennessee Press, 1996); Matt Kramer, *Making Sense of California Wine* (New York: William Morrow, 1992); W. J. Rorabaugh, *The Alcoholic Republic: An American Tradition* (Oxford: Oxford University Press, 1979); Jed Dannenbaum, *Drink and Disorder: Temperance Reform in Cincinnati from the Washingtonian Revival to the WCTU* (Urbana: University of Illinois Press, 1984); Hugh Johnson, *The World Atlas of Wine* (New York: Simon and Schuster, 1977); and H. Warner Allen, *A History of Wine: Great Vintage Wines from the Homeric Age to the Present Day* (n.p., 1961).

9. See also David Vaught, *Cultivating California: Growers, Specialty Crops, and Labor, 1875–1920* (Baltimore: Johns Hopkins University Press, 1999).

10. Definitions found in the *Oxford American Dictionary* and in agricultural journals of the period.

11. Liberty Hyde Bailey, *Cyclopedia of American Horticulture*, 4 vols. (New York: Macmillan, 1900), 755.

12. Ian Tyrrell, in *True Gardens of the Gods: Californian-Australian Environmental Reform, 1860–1930* (Berkeley: University of California Press, 1999), discusses horticulture as a culture in northern California in the early twentieth century. For gardening and horticulture as culture, see also Michael Pollan, *Second Nature: A Gardener's Education* (New York: Atlantic Monthly Press, 1991); Tamara Plakins Thornton, *Cultivating Gentlemen: The Meaning of Country Life Among the Boston Elite, 1785–1860* (New Haven, CT: Yale University Press, 1989); and Douglas Cazaux Sackman, *Orange Empire: California and the Fruits of Eden* (Berkeley: University of California Press, 2005).

13. Harm Jan de Blij, *Wine: A Geographic Appreciation* (Totowa, NJ: Rowman and Allanheld, 1983), xi.

14. John S. Reid, "Grape Cuttings From History—No. 4.," *The Horticulturist* 20 (August 1865), 262. On American neoclassicism, see Caroline Winterer, *The Culture of Classicism: Ancient Greece and Rome in American Intellectual Life, 1780–1910* (Baltimore: Johns Hopkins University Press, 2002); and Carl J. Richard, *The Golden Age of Classics in America: Greece, Rome, and the Antebellum United States* (Cambridge, MA: Harvard University Press, 2009).

15. Andrew Jackson Downing, *The Fruits and Fruit Trees of America: or, The Culture, Propagation, and Management, in the Garden and Orchard, of Fruit Trees Generally; with Descriptions of all the Finest Varieties of Fruit, Native and Foreign, Cultivated in This Country* (New York: John Wiley, 1845), 300.

16. Jim Lapsley, University of California–Davis, Viticulture Department, personal communication January 2012. See also Rebecca K. R. Ambers and Clifford P. Ambers, "Dr. Daniel Norborne Norton and the Origin of the Norton Grape," *American Wine Society Journal* 36:3 (Fall 2004), 77–87; David Mabberly, "*Vitis* x *alexanderi* Prince ex Jacques (*vitaceae*), the First 'American Hybrid' Grapes," *Telopea* 8:3 (1999), 377–379.

17. Lucie T. Morton, *Winegrowing in Eastern America: An Illustrated Guide to Viniculture East of the Rockies* (Ithaca, NY: Cornell University Press, 1985), 55–56, 59.

18. Peters, *American Winescapes*, 65, 150–151. See also Harm J. de Blij, *Geography of Viticulture: Regions, Terroir and Techniques* (Miami: Miami Geographical Society, 1981), 67; Pinney, *History of Wine in America*, 4–5.

19. Barbara Ensrud, *American Vineyards* (New York: Stewart, Tabori & Chang, 1988), 48.

20. "*Sideways*," Box Office Mojo, http://www.boxofficemojo.com/movies/?id=sideways.htm, accessed August 6, 2012.

21. During the same period, "beer consumption jumped from 20.1 to 79.2 liters, [and] spirits fell from 9.5 to 5.7 liters." James Simpson, *Creating Wine: The Emergence of a World Industry, 1840–1914* (Princeton, NJ: Princeton University Press, 2011), 217.

22. Mark O. Morford and Robert J. Lenardon, *Classical Mythology,* 3rd ed. (New York: Longman, 1985), 217, 216.

23. Charles Segal, *Dionysiac Poetics and Euripides'* Bacchae (Princeton, NJ: Princeton University Press, 1982), 66.

24. Andrew Lang, *Custom and Myth* (New York: Harper and Brothers, 1885), 60, 7.

25. Marcel Detienne, *Dionysos Slain* (Baltimore: Johns Hopkins University Press, 1979), x. See also P. E. Easterling, ed., *The Cambridge Companion to Greek Tragedy* (Cambridge: Cambridge University Press, 1997); G. S. Kirk, *The Nature of Greek Myths* (Woodstock, NY: Overlook, 1975); Walter F. Otto, *Dionysus: Myth and Cult* (Bloomington: Indiana University Press, 1965); H. J. Rose, *A Handbook of Greek Mythology* (London: Methuen & Company, 1928).

26. Kolleen M. Guy, *When Champagne Became French: Wine and the Making of a National Identity* (Baltimore: Johns Hopkins University Press, 2003), 41–42. This is just one element of many in the classic image of the vineyard that can be discussed as a fitting example of Marxist overdetermination. This class-specific dream/scene of the vineyard wears very thin in locations further west and with the later-century growth of large industrial vineyards and expendable labor, but it still accompanies it today.

27. David Hancock, *Oceans of Wine: Madeira and the Emergence of American Trade and Taste* (New Haven, CT: Yale University Press, 2009).

28. Peter S. Onuf, *Jefferson's Empire: The Language of American Nationhood* (Charlottesville: University Press of Virginia, 2000), 2, 7, 54, 58. See also Gordon S. Wood, *Empire of Liberty: A History of the Early Republic, 1789–1815* (New York: Oxford University Press, 2009).

29. Thomas R. Hietala, *Manifest Design: American Exceptionalism and Empire,* revised ed. (Ithaca, NY: Cornell University Press, 2003 [1985]), 173. See also Sean Wilentz, *Rise of American Democracy: Jefferson to Lincoln* (New York: W. W. Norton, 2006).

30. Recent works on the "cultures" of U.S. imperialism provide a larger context for this inquiry. They include critical analysis of how empire was practiced, taught, and experienced as an everyday way of life. See Donald Pease and Amy Kaplan, eds., *The Cultures of United States Imperialism* (Durham, NC: Duke University Press, 1994), 14; Amy Kaplan, "Violent Belongings and the Question of Empire Today: Presidential Address to the American Studies Association, Hartford, Connecticut, October 17, 2003," *American Quarterly* 56:1 (March 2004), 1–18. See also Amy Kaplan, *The Anarchy of Empire in the Making of U.S. Culture* (Cambridge, MA: Harvard University Press, 2005); Shelley Streeby, *American Sensations: Class, Empire and the Production of Popular Culture* (Berkeley: University of California Press, 2002). Julie Greene, "The Labor of Empire," *Labor* 2:1 (2004), is an excellent disciplinary map for this sort of inquiry. Slave labor, Native American genocide, and the Mexican-American War are essential referents here, in that they provide just three examples of the literal imperial landscape the horticulturists functioned within and were in dialogue with throughout the century. For "empire over nature," see Donald Worster, *Nature's Economy: The Roots of Ecology* (San Francisco, CA: Sierra Club Books, 1977), 2, 53, 55, and Benjamin R. Cohen, *Notes from the Ground: Science, Soil and Society in the American Countryside* (New Haven, CT: Yale University Press, 2009), 21.

31. Angela Miller, *The Empire of the Eye: Landscape Representation and American Cultural Politics, 1825–1875* (Ithaca, NY: Cornell University Press, 1993), 39.

32. Frieda Knobloch, *The Culture of Wilderness: Agriculture as Colonization in the American West* (Chapel Hill: University of North Carolina Press, 1996). Patricia Limerick has called this the "legacy of conquest"; Patricia Limerick, *The Legacy of Conquest* (New York: W. W. Norton, 1987). See also Sackman, *Orange Empire*; William Cronon, *Changes in the Land: Indians, Colonists, and the Ecology of New England,* revised ed. (New York: Hill and Wang, 2003); and Alfred Crosby's many titles on ecological imperialism.

33. Mary Louise Pratt, *Imperial Eyes: Travel Writing and Transculturation* (New York: Routledge, 1992). The discussion I present here regarding the construction of a powerful cultural nationalism shifts Mary Louise Pratt's critical analysis of eighteenth-century botanist-explorers to nineteenth-century businessmen-horticulturists. Pratt's botanists, through their "gentle herborizing," secured a moral innocence while strengthening their nation's hegemony. The eighteenth-century "planetary consciousness" that gave rise to colonialist competition, and the hegemonic "ethic of exploration" developed by botanist-explorers, were later replaced, I argue, by a nineteenth-century imperialistic ethic of cultivation.

34. See Cronon, *Changes in the Land*; Knobloch, *The Culture of Wilderness*; Erica Hannickel, "Cultivation and Control: Grape Growing as Expansion in Nineteenth Century United States and Australia," *Comparative American Studies* 8:4 (December 2010), 283–299; Rochelle L. Johnson, *Passions for Nature: Nineteenth-Century America's Aesthetics of Alienation* (Athens: University of Georgia Press, 2009). On Australian colonization and wine growing, see Michael Dunn, *Australia and the Empire: From 1788 to the Present* (Sydney: Fontana Books, 1984); Brian Galligan, Winsome Roberts, and Gabriella Trifiletti, *Australians and Globalization: The Experience of Two Centuries* (Cambridge: Cambridge University Press, 2001); Simon Ryan, *The Cartographic Eye: How Explorers Saw Australia* (Cambridge: Cambridge University Press, 1996); Andre Simon, *The Wines, Vineyards and Vignerons of Australia* (London: Paul Hamlyn, 1967); Richard Waterhouse, *The Vision Splendid: A Social and Cultural History of Rural Australia* (Fremantle, Western Australia: Curtin University Books, 2005).

35. Just a few include Pinney, *A History of Wine in America*; Hancock, *Oceans of Wine*; Mark Edward Lender and James Kirby Martin, *Drinking in America: A History* (New York: The Free Press, 1982); Tyler Colman, *Wine Politics: How Governments, Environmentalists, Mobsters, and Critics Influence the Wines We Drink* (Berkeley: University of California Press, 2008); and Tom Standage, *History of the World in Six Glasses* (New York: Walker & Company, 2005).

Chapter 1. Tributaries of the Grape

1. Harold A. Innis, *Empire and Communications* (Toronto: University of Toronto Press, 1972). Also James W. Carey, *Communication as Culture: Essays on Media and Society* (New York: Routledge, 1989), especially his chapter 6, "Space, Time, and Communications: A Tribute to Harold Innis." John Jacob Astor, as just one example, made his fortune from frontier speculation in fur and real estate, all from his New York offices. John D. Haeger, *John Jacob Astor, Business and Finance in the Early Republic* (Detroit: Wayne State University Press, 1991). Also see David Scobey, *Empire City: The Making and Meaning of the New York City Landscape* (Philadelphia: Temple University Press, 2002), and Edward Spann, *The New Metropolis: New York City, 1840–1857* (New York: Columbia University Press, 1981).

2. U. P. Hedrick, *A History of Agriculture in the State of New York* (Albany, NY: J. B. Lyon &

Co., 1933), 387. See also David Scobey, *Empire City*, 26; Tamara Plakins Thornton, *Cultivating Gentlemen: The Meaning of Country Life Among the Boston Elite, 1785–1860* (New Haven, CT: Yale University Press, 1989), 155; U. P. Hedrick, *A History of Horticulture in America to 1860* (New York: Oxford University Press, 1850); and W. H. Upshall and D. V. Fisher, eds., *History of Fruit Growing and Handling in United States of America and Canada, 1860–1972* (Kelowna, BC: Regatta City Press, 1976), especially George L. Slate, "New York," 99–106.

3. Carl Richard, *The Golden Age of the Classics in America: Greece, Rome, and the Antebellum United States* (Cambridge, MA: Harvard University Press, 2009), xi, 63, 85, 112, 115, 117, 136.

4. William R. Prince, "The Vine," in *The Naturalist, Containing Treatises on Natural History, Chemistry, Domestic and Rural Economy, Manufactures, and Arts* (1830–1832, Boston), an article in three parts: 1:1 (December 1830), 22–31; 1:4 (April 1831), 117–125; and 1:9 (September 1831), 276–285. This quote from 1:1 (December 1830), 23–24, 25–29, 31.

5. Hedrick, *A History of Agriculture in the State of New York*, 387. Also see Carlton B. Lees, "The Golden Age of Horticulture," *Historic Preservation* 24:4 (October/November 1972), 35. For a general introduction to U.S. nurserymen in the eighteenth and nineteenth centuries, see Elisabeth Woodburn, "Horticultural Heritage: The Influence of U.S. Nurserymen," in *Agriculture Literature: Proud Heritage—Future Promise, A Bicentennial Symposium, September 24–26, 1975*, ed. Alan Fusconie and Leila Moran (Washington, DC: Associates of the National Agricultural Library, Inc., and the Graduate School Press, 1977). See also James M. Gabler, *Wine into Words: A History and Bibliography of Wine Books in the English Language* (Baltimore: Bacchus Press, 1985), 213; and Daniel J. Kevles, "Fruit Nationalism: Horticulture in the United States—From the Revolution to the First Centennial," in *Aurora Torealis: Studies in the History of Science and Ideas in Honor of Tore Frängsmyr*, ed. Marco Beretta, Karl Grandin, and Svante Lindquist (Sagamore Beach, MA: Science History Publications, 2008).

6. William Prince's father, Robert Prince, started a non-commercial nursery on Long Island in 1737. William Prince turned it into a commercial enterprise in 1765. *A Short Treatise on Horticulture* (1828) was written by William Prince Jr. He also renamed the family nursery the Linnaean Botanic Garden; it remained in production until 1866. *A Treatise on the Vine* (1830) was written by William Robert Prince. See Maynard A. Amerine and Axel E. Borg, *A Bibliography on Grapes, Wines, Other Alcoholic Beverages, and Temperance: Works Published in the United States Before 1901* (Berkeley: University of California Press, 1996), 214. See also Joyce E. Chaplin, "William Prince," in *American National Biography*, ed. John A. Garraty and Mark Carnes (New York: Oxford University Press, 1999), 882-883.

7. William Prince Jr. (1766–1842), *A Short Treatise on Horticulture: Embracing Descriptions of a Great Variety of Fruit and Ornamental Trees and Shrubs, Grape Vines, Bulbous Flowers, Green-House Trees and Plants, &c., Nearly all of Which are at Present Comprised in the Collection of the Linnaean Botanic Garden, at Flushing, near New-York, with Directions for Their Culture, Management, &c.* (New York: T & J Swords, 1828), 70–71, his emphasis.

8. Henry Nash Smith, *Virgin Land: The American West as Symbol and Myth* (New York: Vintage, 1970 [1950]), 39 (reissued with a new preface).

9. A Friend to the National Industry, from Philadelphia, December 10, 1819, published in the *National Intelligencer*, reprinted in *American Farmer: Containing Original Essays and Selections on Rural Economy* 1:41 (January 7, 1820), 323. Andrew Jackson Downing relied on this trope for years: "Living, as we do, in a country whose boundaries extend from the 25th to the 48th degrees of latitude, embracing perhaps a wider range of soil and climate than is possessed by any other

civilized nation," from "Vineyards in the United States," *New-York Farmer* 7:5 (May 1834), 131. Also in Downing's "Notes on the Cultivation of Vineyards in the United States," *Southern Agriculturist* 10:8 (August 1837), 439: "a genial soil and climate in a country that extends from the 25th to the 48th of latitude. We are induced to believe, from observation, that the milder and more temperate portions of the Middle and Western states will become the field of the finest vineyards at no very distant period." Patent commissioner Henry Ellsworth utilized the trope as well, in the previous quote: "From the Gulf of Mexico to our Northern boundary, from the Atlantic to the far West, the peculiarities of climate, soil, and products, are great and valuable." U.S. Patent Office, *Annual Report 1840*, in Wayne D. Rasmussen, ed. *Agriculture in the United States: A Documentary History* Vol. 1 (New York: Random House, 1975), 512. William Robert Prince heavily relies on this trope in *A Treatise on the Vine* (1830), viii, nearly quoting his father's rant in *A Short Treatise on Horticulture* (1828). Viticulturists used it far into the future: in the President's Address to the Proceedings of the Eleventh Session of the American Pomological Society in 1867, he evokes the same: "Throughout an extent of territory running over twenty-five degrees of latitude, and from ocean to ocean, the native vine grows spontaneously; is as hardy as the forests it inhabits, and ripens as surely as the apple." *Proceedings of the Eleventh Session of the American Pomological Society, held in St. Louis, MO, 1867*. Report by Charles Bragdon (Boston: Franklin Printing House, 1868), 41.

10. Botanists use an adapted model of his naming hierarchies today. Details describing Linnaeus as a hilarious, self-promoting oaf are in Patricia Fara, *Sex, Botany and Empire: The Story of Carl Linnaeus and Joseph Banks* (Cambridge, UK: Icon Books, 2003).

11. Mary Louise Pratt, *Imperial Eyes: Travel Writing and Transculturation* (London: Routledge, 1992), 15, 25, 31, 36. Scholars of the U.S. colonial context might add the Bartrams' botanical forays in the Atlantic south and Lewis and Clark's expeditions as examples here. The *Systema Naturae* was fine tuned and republished for decades with two other definitive works, *Philosophica Botanica* (1751) and *Species Plantarum* (1753). Pratt continues, "The systematizing of nature carries this image of accumulation to a totalized extreme, and at the same time models the extractive, transformative character of industrial capitalism" (25).

12. Lisbet Koerner, *Linnaeus: Nature and Nation* (Cambridge, MA: Harvard University Press), 2–7.

13. William Robert Prince, aided by William Prince (Jr.), *A Treatise on the Vine; Embracing Its History from the Earliest Ages to the Present Day, with Descriptions of Above Two Hundred Foreign, and Eighty American Varieties; Together With a Complete Dissertation of the Establishment, Culture, and Management of Vineyards* (New York: T & J Swords, 1830). See also Thomas Pinney, "Wine in America: Twelve Historic Texts" (Part 2), *American Wine Society Journal* 21:2 (1989), 48. Lists of grape names and types are omnipresent in the literature. Nicholas Longworth in Cincinnati, Ohio, as well as operations in southern and northern California, continued to obsess over *vinifera* names, and the tradition continues today as a matter of national propriety and identity. On hybridizing, see David S. Shields, ed., *Pioneering American Wine* (Athens: University of Georgia Press), 24.

14. Hedrick, *A History of Agriculture in the State of New York*, 381.

15. William R. Prince, "The Vine," 120, 123, 125.

16. See Chapter 5 for a discussion of the aesthetic of grapevine flow. I have been inspired by Laura Rigal's attention to matters of flow in U.S. history, approaching the "science of fluid dynamics in the history of U.S. national expansion, examining how eighteenth- and nineteenth-century sciences of fluid motion (electricity, magnetism, plant physiology, blood, hydraulics, and global

weather patterns) underwrote American imperial enterprises." Laura Rigal, Obermann Summer Seminar Proposal, University of Iowa, April 15, 2008.

17. William R. Prince, *A Treatise on the Vine*, vii.

18. *Vitis labrusca*, Isabella, "drawn by W. Prince," frontispiece to *Treatise on the Vine*.

19. C. S. Rafinesque, *American Manual of Grape Vines and the Art of Making Wine: Including An Account of 62 Species of Vines, with Nearly 300 Varieties* (Philadelphia: Printed for the author, 1830), 43–44. Andrew Jackson Downing also estimated five thousand acres of vineyards in the United States in 1834. "Vineyards in the United States," *New-York Farmer* 7:5 (May 1834), 131. I have a feeling this underestimates vineyards in the United States by quite a bit, but these are the published numbers for the time. For more on the geography and location of vineyards in nineteenth-century New York and elsewhere, see W. H. Upshall and D. V. Fisher, eds., *History of Fruit Growing and Handling in United States of America and Canada, 1860–1970* (University Park, PA: Regatta City Press, 1976), especially the section on New York by George L. Slate, 99–106.

20. William R. Prince, "American Vineyards," *The Horticulturist* 1 (March 1847), 397–400.

21. For more on Democratic expansionists of the 1840s, see my Chapter 4, and Thomas R. Hietala, *Manifest Design: American Exceptionalism and Empire*, revised ed. (Ithaca, NY: Cornell University Press, 2003 [1985]), 97.

22. Angela Miller, *The Empire of the Eye*, 2, 13–14. Other key works on nineteenth-century cultural nationalism include Barbara Novak, *Nature and Culture: American Landscape and Painting, 1825–1875* (New York: Oxford University Press, 1980); John F. Sears, *Sacred Places: American Tourist Attractions in the Nineteenth Century* (Amherst: University of Massachusetts Press, 1989); David C. Miller, ed., *American Iconology* (New Haven, CT: Yale University Press, 1993); Albert Boïme, *The Magisterial Gaze: Manifest Destiny and American Landscape Painting c. 1830–1865* (Washington, DC: Smithsonian Institution Press, 1991).

23. Hamilton Traub, "The Development of American Horticultural Literature, Chiefly Between 1800 and 1850" (Part Two), *The National Horticultural Magazine* 8 (January 1929), 13–14.

24. Charles Sellers, *The Market Revolution: Jacksonian America, 1815–1846* (Oxford University Press, 1992); Scott E. Casper, Jeffrey D. Groves, Stephen W. Nissenbaum, and Michael Winship, eds., *A History of the Book in America*, Vol. 3: *The Industrial Book, 1840–1880* (Chapel Hill: University of North Carolina Press, 2007), 4, 7.

25. Donald B. Marti, "Agricultural Journalism and the Diffusion of Knowledge: The First Half-Century in America," *Agricultural History* 54:1 (January 1980), 31. Albert Lowther Demaree, *The American Agricultural Press, 1819–1960* (New York: Columbia University Press, 1941), 17. Shields, *Pioneering American Wine*, 26.

26. Marti's "Agricultural Journalism," *Agricultural History* 54:1 (January 1980), 28–37. For general information on horticultural literature, see also Hamilton Traub, "The Development of American Horticultural Literature, Chiefly Between 1800 and 1850" (Part One), *National Horticultural Magazine* 7 (July 1928), 97–103, and "Part Two," *National Horticultural Magazine* 8 (January 1929), 7–17.

27. Albert Lowther Demaree, *The American Agricultural Press, 1819–1860* (New York: Columbia University Press, 1941), 17.

28. Mrs. H. H. Dodge, "The Cottage of the Vine," *Saturday Evening Post* (March 6, 1830). Republished in *Casket* (April 1830), 162–163.

29. I estimate these numbers and their impact slightly higher. A quick count of the original U.S. works listed in James Gabler's *Wine into Words: A History and Bibliography of Wine Books in*

the English Language (Baltimore: Bacchus Press, 1985), concerning grape growing and dressing (therefore not including works solely on wine) before 1840 comes in at seven titles, but this number includes a "memoir," "essay," "treatise," "guide," "manual," " and "journal," perhaps a larger pool than simply books proper (chronological list of all texts in English in Gabler, with these titles on page 324; I counted original U.S. titles 1820–1840). From 1840 through 1869, I estimate slightly fewer, about thirty-four new U.S. titles (lists of texts in English, separating the ones newly published in the United States, Gabler, *Wine into Words*, 325–329). See also Thomas Pinney, *History of Wine in America from the Beginnings to Prohibition* (Berkeley: University of California Press, 1989), 222. For the most extensive grape and wine bibliographies, see Maynard A. Amerine and Axel E. Borg, *A Bibliography on Grapes, Wines, Other Alcoholic Beverages, and Temperance: Works Published in the United States Before 1901* (Berkeley: University of California Press, 1996), as well as Elisabeth Woodburn, "United States Alcoholic Beverage & Grape Collection, A Historic Collection 1771–1919," unpublished description of collection for sale at Booknoll Farm, Hopewell, New Jersey, undated.

30. Liberty Hyde Bailey, *Cyclopedia of American Horticulture*, Volumes E–M (New York: Macmillan, 1900), 667, 666.

31. "Office of the *American Agriculturist*, No. 41 Park Row, New York City," *American Agriculturist* 19 (October 1860), 304.

32. Some information from Hedrick, *A History of Agriculture in the State of New York*, 318–322. The rest is culled from reading several decades' worth of agricultural journals, and through several directed searches on OCLC FirstSearch.

33. William Wilson, "Art. 1—On the Culture of the Grape." *New-York Farmer and Horticultural Repository* 1:1 (January 1, 1828), 4.

34. The *New-York Farmer* was published 1828–1832, then changed its name to *The Cultivator*. Anonymous, "Art. 48.—Grape Vines—extracted from *Wilson's Economy of the Kitchen Garden, Orchard, and Vinery*, just published by Anderson, Davis, & Co., New York," *New-York Farmer and Horticultural Repository* 1:3 (1828), 55–57, image of grapevine pruning techniques on unnumbered page between 56 and 57.

35. *New-York Farmer and Horticultural Repository* 1:3 (March 1828), 55, 57.

36. "Fig. 88—The Diana Grape" in *The Horticulturist* 4 (November 1849), 224; "The Clinton Grape," *The Horticulturist* 8 (1853), 121; "The Delaware Grape," *The Horticulturist* 8 (1853), 492; and "Rebecca Grape" and "Canadian Chief Grape," *The Horticulturist* 13 (January 1858), 14–15.

37. "Clara," *The Horticulturist* 14 (February 1859), before page 57; "Tokalon, for *The Horticulturist*. Published by C. M. Saxton, Barker & Co., New-York," *The Horticulturist* 14 (July 1859), before page 297; "Golden Hamburgh, Grown by C. P. Bissell & Salter, Rochester, NY," *The Horticulturist* 14 (October 1859), between pages 28 and 29; "Union Village, for the Horticulturist . . . ," *The Horticulturist* 17 (May 1861), foldout between pages 13 and 14; "The Anna," in *The Horticulturist* 17 (June 1861), foldout between pages 15 and 16.

38. *The Horticulturist* 9 (July 1854), 387; *The Horticulturist* 16 (April 1861), 189; *The Horticulturist* 16 (November 1861), 528.

39. "The Grape Mania," *American Agriculturalist* 19 (March 1860), 83.

40. "Wine-making in the West," *The Horticulturist* 3 (January 1848), 317.

41. "American Grapes Two Centuries Ago," *American Agriculturist* 19 (March 1860), 83.

42. Richard Slotkin, *The Fatal Environment: The Myth of the Frontier in the Age of Industrialization, 1800–1890* (New York: HarperPerennial, 1985), 109.

43. Slotkin, *Fatal Environment,* 82–83, 95, 98, 110. Reginald Horsman corroborates that "the growth and acceptance of the Romantic movement in American literature parallels in time the growth and acceptance of the new scientific racialism." Horsman, *Race and Manifest Destiny: The Origins of American Racial Anglo-Saxonism* (Cambridge, MA: Harvard University Press, 1981), 159.

44. Lori Merish, "Melodrama and American Fiction," in *A Companion to American Fiction, 1780–1865,* ed. Shirley Samuels (Oxford: Blackwell, 2004), 192.

45. James Fenimore Cooper, *Gleanings in Europe: Switzerland* (Albany: State University of New York Press, 1980 [1836]), xxvi. See also "Cooper, James Fenimore," in *American National Biography,* ed. John Garraty and Mark Carnes (New York: Oxford University Press, 1999), 443–45.

46. Cooper, *The Headsman,* 91.

47. Cooper, *The Headsman,* 134.

48. Cooper, *The Headsman,* 134.

49. Archibald Alison, *Essays on the Nature and Principles of Taste* (Boston: Cummings and Hillard, 1812 [1790]); see also Rochelle L. Johnson, *Passions for Nature: Nineteenth-Century America's Aesthetics of Alienation* (Athens: University of Georgia Press, 2009), 116–117. Susan Fenimore Cooper, *Pages and Pictures From the Writings of James Fenimore Cooper, with Notes by Susan Fenimore Cooper, Illustrated, on Steel and Wood, from Original Drawings* (Secaucus, NJ: Castle Books, 1980 [1865]), 313–314.

50. On the dangers of weather and travel in Cooper's novels, see Alan Taylor, "Wasty Ways: Stories of American Settlement," *Environmental History* 3:3 (July 1998), 291–309.

51. Cooper, *Gleanings in Europe: Switzerland,* 221.

52. Grape culture figures less so in *France, England,* and *Italy,* perhaps because he so thoroughly addressed it in his first works.

53. Cooper, *Gleanings in Europe: Switzerland,* 10.

54. Cooper, *Gleanings in Europe: Switzerland,* 101, 103.

55. Cooper, *Gleanings in Europe: Switzerland,* 264–266.

56. Cooper, *Gleanings in Europe: The Rhine* (Albany: State University of New York Press, 1986 [1836]), 183.

57. Cooper, *Gleanings in Europe: The Rhine,* xxxi. Ernest Redekop and Maurice Geracht write in the introduction that this volume's real contribution to U.S. travel writing was Cooper's focus on all forms of gardens and planned landscapes throughout the Rhineland.

58. Cooper, *Gleanings in Europe: The Rhine,* 127, 128.

59. Cooper, *Gleanings in Europe: The Rhine,* 177, 178, 184.

60. Cooper, *Gleanings in Europe: The Rhine,* 182.

61. Cooper, *Gleanings in Europe: The Rhine,* 180–181.

62. Cooper, *Gleanings in Europe: Italy* (Albany: State University of New York Press, 1981 [1838]), 20, 205.

63. Cooper, *Gleanings in Europe: Italy,* 68–69.

64. Cooper, *Gleanings in Europe: Italy,* xlii.

65. David Wall, "Andrew Jackson Downing and the Tyranny of Taste," *American Nineteenth Century History* 8:2 (June 2007), 192, 194.

66. Andrew Jackson Downing, founding editor. *The Horticulturist: Journal of Rural Art and Rural Taste, Devoted to Horticulture, Landscape Gardening, Rural Architecture, Botany, Pomology, Entomology, Rural Economy, Etc.* (New York: Luther Tucker, 1846–1875). Some argue that it

continues as the best gardening magazine in the United States, ever. See Hedrick, *A History of Agriculture in the State of New York*, 395. Also see Albert Lowther Demaree, *The American Agricultural Press, 1819–1860* (New York: Morningside Heights, 1941). David Schuyler, *Apostle of Taste: Andrew Jackson Downing, 1815–1852* (Baltimore: Johns Hopkins University Press, 1996), 108, quoted from an advertisement in *The Cultivator* of June 1849, page 200.

67. "Fig. 56—Black Hamburgh Vine grown in a Pot," *The Horticulturist* 2 (July/June 1847–1848), 462; "Pruning the Grape Vine," *The Horticulturist* 12 (August 1857), 367; "Fig. 1. Arbors." *Horticulturist* 8 (1853), 508; and "The Diana Grape," *The Horticulturist* 12 (April 1857), frontispiece, 154, printed in full color.

68. Andrew Jackson Downing, *A Treatise on the Theory and Practice of Landscape Gardening, adapted to North America* (New York: G. P. Putnam, 1852), ix. His italics. Schuyler's *Apostle of Taste* is the best secondary resource on Downing. For this topic, see especially his chapter 5, "Reforming Rural Life." See also Schuyler, "Andrew Jackson Downing," in *American National Biography*, ed. Garraty and Carnes.

69. Downing, *Treatise*, vii, viii.

70. Anonymous, "A Visit to the House and Garden of the Late A. J. Downing," *The Horticulturist* 8 (January 1853), frontispiece, 20–27. The map of Downing's property was drawn by Frederick C. Withers and engraved by Alexander Anderson.

71. Bremer's unpublished letters, XI, 5 (February 1931), 171. In Arthur Channing Downs, Jr., "Downing's Newburgh Villa," *Bulletin of the Association for Preservation Technology* 4:3/4 (1972), 3. I discuss temperance in chapter 3.

72. Anonymous, "A Visit to the House and Garden of the Late A. J. Downing," 28. Downs, "Downing's Newburgh Villa," 16–17.

73. Downing, *Treatise*, 317–318. The first edition of this book was published in 1841; there were multiple editions for decades, and all editions had many reprints.

74. Downing, *Treatise*, 29–30.

75. Chandra Mukerji, *Territorial Ambitions and the Gardens of Versailles* (Cambridge: Cambridge University Press, 1997), 2, 15, 20.

76. "Gigantic Grape Vine at West Hill, Burlington County, New Jersey," *The Horticulturist* 13 (September 1858), frontispiece, 448; "Enormous Grape Vine," *The Horticulturist* 1 (May 1847), 530.

77. Downing, *Treatise*, 324–325.

78. Downing, *Landscape Gardening*, 325. Representative designs include "Design XI. A Cottage for a Country Clergyman," 165, "Design XVII. A Plain House," 187, "Design XXIII. An Architect's Residence," 203. In other writings, he included a picture of a farmhouse "employing the more comfortable and more characteristic verandah," A. J. Downing, "Hints on the Construction of Farm Houses," New York State Agricultural Society, *Transactions* 5 (1846), 236; also "Small Bracketed Cottage," Design II of *The Architecture of Country Houses*, and "Regular Bracketed Cottage," with "arbor-veranda," Design VIII of *The Architecture of Country Houses* (New York, 1850). (Last three reprinted in Schuyler, *Apostle of Taste*, 117, 138, and 140, respectively.)

79. Andrew Jackson Downing, *Victorian Cottage Residences* (New York: Dover, 1981 [1842]), 167. Subsequent editions appeared in 1844, 1847, 1852, and after his death in 1853, 1856, 1860, 1863, 1873, among many others.

80. Downing, *Victorian Cottage Residences*, 33, 312. For more on where these cottages would have been built, see Dolores Hayden, *Building Suburbia: Green Fields and Urban Growth, 1820–2000* (New York: Pantheon Books, 2003). She describes seven patterns of suburban development:

borderlands, picturesque enclaves, streetcar buildouts, mail-order and self-built suburbs, edge nodes, and rural fringes. Each one was successively dominant for about twenty-five years. Downing's houses fit into the "borderlands" and "picturesque enclaves" categories. Hayden specifically treats Downing in chapter 3; landscape gardeners were some of the first professionals to push suburban growth.

81. Some argue that it was a national aesthetic of "variation and discontinuity," and as such was self-consciously democratic. The picturesque deliberately converts landscape into a dramatic incident, and in doing so offered visual literacy to an emerging republic. The voluminous work done on the "beautiful" and the "picturesque" include John Conron, *American Picturesque* (University Park: Pennsylvania State University Press, 2000); David C. Miller, *Dark Eden: The Swamp in Nineteenth-Century American Culture* (New York: Cambridge University Press, 1989); Carrie Tirado Bramen, "The Urban Picturesque," *American Quarterly* 52:3 (September 2000); John Sears, *Sacred Places: American Tourist Attractions in the Nineteenth Century* (Amherst: University of Massachusetts Press, 1989); Kenneth Meyers, "On the Cultural Construction of Landscape Experience: Contact to 1830," in *American Iconology: New Approaches to Nineteenth-Century Art and Literature*, ed. David C. Miller (New Haven, CT: Yale University Press, 1993); and *Home Book of the Picturesque: Or American Scenery, Art, and Literature, Comprising a Series of Essays by Washington Irving, W.C. Bryant, Fenimore Cooper and Others* (New York: G. P. Putnam,1852). I include examples of the picturesque in context in Chapter 3.

82. Downing, *Victorian Cottage Residences*, 48.

83. John Fisk Allen, *A Practical Treatise on the Culture and Treatment of the Grape Vine: Embracing its History, with Directions for its Treatment, in the United States of America, in the Open Air, and under Glass Structures, with and without artificial heat*, 3rd ed. (New York: C. M. Saxton & Co., 1857) (many other editions: 1847, 1853, 1858, 1860).

84. "The Pleasures of Gardening," *The Horticulturist* 7 (September 1852), 397.

85. William R. Prince, "American Vineyards," *The Horticulturist* 1 (March 1847), 393.

86. Benedict Anderson, *Imagined Communities: Reflections on the Origin and Spread of Nationalism* (New York: Verso, 1991).

Chapter 2. Propagating Empire

1. Thomas Bridgeman, *The Young Gardener's Assistant: Containing a Catalogue of Garden & Flower Seeds, With Practical Directions Under Each Head, for the Cultivation of Vegetables and Flowers, also Directions for Cultivating Fruit Trees, the Grape Vine, &c., to which is added, A Calendar* (New York: T. Bridgeman, 1840 [other editions in 1833, 1837, 1845, 1847, 1853, 1857, 1858, 1865]), i, iii. I am citing the "eighth edition, improved," which was written and sold in New York City, as well as in Boston, Baltimore, Washington City, Raleigh, Cleveland, Cincinnati, New Orleans, and St. Louis, and to "other Seedsmen and Florists in various parts of the United States, also, by book-sellers in general."

2. Bridgeman, *Young Gardener's Assistant*, 293–306.

3. Images in the *Annual Report of the Commissioner of Patents for the Year 1858: Agriculture*, U.S. House of Representatives, 35th Congress, Second Session, Executive Document Number 105 (Washington, DC: James B. Steedman, Printer, 1859); hereafter *Report of 1858*. Other details in *Annual Report of the Commissioner of Patents for the Year 1859: Agriculture*, 36th Congress, First Session (Washington, DC: George Bowman, 1860); hereafter *Report of 1859*.

4. *Report of 1858*, 17.

5. S.D., "United States Patent Office, Tea Culture, Grapes, Rare Plants, &c." *Southern Cultivator* 17:8 (August 1859), 249. See also *Report of 1859*, 17; "Patent Office Report for 1859," *The Cultivator* 8:7 (July 1860), 210–212. The *Report of 1859* is also quoted in *The Cultivator* 8:7 (July 1860), 210.

6. Murray Bookchin, *The Ecology of Freedom: The Emergence and Dissolution of Hierarchy* (Oakland, CA: AK Press, 2005 [1982]), 302–355. Bookchin uses a somewhat simpler definition of technics, and critiques Mumford's use of it, but the theoretical end result is the same. See also Georg Lukacs, "The Phenomenon of Reification," in *History and Class Consciousness* (New York: Merlin Press, 1967 [1923]); Herbert Marcuse, "Some Social Implications of Modern Technology" (1941), in *Technology, War and Fascism, Collected Papers of Herbert Marcuse*, Vol. 1, Douglas Kellner, ed. (New York: Routledge, 1998); Teresa de Lauretis, "The Technology of Gender," in *Technologies of Gender* (Bloomington: Indiana University Press, 1987); Lewis Mumford, *Technics and Civilization* (New York: Harcourt, Brace and Co., 1934), 41.

7. Frieda Knobloch, *The Culture of Wilderness: Agriculture as Colonization in the American West* (Chapel Hill: University of North Carolina Press, 1996), 49–50.

8. Vinery details culled from many agricultural journals, including most prominently *The Horticulturist, New York Farmer, Plough Boy,* and *American Agriculturist.* Some details also found in U. P. Hedrick, *A History of Horticulture in America to 1860* (New York: Oxford University Press, 1950), 266. Hedrick cites that by 1858, there were more than forty vineries in Buffalo, New York, as well. See also *Proceedings of the Third Session of the American Pomological Society, held in Boston, 1854* (Boston: Franklin Printing House, 1854), 50, 65, 95, 223; *Proceedings of the Seventh Session of the American Pomological Society, held in New York, 1858* (Brooklyn, NY: George C. Bennett, 1858), 116–117, 232–233; *Proceedings of the Eleventh Session of the American Pomological Society, held in St. Louis, Missouri, 1867,* reported by Charles Bragdon (Boston: Franklin Printing House, 1868), among others.

9. See "A Lean-to Cold Vinery. Scale ten Feet to an inch," in "Culture of Foreign Grapes in Cold Vineries," *The Horticulturist* 8 (1853), 79; and the drawing in "Vine Borders Heated Artificially," *The Horticulturist* 12 (January 1857), 82. See also "View in the Vinery, At Clinton Point" in article "The Vinery at Clinton Point," *The Horticulturist* 4 (October 1949), 179.

10. Georg Kohlmaier and Barna von Sartory, *Houses of Glass: A Nineteenth-Century Building Type* (Cambridge, MA: MIT Press, 1986), 46–47.

11. Kohlmaier and von Sartory, *Houses of Glass,* 36. See also Billie Sherrill Britz, *The Greenhouse at Lyndhurst: Construction and Development of the Gould Greenhouse, 1881* (Washington, DC: The Preservation Press, 1977); and Britz, "The Greenhouse at Lyndhurst," *National Trust for Historic Preservation, Research on Historical Properties,* Occasional Papers, no. 1, 1977.

12. Anne Friedberg details the growth of shopping arcades and other monstrous glass buildings—the nineteenth-century catchall term for structures with artificially warm and humid climates being, tellingly, "winter gardens." Friedberg, *Window Shopping* (Berkeley: University of California Press, 1994), 2, 61, 77.

13. Kohlmaier and von Sartory, *Houses of Glass,* 98, 86.

14. John R. Gold and Margaret M. Gold, *Cities of Culture: Staging International Festivals and the Urban Agenda, 1851–2000* (Burlington, VT: Ashgate, 2005), 62, 63, 4, 31, 1, 25. Kohlmaier and von Sartory argue in *Houses of Glass* that the greenhouse was always a "contrasting" space to the factory and home. While their book is useful and cogent, I disagree with them on this point.

15. Geo. E. Woodward & F. W. Woodward, *Woodward's Graperies and Horticultural Buildings*

(New York: Stephen Hallet, 1865/1867), 94, 124–125. See "Fig. 10—Perspective View," 62, "Fig. 34—Perspective," 95, "Fig. 52—Perspective" and "Fig. 53—Ground Plan." This last grand-scale grapery was also published in *The Horticulturist* 14 (June 1864), 174–175. Many more grapery designs can be found in *The Horticulturist* 18.

16. A. Messer, "The Foreign Grape Under Glass," *The Horticulturist* 7 (December 1852), 567–569. See also Woodward and Woodward, *Woodward's Graperies,* 96–97.

17. Kohlmaier and von Sartory, *Houses of Glass,* 26, quoting Loudon in 1817.

18. Peter B. Mead, *An Elementary Treatise on American Grape Culture and Wine Making* (*Mead's Grape Culture*) (New York: Harper & Brothers, 1867), figures on 77, 90, 103, 104, 113, 125, 127, 129, 136, and 140.

19. Vitis, "New Mode of Ripening Foreign Grapes," *The Horticulturist* 1 (August 1846), 70.

20. Donald H. Parkerson, *The Agricultural Transition in New York State: Markets and Migration in Mid-Nineteenth Century America* (Ames: Iowa State University Press, 1995), 16. Gregory A. Sanford, *A Capacity for Agricultural Change: Indigenous Technical Knowledge and the New York State Agricultural Society in the Transformation of U.S. Agriculture, 1830–1862* (Ames: Iowa State University, 1988), 29. See also Wayne D. Rasmussen, ed., *Agriculture in the United States: A Documentary History,* 4 vols. (New York: Random House, 1975), especially the introductions to each section.

21. "Garden," "horticultural," and "fruit" crops being interchangeable here, including grapes, fruits, vegetables, and other small crops. Larger crops (wheat, cotton, and so on) are defined as agricultural crops. Andrew Jackson Downing, "Cultivators: The Great Industrial Class of America," *The Horticulturist* 2 (June 1848), 538. Downing takes his numbers from Edmund Burke's *Annual Report of the Commissioner of Patents* for 1847. For more, see Paul W. Gates, *The Farmer's Age: Agriculture, 1815–1860* (New York: Holt, Rinehart and Winston, 1960), 329–337, and David Schuyler, *Apostle of Taste: Andrew Jackson Downing, 1815–1852* (Baltimore: Johns Hopkins University Press, 1996), 109.

22. Brooke Hindle and Steven Lubar, *Engines of Change: The American Industrial Revolution, 1790–1860* (Washington, DC: Smithsonian Books, 1986), 105–106. Norman Ware, *The Industrial Worker, 1840–1860: The Reaction of American Industrial Society to the Advance of the Industrial Revolution* (Boston: Houghton Mifflin Co., 1924), 1. See also Sellers, *The Market Revolution: Jacksonian America, 1815–1846* (New York: Oxford University Press, 1991).

23. Sarah T. Phillips, "Antebellum Agricultural Reform, Republican Ideology, and Sectional Tension," 801, 808; see also Eric Foner, *Free Soil, Free Labor, Free Men* (Oxford: Oxford University Press, 1970); and Rasmussen, ed., *Agriculture in the United States,* 523.

24. Hindle and Lubar, *Engines of Change,* 99.

25. The act (5 Stat. L., 353, 354) was passed March 3, 1839, and the Patent Office eventually had help from the Smithsonian Institution. These duties were transferred to the Department of Agriculture in 1862. Gustavus A. Weber, *The Patent Office: Its History, Activities and Organization* (Baltimore: John Hopkins Press, 1924), 11, 12.

26. Harry Kursh, *Inside the U.S. Patent Office: The Story of the Men, the Laws, and the Procedures of the American Patent System* (New York: W. W. Norton & Co., 1959), 26. Kenneth W. Dobyns, *The Patent Office Pony: A History of the Early Patent Office* (Fredericksburg, VA: Sergeant Kirkland's, 1997), 92, 111. Ellsworth was once accompanied on a trip through the Rockies by Washington Irving. Washington Irving wrote about the trip in his *Tour on the Prairies* (published pseudonymously, Philadelphia: Carey, Lea & Blanchard, 1835).

27. U.S. Department of Agriculture, *Yearbook 1902* (Washington, DC: Government Printing

Office, 1903), frontispiece. See also Thomas Pinney, *History of Wine in America from the Beginnings to Prohibition* (Berkeley: University of California Press, 1989), 219, 477. Other details in Stacy V. Jones, *The Patent Office* (New York: Praeger, 1971), 126.

28. *Report of 1859*. Also see Pinney, *History of Wine in America*, 219, 121–123. Williams found a wine industry in El Paso that had been in operation since the seventeenth century. I examine this larger viticultural space, legacy, and its obvious irony in the face of eastern viticultural rhetoric in Chapter 5.

29. Mary Louise Pratt, *Imperial Eyes: Travel Writing and Transculturation* (London: Routledge, 1992), 18, 20, 23.

30. For example, the *Report of 1858* had 210,000 *extra* copies printed (original number unknown); 10,000 were for distribution by the Department of the Interior alone. *Report of 1858*, ii. Dobyns corroborates on other volumes, *Patent Office Pony*, 111.

31. *Report for 1859*, 568–571; Dobyns, *Patent Office Pony*, 113, 114.

32. From the U.S. Patent Office, *Annual Report of 1840*, 4–5, 68–83. Reprinted in Rasmussen, ed., *Agriculture in the United States*, vol. 1, 512, 516–517. The tendency to use sweeping language ("from the Gulf of Mexico to our Northern Boundary") to describe the nation's size and influence was discussed in Chapter 1.

33. Rasmussen, ed., *Agriculture in the United States*, vol. 1, 516.

34. Dobyns, *Patent Office Pony*, 111, 112, 121–128.

35. Siegfried Giedion, *Mechanization Takes Command: A Contribution to Anonymous History* (New York: Oxford University Press, 1948), 131, 139, 140.

36. Historian Tamara Plakins Thornton has argued that in postrevolutionary Boston, gentlemen farming was part of a complex of genteel activities, "a style of living rich." Thornton, *Cultivating Gentlemen: The Meaning of Country Life Among the Boston Elite, 1785–1860* (New Haven, CT: Yale University Press, 1989), 56.

37. Cheryl Lyon-Jenness, "Planting a Seed: The Nineteenth-Century Horticultural Boom in America," *Business History Review* 78:3 (Autumn 2004), 389; Patricia M. Tice, *Gardening in America, 1830–1910* (Rochester, NY: Strong Museum, 1984), 7; Hedrick, *History of Agriculture in the State of New York*, 386. Also see Pinney, *History of Wine in America*, 187ff.

38. Sarah T. Phillips, "Antebellum Agricultural Reform, Republican Ideology, and Sectional Tension," *Agricultural History* 74:4 (Autumn 2000), 801, 808.

39. Schuyler, *Apostle of Taste*, 109.

40. W. J. Rorabaugh, *The Alcoholic Republic: An American Tradition* (Oxford: Oxford University Press, 1979), 101ff. See also Robert C. Fuller, *Religion and Wine: A Cultural History of Wine Drinking in the United States* (Knoxville: University of Tennessee Press, 1996) and Pinney, *History of Wine in America*.

41. Percy Wells Bidwell and John I. Falconer, *A History of Agriculture in the Northern United States, 1620–1860* (New York: Peter Smith, 1925, 1941), 316. See also Charles Van Ravenswaay, *A Nineteenth-Century Garden* (New York: Main Street Press, 1977), 8; David S. Shields, *Pioneering American Wine* (Athens: University of Georgia Press, 2009), 86; Richardson Wright, *The Story of Gardening* (New York: Dodd, Mead & Co., 1934), 403, 406.

42. See Bidwell and Falconer, *The History of Agriculture;* Van Ravenswaay, *A Nineteenth-Century Garden*, and Wright, *The Story of Gardening*.

43. Mead, *An Elementary Treatise*, 474.

44. *Proceedings of the Eleventh Session of the American Pomological Society*, 35–36.

45. Van Ravenswaay, *A Nineteenth-Century Garden*, 10–11; and Bruce Weber, *The Apple of America: The Apple in Nineteenth-Century American Art* (New York: Enterprise, 1993).

46. Mead, *An Elementary Treatise*, 235.

47. Mead, *An Elementary Treatise*, 475–476.

48. Scott E. Casper, Jeffrey D. Groves, Stephen W. Nissenbaum, and Michael Winship, eds., *A History of the Book in America*, Vol. 3: *The Industrial Book, 1840–1880* (Chapel Hill: University of North Carolina Press, 2007), 4, 5. Noel Kingsbury, *Hybrid: The History and Science of Plant Breeding* (Chicago: University of Chicago Press, 2009), 61.

49. "Notes on American Grapes," *The Horticulturist* 2 (September 1847), 122.

50. See Thomas Augst, *The Clerk's Tale: Young Men and Moral Life in Nineteenth-Century America* (Chicago: University of Chicago Press, 2003), 4; Elizabeth B. Keeney, *The Botanizers: Amateur Scientists in Nineteenth-Century America* (Chapel Hill: University of North Carolina Press, 1992), especially chapter 3, "Botanizing and Self-Improvement"; Karen Haltunnen, *Confidence Men and Painted Women: A Study of Middle-Class Culture in America, 1830–1870* (New Haven, CT: Yale University Press, 1982); James B. Salazar, *Bodies of Reform: The Rhetoric of Character in Gilded Age America* (New York: NYU Press, 2010); Scott Sandage, *Born Losers: A History of Failure in America* (Cambridge, MA: Harvard University Press, 2005). For related themes, see also Michael Zakim, *Ready-Made Democracy: A History of Men's Dress in the American Republic, 1760–1860* (Chicago: University of Chicago Press).

51. Andrew Jackson Downing, "The Influence of Horticulture," *The Horticulturist* 2 (July 1847), 9.

52. Augst, *Clerk's Tale*, 65. On the refinement of America, see Richard Bushman, *The Refinement of America: Persons, Houses, Cities* (New York: Vintage, 1993).

53. A Friend to National Industry, "Grape Vine," *National Intelligencer* (1819); reprinted in *American Farmer* 1:41 (January 7, 1820), 323.

54. *The Farmers' Register* 9:7 (July 31, 1841), 385 (this was an American tourist's description of French vineyards); *The Friend* 18:44 (July 26, 1845), 347.

55. *Farmer & Gardener* 4:42 (February 13, 1838), 331.

56. Just a few examples include: "Luxuriant Native Grape Vine," *Archives of Useful Knowledge* 1:3 (January 1811), 276; "The luxuriance with which both foreign and native grapes grow . . . give reason to think that the vine might be cultivated with advantage, on a large scale" *The National Recorder* 2:2 (July 10, 1819), 17; "the United States—where the vine grows luxuriantly," *New Harmony Gazette* (September 6, 1826), 393; "The Grape Vine is a native of the United States, and several varieties of it are found growing in great luxuriance throughout all the forests in the southern, middle, and most of the northern states," *New-York Farmer and Horticultural Repository* 1:1 (1828), 55; "[It] grows with great rapidity and luxuriance," *New Harmony Gazette* (September 13, 1826), 402; "The vine may grow very luxuriantly in a rich, moist soil," Nicholas Herbemont, "Letter to Nicholas Longworth on the Grape Vine, March 19, 1829," *Southern Agriculturist* 2:12 (December 1829), 550–555; "The grape does not do very well with me, though it grows luxuriantly enough," Nicholas Herbemont, "Letter to Alabama Planter, July 9, 1830," *American Farmer* 12:19 (July 28, 1830), 147–148; "flinging its pliant and luxuriant branches over the rustic veranda," *The Naturalist* 1:1 (December 1830), 28; "The cultivation of grapes has been commenced with ardor . . . [grapes and wine] will make an important item in the already numerous catalogue of our home prepared luxuries," *The Genesee Farmer and Gardener's Journal* (February 4, 1832), 37; by Andrew Jackson Downing, "in the Middle States, where now the native vines clamber in wild luxuriance from tree

to tree," *Southern Agriculturist* 10:8 (August 1837), 440; "the roots expand and multiply in all the freedom of unrestrained luxuriance," *American Farmer and Spirit of the Agricultural Journals of the Day* 4:9 (September 28, 1842), 145; "We do not seem aware of the facility with which a luxuriant and fruitful vine may be obtained . . . farmers . . . who do not luxuriate themselves [still grow grape-vines in their cellars], and enable their families to luxuriate in a plentiful supply of this delicious fruit," *The Farmers' Cabinet and American Herd Book* 10:10 (May 15, 1846), 316; "There is nothing that grows more luxuriantly than grape vines, not excepting weeds or wild trees . . . the grape is naturally luxuriant, and it deserves more extensive culture," *Boston Cultivator* 9:27 (July 3, 1847), 208; "our fruits, in their native form, grow wild in the greatest abundance and luxuriance," *The Horticulturist* 1 (November 1846), 222; "the Isabella grape. . . grew in several gardens there, and from its great luxuriance, and the fine flavor of its fruit, I became exceedingly interested in its origin," *The Horticulturist* 6 (September 1851), 410; "the numerous vineyards of the Catawba, dotting the hillsides and valleys . . . around the city, to an eastern man, were truly a luxury to look upon," *The Horticulturist* 6 (September 1851), 411.

57. On anxieties about luxury in the early republic, see Neil Harris, *The Artist in American Society: The Formative Years, 1790–1860* (Chicago: University of Chicago Press, 1982). For the mid-nineteenth century's transition to a love of luxury, and its essential place in cultural debates since generations before, see John Kasson, *Civilizing the Machine: Technology and Republican Values in America, 1776–1900* (New York: Hill and Wang, 1999 [1976]), 15.

58. Herman Melville, "Paradise of Bachelors, Tartarus of Maids," *Harper's New Monthly Magazine* 10 (April 1855), 674.

59. William Cronon, *Nature's Metropolis: Chicago and the Great West* (New York: W. W. Norton, 1991), 68.

Chapter 3. Landscapes of Fruit and Profit

1. Specifically, John Jacob Astor, Cornelius Vanderbilt, and California's "Big Four" (Leland Stanford, C. P. Huntington, Charles Crocker, and Mark Hopkins). Only Gustavus Myers, New York socialist muckraker of the early twentieth century, has compared Longworth with millionaire land barons Astor, Peter Goelet, the Rhinelander brothers, the Schermerhorns (all of New York), and Marshall Field (of Chicago) in his *History of the Great American Fortunes* (New York: Modern Library, 1936 [1910]), in chapter 8, "Other Land Fortunes Considered." On Johnny Appleseed as a fruit speculator, see Michael Pollan, *The Botany of Desire: A Plant's-Eye View of the World,* chapter 1, "Desire: Sweetness/Plant: The Apple" (New York: Random House, 2001).

2. *Memorial of the Golden Wedding of Nicholas Longworth and Susan Longworth Celebrated at Cincinnati on Christmas Eve, 1857* (Baltimore: Hunckel & Son, 1858), n.p.

3. Longworth had many appellations, the "father of American wine" being the most popular. His title "the Western Bacchus" is found in C. M., "American Vineyards and Wine," *Southern Cultivator* 16:6 (June 1858), 22–23. He was also known as "the fifteen millionaire." Ferencz Aurelius Pulszky and Theresa Pulszky, *White, Red, Black: Sketches of American Society in the United States* (New York: Redfield, 1853), 295; Richard Miller Devens, *Cyclopaedia of Commercial and Business Anecdotes* (New York: D. Appleton & Co., 1865), 45. "Nicholas Longworth, Esq. of Cincinnati, and the Vineyards of Ohio," *Harper's Weekly* 2 (July 24, 1858), 472.

4. Paul Lukacs offers this interesting but problematic history of nineteenth-century U.S. wine

in the first two chapters of *American Vintage: The Rise of American Wine* (Boston: Houghton Mifflin, 2000). Thomas Pinney also has a significant, celebratory section on Longworth in *A History of Wine in America: From the Beginnings to Prohibition* (Berkeley: University of California Press, 1989). See also Walter Stix Glazer, *Cincinnati in 1840: The Social and Functional Organization of an Urban Community During the Pre–Civil War Period* (Columbus: Ohio State University Press, 1999), 85–88, and Clara Longworth de Chambrun, *The Making of Nicholas Longworth: Annals of an American Family* (Freeport, NY: Books for Libraries Press, 1933), as well as her *Cincinnati: Story of the Queen City* (New York: Charles Scribner's Sons, 1939).

5. Longworth also paid more real estate tax than any American, save Astor. A short but telling biography of Longworth, by Charles Boewe, is found in John A. Garraty and Mark C. Carnes, eds., *American National Biography,* Vol. 13 (New York: Oxford, 1999), 898–899. The major text on wine history in America is Thomas Pinney's. For wine in America in the eighteenth century, see David Hancock, *Oceans of Wine: Madeira and the Emergence of American Trade and Taste* (New Haven, CT: Yale University Press, 2009). See also Charles L. Sullivan, *Zinfandel: A History of a Grape and Its Wine* (Berkeley: University of California Press, 2003); Leon D. Adams, *The Wines of America,* 3rd ed. (New York: McGraw-Hill, 1985 [1973]). For the fruit industry, see Douglas Cazaux Sackman, *Orange Empire: California and the Fruits of Eden* (Berkeley: University of California Press, 2005), and Steven Stoll, *The Fruits of Natural Advantage: Making the Industrial Countryside in California* (Berkeley: University of California Press, 1998).

6. Frieda Knobloch theorizes a later version of Western agricultural imperialism in *The Culture of Wilderness: Agriculture as Colonization in the American West* (Chapel Hill: University of North Carolina Press, 1996). On the importance of horticulture in the United States, see also Philip J. Pauly, *Fruits and Plains: The Horticultural Transformation of America* (Cambridge, MA: Harvard University Press, 2007); Daniel Kevles, "Fruit Nationalism: Horticulture in the United States— from the Revolution to the First Centennial," in *Aurora Torealis: Studies in the History of Science and Ideas in Honor of Tore Frangsmyr* (Sagamore Beach, CA: Science History Publications, 2008); Cheryl Lyon-Jenness, "Planting a Seed: The Nineteenth-Century Horticultural Boom in America," *Business History Review* 78:3 (Autumn 2004); Cheryl Lyon-Jenness, *For Shade and for Comfort: Democratizing Horticulture in the Nineteenth-Century Midwest* (West Lafayette, IN: Purdue University Press, 2004); Tamara Plakins Thornton, *Cultivating Gentlemen: The Meaning of Country Life Among the Boston Elite, 1785–1860* (New Haven, CT: Yale University Press, 1989). Other fruit entrepreneurs include the William Prince family, "Apple King" Robert Pell, and Ellwanger & Barry (all of New York); Francis Parkman, Marshall Wilder, and Charles Hovey (of Massachusetts); and many others.

7. Frieda Knobloch details the agricultural colonization of the Midwest, as does Wayne D. Rasmussen, ed., in *Agriculture in the United States: A Documentary History,* 4 vols. (New York: Greenwood Press, 1977). See also Brooke Hindle and Steven Lubar, *Engines of Change: The American Industrial Revolution, 1790–1860* (Washington, DC: Smithsonian Institution Press, 1986), 96. In the nineteenth century, federal aid to agriculture increased, as well as money and land for railroads. See Percy Wells Bidwell and John I. Falconer, *A History of Northern Agriculture, 1620–1840* (New York: Peter Smith, 1941), 259, 266, 316; Siegfried Giedion, *Mechanization Takes Command: A Contribution to Anonymous History* (New York: Oxford University Press, 1948), 146. See also Christopher Clark, "The Ohio Country in the Political Economy of Nation Building," in Andrew R. L. Cayton and Stuart D. Hobbs, *The Center of a Great Empire* (Athens: Ohio University Press, 2005), 148; Steven Hahn and Jonathan Prude, *The Countryside in the Age of Capitalist Transformation:*

Essays in the Social History of Rural America (Chapel Hill: University of North Carolina Press, 1985), 3; Robert Price, *Johnny Appleseed: Man and Myth* (Bloomington: Indiana University Press, 1954), 37, 58.

8. Hahn and Prude, *The Countryside in the Age of Capitalist Transformation*, 3; Kim M. Gruenwald, *River of Enterprise: The Commercial Origins of Regional Identity in the Ohio Valley, 1790–1850* (Bloomington: Indiana University Press, 2002), xi, 157.

9. D. W. Meinig, *The Shaping of America: A Geographical Perspective on 500 Years of History*, Vol. 2: *Continental America, 1800–1867* (New Haven, CT: Yale University Press, 1993), 361. See also Andrew R. L. Cayton and Peter S. Onuf, *The Midwest and the Nation: Rethinking the History of an American Region* (Bloomington: Indiana University Press, 1990).

10. Charles Cist, *Cincinnati in 1841: Its Annals and Future Prospects* (Cincinnati: Charles Cist, 1841), 275; Charles Cist, *Sketches and Statistics of Cincinnati in 1851* (Cincinnati: Wm. H. Moore & Co., 1851), 320. Travelers had been writing this for a while: Manasseh Cutler wrote in 1787 that the area between Lake Erie and the Ohio River would be "the garden of the world, the seat of wealth, and the *centre* of a great Empire." Manasseh, *An Explanation of the Map which Delineates that Part of the Federal Lands . . .* (Salem, MA: Dabney and Cushing, 1787), 14. See also Cayton and Hobbs, *The Center of a Great Empire.*

11. Glazer, *Cincinnati in 1840*, 25, 26; Meinig, *The Shaping of America*, 2: 248, 256, 361. See also Richard Wade, *The Urban Frontier: The Rise of Western Cities, 1790–1830* (Urbana: University of Illinois Press, 1996 [1959]). Mammoth growth brought St. Louis even with Cincinnati (at about 160,000 people) by 1860.

12. Jon C. Teaford, *Cities of the Heartland: The Rise and Fall of the Industrial Midwest* (Bloomington: Indiana University Press), 13. He explains: "As early as 1831 Queen City presses were producing books at the rate of 350,000 volumes annually. Ten years later, estimates of production ranged from one to two million volumes annually."

13. Teaford calls this the development of a "heartland consciousness," ix. See also Louis Leonard Tucker, "'Old Nick' Longworth, the Paradoxical Maecenas of Cincinnati," *Cincinnati Historical Society Bulletin* 25 (1967), 253. Longworth was always concerned with how Western culture was faring in comparison to Eastern culture, and he financed many artists' trips east for education and exposure to a wider world. Teaford, *Cities of the Heartland*, 14.

14. Meinig also discusses Porter's daguerreotype in *The Shaping of America*, 2:362. See also Wendy Jean Katz, *Regionalism and Reform: Art and Class Formation in Antebellum Cincinnati* (Columbus: Ohio State University, 2002), 98. Cist, *Sketches and Statistics of Cincinnati in 1859*, frontispiece.

15. Richard Wade, *The Urban Frontier: The Rise of Western Cities, 1790–1830* (Urbana: University of Illinois Press, 1996 [1959]), and Meinig, *The Shaping of America*, 2:248.

16. George W. Pierson, *Tocqueville and Beaumont in America* (New York, 1938), 52.

17. *Memorial of the Golden Wedding of Nicholas Longworth and Susan Longworth celebrated at Cincinnati on Christmas Eve, 1857* (Baltimore: Hunckel & Son, 1858), n.p.

18. Teaford, *Cities of the Heartland*, 6, 7. Quoted from Maria L. Varney, "Letters from the Queen City," *The Herald of Truth* 2 (July 1847), 83–84. *The Horticulturist: Journal of Rural Art and Rural Taste, Devoted to Horticulture, Landscape Gardening, Rural Architecture, Botany, Pomology, Entomology, Rural Economy, Etc.* (New York: Luther Tucker, 1846–1875).

19. A. H. Ernst, "The Vineyards of Ohio," *The Horticulturist* 3 (February 1848), 420.

20. Nineteenth-century viticulturists were in dialogue with major European wine traditions.

See Hancock, *Oceans of Wine*. For how a nationalist identity was constructed through wine in France, see Kolleen M. Guy, *When Champagne Became French: Wine and the Making of a National Identity* (Baltimore: Johns Hopkins University Press, 2003).

21. "Horticultural Department: The Vineyards of the West," *Ohio Cultivator* (October 1, 1850), 300. Reprinted from its previous publication in *The Horticulturist*.

22. Melzer Flagg, *Remarks on the Culture of the Grape, and the Manufacture of Wine, in the Western States, Comprised in a Report Made by the Direction of the Cincinnati Horticultural Society, May 2, 1846* (Cincinnati: L'Hommedieu, 1846), 5, 8.

23. Gary L. Peters, *American Winescapes: The Cultural Landscapes of America's Wine Country* (Boulder, CO: Westview, 1997), 75–76; Harm J. de Blij, *Geography of Viticulture* (Miami: Miami Geographical Society, 1981), 84–85.

24. The Cincinnati Horticultural Society included Longworth, Robert Buchanan, John Mottier, William Resor, C. W. Elliott, A. H. Ernst, and several doctors (Stephen Mosher, Louis Rehfuss, John Aston Warder), all early winegrowers in the region (Pinney, *A History of Wine in America*, 165). Cist, *Sketches and Statistics of Cincinnati in 1851*, 111, and *Sketches and Statistics of Cincinnati in 1859* (Cincinnati: s.n, 1859), 209. Edward S. Wayne, "Extracts from a Report on the Production of Wine, Brandy, and Tartar, in the Vicinity of Cincinnati," *American Journal of Pharmacy* (November 1855), 494. See also Robert Leslie Jones, *History of Agriculture in Ohio to 1880* (Kent, OH: Kent State University Press, 1983), 225, 226. John Frederic von Daacke, *"Sparkling Catawba": Grape Growing and Wine Making in Cincinnati, 1800–1870* (Master's thesis, University of Cincinnati, 1964), 53–60, further details the major vineyardists in the area, including Kentuckian B. F. Sanford, and Cincinnatians Thomas Yeatman, Fredric Disserns, Gabriel Sleath, Sebastian Rentz, John Duhme, John Unholtz, George Bogen, and John Ross.

25. *Cincinnati Horticultural Society: A Brief History, Charter, Constitution, and By-laws* (Cincinnati: L'Hommedieu, 1859), 7, 19, 6.

26. He noted that most of the vineyards were classified as "small," or under three acres. Seventeen were of moderate size (three to five acres), and nine surpassed five acres. Longworth's vineyards spanned twenty-two acres. *Ohio Cultivator*, October 15, 1846, and March 15, 1847. See also Douglas Hurt, "The Vineyards of Ohio, 1823–1900," *Northwest Ohio Quarterly* 55:1 (1982), 6; and Ellen Corwin Cangi, *From Viticulture to American Culture: The History of the Ohio River Valley Meyers Estate, 1845–1965* (n.p., 1983), 10. Robert Jones claims there were more acres under cultivation: there may have been closer to three hundred in Hamilton County in 1844, with Longworth owning eighty to ninety. See Jones, *History of Agriculture in Ohio to 1880*, 226. He cites Robert Buchanan's popular *Culture of the Grape* and the census of 1850.

27. Longworth identifies acreage and a few of his land holdings in his co-authored *A Treatise on the Cultivation of the Grape, in Vineyards* (Cincinnati: Wright, Ferris and Co., 1850): "Number of acres in vineyard culture within a circle of twenty miles around Cincinnati, 743; under charge of 264 proprietors and tenants. Of this, Mr. Longworth owns 122.5 acres, cultivated by 27 tenant [families]" (35–36). He continues, "The oldest vineyard in the county is one of Mr. Longworth's, on Baldface [sic], planted 27 years ago . . . several other vineyards in this country are from 15 to 18, and a few 20, years old" (18). In 1846, he said it had been "sixteen years since I bought an unusually broken piece of ground on Boldface Creek, four miles from the city" (34). The vineyard of his tenant Mr. Rentz was "four miles from town" (35). Longworth's vineyards "at Tusculum, [were] on a high hill" (39). Further, see Robert Buchanan and Nicholas Longworth, *The Culture of the Grape, and Wine-Making* (Cincinnati: Moore & Anderson, 1852), 61.

28. *Proceedings of the Third Session of the American Pomological Society, held in Boston, 1854* (Boston: Franklin Printing House, 1854), 116.

29. Anonymous, "The Vineyards of the West," *Ohio Cultivator* 6:19 (October 1850), 300–301; *DeBow's Review and Industrial Resources, Statistics, etc. Devoted to Commerce, Agriculture, Manufactures* (New Orleans, December 1855), 722–723. Robert Buchanan was also keen to popularize the appellation, discussing it in his book *The Culture of the Grape, and Wine-Making* (1852). See also Cangi, *From Viticulture to American Culture*, 12–15, and Pinney, *A History of Wine in America*, 156. The "Rhine of America" also stuck because of the influx of Germans into Ohio (to be discussed).

30. Cist, *Cincinnati in 1851*; *Ohio Cultivator*, December 1, 1855, 358; *Ohio Farmer*, August 7, 1858; *Annual Report of the Commissioner of Patents for the Year 1854: Agriculture* (Washington, DC: A.O.P. Nicholson, 1855), 265. See also Hurt, "The Vineyards of Ohio," 7–8, and Adams, *The Wines of America*, 92. For another Ohio farmer's experiences with grape culture, see A. N. Prentiss, *My Vineyard at Lakeview* (New York: Lovejoy & Son, 1866). Prentiss discusses his own experiments with vines, how grape growing was socially and regionally "contagious," and the distribution of Cincinnati's grapes to Chicago, Detroit, and New York.

31. Jones, *History of Agriculture in Ohio*, 226.

32. Robert Buchanan, *A Treatise on the Cultivation of the Grape, in Vineyards* (Cincinnati: Wright, Ferris & Co. Printers, 1850), 27. Longworth's collection in 1846 included the Ohio, Catawba, Graham, Elinburg, Clarkson's Eastern Catawba, Indiana, Black Fox, White Fox, Piqua, Herbemont, Giant Catawba, Minor's Seedling, Norton's Virginia Seedling, White Seedling Catawba, Improved Purple Fox, Red Fox, Virginia, Missouri, Helen, Lake, and Guignard.

33. See Cist, *Cincinnati in 1851*, 333–338, and "Nicholas Longworth, Esq. of Cincinnati, and the Vineyards of Ohio," *Harper's Weekly* 2 (July 24, 1858), 472. There is some discrepancy in the records of when Longworth arrived. Lukacs states that he landed in 1803 (Lukacs, *American Vintage*, 10). Glazer (*Cincinnati in 1840*, 85), Pinney (*A History of Wine in America*, 157), and Charles Boewe (in Garraty and Carnes, *American National Biography*, vol. 13, 898) write that it was 1804. Other sources claim 1810 and later. The 1803 date would have had the most symbolic weight as part of the foundational Longworth myth—it is the year that Ohio was admitted as a state.

34. Jed Dannenbaum, *Drink and Disorder: Temperance Reform in Cincinnati from the Washingtonian Revival to the WCTU* (Urbana: University of Illinois Press, 1984), 26, 135. Also see Ohio Writers' Program of the Work Projects Administration, *Cincinnati: A Guide to the Queen City and Its Neighbors* (Cincinnati: Wiesen-Hart Press, 1943), 43–44. The fact that Longworth was never actually offered the stills makes this narrative profoundly mythical. See Cist, *Cincinnati in 1851*, 333–338, and Pinney, *A History of Wine in America*, 156–165.

35. Nicholas Longworth to Mrs. Martha Cook, February 2, 1806. Letters, 1803–1816. Cincinnati History Library and Archives, Mss VF 3601.

36. Nicholas Longworth to Miss Mary Longworth, November 1, 1829. Letters, 1803–1816. Cincinnati History Library and Archives, Mss VF 3601. "I shall take the liberty of mentioning the few mistakes in your [letter], and those arising from carelessness . . . you spell Augusta 'Agusta,' until 'untill,' McLeod 'McCloed.'"

37. Longworth's euchre, drinking, and fairy story are recounted in *Memorial of the Golden Wedding of Nicholas Longworth and Susan Longworth*. Quotes in letters from Nicholas Longworth to Mrs. Martha Cook, October 24, 1807, and April 13, 1811. Letters, 1803–1816. Cincinnati History Library and Archives, Mss VF 3601.

38. *Memorial of the Golden Wedding of Nicholas Longworth*, n.p.

39. Hobhouse, *Seeds of Wealth: Five Plants That Made Men Rich* (Emeryville, CA: Shoemaker & Hoard, 2003), 86.

40. Ohio Writers' Program, *Cincinnati*, 441; Pinney, *A History of Wine in America*, 156–165, and primary sources previously cited. Earlier in the century, there had been local experiments in grape growing in Gallipolis, Ohio, and Vevey, Indiana, begun in 1796 and 1802, respectively. French inhabitants had attempted to cultivate the Red Fox grape in Gallipolis, while the Swiss Colony at Vevey had tried many grapes, settling on the Cape grape.

41. Glazer, *Cincinnati in 1840*, 87. The list enumerates 2,559 property owners in the city—only 6 percent of the city's total population, or less than one-fifth the total adult white male population.

42. DeChambrun, *The Making of Nicholas Longworth*, 28. Many lots cost $10 each. Myers, *History of the Great American Fortunes*, chapter 8.

43. See, for example, Nicholas Herbemont, "Essay on the Culture of the Grape Vine, and Making of Wine; Suited for the United States, and More Particularly for the Southern States," *Southern Agriculturist* 1:7 (January–July 1828), reprinted in *Pioneering American Wine: Writings of Nicholas Herbemont, Master Viticulturist*, ed. David S. Shields (Athens: University of Georgia Press, 2009), 47. Herbemont discusses how vineyards increase land value in the same essay (p. 51), as well as in other articles and speeches (p. 130).

44. *Memorial of the Golden Wedding of Nicholas Longworth*, n.p. Geoffrey J. Giglierano and Deborah A. Overmyer, *The Bicentennial Guide to Greater Cincinnati: A Portrait of Two Hundred Years* (Cincinnati: Cincinnati Historical Society, 1988), 350.

45. Flagg, *Remarks on the Culture of the Grape*, 11, 12.

46. A. A. Mullet, "Report on the Failure of the Grape-Crop in the Vicinity of Cincinnati," November 13, 1858. In *Cincinnati Horticultural Society: A brief history, Charter, Constitution, and By-laws* (Cincinnati: L'Hommedieu, 1859), 101.

47. Myers, *History of the Great American Fortunes*, chapter 8. See also Boewe in Garraty and Carnes, eds., *American National Biography*, vol. 13, 898.

48. *Annual Report of the Commissioner of Patents for the Year 1845: Agriculture*, (Washington, DC: Government Printing Office, 1846), 312; Bidwell and Falconer, *A History of Northern Agriculture*, 381; Nicholas Longworth to Mr. Lytle, House of Representatives, Ohio, March 4, 1852, Cincinnati Historical Society. These numbers are consistent with figures defining a large business, or small industry, in 1850s America. Von Daacke, "*Sparkling Catawba*," 60. See also R. B. Buchanan, "Grape Culture and Vineyards," *The Cincinnatus* 4 (November 1859), 503; and Alan L. Olmstead and Paul W. Rhode, "Quantitative Indices on the Early Growth of the California Wine Industry," Robert Mondavi Institute Center for Wine Economics, Working Paper 0901 (May 2009), http://vinecon.ucdavis.edu/publications/cwe0901.pdf accessed March 12, 2013.

49. Glazer, *Cincinnati in 1840*, 29. Part of the land that Longworth's vineyards were on is now a portion of Eden Park. *Cincinnati Enquirer*, December 1, 1853. See also Steven J. Ross, *Workers on the Edge: Work, Leisure and Politics in Industrializing Cincinnati, 1788–1890* (Los Angeles: Figueroa Press, 1985), 173.

50. "Nicholas Longworth, Esq., of Cincinnati, and the Vineyards of Ohio," *Harper's Weekly* 7:24 (July 24, 1858), 472–474.

51. Longworth's home is preserved and now known as the Cincinnati Taft Museum of Art. Duncanson's murals have been expertly restored, and are "considered the most ambitious surviving pre–Civil War mural paintings for a home," as well as "among the most important nineteenth-century works by an African American artist." Taft Museum of Art Visitors Guide, 2012.

52. On tree stumps, see Barbara S. Groseclose, *Nineteenth Century American Art* (New York: Oxford University Press, 2000), 135–137. Art historians have made much of stumps in Thomas Cole's series *The Course of Empire* (1830s) as well as Andrew Melrose's *Westward the Star of Empire Takes Its Way—Near Council Bluffs, Iowa* (1867).

53. L. F. Allen, "Gossip on Grapes," *The Horticulturist* 6 (1851), 411–412.

54. Pulszky and Pulszky, *White, Red, Black*, 296–297.

55. *Longworth's Wine House* [promotional brochure] (Cincinnati: Miami Printing and Publication Company, 1867), 7.

56. *Longworth's Wine House*, 8, 5. Careful readers will notice that years earlier, Longworth had made it a major point in his battles with the temperance lobby that his wine contained *no* artificial sweeteners (additives to increase palatability and alcohol content of wine from grapes that did not produce enough of their own sugars).

57. "Letters of Hiram Powers to Nicholas Longworth, Esq., 1856–1858," *The Quarterly Publication of the Historical and Philosophical Society of Ohio* 1:2 (April–June 1906), 38.

58. Ross, *Workers on the Edge*, 78. See also Cayton and Onuf, *The Midwest and the Nation*.

59. See W. J. Rorabaugh, *The Alcoholic Republic: An American Tradition* (Oxford: Oxford University Press, 1979) for a longer discussion of this issue, as well as Sharon V. Salinger, *Taverns and Drinking in Early America* (Baltimore: Johns Hopkins University Press, 2002).

60. The story is best told in J. C. Culbertson, M.D., editor and publisher, "What an Advertisement Accomplished," *Cincinnati Lancet-Clinic* (January 20, 1894), 76–80.

61. Glazer, *Cincinnati in 1840*, 57–58; Teaford, *Cities of the Heartland*, 9; Ross, *Workers on the Edge*, 72–73, 172; Katz, *Regionalism and Reform*, 5.

62. Giglierano and Overmyer, *The Bicentennial Guide to Greater Cincinnati*, 83.

63. *Proceedings of the Eleventh Session of the American Pomological Society, held in St. Louis, MO, 1867* (Boston: Franklin Printing House, 1868), 46–47.

64. Mark Edward Lender and James Kirby Martin, eds., *Drinking in America: A History* (New York: The Free Press, 1982), 45–47, 54, 56, 60–63, 84–86, 95; Rorabaugh, *Alcoholic Republic*, 90, 106, 174; Thomas R. Pegram, *Battling Demon Rum: The Struggle for a Dry America, 1800–1933* (Chicago: Ivan R. Dee, 1998). On the history and politics of alcohol in early Ohio, see Dannenbaum, *Drink and Disorder*, especially chapters 3 and 4.

65. See, for example, a discussion in the *Ohio Cultivator* (October 1, 1850, p. 300): "The Catawba[s] of this country . . . contain so little alcohol (only 7 or 8 per ct,) that they are not intoxicating unless drank in a most inordinate manner. . . . They exilerate [*sic*] the spirits, and act in a salutary manner on the respiratory organs." See especially Dannenbaum, *Drink and Disorder*, and Rorabaugh, *The Alcoholic Republic*. Longworth's rhetoric about the "purity" of his wine was not without its own racialized dimensions, which extended to his thoughts on which American grapes to grow in the vineyard. Very early on in viticultural debates over whether to experiment with European varietals on U.S. soil, Longworth took a decidedly nativist stance against "foreign vines," in favor of native rootstock. The larger racialized dimensions of this are discussed in Chapter 4.

66. Ross, *Workers on the Edge*, 173, 181. Cayton and Onuf, *The Midwest and the Nation*, 87–88. For prohibitionists, "demon liquor" included wine.

67. Buchanan and Longworth, *A Treatise on the Cultivation of the Grape*, 32.

68. John Beeston, *A Concise History of Australian Wine* (St. Leonards, Australia: Rathdown, 1994), 21. There are hundreds of books over centuries that implicitly belabor this point. For just a few examples, see Hugh Johnson, *The World Atlas of Wine* (New York: Simon and Schuster, 1977);

H. Warner Allen, *A History of Wine: Great Vintage Wines from the Homeric Age to the Present Day* (n.p., 1961); Julia Flynn Siler, *The House of Mondavi: The Rise and Fall of an American Wine Dynasty* (New York: Gotham Books, 2007); Mike Weiss, *A Very Good Year: The Journey of a California Wine from Vine to Table* (New York: Gotham Books, 2005); Michael Sanders, *Families of the Vine: Seasons Among the Winemakers of Southwestern France* (New York: HarperCollins, 2005).

69. Buchanan and Longworth, *A Treatise on the Cultivation of the Grape*, 20.

70. Buchanan and Longworth, *A Treatise on the Cultivation of the Grape*, 28, 33.

71. Nicholas Longworth, "On the Culture of the Grape, and the Manufacture of Wine," *Annual Report of the Commissioner of Patents for the Year 1847*, Executive Document No. 54, Appendix No. 12 (Washington, DC: Wendell and Van Benthusen, 1848), 469.

72. Buchanan and Longworth, *A Treatise on the Cultivation of the Grape*, 31–32. Longworth details another story of a German tenant "who had a wife, daughter, and three stout boys" in Buchanan's *Culture of the Grape*. Longworth contracted them to "trench and wall with stone, six acres for grapes, in three years, and nine acres in five years. He was also to plant out a peach orchard, and tend an apple orchard I had on the place." Buchanan, *The Culture of the Grape, and Wine-Making*, 56–57. Readers familiar with Jethro Tull's *Horse Hoeing Husbandry* will find similarities here. Tull was hoeing a vineyard, and keeps laborers at a strict distance. Jethro Tull, *The Horse Hoeing Husbandry* (London: William Cobbett, 1829).

73. Dannenbaum, *Drink and Disorder*, 134–135.

74. Nicholas Longworth, open letter to Samuel Cary, *Cincinnati Commercial*, August 2, 15, 1853.

75. Longworth's article, "On the Culture of the Grape and Manufacture of Wine" (December 3, 1847), appears in the *Annual Report of the Commissioner of Patents for the Year 1847: Agriculture* (Washington, DC: Government Printing Office, 1848), Appendix 12, p. 464.

76. Cultural geographers and materialist scholars have theorized the paradoxes of urban capitalist development. See David Harvey, *The Urban Experience* (Baltimore: Johns Hopkins University Press, 1989 [1985]). See also materialist historians and cultural geographers such as Don Mitchell, *The Right to the City: Social Justice and the Fight for Public Space* (New York: Guilford Press, 2003); Mitchell, *The Lie of the Land: Migrant Workers and the California Landscape* (Minneapolis: University of Minnesota, 1996); Alan Kulikoff, *The Agrarian Origins of American Capitalism* (Charlottesville: University Press of Virginia, 1992).

77. Details as to Longworth's estate are in Richard Miller Devens, *Cyclopaedia of Commercial and Business Anecdotes* (New York: D. Appleton & Co., 1865), 45, and *The National Cyclopedia of American Biography*, Vol. 11 (New York: James T. White & Co., 1901), 339. The eulogy was published in "Longworth's School of Vines," *Ohio Farmer* 16:8 (February 23, 1867), 59. It was reprinted from *Horticultural Annual*.

78. Jones, *History of Agriculture in Ohio*, 227; Pinney, *A History of Wine in America*, 169–172.

79. Robert Buchanan, "Correspondence," *The Horticultural Review, and Botanical Magazine* 1:4 (April 1854), 169.

80. *Cincinnati Horticultural Society*, 55. Longworth's letter was dated March 20, 1858.

81. Steven Stoll and others have stated that until 1900, when California took the reins, "no state compared to New York in its importance to American horticulture" (Stoll, *The Fruits of Natural Advantage*, 52–53). He cites Thornton (her book terminates at 1860 and is more focused on the earlier decades) and Ulysses P. Hedrick, himself a booster for New York horticulture through the 1920s. Stoll's book is cogent on the whole, but I believe the Midwest also had a significant role to play in national horticulture.

82. "Creative destruction" was brought into economic discourse via Joseph Schumpeter's book *Capitalism, Socialism and Democracy*, first published in 1942. Max Page discusses it in his book *The Creative Destruction of Manhattan, 1900–1940* (Chicago: University of Chicago Press, 1999).

Chapter 4. Fear of Hybrid Grapes and Men

1. Gladiolus, "Disappointed Hopes," *The Horticulturist* 20 (October 1865), 329–330.

2. See Tamara Plakins Thornton, *Cultivating Gentlemen: The Meaning of Country Life Among the Boston Elite, 1785–1860* (New Haven, CT: Yale University Press, 1989); Elizabeth B. Keeney, *The Botanizers: Amateur Scientists in Nineteenth-Century America* (Chapel Hill: University of North Carolina Press, 1992); Thomas Augst, *The Clerk's Tale: Young Men and Moral Life in Nineteenth-Century America* (Chicago: University of Chicago Press, 2003); Karen Halttunen, *Confidence Men and Painted Women: A Study of Middle-Class Culture in America, 1830–1870* (New Haven, CT: Yale University Press, 1982); James B. Salazar, *Bodies of Reform: The Rhetoric of Character in Gilded Age America* (New York: New York University Press, 2010).

3. For a detailed map of this field, see Donald Pease and Amy Kaplan, eds., *The Cultures of United States Imperialism* (Durham, NC: Duke University Press, 1994).

4. Charles W. Chesnutt, *The Conjure Woman and Other Conjure Tales*, ed. Richard H. Brodhead (Durham: Duke University Press, 1993 [1899]). These quotes are in "The Goophered Grapevine," 31.

5. Julian Mason, "Charles Chesnutt," in *Dictionary of American Bibliography*, ed. John Arthur Garraty, Edward T. James, and Kenneth T. Jackson (New York: Scribner, 1973), 787–790; Christopher Bundrick, "I Shall Leave the Realm of Fiction: Conjure, Genre, and Passing in the Fiction of Charles W. Chesnutt," chapter 3 in *Charles Chesnutt Reappraised: Essays on the First Major African American Fiction Writer*, ed. David Garrett Izzo and Maria Orban (Jefferson, NC: McFarland, 2009), 59; John Edgar Wideman, "The Marrow of Tradition," in *A New Literary History of America*, ed. Greil Marcus and Werner Sollors (Cambridge, MA: Belknap Press, 2012), 465, 467. William L. Andrews, *The Literary Career of Charles W. Chesnutt* (Baton Rouge: Louisiana State University Press, 1980).

6. Liberty Hyde Bailey writes, "The first record of America is also a record of its grapes," in *Sketch of the Evolution of Our Native Fruits* (New York: The MacMillan Company, 1898), 2; Jno. Reid writes, "How beautifully prophetic is the emblematic vine of the destiny of man," in *The Horticulturist* 17 (March 1862), 112; and G. W. Campbell writes, "The vine and the American people are not unlike [one another]. They require room to spread themselves, and do not thrive under restraint," in *The Horticulturist* 29 (February 1874), 50. See also Philip Pauly, *Fruits and Plains: The Horticultural Transformation of America* (Cambridge, MA: Harvard University Press, 2007), 64.

7. This criticism includes work from poststructuralists who detail the stories as ones soaked in capitalist symbolism and racial "masks." Eric Sundquist and Henry Wonham have both argued that grape culture in "The Goophered Grapevine" is a trope for culture itself, mimicking the sociocultural economy and degenerating racial climate of the post-Reconstruction South, respectively. More recently, the scholarship has focused on the physical settings of Chesnutt's tales. William Gleason has described several stories' immediate built environment—the plantation house's piazza—as a symbolically loaded narrative zone. Gleason's attention to architecture reveals Chesnutt's emphasis on a politics of place construction that linked the socioeconomic relationships of

northern (Ohio) capital investment in southern (South Carolina) townscapes. From an ecocritical standpoint, Jeffrey Myers has examined the tales' local forest and swamp and their living inhabitants. Myers argues that "the bodies of the men and women who work the land are conflated with the land itself," and that ultimately, human and ecological oppression are inextricable narratives for Chesnutt. See Craig Werner, "The Framing of Charles W. Chesnutt: Practical Deconstruction in the Afro-American Tradition," in *Southern Literature and Literary Theory*, ed. Jefferson Humphries (Athens: University of Georgia Press, 1990), 339–365; Eric Selinger, "Aunts, Uncles, Audience: Gender and Genre in Charles Chesnutt's *The Conjure Woman*," *Black American Literature Forum* 25 (1991), 665–688; Dean McWilliams, *Charles W. Chesnutt and the Fictions of Race* (Athens: University of Georgia Press, 2002); Eric J. Sundquist, *To Wake the Nations: Race in the Making of American Literature* (Cambridge, MA: Belknap Press, 1993), 362; Henry Wonham, "Plenty of Room for Us All? Participation and Prejudice in Charles Chesnutt's Dialect Tales," *Studies in American Fiction* 26:2 (Autumn 1998), 131–146; William Gleason, "Chesnutt's Piazza Tales: Architecture, Race, and Memory in the Conjure Stories," *American Quarterly* 51:1 (1999), 37; Jeffrey Myers, "Other Nature: Resistance to Ecological Hegemony in Charles W. Chesnutt's *The Conjure Woman*," *African American Review* 37:1 (Spring 2003), 6.

8. Gleason, "Chesnutt's Piazza Tales," 60.

9. Chesnutt, "The Goophered Grapevine," 36, 39.

10. Chesnutt, "The Goophered Grapevine," 42–43.

11. George Husmann, "The New Era in Grape Culture—No. II," *The Horticulturist* 20 (August 1865), 266–267. Other parts in the series ran in May 1865, p. 142-145; October 1865, p. 321-322; and February 1866 (Volume 21), p. 52-54.

12. Lawrence N. Powell, *New Masters: Northern Planters During the Civil War and Reconstruction* (New Haven, CT: Yale University Press, 1980), xii.

13. "Representative Houses and Prominent Men of Fayetteville, N.C., Tokay Vineyard, Hon. Wharton J. Green, Proprietor," *Historical and Descriptive Review of the State of North Carolina, Including the Manufacturing and Mercantile Industries*, Vol. 1 (Charleston, SC: Empire Publishing Co., 1885), 156–157.

14. Wharton J. Green, *Tokay Vineyard, Near Fayetteville, N.C.: With an Essay on Grape-Culture By the Proprietor* (Boston, 188[4?]), 3–5, 9, 17, 24, 36. See also Green's "Essay on American Grape Culture," in *Historical and Descriptive Review of the State of North Carolina*, 42–50.

15. Pinney, *A History of Wine in America: From the Beginnings to Prohibition* (Berkeley: University of California Press, 1989), 140; Sarah T. Phillips, "Antebellum Agricultural Reform, Republican Ideology, and Sectional Tension" *Agricultural History* 74:4 (Autumn 2000); Clarence Gohdes, *Scuppernong: North Carolina's Grape and Its Wines* (Durham, NC: Duke University Press, 1982), 30–32; Rotundifolia, "Is the Scuppernong Grape *the Grape* of America?" *The Horticulturist* 23 (April 1868), 107. Catawba details in "Ohio Grape Vintage for 1855," *Ohio Cultivator* (December 1, 1855), 358. See also Leon D. Adams, *The Wines of America*, 3rd ed. (New York: McGraw-Hill, 1985 [1973]), 42, 72.

16. de Chambrun, *Cincinnati: Story of the Queen City* (New York: Charles Scribner's Sons, 1939), 108–115.

17. de Chambrun, *Cincinnati*, 34, Harriet Beecher Stowe, *Uncle Tom's Cabin* (London: Casseli, 1852), 86, 87, 111–129. Young ironically continued as a servant in Longworth's home until the former slave's death decades later.

18. Eric Foner, *Free Soil, Free Labor, Free Men: The Ideology of the Republican Party Before the Civil War* (New York, 1970), 39; Powell, *New Masters*, 31.

19. Charles Cist, *Sketches and Statistics of Cincinnati in 1859* (Cincinnati: s.n.), 336–339 and 361–362. See also Von Daacke, *Sparkling Catawba: Grape Growing and Wine Making in Cincinnati, 1800-1870* (M.A. Dissertation, Graduate School of the University of Cincinnati, 1964), 63. Von Daacke writes that in this period "sales of the [Cincinnati] grape stock averaged 200,000 roots and 400,000 cuttings each year to the south and southwest. . . . The Catawba stock sold for $25 to $35 per 1000 roots or cuttings, according to age. One [Cincinnati] nursery's sales for 1858 exceeded one million cuttings, enough to start 300 acres of vineyards." See also Gohdes, *Scuppernong,* 28.

20. Gohdes, *Scuppernong,* 4, 6, 7, 8; Alexia Jones Helsley, *A History of North Carolina Wines: From Scuppernong to Syrah* (Charleston, SC: The History Press, 2010), 17, 30.

21. *Proceedings of the Seventh Session of the American Pomological Society, held in the City of New York, September 14, 15, & 16, 1858* (Brooklyn, NY: George C. Bennett, 1858), 212.

22. Powell, *New Masters,* 79.

23. Chesnutt, "The Goophered Grapevine," 43.

24. Peter B. Mead, *An Elementary Treatise on American Grape Culture and Wine Making* (New York: Harper & Bros., 1867), 30. The book's cover states the popular title, *Mead's Grape Culture.* It had several editions, each with several thousand run. The third edition began with 3,000 books printed.

25. Mead, *An Elementary Treatise,* 90–92. George Husmann, "The New Era in Grape Culture—No. 3," *The Horticulturist* 20 (October 1865), 321. See also Ian Tyrell's description of the fetishized orderliness of vineyards in Australia and America in *True Gardens of the Gods: Californian-Australian Environmental Reform, 1860-1930* (Berkeley: University of California Press, 1999), 135.

26. Chesnutt, "The Goophered Grapevine," 32–33.

27. Charles Chesnutt, "The Dumb Witness," 166. Compiled in *The Conjure Woman and Other Conjure Tales,* ed. Richard H. Brodhead (Durham: Duke University Press, 1993 [1899]).

28. "The Goophered Grapevine," 34; "The Dumb Witness," 160, 163, 164. Half-bloods and mulattos populate nineteenth-century fiction. See Sylvia Lyons Render, ed., *The Short Fiction of Charles W. Chesnutt* (Washington, DC: Howard University Press, 1981), 45; William J. Scheik, *The Half-Blood: A Cultural Symbol in Nineteenth-Century American Fiction* (Lexington: University Press of Kentucky, 1979), xi. James Fenimore Cooper's *The Pioneers, or, The Sources of the Susquehanna* (New York: Charles Wiley, 1823) is one of the earliest and most important examples of the trope of bloodline in land title.

29. Michele Mitchell, *Righteous Propagation: African Americans and the Politics of Racial Destiny after Reconstruction* (Chapel Hill: University of North Carolina Press, 2004), 8.

30. Philip J. Pauly, *Fruits and Plains: The Horticultural Transformation of America* (Cambridge, MA: Harvard University Press, 2007), 67.

31. Pauly, *Fruits and Plains,* 65; Reginald Horsman, *Race and Manifest Destiny: The Origins of American Racial Anglo-Saxonism* (Cambridge, MA: Harvard University Press, 1981), 225.

32. Pinney, *A History of Wine in America,* 415–416.

33. Thomas R. Hietala, *Manifest Design: American Exceptionalism and Empire,* rev. ed. (Ithaca, NY: Cornell University Press, 2003), 12, xiii, 7, 108, 170; Horsman, *Race and Manifest Destiny,* 133.

34. Hietala, *Manifest Design,* 171; Horsman, *Race and Manifest Destiny,* 1, 134, 83; Pauly, *Fruits and Plains,* 76.

35. Pinney, *A History of Wine in America,* 203–207, 211; George W. Campbell, "The Grape and Its Improvement by Hybridizing, Cross-Breeding, and Seedlings," *Report of the Commissioner*

of Agriculture, 1862 (Washington, DC, 1863), 216; U. P. Hedrick, *Grapes and Wines from Home Vineyards* (New York, 1945), 149. On Bull, see Pinney, *A History of Wine in America*, 212–215.

36. David Roediger, *The Wages of Whiteness: Race and the Making of the American Working Class* (London: Verso, 1991), 156; *Miscegenation Indorsed By the Republican Party* (New York: s.n., 1864), 8, 7. See also Elise Lemire, *"Miscegenation": Making Race in America* (Philadelphia: University of Pennsylvania Press, 2002), especially chapter 5.

37. Mead, *An Elementary Treatise*, 288–289.

38. Mead and Longworth at times expressed this. See also the discussion of John Lindley (1799–1865), editor of *Gardeners' Chronicle* and sometime opponent of hybridization, as well as Alexander Livingston (1821–1898), an Ohio tomato grower, in Noel Kingsbury's *Hybrid: The History and Science of Plant Breeding* (Chicago: University of Chicago Press, 2009), 93–94.

39. Charles Chesnutt, "The Future American: What the Race Is Likely to Become in the Process of Time," *Boston Evening Transcript*, August 18, 1900. Reprinted in Joseph R. McElrath, Jr., Robert C. Leitz III, and Jesse S. Crisler, eds., *Charles W. Chesnutt: Essays and Speeches* (Stanford, CA: Stanford University Press, 1999), 121–122. See also McWilliams, *Chesnutt and the Fictions of Race*, 49.

40. Arlene A. Elder, "'The Future American Race': Charles W. Chesnutt's Utopian Illusion," *MELUS* 15:3 (Autumn 1988), 121–129.

41. Chesnutt, "The Future American: A Stream of Dark Blood in the Veins of Southern Whites," *Boston Evening Transcript*, August 25, 1900. Compiled in McElrath et al., *Chesnutt: Essays and Speeches*, 126. He repeats the sentiment again in installment three, "The Future American: A Complete Race-Amalgamation Likely to Occur," *Boston Evening Transcript*, September 1, 1900. Compiled in McElrath et al., *Chesnutt: Essays and Speeches*, 133.

42. Eric J. Sundquist, *To Wake the Nations: Race in the Making of American Literature* (Cambridge, MA: Belknap Press, 1993), 361–62. Sundquist argues that John stands in for Chesnutt himself, in that the two men were Northerners returning to exploit the South (John in his grapes, Chesnutt in his writing), and that both John and Chesnutt shared a certain Victorian propriety (John in his Northern white approach to life on the plantation, Chesnutt in censoring the tale's grotesque libidinous origins). I believe John stands for several of Chesnutt's grape-obsessed real-life contemporaries. The central theme in "The Goophered Grapevine" is vineyard ownership and control—and Chesnutt would have had no larger stakes in that arena, whereas Longworth and his associates certainly did.

43. Thomas Volney Munson, "Address on American Grapes, Read Before the American Pomological Society, At Grand Rapids, Michigan, September 10, 1885, And Published in the Transactions of That Society for 1884–5" (Lansing, MI: Thorp & Godfrey, State Printers and Binders, 1886).

44. "On the Improvement of Vegetable Races," *The Horticulturist* 7 (April 1852), 155. The article does not have a cited author, but it is likely the author is *The Horticulturist's* editor, Andrew Jackson Downing. On the last page, there is a plug for Downing's book, *The Fruits and Fruit Trees of North America* (1845, several later editions).

45. "On the Improvement of Vegetable Races," 155.

46. Downing, "American Versus British Horticulture," *The Horticulturist* 7 (1852), 249–251; "Shade Trees in Cities," *The Horticulturist* 7 (1852), 345–349. See also Pauly, *Fruits and Plains*, 170–171.

47. See Pauly, *Fruits and Plains*, 155.

48. Nicholas Longworth, "The Vine," *Cincinnati Republican*, October 20, 1837; reprinted in

The Farmer & Gardener, November 28, 1837, 243–244, and *Horticultural Register, and Gardener's Magazine,* December 1, 1837, 455– 456.

49. Mead, *An Elementary Treatise,* 6.

50. "Editor's Table," *The Horticulturist* 18 (July 1863), 229.

51. Horsman, *Race and Manifest Destiny,* 151, 153-155. See also Lemire, *"Miscegenation,"* especially chapter 4.

52. Chesnutt, "The Future American," in McElrath et al., *Chesnutt: Essays and Speeches,* 123.

53. Horsman, *Race and Manifest Destiny,* 301.

54. Chesnutt, "The Goophered Grapevine," 43.

Chapter 5. California Wine Meets Its "Destiny"

1. Anonymous, "The Way They Talk in California," *The Horticulturist* 12 (July 1857), 314–316.

2. Wine writer Matt Kramer acknowledges this tendency in wine writing: "To those familiar with California today it seems inevitable that California be a wine growing state. . . . Yet wine was not inevitable, at least not fine wine." *New California Wine: Making Sense of Napa Valley, Sonoma, Central Coast, and Beyond* (Philadelphia: Running Press, 2004), 11.

3. California vineyards fit Don Mitchell's definition of the ideological "work" of attractive landscapes: by "hiding" as much as they "revealed." British cultural geographers have long noted that the appreciation of pastoral landscapes became most popular at the height of British society's worry over industrialization. See Don Mitchell, *The Right to the City: Social Justice and the Fight for Public Space* (New York: Guilford Press, 2003) and Mitchell, *The Lie of the Land: Migrant Workers and the California Landscape* (Minneapolis: University of Minnesota Press, 1996). See also David Harvey, *The Urban Experience* (Baltimore: Johns Hopkins University Press, 1989), and Alan Kulikoff, *The Agrarian Origins of American Capitalism* (Charlottesville: University of Virginia Press, 1992).

4. Maynard Amerine, "An Introduction to the Pre-Repeal History of Grapes and Wines in California," *Agricultural History* 43:2 (April 1969), 259.

5. The story of California wine's trek up the coast has been recounted in several texts. See Amerine, "Pre-Repeal History of Grapes," as well as Cleve E. Kindall, "Southern Vineyards: the Economic Significance of the Wine Industry in the Development of Los Angeles, 1831–1870," in *The Historical Society of Southern California Quarterly* 41:1 (March 1959), 29; W. H. Upshall, ed., *History of Fruit Growing and Handling in United States of America and Canada, 1860–1972* (Kelowna, British Columbia, Canada: Regatta Press, 1976); Julius L. Jacobs, "Early California Wine Growing: Priests and Adventurers Lovingly Cultivated the Grape," *American West: The Land and Its People* 20:6 (November–December 1983); Julius L. Jacobs, "California's Pioneer Wine Families," *California Historical Quarterly* 54:2 (Summer 1975); U. P. Hedrick, *A History of Horticulture in America to 1860* (New York: Oxford University Press, 1950); Leon D. Adams, *The Wines of America,* 3rd ed. (New York: McGraw-Hill, 1973 [1985]). Early California wine growing is also discussed in primary texts: T. Hart Hyatt, *Hyatt's Hand-Book of Grape Culture; or, Why, Where, When, and How to Plant and Cultivate a Vineyard, Manufacture Wines, etc., Especially Adapted to the State of California* (San Francisco: H. H. Bancroft and Co., 1867); U.S. Department of Agriculture, *Yearbook of Agriculture 1898* (Washington, DC: Government Printing Office, 1899). Roy Brady critiques the Serra myth in "Alta California's First Vintage," *The University of California/ Sotheby Book of California Wine,* ed. Doris Muscatine, Maynard A. Amerine, and Bob Thompson (Berkeley: University of California Press, 1984), 10–14.

6. Ernest P. Peninou, *History of the Sonoma Viticultural District: The Grape Growers, the Wine Makers and the Vineyards* (Santa Rosa, CA: Nomis Press, 1998), 18. See also Douglas Monroy, "The Creation and Re-creation of *Californio* Society," chapter 7 in *Contested Eden: California Before the Gold Rush*, ed. Ramon Gutierrez and Richard J. Orsi (Berkeley: University of California Press, 1998); Charles W. Bonner, *A Rocky Road: The Pilgrimage of the Grape* (Fresno, CA: Pioneer, 1983), 7–8.

7. Lars Schoultz, *Beneath the United States: A History of U.S. Policy Toward Latin America* (Cambridge, MA: Harvard University Press, 1998), 33–38; Anders Stephanson, *Manifest Destiny: American Expansionism and the Empire of Right* (New York: Hill and Wang, 1995), 36–48; Hedrick, *A History of Horticulture in America to 1860*, 381.

8. *California Farmer and Journal of Useful Sciences* (December 2, 1859), 132; Vincent P. Carosso, *The California Wine Industry: A Study of the Formative Years, 1830–1895* (Berkeley: University of California Press, 1951), 44. For other details on California horticulture as tied up with changing land law and racism, see Ian Tyrell's *True Gardens of the Gods: Californian-Australian Environmental Reform, 1860–1930* (Berkeley: University of California Press, 1999).

9. Julius L. Jacobs, "Early California Wine Growing," *American West: The Land and Its People* 20:6 (November–December 1983), 47.

10. *Plan de la Cuidad de Los Angeles*, map surveyed and drawn by Edward Ord, 1849. Copy held by the Huntington Library, San Marino, California. See also Thomas Pinney, *A History of Wine in America: From Prohibition to Present* (Berkeley: University of California Press, 2005), 247–250.

11. Lawrence J. Jelinek, *Harvest Empire: A History of California Agriculture* (San Francisco: Boyd & Fraser, 1979), 35; Carosso, *The California Wine Industry*, 33; James Curry, *Agriculture Under Late Capitalism: The Structure and Operation of the California Wine Industry* (Ph.D. dissertation, Cornell University, 1994), 79; Liberty Hyde Bailey, *Sketch of the Evolution of Our Native Fruits* (New York: Macmillan, 1898).

12. Jelinek, *Harvest Empire*, 36. See also Carosso, *The California Wine Industry*, 17–18; Kindall, "Southern Vineyards," 35. U.S. Bureau of the Census, *A Compendium of the Ninth Census*, June 1, 1870, comp. F. A. Walker (Washington, DC: Government Printing Office, 1872), 708.

13. Muscatine and Amerine, eds., *The University of California/Sotheby Book of California Wine*, 8. Pinney, *History of Wine in America*, 266–267. For the growth of horticulture in northern California, especially tree crops, grapes, and hops in the Placer County region, see David Vaught's incisive *Cultivating California: Growers, Specialty Crops, and Labor, 1875–1920* (Baltimore: Johns Hopkins University Press, 1999).

14. *Semi-Tropic California and Southern California Horticulturist* and *Rural Californian* (Los Angeles) have not been sufficiently catalogued. Most catalogues display its date range as "1880s–1914."

15. George Ordish, *The Great Wine Blight* (London: Sidgwick & Jackson, 1987 [1972]), 6, 15. Oidium still blights vineyards today. Scholars are relatively certain the United States was the home of oidium, and are positive of the U.S. provenance of phylloxera.

16. Leon D. Adams, *The Wines of America*, 3rd ed. (New York: McGraw-Hill, 1985 [1973]), 22.

17. A. Millardet, *Notes sur les vignes américaines* (Bordeaux, 1881), 73. Found in Christy Campbell, *Phylloxera: How Wine Was Saved for the World* (London: HarperCollins, 2004), 191. See also James Simpson, *Creating Wine: The Emergence of a World Industry, 1840–1914* (Princeton, NJ: Princeton University Press, 2011), especially chapter 2, "Phylloxera and the Development of Scientific Viti-Viniculture."

18. Kolleen M. Guy, *When Champagne Became French: Wine and the Making of a National Identity* (Baltimore: Johns Hopkins University Press, 2003).

19. George Husmann, *American Grape Growing and Wine Making, With Contributions from Well-Known Grape Growers, Giving a Wide Range of Experience* (New York: Orange Judd Co., 1880), xii. Napa growers were hard-hit by the 1890s. Pinney, *History of Wine in America*, 343–346 and 392–394.

20. Ordish, *Great Wine Blight*, 144, 114–115. For difficulties securing rootstock, also see Campbell, *Phylloxera*, 222–223.

21. Simpson, *Creating Wine*, 196; *Report of the California State Board of Agriculture for the Year 1911* (Sacramento, 1912), 184, 185, 179, 187, 191. (See also the *Report* from 1914.) For detail on California's outstripping of other agricultural states in this period, see Paul W. Rhode, "Learning, Capital Accumulation, and the Transformation of California Agriculture," *Journal of Economic History* 55:4 (December 1995), 773–800.

22. *Official Report of the Sessions of the International Congress of Viticulture, Held in Recital Hall at Festival Hall Panama-Pacific International Exposition, San Francisco, California, July 12 and 13, 1915* (San Francisco: Dettner Printing Co., 1915), 34 (hereafter *Official Report*).

23. Alfred W. Crosby, *The Columbian Exchange: Biological and Cultural Consequences of 1492*, 30th anniversary ed. (New York: Praeger, 2003). See also Crosby, *Ecological Imperialism: The Biological Expansion of Europe, 900–1900* (London: Cambridge University Press, 1986); Crosby, *Germs, Seeds and Animals: Studies in Ecological History* (London: M. E. Sharpe, 1994); Carosso, *The California Wine Industry*, 99.

24. Alan L. Olmstead and Paul W. Rhode, *Creating Abundance: Biological Innovation and American Agricultural Development* (New York: Cambridge University Press, 2008), 223, 242–244.

25. Schoultz, *Beneath the United States*, 83.

26. Muscatine and Amerine, eds. *The University of California/Sotheby Book of California Wine*, 17; Victor W. Geraci, "Fermenting a Twenty-first Century California Wine Industry," *Agricultural History* 78:4 (2004), 446; Pinney, *History of Wine in America*, 311. Investors established several wineries in Alameda County: Chateau Bellevue, Mont Rouge, Ravenswood, and La Bocage were built at this time.

27. Richard Rayner, *The Associates: Four Capitalists Who Created California* (New York: W. W. Norton, 2008), 36, 79, 120; Norman E. Tutorow, *The Governor: The Life and Legacy of Leland Stanford, A California Colossus* (Spokane, WA: Arthur H. Clark Co., 2004), 237; Norman E. Tutorow, "California Wine King," chapter 9 in *Leland Stanford: Man of Many Careers* (Menlo Park, CA: Pacific Coast Publishers, 1971), 184.

28. Hubert Howe Bancroft, *History of the Life of Leland Stanford: A Character Study* (Oakland, CA: Biobooks, 1952 [1888]), 147. William Deverell, "Stanford, Leland," in *American National Biography*, ed. John Garraty and Mark Carnes (New York: Oxford University Press, 1999), 539–541.

29. Tutorow, *The Governor*, 519; Tutorow, *Leland Stanford*, 192–193.

30. Bancroft, *History of the Life of Leland Stanford*, 149–150.

31. See Leland Stanford's Great Vina Ranch, "3500 acres in vines" (San Francisco: City Argus, 1889). California State Library, Picture Catalog. Rayner, *The Associates*, 187. "Stealand Landford" detail in Tutorow, *The Governor*, 923.

32. Tutorow, *Leland Stanford*, 190.

33. Ernest P. Peninou, *Leland Stanford's Great Vina Ranch, 1881–1919* (San Francisco: Yolo Hills Viticultural Society, 1991), 55, 63. See also Geraci, "Fermenting a Twenty-first Century California Wine Industry," 446.

34. Hubert Howe Bancroft, *History of the Life of Leland Stanford: A Character Study* (Oakland, CA: Biobooks, 1952 [1888]), 147. Stanford's vineyard was "on the east bank of the Sacramento, with Deer Creek as the northern boundary, the tract being three by three and a half miles in extent, and the California and Oregon railway passing through it," 149. See also Pinney, *History of Wine in America*, 324–325.

35. Steven Stoll, *The Fruits of Natural Advantage: Making the Industrial Countryside in California* (Berkeley: University of California Press, 1998), 184. See also Carroll Pursell, *The Machine in America: A Social History of Technology*, 2nd ed. (Baltimore: Johns Hopkins University Press, 2007 [1995]), chapter 5.

36. See also Ian Tyrell, *True Gardens of the Gods: Californian-Australian Environmental Reform, 1860–1930* (Berkeley: University of California Press, 1999).

37. Charles A. Wetmore, "Physical and Moral Influence of the Vine," *Californian* 1:1 (January 1880), 47. The tie between gold and wine continued through the fin de siècle. See *Report of Special Committee on the Culture of the Grape-Vine in California, Introduced by Mr. Morrison Under Resolution of Mr. Gillette* (Sacramento: Charles Botts, State Printer, 1906), 3–4.

38. Wetmore, "Physical and Moral Influence," 48. T. Hart Hyatt was also former consul to Morocco and China. *Hyatt's Hand-Book of Grape Culture* (San Francisco: H. H. Bancroft, 1867), 264.

39. Wetmore, "Physical and Moral Influence," 51.

40. Paul Lukacs, *American Vintage: The Rise of American Wine* (Boston: Houghton Mifflin, 2000), 53.

41. Charles L. Sullivan, "The Great Wine Quake," *Wayward Tendrils Quarterly* 16:2 (April 2006), 2.

42. Schoultz, *Beneath the United States*, 87, quoting Robert W. Shufeldt, *The Relation of the Navy to the Commerce of the United States: A Letter Written By Request to Hon. Leopold Morse, M.C.* (Washington, DC: John L. Ginck, 1878), 3, 6, 8, and Evarts to Thompson, March 31, 1880, Domestic Letters of the Department of State, 1784–1906, National Archives, College Park, MD, Microform 40, Reel 91. See also Stephanson, *Manifest Destiny*, 72.

43. Paul Greenhalgh, *Ephemeral Vistas: The Expositions Universelles, Great Exhibitions and World's Fairs, 1851–1939* (New York: St. Martin's Press, 1988), 54; T. J. Jackson Lears, *No Place of Grace: Antimodernism and the Transformation of American Culture, 1880–1920* (Chicago: University of Chicago Press, 1994), 16–17.

44. Robert W. Rydell, "The Culture of Imperial Abundance: World's Fairs in the Making of American Culture," in *Consuming Visions: Accumulation and Display of Goods in America 1880–1920*, ed. Simon J. Bronner (New York: W. W. Norton, 1989), 191–216; quotes from 192, 195, 198, 202, 215. Also see Rydell, *All the World's a Fair: Visions of Empire at American International Expositions, 1876–1916* (Chicago: University of Chicago Press, 1984), and Frieda Knobloch, *The Culture of Wilderness: Agriculture as Colonization in the American West* (Chapel Hill: University of North Carolina Press, 1996). For an excellent introduction to the Panama-Pacific Exposition's hegemonic thrust and agricultural techniques of display, see Burton Benedict, ed., *The Anthropology of World's Fairs: San Francisco's Panama Pacific International Exposition of 1915* (Berkeley, CA: Scholar Press, 1983), especially pages 15–17, 27–29.

45. Adams, *Wines of America*, 568.

46. *Viticulture and viniculture in California. Statements and extracts from reports of the Board of State Viticultural Commissioners, prepared specially for distribution at the New Orleans World Fair, 1885* (Sacramento: James J. Ayres, Supt. State Printing, 1885).

47. University of California–Davis Special Collections Blanchard Reading Room, found in a compiled scrapbook called *California Wine Clippings*. This article is from an unknown source, but is titled "The Largest Grape-Vine." It quotes the *Stockton Herald*, and is placed in a section of dated materials between August 18 and 25, 1883. The article cites the massive grapevine at the Philadelphia Fair because Captain W. G. Phelps of Stockton in 1883 claimed to have an even larger vine.

48. Carosso, *The California Wine Industry*, 98. See also Edward Roberts, "California Wine-Making," *Harper's Weekly* (March 9, 1889), 197; *San Francisco Call* (September 15, 1875).

49. "Centennial Exposition Memoranda," *Potter's American Monthly* (December 1876), 480. The article states, "It has grown to the dimensions of a good size apple-tree, from 18 to 22 inches diameter in its trunk."

50. Joseph Henry Jackson, "The Mammoth Vine," number 7 in a series entitled *The Vine in Early California*, published by the Book Club of California for its members in 1955 (San Francisco: Book Club of California, 1955), n.p.

51. N.G.F., "A Boy's Trip to the Centennial," *Prairie Farmer* (December 16, 1876), 406.

52. "The Century—Its Fruits and Its Festival, XI: Agriculture and Horticulture" *Lippincott's Magazine of Popular Literature and Science* 18 (November 1876), 527.

53. Adams, *The Wines of America*, 21.

54. Linda Walker Stevens, *What Wondrous Life: The World of George Husmann: A Photographic Exhibit on the Life and Achievement of Horticulturist and Winemaker George Husmann* (Hermann, MO: Hermann University Press, 2002), 14.

55. *Final Report of the California World's Fair Commission, Including a Description of all Exhibits from the State of California, Collected and Maintained Under Legislative Enactments, at the World's Columbian Exposition, Chicago, 1893* (Sacramento: State Office Building, A. J. Johnston, Supt. State Printer, 1894), 84, 19, 102, 108. Stanford detail in Tutorow, *The Governor*, 527.

56. California State Board of Viticultural Commissioners, *Annual Report*, 1893–94, 10. See also Pinney, *History of Wine in America*, 349, and Carosso, *The California Wine Industry*, 163.

57. *Pacific Wine and Spirit Review* was its title 1889–1912; its name was changed to *Pacific Wine, Brewing & Spirit Review* in 1913 and continued to be printed through 1935 (San Francisco: R. M. Wood). Hereafter *PWBSR*.

58. Anonymous, "California's 1915 Wine Exhibit," *Pacific Wine, Brewing & Spirit Review* (May 1913), 12.

59. *Final Report of the California World's Fair Commission*, 84.

60. *Final Report of the California World's Fair Commission*, 12.

61. Report of State Board of Viticultural Commissioners, "Viticulture in California," Bulletin No. 1 (March 15, 1914), 14–15.

62. Liberty Hyde Bailey, *Sketch of the Evolution of Our Native Fruits* (New York: Macmillan, 1898), 87.

63. Report of State Board of Viticultural Commissioners, "Viticulture in California," 14.

64. Ben Macomber, *The Jewel City: Its Planning and Achievement; Its Architecture, Sculpture, Symbolism, and Music; Its Gardens, Palaces, and Exhibitions* (San Francisco: John H. Williams, 1915), 13. See also Charles L. Sullivan, "The Great Wine Quake," *Wayward Tendrils Quarterly* 16:2 (April 2006), 10. Grape and wine displays at the Pan-Pacific Expo have received scant attention from historians, due to Prohibition taking effect while the fair's retrospective annals were being written. The exposition's major anthology, *The Story of the Exposition* (1921), written by Frank Morton Todd in five volumes, effectively erased the presence of wine at the fair by summing up a painfully short

exhibit description: "This is history—closed by the Eighteenth Amendment." Frank Morton Todd, *The Story of the Exposition*, vol. 4 (New York, 1921), 302. The illegality of the commercial production and sale of alcohol in the 1920s led to, it seems, the erasure of the records and displays of winemaking in previous years. Nevertheless, some striking descriptions and visual evidence of the fair's displays can be found in other primary sources, especially the major Californian wine trade publication of the 1910s, the *California Wine, Brewing & Spirit Review* (1889–1935). I would like to thank Ja Rue Manning, John Skarstad in Special Collections, and wine bibliographer Axel Borg, all at University of California–Davis, for pointing me to this treasure trove and many other fascinating and invaluable documents. This and other articles and ephemera provide evidence to illustrate that California viticulturists believed the Pan-Pacific Expo was U.S. viticulture's crowning achievement, fulfilling a plan of cultural empire through grapes that had been laid generations earlier.

65. Erik Mattie, *World's Fairs* (New York: Princeton Architectural Press, 1998), 132.

66. Todd, *Story of the Exposition*, 301. See also *Official Report*.

67. "California's Wine Exhibit," *PWBSR* (May 1913), 12–13.

68. "Splendid Collective Wine Display," *PWBSR* (March 1915), 12.

69. Paul Welschmeyer, "Spanish Revival Unraveled: The Risk of Cultural Deception," architectural position paper, www.pwarchitects.biz, accessed November 15, 2012. Also see Mike Davis, *City of Quartz: Excavating the Future in Los Angeles* (New York: Vintage Books, 1992), 26–27.

70. Lears, *No Place of Grace*, 26. Karen J. Weitze, *California's Mission Revival* (Los Angeles: Hennessey & Ingalls, 1984), 7, 10, 18, 21, 51. *Final Report of the California World's Fair Commission*, 104.

71. Weitze, *California's Mission Revival*, 51.

72. "Mission History," in *Prospectus of the 1915 Exposition*, San Diego Historical Society, Library and Manuscripts Collection. Cited in Rydell, *All the World's a Fair*, 208.

73. Macomber, *The Jewel City*, 25–26, 29.

74. Macomber, *The Jewel City*, 171.

75. George Sterling, *The Evanescent City* (San Francisco: A. M. Robertson, 1916), 3, 6, 12.

76. "Panama-Pacific Exposition Rising in Increasing Glory," *Overland Monthly* 62:6 (June 1914), 618.

77. *Official Report*, 323–324. Sources attest that there were a greater number of foreign nations participating, and a greater number of foreign attendees at the Pan-Pacific Expo, than in any previous U.S. exposition. See Edward H. Hurlburt, "Features of the Panama-Pacific Exposition," *Overland Monthly* 66:5 (November 1915), 18.

78. Macomber, *The Jewel City*, 146.

79. Hamilton Wright, "Panama-Pacific Exposition: The Mecca of the Nation," *Overland Monthly and Out West Magazine*, 66:3 (September 1915), 12, 16.

80. *Official Report*, 26–27, 42. The only name associated with the film is H. F. Stoll, a major industry player and organizer for the California wine exhibit. As far as I know, the film has been lost. I and other scholars have hunted for this film and cannot find any piece of it. This may be due to the probability that it was filmed on nitrate stock, and therefore very volatile, or due to the possibility that it was sent around to the groups that had requested it and was never returned.

81. Charles L. Sullivan, "The Great Wine Quake," *Wayward Tendrils Quarterly* 16:2 (April 2006), 11.

82. Todd, *Story of the Exposition*, 302. See also "California Wine Exhibit at the World's Fair," *PWBSR* (February 1915), 40, and "Splendid Collective Wine Display," *PWBSR* (March 1915), 12.

83. "Latest Data on the Progress of the Great Panama-Pacific International Exposition," *PWBSR* (January 1915), 54. See also Erik Mattie, *World's Fairs* (New York: Princeton Architectural Press, 1998), 132; and Rydell, *All the World's A Fair*, 227. Fred McClellan, designer, originally wanted to build a model large enough to have visitors ride in boats through locks; this was a scaled-down version.

84. As an imperial apparatus, the canal itself was thought to have finally resolved an "international conflict with clear U.S. hemispheric domination" as its real triumph. Bill Brown has argued that both the canal and the fair that were constructed to celebrate its completion helped build a new American "mode of imperialist perception . . . [and celebrate] the triumph of American artifice." The presence of the new, popular medium of film at the fair also compelled visitors to reflect upon the feeling of fluid movement they garnered from the experience. In the service of this new mode of perception, the latest optical technologies were on display, creating new modes of vision—including both electric lighting and motion pictures. Bill Brown, "Science Fiction, the World's Fair, and the Prosthetics of Empire, 1910–1915," in *Cultures of U.S. Imperialism*, ed. Amy Kaplan and Donald Pease (Durham, NC: Duke University Press, 1993), 129–163. Anne Friedberg has called this the "mobile gaze." See Anne Friedberg, *Window Shopping: Cinema and the Postmodern* (Berkeley: University of California Press, 1993), for a discussion of the "mobile gaze" constructed through the new experiences of film and department store shopping.

85. Geddes Smith, "A Shop Window of Civilization," *The Independent* (June 28, 1915), 535, 538.

86. *PWBSR* (May 1913), 12.

87. "Physiological Influence of Alcohol," *The Friend; a Religious Literary Journal* (September 18, 1875), 37; continued on September 25, 1875, pp. 41–42. See also "The Physiological Influence of Alcohol," *Littell's Living Age* (October 30, 1875), 259. Horatio F. Stoll, "A Campaign of Wine Education," *Official Report*, 24–29, and Bancroft, *History of the Life of Leland Stanford*, 152.

88. *Official Report*, 13, 324, 26–27.

89. "Splendid Collective Wine Display," *PWBSR* (March 1915), 12.

90. F. E. Gladwin, "Pruning and Training American Grapes," in *Official Report*, 51.

91. Chas W. Stevenson, "Value of Exposition to Agriculture: What the Panama-Pacific Exposition Will Do for the Farmers of the World," *Colman's Rural World* (September 10, 1914), 6.

92. Mary Louise Pratt, *Imperial Eyes: Travel Writing and Transculturation* (New York: Routledge, 2007).

93. Stevenson, "Value of Exposition," 6; see also "Preserve the Vineyards," *PWBSR* (April 1913), 28.

Chapter 6. The Danger of a Vineyard Romance

1. Barbara Ensrud, *American Vineyards* (New York: Stewart, Tabori & Chang, 1988), 11.

2. *Blood into Wine*, dir. Ryan Page and Christopher Pomerenke (Semi Rebellious/True Story Films, 2010). Keenan is the lead vocalist in the bands Tool and Perfect Circle.

3. Ensrud, *American Vineyards*, 11.

4. Advertisement for Bridlewood Estate Winery, *Wine Spectator* 36:10 (November 15, 2011), 99.

5. Advertisement for Beringer Knights Valley wine, *Wine Spectator* 36:12 (December 15, 2011), 61.

6. MaryAnn Worobiec, "Head to the Foothills: Viticulturist Ann Kraemer Shows Amador's Potential," *Wine Spectator* 36:15 (March 31, 2012), 100.

7. Just a few include Mrs. Ann S. Stephens, "Annette Delarbre," *The Ladies Companion, a Monthly Magazine* (November 1837), 3–7; Miss H. L. Beasley, "Castle Garden," *The Ladies Companion* (December 1837), 75–76; Catharine A. Janvier, "A Poet's Wedding in Provence," *The Critic: a Weekly Review of Literature and the Arts* (March 30, 1895); E. Braddon, "My Sister Caroline: A Novelette: The Whits House Among the Vineyards," *Harper's Bazaar* (March 19, 1870), 186; M. Topham Evans, "Count Otto of Harpsburg: A Romance of the Rhine," *The American Museum of Literature and the Arts, A Monthly Magazine* (May 1, 1839), 411; Richard Faulkner, "The Vine-Dresser's Daughter," *Dollar Monthly Magazine* (December 1, 1864), 478; Susan Coolidge, "In the Chateaux Country: A Pleasant Land of Romance," *The Independent . . . Devoted to the Consideration of Politics, Social and Economic Tendencies, History, Literature, and the Arts* (September 5, 1895), 3; "Romance of the Wine Press," *Phrenological Journal and Science of Health* 77:2 (1883), 105; "Window Love," *Home Journal* (May 17, 1851), 1; "Wines of the Ancients," *The Albion, A Journal of News, Politics and Literature* (December 24, 1836), 412. John S. Reid completed a six-part series titled "Grape Cuttings from History" for *The Horticulturist* from March 1865 through April 1867. In it, he detailed the global history of wine growing. George Husmann, *The Cultivation of the Native Grape, and Manufacture of American Wines* (New York: The American News Company, 1866), also opens his viticultural guide with a romantic story of the Vikings bringing grapevines to the New World.

8. Helen Hunt Jackson, *Ramona* (New York: Grosset and Dunlap, 1884), 19.

9. Jackson, *Ramona*, 197, 285.

10. See John Moran Gonzalez, *The Troubled Union: Expansionist Imperatives in Post-Reconstruction American Novels* (Columbus: Ohio State University Press, 2010), 19; Robert McKee Irwin, "*Ramona* and Postnationalist American Studies: On 'Our America' and the Mexican Borderlands," *American Quarterly* 55:4 (December 2003), 539–567.

11. Gonzalez, *The Troubled Union*, 3, 19; see chapter 3.

12. Maria Amparo Ruiz de Burton, *The Squatter and the Don* (San Francisco: S. Carson and Co., 1885), 52, 343.

13. Lazaro Lima, *The Latino Body: Crisis Identities in American Literary and Cultural Memory* (New York: New York University Press, 2007), 47–48.

14. Frank Norris, *The Octopus: A Story of California* (Garden City, NY: Doubleday, 1901), 18–20.

15. Thomas J. Vivian, "The Commercial, Industrial, Agricultural, Transportation, and Other Interests of California, Being a Report on That State for 1890 Made to S. G. Brock, Chief of the Bureau of Statistics, Treasury Department," Washington, DC: Bureau of Statistics, Treasury Department, 1891), 118.

16. Victor W. Geraci, "Fermenting a Twenty-first Century California Wine Industry," *Agricultural History* 78:4 (Autumn 2004), 439, 447.

17. For more scholarship on these three works, see Jose David Saldivar, *Border Matters: Remapping American Cultural Studies* (Berkeley: University of California Press, 1997); Manuel M. Martin Rodriguez, "Textual and Land Reclamations: The Critical Reception of Early Chicana/o Literature," in *Recovering the U.S. Hispanic Literary Heritage*, vol. 2, ed. Erlinda Gonzales-Berry and Charles M. Tatum (Houston, TX: Arte Publico, 1996), 40–58; John M. Gonzalez, "Romancing Hegemony: Constructing Racialized Citizenship in Maria Amparo Ruiz de Burton's *The Squatter and the Don*," in *Recovering the U.S. Hispanic Literary Heritage*, vol. 2, ed. Erlinda Gonzales-Berry and Charles M. Tatum (Houston, TX: Arte Publico, 1996), 22–39; Gonzales, *The Troubled Union*; David Luis-Brown, "'White Slaves' and the 'Arrogant Mestiza': Reconfiguring Whiteness in *The*

Squatter and the Don and Ramona," *American Literature* 69:4 (December 1997), 813–839; Deborah Moreno, "'Here the Society Is United': 'Respectable' Anglos and Intercultural Marriage in Pre-Gold Rush California," *California History* 80:1 (Spring 2001), 2–17; Robert McKee Irwin, "*Ramona* and Postnationalist American Studies: On 'Our America' and the Mexican Borderlands," *American Quarterly* 55:4 (December 2003), 539–567; Chimène I. Keitner, "The Challenge of Building an Inter-Communal Rule of Law in Helen Hunt Jackson's *Ramona*," *Law and Literature* 15:1 (2003), 53–86; Martin Padget, "Travel Writing Sentimental Romance, and Indian Rights Advocacy: The Politics of Helen Hunt Jackson's *Ramona*," *Journal of the Southwest* 42:4 (Winter 2000), 833–876; Donald J. Pisani, "The Squatter and Natural Law in Nineteenth-Century America," *Agricultural History* 81:4 (Fall 2007), 443–463; George Henderson, *California and the Fictions of Capital* (Philadelphia: Temple University Press, 2003).

18. Nathan Hoyt Sheppard, *Lucile of the Vineyard: A Temperance Romance* (Los Angeles, CA: N. H. Sheppard, 1915), 8.

19. Sheppard, *Lucile of the Vineyard*, 11.

20. Sheppard, *Lucile of the Vineyard*, 25.

21. Sheppard, *Lucile of the Vineyard*, 69–70.

22. Sheppard, *Lucile of the Vineyard*, 44, 71, 129–130.

23. Sheppard, *Lucile of the Vineyard*, 134, 152.

24. Maynard A. Amerine, "An Introduction to the Pre-Repeal History of Grapes and Wines in California," *Agricultural History* 43:2 (April 1969), 262. Thomas Pinney, "The Junior Enologist and the Banker's Wife: Maynard Amerine and Frona Eunice Wait," *Wayward Tendrils Quarterly* 15:3 (July 2005), 13–15.

25. Frona Eunice Wait, *Wines and Vines of California, or a Treatise on the Ethics of Wine Drinking* (San Francisco: The Bancroft Company, 1889), 11–12.

26. Frona Eunice Wait (Colburn), *In Old Vintage Days* (San Francisco: John Henry Nash, 1937), 160.

27. Wait, *In Old Vintage Days*, 168.

28. Wait, *In Old Vintage Days*, 46.

29. Wait, *In Old Vintage Days*, 177.

30. On "appear to disappear," see Eric Cheyfitz, "Savage Law: The Plot Against American Indians in *Johnson and Graham's Lessee Vs. M'Intosh* and *The Pioneers*," in *Cultures of United States Imperialism*, ed. Amy Kaplan and Donald Pease (Durham, NC: Duke University Press, 1993). Tellingly, Cheyfitz locates the most prominent examples of "appearing to disappear" in James Fenimore Cooper's *The Pioneers*, his best-known historical frontier romance.

31. For how ethnic characters, especially ethnic women, have been constructed in literature as irrational and not prepared for U.S. citizenship, see Melanie V. Dawson, "Ruiz de Burton's Emotional Landscape: Property and Feeling in *The Squatter and the Don*," *Nineteenth-Century Literature* 63:1 (June 2008).

32. Stanley Corkin, *Cowboys as Cold Warriors: The Western and U.S. History* (Philadelphia: Temple University Press, 2004), 51–53.

33. Wait, *In Old Vintage Days*, 58.

34. Gonzalez, *The Troubled Union*, 6, 7, 8; Corkin, *Cowboys as Cold Warriors*, 67.

35. Corkin, *Cowboys as Cold Warriors*, 53–53, quoting Amy Kaplan. See also Gonzalez, *The Troubled Union*, 3.

36. Geraci, "Fermenting a Twenty-first Century California Wine Industry," 450–451, 453.

Thomas Pinney, *A History of Wine in America: From Prohibition to Present* (Berkeley: University of California Press, 2005), 212.

37. Alice Hobart, *The Cup and the Sword* (New York: Bobbs-Merrill Co., 1942), 65. The book was loosely based on the life of Georges de Latour, founder of Baeulieu Vineyards. Louis Gomberg, *Analytical Perspectives on the California Wine Industry, 1935–1990*, interviewed by Ruth Teiser (Berkeley: Regional Oral History Office, Bancroft Library, University of California, 1990), 54–56.

38. Hobart, *The Cup and the Sword*, 54.

39. Hobart, *The Cup and the Sword*, 335–336.

40. Hobart, *The Cup and the Sword*, 231.

41. Hobart, *The Cup and the Sword*, 206.

42. *This Earth Is Mine*, dir. Henry King (Vintage Productions, Inc., Universal-International Pictures, 1959). "This Earth Is Mine [review]," *Variety* (December 31, 1958). In the film, John Rambeau is innocent of most character flaws he is guilty of in the book, including impregnating Buz. He is also revealed to not be a blood relative of Elizabeth. Elizabeth and Andrew never marry in the film, for he is haughty and unattractive; there is no Henri de Swanaña character at all. Still, ethnic characters are pushed to the side, and John and Elizabeth come together at the end of the film and inherit Philippe's vineyards, sealing the vineyard romance. See also Louis Gomberg, *Analytical Perspectives on the California Wine Industry 1935-1990* (Berkeley, University of California Press, 1990), 54-56.

43. Pinney, *A History of Wine in America*, 218, 225–226, 231, 239, 241.

44. Geraci, "Fermenting a Twenty-first Century California Wine Industry," 452.

45. Anita Clay Kornfeld, *Vintage* (New York: Simon and Schuster, 1980), 561.

46. Kornfeld, *Vintage,*163.

47. *Sideways*, dir. Alexander Payne, Jim Taylor (Fox Searchlight, 2004). Screenplay adapted from Rex Pickett's novel *Sideways* (New York: St. Martin's Press, 2004).

48. There are some significant differences between the novel and the film: there are no central ethnic characters in the book (the Stephanie character is white), and Jack pays Maya to sleep with Miles, among other different plot twists. Jack still ultimately returns to his wealthy fiancée.

49. *Bottle Shock*, dir. Randall Miller (Twentieth Century Fox, 2008).

50. Employees at Chateau Montelena report that liberties were taken with the characterization of many members of the cast, especially the character of Sam. (Personal discussion with employees of Chateau Montelena, October 2010.)

51. This brief scene was deleted from the film's theatrical release (it is included in the DVD's "Deleted Scenes").

52. Idwal Jones's *The Vineyard* (Berkeley: University of California Press, 1942) takes a different socioeconomic tack than most novels of its type, but includes no characters of color. For all its attention to critiquing the issues of class and land ownership typical of the vineyard romance, the novel still ends with happily married white couples taking possession of vineyards in which they have labored all their lives.

Epilogue: An Empire of Wine

1. George Husmann, *The Cultivation of the Native Grape, and Manufacture of American Wines* (New York: American News Company, 1866), 24, 25.

2. "Bacchus America: The Old Wine God and the New," W. J. Linton after Hennessy, 1872 [1869]. Originally an advertisement for "Perkins, Stern, and Co., 14 + 16 Vesey St., New York; 108 Tremont St., Boston; and 34 + 36 La Salle St., Chicago." Found reprinted in *Our Young Folks*, a double advertisement for Prang's American Chromos and the Travelers' Insurance Company, 1972 (no other publication information available). Courtesy Minneapolis Institute of Arts, Gift of Timothy Cole, 1919, Box 106, Reg. No. P. 5926. Other sources unknown, possibly Linton's *American Enterprise* 1 (August 1870). Linton described the 25 × 16" work as "the largest wood engraving ever done as a studied work of art (larger cuts not artistic there certainly are)." William James Linton, *The History of Wood-Engraving in America* (Boston: Estes and Lauriat, 1882), 31.

3. C. Scott Littleton, ed., *Gods, Goddesses, and Mythology* (New York: Marshall Cavendish, 2005), 1305–1306. See also F. B. Smith, *Radical Artisan: William James Linton, 1812–97* (Manchester, UK: Manchester University Press, 1973), 178.

4. Gustav Eisen, "Why Some Raisin Vineyards Pay More Than Others," *California—A Journal of Rural Industry* 3 (March 22, 1890), also in Stoll, *The Fruits of Natural Advantage: Making the Industrial Countryside in California* (Berkeley, University of California Press, 1998), 52.

5. David Dunstan wrote his history of wine in Victoria in large part to discover why the Australian wine business failed in the nineteenth century. The fact that Australia's wine industry failed for decades, but regained its prominence in the twentieth century, is further evidence of the fact that terroir has quite little to do with wine industry success. No one today would say that many regions of Australia don't have fabulous terroir, yet U.S. Midwestern wines have been laughed at for years, because of California's unquestioned claim to terroir. David Dunstan, *Better Than Pommard! A History of Wine in Victoria* (Victoria: Australian Scholarly Publishing, 1994).

6. Mark Hertsgaard, "In Vino Veritas: The Delicate Wine Grape Has Become Our Best Early-Warning System for the Effects of Global Warming," *Slate.com*, http://www.slate.com/articles/health_and_science/climate_desk/2010/04/in_vino_veritas.html, accessed April 27, 2010.

7. Henry Hobhouse, *Seeds of Wealth: Five Plants That Made Men Rich* (New York: Macmillan, 2003), 88.

8. Reginald Horsman, *Race and Manifest Destiny: The Origins of American Racial Anglo-Saxonism* (Cambridge, MA: Harvard University Press, 1981), 4–5, 59.

9. *Wine Spectator* 37:1 (April 30, 2012), 9; *Spotlight's Wine Country Guide* 22 (2007): 11/12, 42, 32. I picked up the *Spotlight* on a trip through Sonoma in October 2010.

10. *Wine Spectator* 36:15 (March 31, 2012), 45; *Wine Spectator* 36:13 (December 31, 2011–January 15, 2012), 18.

11. Timothy Tomasik, "De Certeau à la carte: Translating Discursive *Terroir* in *The Practice of Everyday Life: Living and Cooking*," *South Atlantic Quarterly* 100:2 (Spring 2001), 526.

12. Michael Sanders, *Families of the Vine: Seasons Among the Winemakers of Southwest France* (New York: HarperCollins, 2005), 88.

13. Jonathan Swinchatt and David G. Howell, *The Winemaker's Dance: Exploring Terroir in the Napa Valley* (Berkeley: University of California Press, 2004), 7–8.

14. Claire Hope Cummings, *Uncertain Peril: Genetic Engineering and the Future of Seeds* (Boston: Beacon Press, 2008), 72. See also *The Future of Food*, dir. Deborah Koons Garcia (Lily Films, 2004), and Glenn E. Bugos and Daniel J. Kevles, "Plants as Intellectual Property: American Practice, Law, and Policy in World Context," *Osiris*, 2nd series, vol. 7 (1992), 74–104.

15. Jenny Barchfield, "Scientifically Delicious: Pinot Genome Mapped," *MSNBCNews.com*, September 27, 2007, http://www.msnbc.msn.com/id/21017541/ns/technology_and_science-science/t/

scientifically-delicious-pinot-genome-mapped, accessed August 27, 2012. See also "Fingerprinting Helps Make Great Grapes," September 2, 2008, *ScienceDaily*, http://www.sciencedaily.com/re leases/2008/08/080830160454.htm, accessed August 27, 2012.

16. Cummings, *Uncertain Peril*, 77. For example, George W. Bush's Secretary of Agriculture, Ann Veneman, was formerly a leading agribusiness lawyer; Linda Fisher, Deputy Director of the Environmental Protection Agency, was previously a major lobbyist for Monsanto. In an agricultural patent case that went before the Supreme Court in 2001, the opinion of the court was written by Justice Clarence Thomas—who was himself a lawyer for Monsanto before being selected for the national bench.

BIBLIOGRAPHY

Primary Sources

Alison, Archibald. *Essays on the Nature and Principles of Taste.* Boston: Cummings and Hillard, 1812 [1790].

Allen, John Fisk. *A Practical Treatise on the Culture and Treatment of the Grape Vine: Embracing its History, with Directions for its Treatment, in the United States of America, in the Open Air, and under Glass Structures, with and without artificial heat.* 3rd ed. New York: C. M. Saxton & Company, 1847, 1853, 1857, 1858, 1860.

Annual Report of the Commissioner of Patents for the Year 1840: Agriculture. Washington, DC: Government Printing Office, 1841.

Annual Report of the Commissioner of Patents for the Year 1845: Agriculture. Washington, DC: Government Printing Office, 1846.

Annual Report of the Commissioner of Patents for the Year 1847: Agriculture. Washington, DC: Government Printing Office, 1848.

Annual Report of the Commissioner of Patents for the Year 1854: Agriculture. U.S. House of Representatives, 33rd Congress, Second Session, Executive Document Number 59. Washington, DC: A.O.P. Nicholson, 1855.

Annual Report of the Commissioner of Patents for the Year 1858: Agriculture. U.S. House of Representatives, 35th Congress, Second Session, Executive Document Number 105. Washington, DC: James B. Steedman, Printer, 1859.

Annual Report of the Commissioner of Patents for the Year 1859: Agriculture. U.S. House of Representatives, 36th Congress, First Session. Washington, DC: George Bowman, 1860.

Annual Report of the Commissioner of Patents for the Year 1860: Agriculture. Washington, DC: Government Printing Office, 1861.

Annual Report of the Commissioner of Patents for the Year 1862: Agriculture. Washington, DC: Government Printing Office, 1863.

Annual Report of the State Board of Viticultural Commissioners. Bulletin No. 1, "Viticulture in California." Sacramento: State Office, March 15, 1914.

Atkinson, Eleanor. *Johnny Appleseed: The Romance of the Sower.* New York: Harper & Brothers, 1915.

Bailey, Liberty Hyde. *Cyclopedia of American Horticulture.* 4 vols. New York: The MacMillan Company, 1900.

———. *Sketch of the Evolution of Our Native Fruits.* New York: The MacMillan Company, 1898.

Bear, J. W. *The Coming Industry of Victoria: Viticulture: With a Dictionary Describing One Hundred Varieties of the Vine and Various Notes and Comments.* Melbourne: Melville, Mullen and Slade, 1894.

Bleasdale, Rev. J. J. *On Colonial Wines.* Melbourne: Stillwell & Knight, 1867.

Blood into Wine. Dir. Ryan Page and Christopher Pomerenke. Perf. Maynard James Keenan and Eric Glomski. Semi Rebellious/True Story Films, 2010.

Book Club of California. *The Vine in Early California*. San Francisco: Book Club of California, 1955.

Bottle Shock. Dir. Randall Miller. Perf. Chris Pine, Alan Rickman, and Bill Pullman. Twentieth Century Fox, 2008.

Bridgeman, Thomas. *The Young Gardener's Assistant: Containing a Catalogue of Garden & Flower Seeds, With Practical Directions Under Each Head, for the Cultivation of Vegetables and Flowers, also Directions for Cultivating Fruit Trees, the Grape Vine, &c., to which is added, A Calendar*. New York: T. Bridgeman, 1833, 1837, 1840, 1845, 1847, 1853, 1857, 1858, 1865.

Buchanan, Robert. *A Treatise on the Cultivation of the Grape, in Vineyards*. Cincinnati: Wright, Ferris & Company Printers, 1850.

Buchanan, Robert, and Nicholas Longworth. *The Culture of the Grape, and Wine-Making*. Cincinnati: Moore & Anderson, 1852.

Busby, James. *A Manual of Plain Directions for Planting and Cultivating Vineyards, and for Making Wine, in New South Wales*. Sydney: R. Mansfield, 1830.

———. *Journal of a Tour Through Some of the Vineyards of Spain and France*. Sydney: Stephens and Stokes, 1833.

California State Board of Viticultural Commissioners. *Annual Report for 1893–1894*. Sacramento: State Publisher, 1894.

California Wine Clippings. A compiled scrapbook from the late nineteenth century. University of California–Davis, Library Special Collections, Blanchard Reading Room.

Chapin, Henry. *The Adventures of Johnny Appleseed*. New York: Coward-McCann, 1930.

Chavez, Cesar. "The Wrath of Grapes." In *American Earth: Environmental Writing Since Thoreau*. Ed. Bill McKibben. Washington, DC: Library of America, 2008.

Chesnutt, Charles W. *The Conjure Woman and Other Conjure Tales*. Ed. Richard H. Brodhead. Durham, NC: Duke University Press, 1993 [1899].

———. "The Future American: What the Race Is Likely to Become in the Process of Time." *(Boston) Evening Transcript*, August 18, 1900. In *Charles W. Chesnutt: Essays and Speeches*, ed. Joseph R. McElrath, Jr., Robert C. Leitz III, and Jesse S. Crisler. Stanford, CA: Stanford University Press, 1999.

Cincinnati Horticultural Society: A brief history, Charter, Constitution, and By-laws. Cincinnati: L'Hommedieu, 1859.

Cist, Charles. *Cincinnati in 1841: Its Annals and Future Prospects*. Cincinnati: Charles Cist, 1841.

———. *Sketches and Statistics of Cincinnati in 1851*. Cincinnati: Wm. H. Moore & Company, 1851.

Cooper, James Fenimore. *Gleanings in Europe: England*. Albany: State University of New York Press, 1982 [1837].

———. *Gleanings in Europe: France*. Albany: State University of New York Press, 1983 [1837].

———. *Gleanings in Europe: Italy*. Albany: State University of New York Press, 1981 [1838].

———. *Gleanings in Europe: The Rhine*. Albany: State University of New York Press, 1986 [1836].

———. *Gleanings in Europe: Switzerland*. Albany: State University of New York Press, 1980 [1836].

———. *The Headsman, or The Abbaye des Vignerons*. Philadelphia: Carey, Lea & Blanchard, 1833.

———. *The Pioneers, or, The Sources of the Susquehanna*. New York: Charles Wiley, 1823.

Cooper, Susan Fenimore. *Pages and Pictures From the Writings of James Fenimore Cooper, with Notes by Susan Fenimore Cooper, Illustrated, on Steel and Wood, from Original Drawings*. Secaucus, NJ: Castle Books, 1980 [1865].

The Cultivated Life: Thomas Jefferson and Wine. Dir. John Harrington. PBS, Madisonfilm, 2005.

Cutler, Manasseh. *An Explanation of the Map which Delineates that Part of the Federal Lands.* Salem, MA: Dabney and Cushing, 1787.

de Castella, Hubert. *John Bull's Vineyard: Australian Sketches.* Melbourne: Sands & McDougal, 1886.

de Chambrun, Clara Longworth. *Cincinnati: Story of the Queen City.* New York: Charles Scribner's Sons, 1939.

———. *The Making of Nicholas Longworth: Annals of an American Family.* Freeport, NY: Books for Libraries Press, 1933.

Devens, Richard Miller. *Cyclopaedia of Commercial and Business Anecdotes.* New York: D. Appleton & Company, 1865.

Downing, Andrew Jackson. *The Architecture of Country Houses.* New York, 1850.

———. *The Fruits and Fruit Trees of America: or, The Culture, Propagation, and Management, in the Garden and Orchard, of Fruit Trees Generally; with Descriptions of all the Finest Varieties of Fruit, Native and Foreign, Cultivated in this Country.* New York: John Wiley, 1845.

———. *A Treatise on the Theory and Practice of Landscape Gardening, adapted to North America.* New York: G. P. Putnam, 1852.

———. *Victorian Cottage Residences.* New York: Dover, 1981 [1842].

Final Report of the California World's Fair Commission, Including a Description of all Exhibits from the State of California, Collected and Maintained Under Legislative Enactments, at the World's Columbian Exposition, Chicago, 1893. Sacramento: State Office Building, A. J. Johnston, Supt. State Printer, 1894.

Gilpin, William. *Mission of the North American People: Geographical, Social and Political.* Philadelphia: J. B. Lippincott and Company, 1846.

Green, Wharton J. *Tokay Vineyard, Near Fayetteville, N.C.: With an Essay on Grape-Culture By the Proprietor.* Boston, 188[?].

Hill, N. N. *History of Knox County, Ohio, Its Past and Present.* Mount Vernon, OH: A. A. Graham and Company, 1881.

Historical and Descriptive Review of the State of North Carolina, Including the Manufacturing and Mercantile Industries. Charleston, SC: Empire Publishing Company, 1885.

Hobart, Alice. *The Cup and the Sword.* New York: Bobbs-Merrill, 1942.

Husmann, George. *American Grape Growing and Wine Making, With Contributions from Well-Known Grape Growers, Giving a Wide Range of Experience.* New York: Orange Judd Company, 1880.

———. *The Cultivation of the Native Grape, and Manufacture of American Wines.* New York: American News Company, 1866.

Hyatt, T. Hart. *Hyatt's Hand-Book of Grape Culture; or, Why, Where, When, and How to Plant and Cultivate a Vineyard, Manufacture Wines, etc., Especially Adapted to the State of California.* San Francisco: H. H. Bancroft and Company, 1867.

Irving, Washington. *Home Book of the Picturesque: Or American Scenery, Art, and Literature, Comprising a Series of Essays by Washington Irving, W. C. Bryant, Fenimore Cooper and Others.* New York: Putnam, 1852.

———. *A Tour on the Prairies.* Philadelphia: Carey, Lea & Blanchard, 1835.

Jackson, Helen Hunt. *Ramona.* New York: Grosset and Dunlap, 1884.

Jones, Idwal. *The Vineyard.* Berkeley: University of California Press, 1942.

Kelly, A. C. *The Vine in Australia.* Melbourne: Sands, Kenny & Company, 1861.

Kornfeld, Anita Clay. *Vintage.* New York: Simon and Schuster, 1980.

Lang, Andrew. *Custom and Myth.* New York: Harper and Brothers, 1885.

Longworth, Nicholas. *A Treatise on the Cultivation of the Grape, in Vineyards.* Cincinnati: Wright, Ferris and Company, 1850.

Macomber, Ben. *The Jewel City: Its Planning and Achievement; Its Architecture, Sculpture, Symbolism, and Music; Its Gardens, Palaces, and Exhibitions.* San Francisco: John H. Williams, 1915.

McEwin, George. *The South Australian Vigneron and Gardener's Manual.* Adelaide: James Allen, 1843.

Mead, Peter B. *An Elementary Treatise on American Grape Culture and Wine Making (Mead's Grape Culture).* New York: Harper & Brothers, 1867.

Melville, Herman. "Paradise of Bachelors, Tartarus of Maids." *Harper's New Monthly Magazine* 10 (April 1855).

Memorial of the Golden Wedding of Nicholas Longworth and Susan Longworth celebrated at Cincinnati on Christmas Eve, 1857. Baltimore: Hunckel & Son, 1858.

Miscegenation Indorsed By the Republican Party. New York: s.n., 1864.

Munson, Thomas Volney. "Address on American Grapes, Read Before the American Pomological Society, At Grand Rapids, Michigan, September 10, 1885, And Published In the Transactions of That Society For 1884–5." Lansing: Thorp & Godfrey, State Printers and Binders, 1886.

Myers, Gustavus. *History of the Great American Fortunes.* New York: Modern Library, 1936 [1910].

Naglee, Henry M. "The Report of a Jury of Experts on Brandy . . . Together with Testimonials of Physicians and Gentlemen as to its Purity and Wholesomeness: to which is added a short essay upon it, and other Spirits, both pure and adulterated, and their affects on the Human System, in Health, Disease, and Convalescence." San Francisco: San Jose, San Francisco Mechanics Institute, Spaulding, Barto & Company, Steam Book, Card and Job Printers, 1879. (Found in University of California–Davis Special Collections.)

Norris, Frank. *The Octopus: A Story of California.* Garden City, NY: Doubleday, 1901.

Norton, A. Banning. *A History of Knox County, Ohio.* Columbus, OH: R. Nevins, 1862.

Official Report of the Sessions of the International Congress of Viticulture, Held in Recital Hall at Festival Hall Panama-Pacific International Exposition, San Francisco, California, July 12 and 13, 1915. San Francisco: Dettner Printing Company, 1915.

Prentiss, A. N. *My Vineyard at Lakeview.* New York: Lovejoy & Son, 1866.

Prince, William. *A Short Treatise on Horticulture: Embracing Descriptions of a Great Variety of Fruit and Ornamental Trees and Shrubs, Grape Vines, Bulbous Flowers, Green-House Trees and Plants, &c., Nearly all of Which are at Present Comprised in the Collection of the Linnaean Botanic Garden, at Flushing, near New-York, with Directions for Their Culture, Management, &c.* New York: T & J Swords, 1828.

Prince, William Robert, aided by William Prince. *A Treatise on the Vine; Embracing Its History from the Earliest Ages to the Present Day, with Descriptions of Above Two Hundred Foreign, and Eighty American Varieties; Together With a Complete Dissertation of the Establishment, Culture, and Management of Vineyards.* New York: T & J Swords, 1830.

Proceedings of the Third Session of the American Pomological Society, held in Boston, 1854. Boston: Franklin Printing House, 1854.

Proceedings of the Seventh Session of the American Pomological Society, held in New York, 1858. Brooklyn, NY: George C. Bennett, 1858.

Proceedings of the Eleventh Session of the American Pomological Society, held in St. Louis, Missouri, 1867. Boston: Franklin Printing House, 1867.

Pulszky, Ferencz Aurelius, and Theresa Pulszky. *White, Red, Black: Sketches of American Society in the United States*. New York: Redfield, 1853.

Rafinesque, C. S. *American Manual of Grape Vines and the Art of Making Wine: Including An Account of 62 Species of Vines, with Nearly 300 Varieties*. Philadelphia: Printed for the author, 1830.

Report of the California State Board of Agriculture for the Year 1911. Sacramento, Superintendent of State Printing, 1912.

Report of the Commissioner of Agriculture, 1862. Washington, DC: Government Printing Office, 1863.

Report of Special Committee on the Culture of the Grape-Vine in California, Introduced by Mr. Morrison Under Resolution of Mr. Gillette. San Francisco: Charles Botts, State Printer, 1906.

Rose, H. J. *A Handbook of Greek Mythology*. London: Methuen & Company, 1928.

Ruiz de Burton, Maria Amparo. *The Squatter and the Don*. San Francisco: S. Carson, 1885.

Sheppard, Nathan Hoyt. *Lucile of the Vineyard: A Temperance Romance*. Los Angeles: N. H. Sheppard, 1915.

Shields, David S., ed. *Pioneering American Wine: Writings of Nicholas Herbemont, Master Viticulturist*. Athens: University of Georgia Press, 2009.

Shufeldt, Robert W. *The Relation of the Navy to the Commerce of the United States: A Letter Written By Request to Hon. Leopold Morse, M.C.* Washington, DC: John L. Ginck, 1878.

Sideways. Dir. Alexander Payne. Perf. Paul Giamatti, Thomas Haden Church, and Virginia Madsen. Fox Searchlight, 2004.

Sterling, George. *The Evanescent City*. San Francisco: A. M. Robertson, 1916.

Stowe, Harriet Beecher. *Uncle Tom's Cabin*. London: Casseli, 1852.

Todd, Frank Morton. *The Story of the Exposition*. New York: Putnam, 1921.

Traub, Hamilton. "The Development of American Horticultural Literature, Chiefly Between 1800 and 1850, Part One." *National Horticultural Magazine* 7 (July 1928): 97–103. "Part Two." *National Horticultural Magazine* 8 (January 1929): 7–17.

Tull, Jethro. *The Horse Hoeing Husbandry*. London: William Cobbett, 1829.

U.S. Bureau of the Census. *A Compendium of the Ninth Census*. June 1, 1870, F. A. Walker, comp. Washington, DC: Government Printing Office, 1872.

U.S. Department of Agriculture. *Yearbook of Agriculture 1898*. Washington, DC: Government Printing Office, 1899.

———. *Yearbook of Agriculture 1902*. Washington, DC: Government Printing Office, 1903.

The Vine; With Instructions for its Cultivation, for a Period of Six Years; the Treatment of the Soil, and How to Make Wine from Victorian Grapes, essays by multiple authors. Geelong, Australia: Heath and Cordell, 1859.

Viticulture and viniculture in California. Statements and extracts from reports of the Board of State Viticultural Commissioners, prepared specially for distribution at the New Orleans World Fair, 1885. Sacramento: James J. Ayres, Supt. State Printing, 1885.

Wait (Smith Colburn), Frona Eunice. *In Old Vintage Days*. San Francisco: John Henry Nash, 1937.

———. *Wines and Vines of California, or a Treatise on the Ethics of Wine Drinking*. San Francisco: Bancroft Company, 1889.

Ward, Ebenezer. *The Vineyards and Orchards of South Australia: A Descriptive Tour by Ebenezer Ward in 1862*. Sullivan's Cove: Giffin's Press Limited, 1979 [1862].

Wekey, S. *The Land, Importance of its Culture to the General Prosperity of Victoria; With a Special Reference to the Cultivation of the Vine, its Advantages and Prospects.* Melbourne: James J. Blundell and Company, 1854.

Wilson, William. *Economy of the Kitchen Garden, the Orchard, and the Vinery.* New York: Anderson, Davis, and Company, 1828.

Wine Spectator, The. San Diego: Wine Group, 1970s–present.

Woodward, Geo. E., & F. W. *Woodward's Graperies and Horticultural Buildings.* New York: Stephen Hallet, 1865/1867.

Nineteenth-Century Journals

The Albion. New York: J. S. Bartlett, 1822–1856.

American Agriculturist. New York: Geo. A. Peters, 1842–1912.

American Farmer and Spirit of the Agricultural Journals of the Day. Baltimore: Samuel Sands, 1839–1849.

American Farmer: Containing Original Essays and Selections on Rural Economy. Baltimore: S. Sands & Son, 1819–1834.

American Gardener's Magazine. New York: Hovey & Company, 1835–1836.

American Journal of Pharmacy. Philadelphia: Philadelphia College of Pharmacy, 1835–1936.

The American Museum of Literature and the Arts, A Monthly Magazine. Baltimore: Brooks & Snodgrass, 1838–1839.

Archives of Useful Knowledge. Philadelphia: David Hogan, 1810–1813.

Boston Cultivator. Boston: Otis Brewer, 1839–1850.

Boston Evening Transcript. Boston: Dutton, 1830–1872.

California—A Journal of Rural Industry. San Francisco: California Company, 1890–1900.

California Farmer. San Francisco: John F. Morse and Company, 1854–1889.

Californian. San Francisco: A. Roman Publishing Company, 1880–1882.

California Rural Home Journal. San Francisco: T. Hart Hyatt, 1865–1866.

Casket. Philadelphia: Atkinson & Alexander, 1826–1843.

Cincinnati Commercial. Cincinnati: M. D. Potter and Company, 1865–1883.

Cincinnati Enquirer. Cincinnati: Day, Farran & McLean, 1841–1921.

The Cincinnati Lancet-Clinic. Cincinnati: J. C. Culbertson, 1878–1916.

Cincinnati Republican. Cincinnati: Geo. W. Bradbury and Company, 1838-1842.

The Cincinnatus. Cincinnati: Applegate and Company, 1856–1860s.

Colman's Rural World. St. Louis: Norman J. Colvin, 1865–1916.

The Critic: A Weekly Review of Literature and the Art. New York: The Critic, 1865–1916.

The Cultivator. Albany: New York State Agricultural Society, 1834–1865.

DeBow's Review and Industrial Resources, Statistics, etc. Devoted to Commerce, Agriculture, Manufactures. New Orleans: J. D. B. DeBow, 1853–1864.

Dollar Monthly Magazine. Boston: M. M. Ballow, 1855–1865.

The Farmer & Gardener. Baltimore: Sinclair & Moore, 1835–1839.

The Farmers' Cabinet, and American Herd Book. Philadelphia: Kimber & Sharpless, 1836–1848.

The Farmers' Register. Petersburg, VA: Edmund Ruffin, 1833–1843.

The Friend: A Religious Literary Journal. Honolulu: S. C. Damon, 1845–1854.

Gardener's Chronicle. London: Gardener's Chronicle Ltd., 1874–1956.

The Genesee Farmer and Gardener's Journal (becomes *American Agriculturist*). New York: Allen & Company, 1853–1912.

Harper's Weekly. New York: Harper's Magazine Company, 1857–1976.

The Herald of Truth. Cincinnati: L. A. Hine, 1847–1848.

Home Journal. New York: 1851–1891.

Horticultural Register, and Gardener's Magazine. Boston: George C. Barrett, 1835–1838.

The Horticultural Review, and Botanical Magazine. Cincinnati: H. W. Derby, 1850–1854.

The Horticulturist: Journal of Rural Art and Rural Taste, Devoted to Horticulture, Landscape Gardening, Rural Architecture, Botany, Pomology, Entomology, Rural Economy, Etc. New York: Luther Tucker, 1846–1875.

Illustrated Australian News. Melbourne: Ebenezer and David Syme, 1876–1889.

The Independent . . . Devoted to the Consideration of Politics, Social and Economic Tendencies, History, Literature, and the Arts. New York: S. W. Benedict, 1848–1928.

The Ladies Companion, a Monthly Magazine. New York: William W. Snowden, 1834–1844.

Lippincott's Magazine of Popular Literature and Science. Philadelphia: J. B. Lippincott & Company, 1871–1880.

Littell's Living Age. Boston: T. H. Carter & Company, 1844–1896.

The Magazine of Horticulture, Botany, and all Useful Discoveries and Improvements in Rural Affairs. Boston: Hovey and Company, 1837–1868.

The National Horticultural Magazine. Washington, DC: American Horticultural Society, 1922–1959.

National Intelligencer. Washington, DC: Joseph Gales, 1810–1869.

The National Recorder. Philadelphia: Littell & Henry, 1819–1821.

The Naturalist, Containing Treatises on Natural History, Chemistry, Domestic and Rural Economy, Manufactures, and Arts. Boston: Pierce & Parker, 1830–1832.

New Harmony Gazette. New Harmony, IN: s.n., 1825–1828.

New York Farmer. New York: D. K. Minor, 1833–1837.

New-York Farmer and Horticultural Repository. New York: New York Horticultural Society, 1828–1832.

New York Journal of Commerce. New York: A. Tappan, 1827–1893.

Northwest Ohio Quarterly. Maumee, OH: Lucas County, 1929–1943.

Ohio Cultivator. Columbus: M. B. Bateham, 1845–1866.

Ohio Farmer. Cleveland: s.n., 1852–1876.

Overland Monthly. San Francisco: A. Roman & Company, 1868–1923.

Pacific Wine and Spirit Review. San Francisco: R. M. Wood, 1889–1913.

Pacific Wine, Brewing and Spirit Review. San Francisco: R. M. Wood, 1913–1935.

The Phrenological Journal and Science of Health. New York: Fowler & Wells, 1889–1911.

Plough Boy. New York: Solomon & Southwick, 1820–1822.

Potter's American Monthly. Philadelphia: John E. Potter & Company, 1875–1882.

Prairie Farmer. Chicago: John S. Wright, 1843–1858.

Quarterly Publication of the Historical and Philosophical Society of Ohio. Cincinnati: University of Cincinnati Press, 1906–1923.

Rural Californian. Los Angeles: s.n., 1880s–1914.

Rural New Yorker. Rochester, NY: D. D. T. Moore, 1850–1878.

Saturday Evening Post. Philadelphia: Atkinson & Alexander, 1821–1839.

Semi-Tropic California and Southern California Horticulturist. Los Angeles: s.n., 1880s–1914.

Southern Agriculturist. Charleston, SC: A. E. Miller, 1828–1846.

Southern Cultivator. Augusta, GA: J. W. & W. S. Jones, 1843–1880s.

Stockton Herald. Stockton, IL: J. Nellis Klock, 1888–1919.

INDEX

Italicized page numbers indicate illustrations.

ACKNOWLEDGMENTS

I would like to thank my families, the Hannickels, Andersons, and Vander-wolds, for creating a stimulating and loving intellectual environment throughout my life. They have supported me and modeled a dedication to critical, liberal thought and higher learning in ways I fear are now ebbing from the American tradition.

This project has its roots in the Ethnic Studies Department at University of California–San Diego, an exacting and brave department in immigrant fear-obsessed 1990s Southern California. The American Studies programs at California State University, Fullerton, and the University of Iowa were both ideal scholarly environments: rigorous, but kind. I would especially like to thank my colleague at Iowa, Laura Rigal, for her unwavering excitement about this project, her brilliant insight, and her attention to detail on all levels. My colleague at Fullerton, Pamela Hunt-Steinle, offers constant good counsel and friendship as I continue my career.

I could not have completed this project without the help of many wonderful librarians and fellowships. Librarian and wine bibliographer Axel Borg at the University of California–Davis was a fantastically invaluable and friendly resource. University Archivist John Skarstad, professor emeritus of microbiology Ja Rue Manning, and Jim Lapsley, all also at UC Davis, pointed me to important images and resources for the project. In addition, Dr. Lapsley read several chapters and offered his critique. Although we are historians of different stripes and disagree on the implications of much of my work, his help was invaluable. Librarians at the Cincinnati History Library and Archives were swift to lend assistance. The yearlong national fellowship I was awarded by the American Association of University Women (AAUW) was a gift like none I have ever received. It, in addition to smaller fellowships from the National Gallery of Art and the University of Iowa, as well as several course releases from Northland College through the Frances Werner Altenburg Professorship in Environmental Studies, made the completion of this book possible. Northland College librarians Julia Waggoner, Elizabeth Madsen-Gensler, and

Kyle Neugebauer may work in a very small library, but exercise tremendous skill in finding resources for faculty from far outside the confines of northern Wisconsin. They saw to my repeated "last pushes" of research with expertise, humor, and kindness. Northland continues as an amazingly collegial place, as well as a pedagogically and environmentally forward-thinking institution—a lovely spot on Lake Superior to call home.

My editors at the University of Pennsylvania Press, Bob Lockhart and Peggy Schaffer, have been unflaggingly engaged and helpful with this work. Since our initial conversations about the manuscript, I've appreciated how deeply they understood where this book was coming from intellectually, and where I have wanted it to go in the broader field of American studies. Several friends and colleagues also supported, critiqued, and edited this book. I'd like to thank the blind reviewers, Cynthia Belmont, Paul Bogard, Claudia Curran-Broman, Barbara Eckstein, Rick Fairbanks, Claire Fox, Billy Knoblauch, Paul Knox, Rob Latham, Emily Pawley, Dana Quartana, John Raeburn, David Saetre, Paul Schue, Traci Sinclair, Amy Spellacy, Talia Starkey, Michael Steiner, Jason Terry, Megan Threlkeld, Jim Throgmorton, Mark Warburton, and Charlie Williams.

For the friends and colleagues that buoy me, challenge me, and make me laugh on a daily basis, thank you.